Northwest Vista College
Learning Resource Center
3535 North Ellison Drive
San Antonio, Texas 78251

D1713464

THE WORKING CLASS IN AMERICAN HISTORY

Editorial Advisors
  David Brody
  Alice Kessler-Harris
  David Montgomery
  Sean Wilentz

Duquesne and the Rise of Steel Unionism

JAMES D. ROSE

University of Illinois Press

URBANA AND CHICAGO

Library of Congress Cataloging-in-Publication Data
Rose, James Douglas.
Duquesne and the rise of steel unionism / James D. Rose.
p.   cm.
Includes bibliographical references and index.
ISBN 0-252-02660-8 (cloth : alk. paper)
1. Iron and steel workers—Labor unions—Pennsylvania—
Duquesne—History. 2. Duquesne (Pa.)—History. I. Title.
HD6515.I52D87   2001
331.88'169142'0974885—dc21   00-012304

In memory of James R. Rose and Iris C. Rose

Contents

Acknowledgments

MANY INDIVIDUALS and institutions deserve a great deal of thanks for making this book possible.

The archivists and staffs at numerous libraries and archives provided me with much professional and friendly help: the Archives of Industrial Society and Hillman Library at the University of Pittsburgh; Archives of Labor and Urban Affairs, Wayne State University; Carnegie Library of Pittsburgh; Department of Archives and Manuscripts, Catholic University of America; Diana Shenk, Peter Gottlieb, Jim Quigel, and Denise Conklin at the Historical Collections and Labor Archives, Pennsylvania State University; Interlibrary Loan, Shields Library, University of California at Davis; Library of Congress, Washington, D.C.; Barbara Huff-Duff, Management Library, Industrial Relations Center, California Institute of Technology; Manuscript Division, Special Collections, University of Virginia Library; Cynthia McClain at the McKeesport (Pennsylvania) Heritage Center; Tab Lewis and the staffs at the National Archives, Washington, D.C.; Kellee Green at the National Archives—Mid-Atlantic Region, Philadelphia; Pennsylvania State Archives, Harrisburg; Rockefeller Archive Center, North Tarrytown, New York; State Historical Society of Wisconsin in Madison; Doris Dyer at the Steel Industrial Heritage Task Force, Homestead, Pennsylvania; and Washington National Records Center, Suitland, Maryland. And, above all, David Rosenberg at the UE/Labor Archives at the University of Pittsburgh made this study possible. He accommodated my many requests and needs, made the archives readily accessible during my trips in and out of the state, and shared with me his friendship and historical knowledge of the region.

I owe a large debt to many teachers. They shared their ideas, gave me encouragement, and had the patience to allow for my intellectual growth. They include Paul Goodman, Howell Harris, Wells Keddie, Mike McClain, Norman Markowitz, William Sullivan, Al Syzmanski, and Clarence Walker. This book grew out of my dissertation at the University of California at Davis. My dissertation director was David Brody, and anyone familiar with his work immediately will recognize his influence. Through seminars and individual readings he shared his wealth of knowledge of labor history, and then he steered me toward Duquesne. At that point he stepped back, allowing me to ask my own questions and find my own answers. He then continually encouraged me to refine my arguments, rewrite, and then rewrite some more. My committee also included Mort Rothstein and Roland Marchand. Mort served as a model member, offering advice, criticism, sources, and encouragement, all in a friendly manner. Roland guided my writing, served as a model teacher, and imparted to me an appreciation for management's side of history. He died a month after I completed the dissertation, and we all still miss him deeply.

At the University of Illinois Press I would like to thank Richard L. Wentworth for showing his support and encouragement for my work. I also want to thank Bruce Nelson and Ron Schatz, who read the initial manuscript, encouraged its publication, and offered invaluable advice about strengthening it. Series editor David Montgomery provided a series of questions and comments, both large and small, that greatly improved this work. Theresa L. Sears, the managing editor, made this process efficient and productive, and Polly Kummel, my copy editor, made this book much more readable and concise.

Others provided much help and support along the way. I thank Lou Bortz for his remembrances; Joan Striegle for sharing the personal papers of her father, Elmer Maloy; and especially Phillip Bonosky, who graciously provided me with documents and his insights and remembrances of Duquesne in the 1930s. I also want to thank Burris Esplen for serving as a research assistant; Pat Naugle for putting me up in Pittsburgh; and René, Ev, Sophia, and Val, who provided me with a family and home away from home. As I worked on this project, I met numerous scholars who generously shared their knowledge of the steel industry. Thank you to Ric Dias, Vic Forberger, John Hinshaw, Elizabeth Jones, Jim Kollros, Irwin Marcus, Karen Olson, Jonathan Rees, Rob Ruck, and Joel Sabadasz.

I deeply appreciate the generous support and friendship of many at the University of California at Davis, including Tom Addams, Karen Hairfield, Kevin Leonard, Debbie Lyon, Kathy Olmstead, and Eteica Spencer. I especially want to thank my two dear friends, Jeff Kolnick and Dave Vaught, with whom I have had the good fortune to spend time in both California and Texas. Jeff read various versions of this book and always took the time to provide comments and suggestions, along with much-needed help when teaching and revisions consumed my life. I will always be indebted to Dave, who has read the entire work and continually given support, suggestions, criticism, and editing suggestions too numerous to mention.

I owe my deepest thanks to my family. My parents, Jim and Iris, along with my sisters, Sharon and Kath, and brother-in-law, Mike, always offered me encouragement and love at each and every step of the way. My daughter, Hannah, was born three months before I began graduate school, and my son, Nick, arrived a month after I chose to write about Duquesne. Although they extended the length of this project by years, they have extended my happiness and pride beyond measure. They have grown up with steel and they are all the stronger for it. To Kate, my wife, I simply owe everything and more, and that is still not enough.

Duquesne and the Rise of Steel Unionism

Introduction

IN THE SPRING and early summer of 1934, Duquesne, Pennsylvania, braced for a steel strike. The Amalgamated Association of Iron, Steel, and Tin Workers had established a lodge at U.S. Steel's Duquesne Works in late 1933. By February the Fort Dukane Lodge had enrolled approximately one quarter of the mill's workforce, mostly unskilled immigrants and their sons, and blacks. Fort Dukane formed one of the many militant lodges that had sprung up across the nation early in the New Deal. Together these lodges, as the union locals were called, had coalesced into the rank-and-file movement within the Amalgamated, which challenged the older conservative leadership to act decisively.

The Amalgamated faced a daunting task in trying to pull off a strike. Forty-two years earlier Andrew Carnegie and Henry Clay Frick had delivered a stunning blow to the steelworkers' union when they crushed the famous Homestead Strike in 1892. Nine years later, in 1901, the newly formed United States Steel Corp. defeated another strike, and by 1909 the union had no presence at U.S. Steel or in most American steel mills. Nevertheless, the Amalgamated, spurred by conditions created by World War I, rose once again. But in the Great Steel Strike of 1919 workers went down to total defeat. By the end of the 1920s the Amalgamated represented approximately five thousand workers in an industry that employed more than a half million. In the early 1930s conditions for unionism appeared even worse. The Great Depression had devastated the ranks of steelworkers. About one quarter had been laid off, and a majority of the rest worked only part time. The Amalgamated's leadership had become defensive, overly cautious, and isolated.

Then came the New Deal. President Franklin Roosevelt's National Recovery Administration promised workers the right to organize and bargain collectively with management. Steelworkers responded by flooding into the Amalgamated and in the process pushed to the forefront at the local level a new brand of militant rank-and-file leadership. Throughout the spring of 1934 the rank-and-file leaders pushed for a summer showdown with the steel industry. But the steel industry answered in kind. The Duquesne Works management prepared for the threatened strike by campaigning to rally loyal workers to its side, stocking the mills with guns and tear gas, and mobilizing the town's Republican political leaders and police force in defense. Management also had scores of workers serve as guards within and around the mill. Seven of those men were worker-elected employee representatives for the company's employee representation plan (ERP), or, as it was frequently called, company union. Unlike the Amalgamated supporters, the ERP men had been born in the United States and held high-paying jobs.

As the strike deadline neared, the rank-and-file movement collapsed. Inadequate organization, the obstructionist policies of the Amalgamated's conservative national leadership, determined opposition of the steel industry, and failure of the New Deal to support the workers combined to force the rank-and-file leaders to call off the strike. The dream of unionization had once again been deferred.

Remarkably, however, it was resurrected within two years. The Committee for Industrial Organization (CIO) split off from the older American Federation of Labor in 1935. The CIO then created a new steel union in 1936, the Steel Workers Organizing Committee (SWOC), which quickly absorbed the old Amalgamated. Then, in 1937, without a strike or even a threat to strike, SWOC signed a collective bargaining agreement with U.S. Steel after an eight-month organizing drive. Duquesne's steelworkers finally had union protection, formalized in a written contract that they had lacked for five decades.

When I began this study, I wanted to locate the origins of steel unionism in the 1930s. I expected to find them in the blending of the old and the new, both in the structure and membership of the older Amalgamated and in the structure and leadership of SWOC. The rank-and-file activism and militancy that erupted inside the Amalgamated early in the New Deal especially interested me, and I wanted to see how that became submerged within SWOC, perhaps the CIO's most centralized and least democratic union. As for those seven ERP men who guarded the mill against the Amalgamated, they were, in most historical accounts, an obstacle to unionization. The ERP men were skilled workers who cast their lot with an organization created and controlled by management in an effort to defeat trade unionism. Most Amalgamated and SWOC activists had belittled the ERPs, dismissing them as "mostly window-dressing" that "couldn't get me anything." And if they did accomplish anything, "it was only a sop."[1]

The setting of this study is U.S. Steel's Duquesne Works. The roots of steel unionism and its early history are especially traceable at this mill. Located just south of Pittsburgh along the Monongahela River, the Duquesne Works was in the center of the greatest steel-producing region in the world. Built in the 1880s, it formed—along with the Edgar Thomson and Homestead Works—the core of the old Carnegie Steel Co. empire and, after 1901, the core of U.S. Steel. After World War I, the Duquesne Works employed approximately six thousand workers and was a fully integrated basic steel mill, with blast-furnace, open hearth, and rolling mill departments.

In addition to its size, importance, and representativeness, the Duquesne Works holds another important advantage for the scholar: rich archival records. In the 1980s, when U.S. Steel abandoned most of its steelmaking facilities in the Pittsburgh region, it closed the Duquesne Works and walked away from the mill, its workforce, and the town. Left behind and literally scattered on the floor were massive amounts of company records. Archivists from the UE/Labor Archives at the University of Pittsburgh have preserved many of these records, including those from the personnel department—company memos, union grievances, and ERP materials. Such corporate records seldom are available to the public and are singularly rare for the steel industry, which is well known for its secrecy. Combined with other more traditional sources, they allow for an examination of the rise of steel unionism from the shop floor of one of the nation's most important steel mills.

What this study demonstrates above all else is the centrality of the ERP in shaping steel unionism in the 1930s, despite what SWOC activists and historians have argued. The ERP, in fact, produced as many SWOC leaders as the old Amalgamated, including the Duquesne local's first three presidents. Moreover, the grievances and grievance processes of both the ERP and SWOC were decidedly similar. Even the first SWOC collective bargaining agreement with U.S. Steel all but reproduced what the ERP and the company had developed over the years. Had the ERP been under the early union influence of the Amalgamated? No. In fact, the leaderships of the two organizations deeply despised each other. Had the CIO managed to influence the ERP before SWOC was formed? For the Duquesne Works the answer again is no. Although the ERP began as a closely controlled organization of loyal company workers, it quickly evolved into a quite independent group of militant employees. Despite their isolation from the union movement through early 1936, the ERP representatives and management had created a sophisticated bargaining structure that represented the shop-floor interests of the mill's skilled workforce. The roots of steel unionism, it turns out, are to be found not only in the Amalgamated but also in an organization that most labor historians would associate with management, not workers.

This piece of history becomes clear only by focusing on the shop floor and uncovering the life of the ERP within the mill. The majority of recent steel histories have focused primarily on management, technology, the community, or workers' racial or ethnic identities.[2] The shop floor has not always been absent in these studies. However, its location on the periphery has meant that no one has ever adequately explored the continuities and discontinuities of labor relations within the mill, especially between the nonunion and union periods.[3] But by focusing on the shop floor, I was able to explore all the factors affecting unionization as they interacted in the one arena all workers occupied simultaneously. As important, the shop floor was the one arena the workers shared with management. Corporate decision making; federal labor policy; local, state, and national political shifts; and workers' ethnic and racial identities and skill levels all profoundly affected the course of steel unionism. Approaching labor history through the shop floor reveals how these various factors directly influenced the relations between workers and managers and, consequently, workers' attempts at unionization.

Most important, focusing on the shop floor reveals the centrality of the production process in shaping workers' interests. Steel mills employed a highly segmented and hierarchical workforce. Within this hierarchy were skill divisions that were reinforced by wage compensation systems, such as hourly wage rates and tonnage incentive plans. Layered onto these skill divisions were racial and ethnic hierarchies. However, the divisions based on work and cultural identity did not always correspond. Workers who shared a common racial or ethnic identity often experienced sharply different work lives. They felt the effects of management policies in dissimilar ways and harbored starkly different grievances. Working-class fragmentation therefore is a central theme of this study.

Working-class fragmentation calls into question the culture-of-unity arguments in labor history. Gary Gerstle and Lizabeth Cohen argue that by the 1930s economic, political, and cultural changes at the national level had created a largely unified working class. Gerstle, in his study of textile workers in Woonsocket, Rhode Island, argues that these changes fostered a common and broad "language of Americanism," which the Independent Textile Union used to organize workers of vastly different ethnic and skill backgrounds into one union in the 1930s. Cohen, in her study of Chicago workers, finds working-class fragmentation existed through the 1920s, largely caused by the insular nature of most ethnic working-class cultures. This changed in the 1930s when the depression destroyed the economic backbone of their communities. Both immigrant and native-born workers were forced to look to the federal government and national unions for relief. Increasingly common social and cultural experiences between workers, combined with a decrease in their skill divisions, reinforced this convergence of workers' interests. Both Gerstle and Cohen thus show the New Deal and unions acting as unifying agents that break down the divisions between workers.[4]

Just the opposite occurred in the steel industry early in the depression. Divisions between workers on the shop floor actually deepened, as the combined effects of the depression and early New Deal labor policies intensified differences rooted in skill and wage compensation. The early New Deal actually set in motion two conflicting conceptions of workplace representation—trade unionism and company-sponsored employee representation. Divisions between workers became institutionalized through the creation of two competing organizations: the Amalgamated and the ERP. The Amalgamated represented largely unskilled hourly workers, mostly blacks and eastern and southern Europeans; the ERP appealed to skilled tonnage workers and skilled tradesmen of northern and western European heritage, most of whom had been born in the United States. Between 1933 and 1935 these organizations battled for supremacy and divided further an already deeply fragmented workforce.

This fragmentation also calls into question a second recent theme in 1930s labor history. The rank-and-file school, the most forceful proponent of which is Staughton Lynd, emphasizes the radical and localized activity of workers early in the depression. This approach builds on earlier New Left histories and deemphasizes the importance of the early New Deal. It argues that workers, not changes in federal policy, began the revival of the labor movement. But this school is highly critical of the later New Deal, especially the National Labor Relations Act of 1935 (Wagner Act), for subverting worker militancy and channeling the labor movement toward bureaucratic unionism. This school then criticizes national "bureaucratic" trade unions, such as SWOC, for undermining an "alternative unionism" that grew out of a more community-oriented and radical approach to trade unionism.[5]

But the steel industry experienced precious little militant worker activity until the New Deal. Only when Congress passed the National Industrial Recovery Act (NIRA) in June 1933 did steel unionism revive after nearly a half-century of failures. Workers eventually felt a deep resentment toward the early New Deal, but they criticized it for not exercising greater centralized authority. Union militants at the local level wanted stronger federal intervention. The relationship of worker militants and the Amalgamated was similar. A union did not arise in Duquesne simply because workers got themselves organized; it was born only after months of organizing by the national Amalgamated representatives. The Amalgamated's national leadership ultimately proved quite inept, and destructive, in its attempt to organize the nation's steelworkers. And the national union did try to destroy militant locals and their leaders. However, local militancy was in large part a result of the frustration that workers and rank-and-file leaders experienced in their dealings with the national union. Local leaders always wanted a greater national coordination of their efforts, something the Amalgamated did not provide. Further, as events in Duquesne show, localized militancy simply could not defeat U.S. Steel. It could not overcome the divisions between workers and the power of an open-shop industry that extended across the nation.

Community-based movements could not have unionized the steel industry; only a national movement coordinated by a centralized union with the aid of the federal government made unionization possible. Although the National Industrial Recovery Act and the Amalgamated revived steel unionism, their efforts were not enough to defeat the open-shop industry. Workers soon realized that they needed more national coordination, aid, and intervention. To understand why SWOC had to be a top-down, highly centralized organization that minutely directed organizing in the steel industry, one must first understand the failures of the Amalgamated. And to understand why passage of the National Labor Relations Act and its bureaucratic approach to labor organizing were crucial to the success of organized labor, one must understand the failures of the NIRA. And even with greater union centralization and federal authority, steel still proved a difficult industry to organize.

Management's support of ERPs, as well as the divisions between workers, hampered union efforts. ERPs arose in the United States at the turn of the century but did not gain widespread application until World War I. Companies found that ERPs were a good way to avoid recognizing trade unions and still meet federal requirements to bargain with organized committees of workers. The ERP movement waned after the war but rebounded in 1933 as a way to fend off unions and the NIRA. During the 1920s and 1930s industrialists and academics praised ERPs as a means of restoring personal relations between employers and employees, increasing labor-management cooperation, providing workers with a voice, and improving management standards.[6] Labor leaders and radicals, on the other hand, attacked ERPs as antiunion devices that sowed divisiveness among workers and created a false sense of liberty.[7]

Labor historians have viewed ERPs harshly, especially those created in the wake of the NRA. In his pioneering revisionist study of ERPs, Daniel Nelson called these 1930s creations "the classic company unions . . . , the bogey-men of the traditional accounts. With few exceptions their impact was inconsequential."[8] The underlying assumption of most of these studies is that ERPs never amounted to more than a crude antiunion tool for thwarting industrial unionism and providing workers with only token concessions. Because ERPs were counterfeit labor organizations, trade unions needed to defeat them. Most accounts of the steel industry's ERPs in the 1930s therefore focus largely on SWOC's attempts to capture U.S. Steel's ERPs and the company's efforts to resist.[9] Labor historians depict steel industry ERPs as, at best, transitional organizations that bridged the nonunion and union eras, acting as schools of independent unionism for a few militant workers.[10] Much of the basis for these views of steel ERPs derives from oral histories of workers who actively sought to discredit the ERPs, that is, workers who served as ERP representatives and later joined SWOC.

Although U.S. Steel's ERPs clearly originated as crude antiunion tools, they evolved into largely independent, worker-led organizations at many steel mills. Skilled tonnage workers in particular found them a useful mechanism for resolving shop-floor grievances. The opposition of trade unions to ERPs does not mean that ERPs were not viable worker organizations. Many steelworkers did not join trade unions during the critical years of 1933 to 1937, and many opposed those unions outright. They were deeply concerned with shop-floor issues and found the ERPs better equipped to meet their needs. Further, the remembrances of former ERP militants who joined SWOC did not always correspond to the reality of the majority of ERP representatives. Even the militants' experiences with the ERPs were not always as negative as they later sought to portray them. The historical record and their recorded memories do not always correspond.

Ultimately, SWOC needed the federal government to overcome the ERPs' hold on workers. The Wagner Act finally cleared ERPs from the scene by declaring them illegal and by holding highly publicized hearings that exposed attempts by management to manipulate the ERPs. The Wagner Act has come under increasing criticism as a constraint on the abilities of workers and unions to organize workplaces today.[11] This is a well-founded criticism, but at times critical legal scholars and others, seeking to dismiss the entire Wagner Act, read the contemporary problems with the law backward into history.[12] Many of the law's consequences, however, were unforeseen in the 1930s and were partially the result of historical contingencies that occurred after the passage of the act.[13] More pertinent in the 1930s was that many workers preferred the ERPs until the Wagner Act outlawed them and thus made unions more attractive.

The failures of industrial unionism and labor law in recent years should not be the lens through which to view the labor history of the 1930s. It is important to remember why many, though not all, industrial workers joined unions during that decade. For them the standard of comparison was the open shop of the 1920s and the Great Depression.[14] Steelworkers labored under horrible conditions, many earning a bare subsistence for themselves and their families. They constantly experienced the arbitrary authority of foremen who could hire and fire them at will. And workers had no contractual, legal, or organizational mechanisms for redressing these and countless other grievances.

The New Deal opened up new hope and possibilities for steelworkers, but they became divided about how best to proceed. The Amalgamated and the ERP, responding to the particular needs of different constituencies of workers, fought each other, weakening and foreclosing any kind of unified response to management early in the New Deal. For all its weaknesses and problems, SWOC was able to bring the former Amalgamated and ERP activists together. From their divergent pasts—trade unionism and employee representation—came the roots of steel unionism. Still, fragmentation and division within the ranks of workers ran deep. SWOC would find it was one thing to create a union in steel but quite another to maintain it.

1. The Steel Strike of 1919

THE GREAT STEEL STRIKE of 1919 spread fear across the United States. The specter of bolshevism, riots, and bombings gripped the nation during the early fall, fanned by sensational headlines in the nation's newspapers.[1] But the reality of the strike was quite different. The walkout proved remarkably nonviolent, despite the hysteria whipped up by the press and steel industry officials. The sensationalism also did not deter large numbers of steelworkers around the country from joining the strike. In the Pittsburgh region the U.S. Steel Corp.'s Carrie blast furnaces in Rankin completely shut down and its Clairton Works ground nearly to a halt. The strike also found strong support at U.S. Steel's National Tube Works in McKeesport, Edgar Thomson Works in Braddock, and Homestead Works.[2]

U.S. Steel's Duquesne Works, however, did not follow. By all accounts, the Duquesne Works had the fewest strikers of all the corporation's Pittsburgh mills. Lost wages at Duquesne were significantly less than at other Pittsburgh-area U.S. Steel mills of comparable size.[3] The strike did not shut down any significant portion of the mill, and by the end of its first week, production remained nearly normal. During the second week the strikers numbered only 438 out of a workforce of 5,700.[4]

"The strike has been a strike of fear," A. F. Diehl, the general superintendent of the Duquesne Works, told a U.S. Senate committee investigating the strike. According to Diehl, most workers who left their jobs during the first week did not support the walkout at all but instead feared violence and retribution from the union. Just before the strike he noted that workers discussed whether to go to work.

They [the immigrants] were saying, "If there is going to be a strike, I am not going to work; I am going to wait until it is all over." Many of the Americans said the same thing, and the result was that on Monday morning there was an absolute condition of fear. . . . We had men rushing up to the plant gates and expecting aeroplanes blowing up the plants, and we had women that were saying that their men—that they would never see them again. Our visiting nurse told me that she had talked with a woman in an upper ward; and she had four men locked in a room and would not let them get out—a son-in-law, husband, father, and a boarder.

In fact, Duquesne saw little violence. Diehl knew of only one man who had been hit by a brick. And what of the radical tendencies that newspapers reported that the large immigrant workforce harbored? Diehl believed that few workers had any radical inclinations. He commented that most immigrant workers took their earnings and "put it down in their socks" to save for homes, many of which were built by U.S. Steel.[5]

How did management shield the Duquesne Works from the strike? Although Diehl never mentioned it to the Senate, most workers feared the Duquesne Works management and town authorities, not violence and retribution from the union. Mill managers, businessmen, and large landowners created an imposing political, economic, and legal structure that effectively blocked nearly all union activity and made using violence to crush the strike unnecessary. But this explains only half the reason for Duquesne's success. Diehl touched on the other half when he spoke of corporate housing. Duquesne offered the most extensive welfare capitalist programs of all the Pittsburgh-area U.S. Steel plants. The programs, which included stock option plans, health and safety measures, English classes, recreation facilities, and housing, were designed to ensure the loyalty of skilled workers and provide enough aid to unskilled and semiskilled workers to help dampen enthusiasm for a union. The singular success of the Duquesne management in the steel strike of 1919 was its ability to use what Charles Gulick in the 1920s called the essence of U.S. Steel's labor policy: paternalism and autocracy.[6]

Building a Mill

The Duquesne Works underwent several transformations between 1886 and 1919, each with a profound effect on workers and labor relations. The Duquesne Steel Co. first built a steel mill in 1886 at the site that would become the town of Duquesne. Situated on the western bank of the Monongahela River, approximately ten miles south of Pittsburgh, it lay across the river from McKeesport and the National Tube Works. Just north by a few miles stood the giant Edgar Thomson and Homestead mills. The first Duquesne Works contained a Bessemer mill, which converted pig iron into steel, and a blooming mill, which rolled steel ingots into various shapes. However, the mill never started up, and the Allegheny Bessemer Co. bought the abandoned plant in 1888.[7] Allegheny Bessemer then attempted to do what no other steel company had been able to do: beat Andrew Carnegie in the basic steel market.

Carnegie had pioneered large-scale steelmaking in the Pittsburgh region with the construction of the Edgar Thomson Works at Braddock in 1875. The Edgar Thomson Works combined the latest steelmaking technology with a hard-driving management style and innovative accounting procedures. The results were high profits and record steel production. The most notable effort to challenge Carnegie, the Pittsburgh Steel Co.'s plant at Homestead, failed. The Homestead Works surpassed the Edgar Thomson Works in engineering design, but the new plant became embroiled in labor conflicts, including a successful strike by the Amalgamated Association of Iron and Steel Workers in 1882. Pittsburgh Steel sold the mill to Carnegie in 1883, which made him the owner of the two most advanced steel plants in the world.[8]

Allegheny Bessemer had used two strategies to make its Duquesne Works competitive with Carnegie: modern technology and a brutal labor policy. The company kept the Bessemer converting mill but built new blooming and rail mills. When production began in February 1889, its new direct rolling process, which reduced the need to reheat railroad rails during rolling, gave the Duquesne Works a competitive edge over Carnegie's Edgar Thomson Works. Allegheny Bessemer also saved money by paying its workers less than union wages. In order to make its labor policies explicitly clear, management enforced an ironclad, or "yellow dog," contract that banned union men. The company hung signs throughout the mill proclaiming "NO UNION MEN ARE ALLOWED IN THE WORKS."[9]

From the moment of its start-up, the company experienced serious problems. Production difficulties plagued the mill during its first few months, forcing management to scrap tons of finished product. Andrew Carnegie further undermined Allegheny Bessemer by mailing a letter to railroad purchasing agents around the country, warning them against buying Allegheny's steel rails. He claimed that rails rolled by the company's new technology lacked homogeneity. Carnegie fabricated the term *homogeneity,* but the lie worked and it shut Allegheny Bessemer out of the lucrative rail pool, forcing the company to accept smaller and less profitable contracts. In addition, after only two months of production workers formed an Amalgamated lodge and struck the plant because of the low wage scale, twelve-hour day, and ironclad agreement. The strike failed but not before it stopped production for

more than a month. Allegheny Bessemer could not recover from these problems, and the financially strapped owners sold out to Carnegie in 1891.[10]

The mill paid for itself in less than a year, attesting to Carnegie's managerial and financial savvy.[11] Still, Carnegie was not content to keep the Duquesne
Works a small but highly efficient Bessemer converting mill and rail plant.
Between 1893 and 1901 he transformed the Duquesne Works into a fully integrated basic steel plant. The work of expanding the plant proceeded at
various levels, beginning with the purchase of two hundred acres of river-
front property that included a bankrupt tube mill and a glassworks. By 1901
the plant covered more than 240 acres, or just slightly more than a quarter
of the town's acreage, and stretched two miles along the river bank. In one
of the first changes to the mill, Carnegie built a four-furnace blast-furnace
department, which quickly broke, then held for four years, the world record
for monthly iron production. In keeping with Carnegie's drive for reduced
costs, the department pioneered new raw material delivery systems that automatically loaded raw materials and delivered them into the furnaces. Automated systems also poured the molten iron into casts and dumped the
cooled ingots into waiting railroad cars. Dubbed the "Duquesne revolution,"
this new system cut blast-furnace labor costs by half.

Carnegie also converted the plant from Bessemer to open hearth steel.
Open hearth steel, pioneered at the Homestead Works in 1888, produced
better and more varied grades of steel in less time. In 1890 Duquesne workmen put on line a twelve-furnace open hearth plant. Later known as the Open
Hearth Shop #1, it was enclosed within a building that covered 107,000 square
feet. Each furnace could produce fifty tons of steel, two to three times a day.

Rebuilding and expanding the rolling department in the late 1890s completed the transformation of the Duquesne Works. It consisted of four separate mills: blooming, roughing, finishing, and continuous. Huge steel ingots
from the open hearth department, kept hot in a series of hot-air soaking pits,
first proceeded to the blooming mill. The steel passed through a series of
enormous rollers that squeezed the steel into a long bloom that measured
four inches on each side. The bloom then passed to the roughing mill, which
further reduced the diameter of the steel and cut it into lengths. The finishing and continuous mills rolled the steel into various semifinished and
finished bars and square billets. Duquesne did not specialize in finished products but instead shipped much of its semifinished steel to finishing mills for
further milling. Two years after completion of the rolling department, Carnegie added a new blooming mill. The first blooming mill, now only two years
old, became known as the "old mill," a name that bespoke the innovation
and expansion of this early stage of steelmaking.[12]

The expansion program proceeded along with the integration of Carnegie's big three plants: the Duquesne, Homestead, and Edgar Thomson Works. Duquesne and the Edgar Thomson Works, along with the two Carrie blast furnaces in Rankin and the two Lucy blast furnaces in Pittsburgh, produced all the iron for the Carnegie Steel Co. In these four blast-furnace departments resided one-fifth of the iron production capacity of the United States in 1900. Duquesne, Homestead, and Edgar Thomson also produced most of the steel for Carnegie, and more than a quarter of the U.S. supply. In addition, the three mills rolled the majority of the company's steel. The modernization of the Duquesne Works now provided Carnegie with a new mix of finished and semifinished steel products. The Duquesne and Homestead Works, both of which began as rail mills, dropped this product line, leaving it for the Edgar Thomson Works. The Homestead Works came to concentrate on structural shapes, plates, blooms, and billets, whereas the Duquesne Works specialized in blooms, billets, and bars. Carnegie linked the three mills with the Union Railroad (a Carnegie subsidiary), which allowed him to ship unfinished and semifinished products from one plant to another for processing. This allowed Carnegie not only to avoid unnecessary duplication but gave him the ability to shuffle work between one plant and another during a strike.[13]

In only nine years Carnegie had built one of the world's greatest steelworks at Duquesne. Simply to connect the plant's various mills and departments took twenty-five miles of railroad track. The editor of the local newspaper, who proudly called Duquesne a "Carnegie Town," likened the town and its mill to a meteor that "darted out of space and cut a brilliant path across the horizon." Not satisfied with this heavenly comparison, he added, "An infant in years, it is the acknowledged young giant and the mastodon of the unconquered and unconquerable Monongahela valley."[14]

Even before Carnegie finished construction of the blast furnaces, open hearth shop, and rolling mills, he had made plans to extend the Duquesne Works into finished steel products. This expansion owed to the increasing competition between Carnegie and J. P. Morgan. Carnegie's empire rested on his dominance of the basic steel market; his mills produced primarily iron, and unfinished and semifinished steel, which he sold to other steel companies for finishing. By the end of the century, however, many finishing-steel companies, including Federal Steel and J. P. Morgan's National Tube Works, planned to increase basic iron and steel production. Carnegie feared that as these companies came to produce their own iron and steel, his position in the industry would be threatened. As a defensive measure, he planned to move into the finished steel business. Duquesne would benefit with the construction of a nail and wire mill. Morgan, threatened by Carnegie's growing empire and opposed to Carnegie's penchant for brutal competition, saw nothing but increased and destructive competition ahead. Hoping to avoid it, Morgan offered to buy out Carnegie and other competing steelmakers and unite them into one company. Carnegie agreed and sold his company for $492 million in 1901. Morgan combined it with seven other companies to form the United States Steel Corp., the world's first billion-dollar corporation.[15]

U.S. Steel spent the next twenty years consolidating and integrating these eight steel companies. The corporation disposed of unprofitable plants, built new ones, bought others, and acquired and integrated in its empire shipping companies, coal lands, and railroad lines. The corporation also spent millions on plant expansion, including significant improvements to the Duquesne Works. Duquesne remained within the Carnegie Steel Co., which kept its corporate identity and continued its role as a provider of the industry's basic iron and steel needs.[16] Although the buyout ended plans for a wire and nail mill at Duquesne, U.S. Steel increased the iron, steel, and rolling capacities of the mill. Between 1902 and 1918 the Duquesne Works added two blast furnaces and twenty-one open hearth furnaces. The plant now contained six blast furnaces, and thirty-three open hearth furnaces housed in two open hearth shops. The rolling mills expanded to include three mills for blooms, large billets, and slabs; two mills for small billets and sheet bar; and seven bar mills.[17]

By World War I the Duquesne Works stood as an imposing feature of the western Pennsylvania industrial landscape. The mill represented the early stage of steelmaking in the United States, when steelmakers lavished money on their mills, increased steelmaking capacity, and pioneered technological innovations. Duquesne had been rebuilt twice by 1901, and during the next two decades was expanded and upgraded further. These changes not only altered the mill physically but brought profound changes to the social and cultural makeup of the workforce, labor relations within the mill, and the power structure of the town.

A Fragmented Workforce

Andrew Carnegie's and U.S. Steel's bold rebuilding of the Duquesne Works fundamentally altered both the size and social composition of the mill's workforce. Although the rebuilding added great numbers of workers to the mill, it also fragmented the large workforce along several different lines. Workers were divided by ethnicity and race but also by skill, department, and even shift. In turn, this affected both the amount of control workers had over the production process and their ability to mount strikes.

Before Carnegie took over the mill, the workers at Duquesne formed a smaller and more cohesive unit. The plant consisted of only three mills (Bessemer, blooming, and rail) and had only five hundred workers. Much of the production depended heavily on skilled workers, who held a great amount of bargaining power because of their production knowledge. The workers also formed a more homogeneous social grouping. Although eastern European workers had begun working in the mill by 1890, the majority of the workforce had been born in the United States, Scotland, Wales, Ireland, and Germany.[18]

The rebuilding of the Duquesne Works vastly increased the company's labor needs. The original workforce of 500 grew to 2,400 in 1901, 3,000 in 1905, 4,000 in 1910, and roughly 6,000 by 1920.[19] As the number of workers increased, the social composition of the workforce changed. Employment in the Pennsylvania iron and steel industry doubled between 1880 and 1910, and the industry increasingly depended on southern and eastern European immigrants to staff its mills. By the 1890s Duquesne management was hiring more Slovaks, Magyars, Poles, Lithuanians, Italians, Croats, Czechs, and Russians than Americans, British, and Germans.[20]

As in all steel mills, men dominated not only production jobs but also clerical work. Both workers and managers viewed steel work as too dangerous and heavy for women. Although other industries were undergoing a feminization of clerical work, steel mills held firm to the older ideal of the male clerical worker. Female employment at the Duquesne Works before World War I was limited primarily to hospital work. Although women broke into clerical jobs during the war, only about forty-five of six thousand workers were women. By the end of the 1920s, only nineteen women worked at the mill—six hospital workers, seven clerks, three telephone operators, and three stenographers. At the same time, hundreds of men held clerical positions there. Female employment declined further during the 1930s.[21]

World War I brought more changes to the male labor force, contributing to a deeper fragmentation. Steel mills experienced a severe labor shortage during the war, caused by increased labor needs, lower immigration rates from traditional labor sources in southern and eastern Europe, and a loss of workers to the military. To fill its labor needs Duquesne recruited from new labor pools, which further complicated the mill's ethnic mixture. Beginning in 1918, the mill hired Turks, Macedonians, Dalmatians, and Armenians, ethnic groups that had no previous representation at the mill. They remained both ethnically and spatially separate from the other workers, housed in a large labor camp.[22] A more important and long-lasting effect of the labor shortage was the introduction of large numbers of black workers. The Duquesne Works, which employed only fifteen blacks in 1915, had 344 on the payroll by the beginning of the Great Steel Strike four years later.[23]

By 1919 immigrant workers from more than thirty different ethnic groups accounted for 60 percent of the workforce at the Duquesne Works. Slovaks and Magyars, the two largest groups, accounted for 15 percent and 12 percent, respectively. Russians, Lithuanians, Croats, Serbs, and Poles each accounted for 3 percent to 4 percent of the workforce. The foreign-born Irish, Germans, Scots, Welsh, and English, who once held a majority of jobs at the mill, now accounted for just 5 percent of the workforce. Thirty-five percent of workers were white and had been born in the United States; approximately half were second-generation immigrants, the vast majority with parents from northern and western Europe. Blacks held 6 percent of the jobs by 1919.[24]

As newer immigrants entered the steel mill, workers from western and northern Europe, along with U.S.-born white workers, became concentrated in skilled and supervisory positions. At Carnegie mills almost all unskilled workers were southern and eastern Europeans by 1907. Immigrants from western and northern Europe and American workers with the same heritage accounted for 39 percent of the mill's workforce in 1920 but held 73 percent of the skilled trades jobs (carpenter, bricklayer, boilermaker, machinist, millwright, etc.), 88 percent of the highest-paying skilled positions (first helper, heater, finisher, and roller), and 85 percent of the lower management positions (see table 1). Still, as these percentages suggest, the more recent immigrants had risen into higher-skilled positions by World War I, breaking down job discrimination barriers. This was especially true of semiskilled work. Fifty-five percent of Duquesne's crane operators in 1920, for example, had been born in eastern and southern Europe, and their U.S.-born sons held another 20 percent of these jobs.[25] According to steelworker John Hovanec, "A lot of the people [newer Catholic immigrants] were making break-throughs in the 1920s and early 1930s."[26]

But job mobility for the newer immigrant workers had clear limitations. They made inroads into skilled and skilled trades jobs but in small numbers. The preponderance of American and western and northern European workers in higher-paying and skilled jobs did not result from seniority but from management's privileging of one ethnicity over another. By 1920 immigrant workers from southern and eastern Europe had been in the mill for decades. For workers with sixteen or more years of seniority, immigrant Slovaks alone outnumbered immigrant British and German workers nearly 2 to 1 in 1920.[27]

The rebuilding of the mill changed not only the ethnic composition of the workforce but also its skill levels. As the Duquesne Works grew, it came to depend much less on skilled labor. By 1910 the typical integrated basic steel

Table 1. Skilled Workers and Management at Duquesne, Percentages by Ethnicity and Race, 1920

	Total Male Workforce (N = 1006)	Skilled Trades (N = 137)	Skilled Jobs[1] (N = 24)	Lower Management (N = 20)	Upper Management (N = 4)	Skilled, Skilled Trades, and Management (N = 185)
U.S.-born whites with U.S.-born parents	19%	38%	46%	50%	100%	42%
U.S.-born whites whose parents migrated from western and northern Europe	11	26	21	20	0	24
Immigrants from western and northern Europe	9	9	21	15	0	11
Immigrants from southern and eastern Europe	46	19	13	15	0	17
U.S.-born whites whose parents migrated from southern and eastern Europe	7	8	0	0	0	6
Blacks	8	0	0	0	0	0
	100%	100%	101%[2]	100%	100%	100%

Sources: U.S. Census, Fourteenth Census of the United States: 1920, Manuscript Schedules, vol. 10, Pennsylvania, Allegheny County, reel 1511.

1. Skilled jobs in this category included first helper, finisher, roller, and heater.
2. Exceeds 100 percent due to rounding.

mill employed 33 percent of its workforce in skilled jobs, 28 percent in semi-skilled positions, and 39 percent in unskilled jobs. However, each department varied in its skill composition. Blast furnaces, which used automated delivery systems to unload raw materials into furnaces, employed a high percentage of both semiskilled workers (41 percent) to direct and monitor the flow of materials, and unskilled workers (51 percent) to do common laboring jobs, but few skilled workers (7 percent). In contrast, rolling mills used the highest percentage of skilled workers (40 percent) and the lowest percentage of semiskilled workers (20 percent). The open hearth department had the most even distribution of workers, with approximately 36 percent skilled, 32 percent unskilled, and 32 percent semiskilled.[28]

Because skill divisions varied by department, the fragmentation of the workforce along skill and ethnic lines did not occur evenly throughout the Duquesne Works. Each department had its unique skill and ethnic identity because of its particular labor needs. The blast-furnace department, with its large numbers of unskilled and semiskilled workers, had a large number of eastern and southern European immigrants and blacks. But because of the high number of semiskilled positions, this department also afforded unskilled workers the greatest job mobility into semiskilled positions. The rolling mill, with its dependence on skilled labor, had a large percentage of Americans and northern and western European immigrants. Highly skilled rollers, for instance, tended to be Swedes. Because the open hearth department had a relatively even mix of skill levels, it had a greater mix of workers.[29]

Compounding the ethnic and skill fragmentation of the workforce were the size and layout of the mill and its departments, which led to a further spatial separation. The Duquesne Works covered more than two hundred acres. An eight-block residential neighborhood in the middle split the mill into two sections—the upper works (blast furnaces and open hearth) and the lower works (rolling mills). Workers in various departments labored miles from each other, entered and left work through separate gates, and had no regular contact on the job. But workers in the same department did not necessarily have contact, either. The open hearth department was divided into two shops, each with its own building, workforce, and work rotation schedule. The rolling mill department experienced the greatest dislocation, with seven bar mills, three blooming mills, and several other mills, most of which were housed in separate buildings.[30] In addition, the use of shift work, complicated work rotations between day and night, and varied days off further divided the workforce.[31]

The ethnic, skill, and spatial fragmentation of Duquesne's workforce gave management an advantage whenever workers tried to unionize. Before the first rebuilding of the Duquesne Works, the more cohesive nature of the workforce and the small size of the mill allowed workers to shut the plant down on two occasions. Workers accomplished this first during the 1889 Allegheny Bessemer strike, although management finally gained the upper hand and ended the strike when it secured court injunctions that sent the strike leaders to jail with heavy fines. Andrew Carnegie also faced a strike at Duquesne a year after he bought the plant and before he began his rebuilding program. When Homestead workers struck Carnegie in the famous 1892 strike, Duquesne workers were highly supportive of the labor action. Steelworkers at the Duquesne and Edgar Thomson Works joined the Amalgamated and shut their mills down in sympathy. They also took up arms alongside the Homestead workers against the Pinkertons whom Henry Frick had brought to the plant by barge. The sympathy strike at Duquesne lasted two weeks and was not without violence. When the company tried to reopen the plant with loyal workers, the strikers waged a street battle that kept the mill closed. As management had during the Allegheny Bessemer strike, Carnegie looked to the government to suppress the strike. Federal troops arrived shortly after the violent clash; their orders were to reopen the mill. The strikers attempted one more battle to keep the plant shut down, but they were routed. The day ended with federal troops scouring the hills around Duquesne for the fleeing strike leaders.[32]

After the formation of U.S. Steel in 1901, another labor conflict at the Duquesne Works revealed the long-term effects of the mill's expansion. Within the first few months of its formation U.S. Steel faced negotiations with the Amalgamated about the renewal of contracts at the company's tin plate, hoop, and sheet steel mills. During early negotiations the corporation appeared to step back from the labor policy of the old Carnegie managers, who believed that "if a workman sticks up his head, hit it."[33] Corporate officials did not want a disruption of production during the first year; thus they directed the presidents of U.S. Steel's subsidiaries to be cautious. The presidents could sign reasonable wage scales with the union where it already existed, but they could not allow the unionization of nonunion mills. Bargaining between the corporation and the Amalgamated quickly deteriorated, although U.S. Steel signaled a major policy shift by expressing a willingness to allow a minor extension of the union. The Amalgamated, completely misreading its own strength and U.S. Steel's resolve, pushed for unionization well beyond what U.S. Steel would grant. When U.S. Steel balked, the Amalgamated called a strike, hoping to include all U.S. Steel plants. The strike lasted two months and ended in total defeat for the Amalgamated.[34]

The strike mostly affected the corporation's smaller mills and almost completely missed the large basic steel plants. However, the Duquesne Works was an exception. Toward the end of the Amalgamated's walkout, fifty to sixty skilled open hearth workers struck Duquesne in response to a desperate strike call from the Amalgamated lodge at the McKeesport Tube Works across the river. Despite a parade, rally, and door-to-door canvassing by the strikers, they failed to expand the strike. The small group of striking Duquesne workers came from only one shift and found themselves isolated. Management fired them and temporarily placed supervisors and clerical workers in their jobs.[35]

Had the open hearth workers at Duquesne been able to shut down their department, U.S. Steel planned to keep the rest of the mill open. Iron from Duquesne's blast furnaces would travel by rail to Homestead. Open hearth furnaces there would turn the iron into steel, and it would be shipped back to Duquesne as ingots to be rolled.[36] Duquesne Works management also intended to borrow skilled open hearth workers from Homestead to reopen the Duquesne furnaces if the strike spread within the department. Whether Homestead steelworkers would have scabbed on their Duquesne brothers remains an open question. But the Duquesne workers must have noticed that the company used Coal and Iron Police from Homestead to guard the Duquesne plant's gates during the strike. The Commonwealth of Pennsylvania allowed coal and steel companies to petition the governor during labor troubles to swear in company-appointed workers and managers as police. If the governor approved, a minor formality until the 1930s, Pennsylvania deputized the company guards, providing them with full police powers. During the 1901 strike U.S. Steel appointed workers from the Homestead and Edgar Thomson Works to serve as police at Duquesne.[37] The interplant solidarity of the Homestead strike of 1892 had vanished.

The defeat of the Duquesne workers demonstrated the difficulty the Amalgamated now faced in mounting strikes. Gone was the relative cohesiveness born of common ethnic ties and skill levels. Workers were now divided not only by ethnicity and skill throughout the mill but also by skill and ethnicity within the different departments. In addition, each department and mill was a separate work area, and the shift schedule reinforced the separation of workers. Because of the complex fragmentation of the workforce, in 1901 the union could bring workers from only one department out on strike and only the skilled workers from one shift at that.

Welfare Capitalism

The 1901 strike profoundly affected U.S. Steel's labor policy. Although the corporation negotiated with the Amalgamated, the strike convinced the board of directors that it had to remove the union from its plants. In 1909, more confident of its position, U.S. Steel stopped negotiating with all unions.

But edict alone could not banish unions or ensure labor peace. U.S. Steel combined its anti-union policies with welfare capitalism, which tied the economic and social interests of the worker to the corporation. Although centrally planned, implementation of welfare capitalist measures, such as stock option plans, pension benefits, accident insurance, health and safety programs, and housing plans, remained largely the province of relatively autonomous individual plant managers. At Duquesne an enthusiastic and creative management approach to welfare capitalism would be a key element in the mill's relative labor peace.

When U.S. Steel stopped negotiating with unions, corporate officials announced that all plants would be operated as open shops. U.S. Steel claimed that the open-shop policy did not discriminate against a man who belonged to a union. According to the corporation, a worker could join a union; however, the corporation refused to recognize, or bargain with, that union. In practice, the primary tactic for upholding the open shop and keeping the company nonunion became the firing and blacklisting of all known or suspected union men. This had been the policy followed by the Duquesne Works during the 1901 strike. And when boilermakers at the mill organized a craft local in 1907, they met the same fate. Management also used spies throughout its mills to uncover any union sympathies. The corporation's efforts bred distrust and silence among workers and effectively stifled any union efforts.[38]

However, an open-shop labor policy, combined with a highly divided workforce, did not ensure labor peace in the corporation's mills. Management needed to create a new labor strategy to deal with its complex grouping of workers. As David Brody has shown, the strategy for stabilizing labor relations in the industry during the early twentieth century was three pronged. First, management induced skilled workers into a dependent relationship. Mixing the threat of firings for union activity with welfare policies, management both forced and reinforced allegiance to the company. Second, mobility ensured that immigrant workers did not have to languish in unskilled jobs, thus reducing a potential area of tension and conflict within the industry. Third, mill managers forged business, social, and political alliances within the community in order to maintain local power over the mill's workforce.[39]

In 1902 U.S. Steel introduced such welfare capitalist measures as stock options, pensions, accident insurance, health and safety measures, and housing programs. The reasons were diverse. In part, they represented the paternalistic views of Judge Elbert H. Gary, the chairman of the board of U.S. Steel who had once been a county judge. The programs also served to boost U.S. Steel's public image, especially after it came under attack for its lengthy work-

week and twelve-hour workday. But the programs also served a more practical purpose: to steer the skilled workforce away from unionism.[40]

U.S. Steel's welfare programs sought to make the skilled worker dependent
on the corporation. It achieved this through stipulations. The stock plan allowed workers to buy U.S. Steel stock on an installment plan, which, in addition to dividends, paid the worker $5 per year for five years on each share
of stock purchased. The incentive encouraged workers to hold on to the stock
and continue to work for the corporation in order to receive the bonus. But
to obtain the yearly bonus, workers also had to produce a letter from their
boss stating that they had "shown a proper interest in [the] welfare and
progress" of the company. Similarly, the corporation's pension plan provided pensions only for "faithful" employees. Workers who struck the company or favored unions could be denied a pension. Housing programs, which
offered loans and company-built houses to workers, operated in the same
way. To receive the benefits of welfare capitalism, the worker had to remain
employed and compliant with the company's policies.[41]

It is a mistake, however, to view U.S. Steel's welfare capitalist measures as
aimed solely at the skilled workforce. Although this had been the planned
effect of these programs in their early conceptualizations, welfare capitalism
also affected the unskilled and semiskilled worker, especially immigrants. U.S.
Steel, which at first had assumed only skilled workers would provide the bulk
of the long-term labor force and therefore were the focus of its welfare programs, did not necessarily distinguish skill as a factor in its programs. Managers at the individual plants also could provide pensions and company housing for unskilled and semiskilled immigrant workers. The corporation's
welfare programs affected the immigrant labor force precisely because these
workers came to view their steel employment as permanent. Although many
had come to the United States with plans to make money and return to their
homeland, Frank Huff Serene has shown that by the end of the 1910s greater
numbers of immigrant steelworkers had settled permanently in the Monongahela Valley than previously had been suspected. Even during hard economic times these workers remained in the mill towns and did not return to their
homelands.[42] Further, John Bodnar has shown that these immigrant steelworkers in Pennsylvania sought stability and security from their jobs.[43] Because welfare programs offered housing and pension programs that helped
provide security, they appealed to immigrant workmen. At Duquesne in 1919,
31 percent of the workers with more than twenty years' seniority were born
in eastern and southern European countries. Because of their persistence,
many had advanced into semiskilled jobs. As important was that corporate
pensions, paid to retired workers with thirty years' seniority, were within their

reach. Foreign-born Duquesne workers, who bought houses at more than twice the rate of U.S.-born workers, also sought out corporate welfare programs that provided housing.[44] Diehl, the general superintendent, found himself swamped with requests from these workers; they wanted to buy company houses. His waiting list for company homes in 1919 included about two hundred immigrants.[45]

Duquesne management's success in incorporating unskilled and semi-skilled workers in its welfare programs rested on U.S. Steel's corporate structure and the relative autonomy of individual plants. The corporation's welfare programs, like its open-shop policy, mixed centralization with local autonomy. Corporate officials set basic policy but left implementation up to the individual plant superintendents. Even when U.S. Steel centralized its welfare programs in the Bureau of Safety, Sanitation, and Welfare in 1911, the new bureau did not direct the welfare programs. Instead, it provided a central office that would obtain information and disseminate it among the subsidiary companies. When the bureau soon broadened its interests to plant sanitation and community welfare programs, it provided guidelines for the individual plants but again allowed plant managers to direct the programs.[46]

Duquesne managers already had shown how local autonomy could affect immigrant workers in relation to job promotion. It appears from evidence at other Pittsburgh-area U.S. Steel mills that advancement into semi-skilled and skilled trades positions was more frequent at Duquesne than at the other mills.[47] However, where Duquesne showed its greatest autonomy and leadership was in both creating and sustaining welfare programs aimed at immigrant workers. In 1914 the Pittsburgh *Gazette Times* singled out the Duquesne Works as having a welfare program "probably unequaled in any other mill town in the United States." The industry trade journal *Iron Age* also found the Duquesne program to be "further advanced . . . than elsewhere."[48]

Much of the credit for this success goes to Homer Williams, the general superintendent of the plant during the 1900s and 1910s, before Diehl. Williams began his steel career at seventeen in the Cambria Iron Works. He left his job to attend college, then returned to the industry as a chemist. He quickly worked his way up through several companies, becoming assistant superintendent of the Homestead Works in 1903. That same year U.S. Steel appointed him general superintendent of the Duquesne Works. Williams was one of the new breed of corporate manager, responsible for achieving not only high production levels at low costs but also labor peace and a reservoir of goodwill within the community. Technical expertise, broad-based experience, and managerial leadership, gained both on the job and in college, were only a few of his skills. He also was an adept town booster, civic leader, and political strategist. Under Williams's stewardship the Duquesne Works became the supreme power in town, enjoying widespread support within the business and middle classes. Williams's success would not go unnoticed; in 1915 he was named president of the Carnegie Steel Corp.[49]

Duquesne's welfare programs began in 1904, the year after Williams arrived, with the completion of the town's Carnegie Library. The building also housed a gymnasium, swimming pool, bowling alleys, meeting rooms, and auditorium. Although the library officially was a public institution, a gift from Andrew Carnegie to the people of Duquesne, mill managers oversaw all facets of the library, deciding which books would appear on its shelves and which organizations could hold meetings in its rooms. As in other Carnegie towns, the library became the focal point for company-directed recreation, sporting leagues, lectures, and holiday programs.[50] With the inauguration of the library programs Williams also instituted safety and sanitation changes at the plant that improved working conditions. He formed safety committees, installed sanitary water fountains, showers, and lunchrooms and improved toilets and lockers. These programs were not atypical of U.S. Steel's early welfare work, much of which centered on the Carnegie libraries and improving plant conditions to cut down on the high accident rate.

Williams's pioneering work came from his inclusion of less-skilled immigrant workers in Duquesne's plant-level welfare programs. Instead of viewing these workers as a floating labor force, the company sought to integrate the foreign born in the plant and community. Thus Williams introduced education classes aimed directly at the immigrant workers. In conjunction with various citizens' groups, he established English classes for foreign-born workers in 1907, years ahead of the other area plants. The popular English classes were soon complemented by drawing, math, and chemistry courses, which could be beneficial for job advancement.[51]

The courses served a number of purposes for the mill managers. Based on the Roberts Method of teaching English, the courses stressed language necessary for working in the mill. In learning the language, foreign-born workers also learned plant rules and expectations, such as safety rules and how to punch their time cards for work. Other lessons taught workers what to do in case of accidents and how to perform various unskilled and semiskilled jobs.[52] English classes also sought to integrate workers in the broader non-immigrant community. But the company did this in a way that included local businessmen. Raymond Hofen, the director of the foreign department of the Duquesne Trust Co., a bank established by Carnegie Steel Co. managers, served as a leader of the foreign-language program. Hofen drummed up community support for the program by inviting the Reverend David M. Cleveland, director of the Western Pennsylvania Training School for Adult Foreigners, to Duquesne. In a speech that appealed to businessmen, Cleveland noted that English classes would decrease foreign-born workers' use of immigrant businesses and banks and increase their dependence on "American" stores. Ties between the steel company and community groups were solidified further through an arrangement whereby the mill paid for the English classes, and various community groups, including the Board of Trade (a chamber of commerce organization), organized the classes. In this way the company built goodwill and support among local businessmen, which translated into greater political power for Duquesne Works managers.[53]

English and technical classes for workers formed only one part of a broader Americanization program practiced at Duquesne and later at other U.S. Steel facilities. The company also offered English classes for workers' wives, although these classes stressed different lessons. In addition, the Duquesne Works managers provided an extensive summer program for its workers and their families that included films, slide shows, and lectures. Aimed at immigrant families, the programs stressed lessons in civics ("How to Become an American Citizen"), virtue ("Honesty Is the Best Policy"), and politics ("A Day in Washington, D.C."). Programs also stressed safety and health issues, such as preventing the spread of disease. The Duquesne Works management, however, did not subscribe to the notion that it was necessary to aggressively socialize immigrants as Americans; mill officials showed an acceptance of and appreciation for eastern and southern European cultures. The company's summer programs included classes in folk dancing and travel films of Europe, and the Christmas festival included the participation of organized ethnic groups.[54]

The mill provided other services and programs that bettered the lives of workers and their families. The plant supplied a gardener to assist workers' children in raising plants and to supervise a large community garden, both of which provided food for mill families. The company hired a visiting nurse to check on sick workers and their families and make referrals to hospitals. The company provided day-care centers for children whose fathers had died in mill accidents. The company's yearly summer playground program became one of the centerpieces of the plant's welfare efforts. The company hired full-time workers to supervise two playgrounds, including one located in the heart of the immigrant community. The summer programs offered films, festivals, hikes, and classes in carpentry, folk dancing, sewing, and other arts and crafts. The elaborate playground programs, which served more people at Duquesne than at any other Carnegie mill, were used by more than six hundred people a day during the summer.[55]

The playground program further demonstrated how the mill gained business allies within the city. The Chamber of Commerce had established a similar program but found itself unable to pay for it. The mill simply took over the program and expanded it. In a similar situation Williams took over management of the town's poor relief from the Associated Charities run by the Board of Commerce (whether this was the Board of Trade under a new name is not clear). These maneuvers brought the company greater community support, especially among businessmen, but they also provided the company with greater social control of its workforce and the town. The search for middle-class support was also evident in the mill's city beautification projects. The Duquesne Works sponsored annual city clean-up drives and handed out awards to mill employees with the best-kept yards and gardens in town, programs that appealed to a middle-class sense of order.[56]

When World War I led to the hiring of hundreds of black workers, the Duquesne Works reproduced its welfare programs for the new workforce, although on a segregated basis. Seeking to integrate black workers in the company as it had unskilled immigrant workers, the Duquesne Works hired a black welfare worker. First proposed as a solution to the problem of high black turnover rates by the Pittsburgh Urban League, the new position itself suffered from high turnover during the early 1920s, until the appointment of Charles Broadfield, an African American steelworker. Broadfield then held the position for several decades, providing several services for black workers and the mill. He recruited black workers from the South, ran a boardinghouse for blacks, and at times acted as a community spokesperson for the black community in such matters as police affairs. He also provided black workers with many of the services that the regular welfare programs provided for immigrant workers. Broadfield began remedial classes for black workers and their families, gave talks on various subjects related to the mill and community, and helped organize sports teams. When he was not conducting these activities, however, the company used him as a chauffeur and "messenger boy." The mill also hired two black nurses, who aided black patients in the plant's hospital and visited sick workers and their family members in their homes.[57]

Although welfare capitalism allowed the Duquesne management to secure broader business-class support for its policies, the company had less luck with the town's wealthy landowners, who were the oldest residents of the Duquesne area and remained a bitter political enemy of the mill through the early 1900s. The mill's efforts to build support from business interests based on common economic and social goals did not work with the landowners. Instead, mill managers found it necessary to engage them in a bruising political battle for control of the town.

Duquesne Politics

Before the construction of the Duquesne Works, the region was rural, inhabited by approximately three hundred immigrant Scottish, Irish, and English farmers and German farmers and miners who arrived in the eighteenth and nineteenth centuries. In the late 1880s and early 1890s the building of the steel mill, glass factory, and tube mill created a boomtown and social chaos. Haphazard development and little social control led to surges in crime. Without a police force, older citizens formed "vigilance committees" to patrol the town, but they soon tired of the effort. Concerned with the growing anarchy, older landed and established residents petitioned the state legislature for incorporation. They wanted above all else to form a police force. Both the Allegheny Bessemer Steel Co. and, subsequently, Andrew Carnegie opposed incorporation. Steel companies preferred to build in unincorporated areas, not just to provide room for growth but also to avoid taxation. Carnegie also had wanted the Duquesne Works precisely because it provided him with direct control of the workforce, both on and off the job. Incorporation would lessen his control, and might, as in the case of Homestead, allow workers to gain political power. After protracted legal stalling, the industrialists lost the battle, and the city of Duquesne became incorporated in 1891.[58]

Incorporation did not end the conflict between the mill and landed families. It intensified it. Leading the incorporation effort were the Crawfords, a long-established landowning family. Since the 1790s the Crawfords, descendants of Scottish Presbyterians, had owned land in what was to become Duquesne. Over the years the Crawford lands became one of the largest holdings in the area. The Crawford family's wealth increased greatly in 1888 when the Howard Glass Co. bought twenty acres of choice river bottom from the family. Ironically, the land sale furthered the industrialization of Duquesne, the effects of which the Crawfords would spend years fighting.

James C. Crawford, Sr., and his son John Crawford led the movement for incorporation of the new town. When the town held its first election in 1892, the senior Crawford served as election judge, and his son became burgess, a municipal office equivalent to mayor. John Crawford soon won election as a state senator, but he remained active in local politics as a member of the city council. John's brother James S. Crawford followed him as burgess, becoming the family's leading local political figure. The Crawfords controlled local politics for the town's first thirteen years, easily winning a city council majority with the solid backing of other established landed families. In addition to their political power, the Crawford brothers, Edwin, James, and John, gained considerable economic influence by opening the town's first bank, the First

National Bank of Duquesne. Edwin Crawford also purchased the United States Iron and Tin Plate Manufacturing Co. in nearby McKeesport.[59]

The Crawfords' political and economic power faced continual challenge from the Carnegie Steel Co. In order to counter the Crawfords, Carnegie Steel's managers established a rival bank, the Duquesne Trust Co., and bought one of the two local newspapers, the *Duquesne Observer*. Aiming a steady barrage of charges against the "Crawford Ring," the mill forces mounted an effective political opposition within the Republican Party in 1905. After winning some minor races that year, the "mill crowd" launched a frontal assault on the Crawfords in 1906. Charging the Crawford Ring with corruption and incompetence, the mill ticket also attacked James S. Crawford for his treatment of the local workforce. The company-owned newspaper argued that Crawford's police officers regularly arrested workmen on trumped-up charges, and that Crawford refused to allow the company to build an overpass into the plant that would save workers from walking across dangerous railroad tracks. The mill ticket routed the Crawford forces in the general election, with four mill superintendents and skilled workers winning a majority of seats on the city council. Their victory was aided by mill foremen and superintendents, who marched their work crews into the polling places on election day.[60]

The defeat of the Crawford faction in the Republican Party marked the culmination of the mill management's control of the town. The political victory coincided with the expansion of Carnegie Steel's welfare programs, which cemented the mill's middle-class and business support. Around this time the company also bought the other local newspaper, the *Duquesne Times*, and merged it with its own paper, silencing a voice once critical of the steel mill and its labor policies.[61] Eager to reunite the Republican Party, the Carnegie managers also allowed the Crawfords back into the political fold. The two factions united in 1909 when the mill openly supported James Crawford for a council seat. When Duquesne became a city and elected its first mayor in 1918, Crawford received the mill's endorsement. And the mill management's support kept him in the mayor's office through 1937. The two factions also found a common economic interest when Edwin Crawford's tin plate plant announced that it would begin buying its steel exclusively from the Duquesne Works.[62]

The management of the Duquesne Works had positioned itself well before the strike of 1919. It had built a highly successful welfare program, which not only reached out to the mill's unskilled and semiskilled immigrant workforce and skilled U.S.-born workers but secured middle-class and business support. Paternalism was complemented by the threat of repression, which had a long history at the Duquesne Works. And after intense political feuding, mill managers had formed an imposing political alliance with the Craw-fords. This alliance would have far-reaching consequences for the mill and its workers, as became abundantly clear in 1919.

The Great Steel Strike

When the Great Steel Strike began, Duquesne experienced only a temporary disruption of production. The strike was like a tornado, touching down in towns such as Rankin and Clairton and sparing Duquesne. But nothing was random about the low level of strike activity in Duquesne. Management had established a system of labor control that put a damper on worker unrest. Although Duquesne shared much in common with other steel mills, the strike revealed how management had inoculated its workforce against the steel rebellion.

The Steel Strike of 1919 was the result of long-standing worker grievances and the disruption caused by World War I.[63] The steelworkers' greatest complaint was the length of their workday. U.S. Steel generally scheduled work-ers for twelve-hour days, seven days a week, with workers rotating from day to night and back every one to two weeks. At least once a month they had to work the "long turn" when they changed shifts, which entailed working two back-to-back shifts, twenty-four hours straight, resting for twelve hours, and then returning for the regular twelve-hour shift. The only solace came two weeks after the long turn, when the shift change provided them with a full twenty-four hours off. Thomas Bell, in his novel *Out of This Furnace,* cap-tured the brutality and monotony of this work schedule: "When human flesh and blood could stand no more it got up at five in the morning as usual and put on its work clothes and went into the mill; and when the whistle blew it came home."[64]

Despite various private and public crusades challenging the twelve-hour day, U.S. Steel remained doggedly committed to it. Another crusade against the seven-day workweek, led within U.S. Steel by one of its vice presidents, William Dickson, proved more successful. U.S. Steel officially abolished the seven-day week in 1910, although not all departments ended the practice. During the war, however, the seven-day week returned to most mills. The corporation argued that it had to reinstate the practice because of the war-time labor shortage. But by the summer of 1919 the seven-day week and twelve-hour day were still in place, and steelworkers viewed them as perma-nent fixtures.[65]

Next to hours of work, low wages angered steelworkers most. But unlike hours, wages were not a universal complaint. Skilled workers in steel mills could earn high wages, well above the minimum comfort standards of the day. These were the workers who had enough income to invest in U.S. Steel stock-buying plans. But for the majority of steelworkers, wages proved quite low. U.S. Steel granted a series of raises during World War I that doubled the rate for unskilled laborers, but this proved to be insufficient. First, the raises only tended to bring rates into line with other manufacturing industries. Second, wartime inflation ate up the increases. In both 1918 and 1919 the typical unskilled worker in the industry earned less than the minimum subsistence level for a family of five. In addition, any money a steelworker saved for returning to his homeland or for buying a house could be wiped out during the many frequent layoffs that unskilled workers experienced.[66]

Neither of these grievances—long hours or low wages—had led to a large-scale rebellion of steelworkers before World War I. But the war both sharpened these grievances and changed the worldviews of immigrant steelworkers. Shut off from the option of returning to their homeland, most now regarded the United States as their permanent home. Intensive Americanization drives by the federal government and the steel industry facilitated this change. Steelmakers praised immigrant workers and noted their participation in the democratic war. Many immigrant steelworkers now bought Liberty bonds and became more assertive of their rights as U.S. residents. This assertion of rights became even more pronounced when the war ended and the government and steelmakers retreated to their prewar treatment of these workers.[67]

Steelworkers still were not organized. The American Federation of Labor (AFL), bolstered by large membership gains and union advances in the meat-packing industry, decided to take on the task. It established the National Committee for Organizing Iron and Steel Workers in 1918, composed of twenty-four unions, including the Amalgamated Association of Iron, Steel, and Tin Workers. Heading the National Committee were John Fitzpatrick and William Z. Foster, leaders in the Chicago labor movement. The National Committee did not support industrial unionism but instead sought to organize all steelworkers and later divide them into the various craft unions; the majority of the industry's workforce fell into the Amalgamated or the International Union of Mine, Mill, and Smelter Workers. The effort was financed by a tax on each participating union. By the end of the strike, the flaws in the National Committee's structure were painfully clear, as were its misguided commitment to craft unionism and the inadequacy of its financing.[68]

The strike began on September 22, 1919. With the steel companies unwilling to negotiate, and no longer able to forestall the inevitable strike, the National Committee called out all 500,000 steelworkers across the country; how many went out is not clear. It first appeared that Duquesne workers might support the strike, with fully one quarter of the workforce of 5,700 skipping work the first day. Would the strike movement grow? On the second day came the answer: strike support was vanishing. By the end of the first week the number of workers staying away from work dropped by more than half, from fourteen hundred to six hundred. Company spokesmen even noted that not all six hundred could be considered strikers. Many stayed away out of fear, while others just decided to sit the strike out. Production levels during the second week returned to near normal, and by all measures the strike had failed miserably.[69]

Skilled and U.S.-born workers continued to work through the strike at Duquesne and most other Pittsburgh-area mills. U.S. Steel's welfare policies had successfully tied the interests of these workers to the company. Many had invested their savings in U.S. Steel stock, bought Carnegie homes, or expected to retire on company pensions. Honoring the strike would have imperiled these investments. Older skilled steelworkers also had the most to lose from a strike. They had few transferable skills and could lose a well-paying job and have their name placed on an industry blacklist. In addition, the industry exploited the deep ethnic divisions between the immigrant and U.S.-born workforces. Steel managers, aided by public officials and newspapers, effectively smeared the strikers as foreign-born radicals. Finally, skilled and U.S.-born workers had historic reasons for not striking. Many still felt betrayed by the Amalgamated for the 1901 debacle, when dozens of skilled workers lost their jobs in that futile walkout.[70]

The strike also found no support from Duquesne's newest workers. The hiring of blacks, Turks, Macedonians, Dalmatians, and Armenians, strictly the result of labor force needs, had the unintended effect of providing the company with additional loyal workers during the strike. Of the 474 new ethnic and black workers hired at the mill during the war, only ten went on strike. Black workers proved the least supportive of the strike throughout the Carnegie mills, and at Duquesne only one struck. According to Pittsburgh-area black welfare workers, African Americans did not join the strike because of the Amalgamated's historic animosity toward blacks, and because African American workers wanted to prove to employers that they were good workers worthy of advancement.[71]

What most distinguished Duquesne from other steel towns was that so few of its foreign-born workers struck. At mills such as Clairton and Homestead, nearly all the foreign-born workforce went on strike. Although a majority of the strikers at Duquesne were immigrants, a much smaller percentage of its immigrant workers went on strike. At Duquesne 94 percent of the strikers had been born in southern and eastern Europe; most had not become U.S. citizens and probably were unskilled. However, only 438 workers stayed out past the second week. At Duquesne fewer than 1 in 6 immigrant workers honored the strike past the first few days.[72]

The lack of strike support by the immigrant workforce was partly the result of Duquesne's welfare programs and its job advancement policies. Foreign-born workers had become rooted in both Duquesne and the mill. Management's policies had offered them enough inducement to tie their futures to the company, not the labor movement. Many older workers were approaching retirement with the promise of a pension. Others were buying homes in the town. Company programs also provided a certain level of health care, along with free summer recreation programs. In addition, the opportunity for foreign-born workers to gain promotion into semiskilled and skilled trades jobs offered a way to break out of poverty. And gaining advancement and the benefits of the welfare programs depended on loyalty to the company.

But those were not the only reasons that immigrant workers failed to sustain the strike. The alliance of mill managers and the Crawford family and management's use of repression were the other reasons. The National Committee began organizing the Pittsburgh region in the spring of 1919, conducting union meetings with varying degrees of success. In McKeesport, after several illegal street meetings, the National Committee gained the right to hold indoor meetings, although only if speeches were given in English. After a month the mayor canceled the meetings, although the National Committee continued to hold street meetings before the strike. Homestead organizers won the rights to hold indoor meetings without a permit and to include foreign-language speakers. Braddock allowed both indoor and outdoor meetings before the strike. But Duquesne proved to be the most difficult town for the National Committee to penetrate.[73]

During the year leading up to the strike, the National Committee found itself unable to hold a single meeting in Duquesne or to open a union office in the town. Mayor Crawford and the city council (of which the mayor was a voting member) passed a resolution in March 1919 that forbade all public meetings, parades, and street assemblages, unless the organizers made a request in writing and it was approved by the mayor. Crawford then simply denied all requests for meetings by the National Committee.[74] Frustrated by the mayor's actions, the AFL organizer J. G. Brown secured an appointment with Crawford and sought permission for a labor meeting in town. Crawford replied, "There will be no meeting held in Duquesne. I'll tell you that Jesus Christ can't hold a meeting in Duquesne." Brown said he believed the claim.[75]

The National Committee tried several times to evade the Duquesne ordinance, but Crawford and the mill quickly blocked the union each time. When organizers rented a lot for a meeting, they found that the Carnegie Land Co. had leased the property before the meeting and posted it with "No Trespassing" signs. With time running out the National Committee decided to hold a mass outdoor meeting in Duquesne just weeks before the strike. Nearly one thousand workers gathered for the illegal assembly, but it ended almost immediately. As the National Committee organizers rose to speak, Duquesne police officers arrested them. Among them were the National Committee's secretary-treasurer, William Z. Foster, and the popular and flamboyant labor organizer and socialist Mother Jones. The police also arrested approximately forty workers on charges of disorderly conduct. The National Committee organizers were temporarily jailed and fined $100, and the workers were fined $25 to $50.[76]

Foster and the other union leaders were especially incensed at Crawford's near-dictatorial control of the community. Crawford wrote the law forbidding meetings, introduced it at a city council meeting, and then voted for it. As mayor he decided that the National Committee could not hold a meeting. Serving as director of public safety, he ordered the arrests of the organizers, and, sitting as city magistrate, he presided over the court that convicted and sentenced them. Crawford also was not one to keep his feelings about unions and labor organizers to himself. When he sentenced one organizer, he told the defendant, "If I had my way you would be sent to the penitentiary for 99 years and when you got out you'd be sent back for 99 years more."[77] But Crawford did not act alone; he had the full support of the Duquesne Works management. When the U.S. Senate committee investigating the steel strike asked Diehl, the mill superintendent, about the attempted meeting, he gave a telling answer: "Well, we simply prohibited it."[78] Management's decision to align politically with James Crawford after the bitter feud had begun to pay huge dividends for the company.

Whatever maneuvering room the National Committee had gained in the various Pittsburgh-area steel towns before the strike, authorities quickly took it away during the strike. Repression by industry, civic, and public leaders was more pronounced in Pittsburgh than in any other steel-producing region. Almost all the Monongahela Valley steel towns prohibited meetings within the first two weeks of the strike. Allegheny County authorities aided the town authorities by issuing an emergency proclamation banning the congregation of three or more people in public. At Duquesne the ban on all unauthorized meetings continued during the strike.[79]

Duquesne had a wide array of public and private authorities to enforce the law during the strike. Crawford bolstered the regular police force by swearing in twenty-two special officers just before the strike. Once the strike began, a group of one hundred "prominent citizens" held a special meeting to discuss protecting themselves and the community. At the end of the meeting Crawford swore all of them in as special officers. Under authority of the Allegheny County sheriff, the Duquesne Works also deputized 143 supervisors and skilled workers to patrol the town. Between the special police sworn in by Crawford and the worker-deputies used by the steel company, the town required no outside police. The state constabulary, which numbered fifty officers for Allegheny County, did not establish a substation in Duquesne, nor did it have to patrol the town.[80]

Mill managers and civic leaders used a combination of persuasion, threats, harassment, and physical intimidation to dissuade people from supporting the strike. At a mass meeting of merchants and property owners, Crawford urged the attendees to refuse all credit to steelworkers, to make workers pay their rent in advance, and to evict any strikers. A "Citizens' Committee," made up of prominent businessmen and town leaders, visited the homes of workers who stayed away from work. In addition, mill officials paid visits to striking workers. The visits played an important role in the first days of the strike, as the company determined who supported the strike and who stayed away from work out of fear. Mill officials assured workers of their safety if they returned to work and warned veteran workers of the loss of their pension benefits if they continued to stay away.[81]

If persuasion failed, arrests followed. On the first day of the strike, police arrested four steelworkers who were sitting on a porch and threw them in jail. Crawford fined each $27.75. Undercover spies also circulated through town in an attempt to entrap striking workers. Frank Lopashanki, a striker, met a stranger in town who struck up a conversation. When the man asked whether a particular worker walking to the plant was a scab, Lopashanki replied that he was. The stranger then showed Lopashanki his badge and hauled him into the mill. From there he was sent to jail for two days without bail. At his hearing he was convicted of "calling a man a scab," fined, and sent back to jail. The arrests served as a pressure tactic. In each instance the company offered to allow the men to return to work if they renounced the strike. Like the company's overall policy of repression and paternalism, the arrests combined suppression and clemency. In Lopashanki's case the company's offer came after he had been on strike for a month. Lopashanki refused and instead languished in jail.[82]

In nearly all the steel-producing regions of the United States the strike had begun to wane by late October. Repression, strikebreakers, and hostile press coverage had taken their toll. Weaknesses within the structure of the National Committee also emerged, exposing financial problems and strategic divisions between the National Committee and the Amalgamated. Steelmakers broke the rebellion at Clairton, Homestead, and Braddock, and the Pittsburgh region returned to near-normal production schedules by late October. The strike officially dragged into winter, but by January it remained visible only in scattered towns. On January 8, 1920, the National Committee officially conceded defeat.[83]

Although the strike was over, Crawford continued to rein in working-class behavior. In early 1920 he introduced an ordinance that required "all able-bodied persons between the ages of eighteen and fifty-five to engage in some useful employment, occupation, business, trade or profession." Failure to work became a crime. Another Crawford ordinance was designed to more strictly enforce all liquor, prostitution, and gambling laws in the city.[84]

As Duquesne became even more repressive, William Z. Foster could not resist one more attempt at opening up the town. In the spring of 1920 the National Committee chose Duquesne as the symbolic target for a renewed organizing campaign. If the union secured the right to meet in Duquesne, the most closed town in the valley, the workers in other steel towns would be less fearful and the union would establish a legal precedent for public union meetings. Supported by the Pittsburgh Central Labor Union and the American Civil Liberties Union, the National Committee used a tactic borrowed from the Industrial Workers of the World (also known as the Wobblies), who would begin an organizing drive with a free speech movement. Clearly, unionism would fail without the ability to hold meetings or open a union headquarters.[85]

The city of Duquesne rejected the National Committee's repeated legal efforts to secure a meeting site at Duquesne; Mayor Crawford deemed the time "inopportune." In early May the National Committee sent six speakers, including a former Presbyterian minister, to hold a rally in the town anyway. A reported crowd of one thousand gathered to hear the speakers, whom police immediately arrested. Regular and specially sworn city police, guards from the steel mill, and a state constable circulated through the crowd and arrested eight more on such charges as blocking the sidewalk. Crawford found the speakers guilty of holding a meeting without a permit and sentenced them to thirty days in jail. Thus ended the last organizing effort of the National Committee.[86]

The National Committee appealed the convictions to the Allegheny County Court in 1920. Ironically, the appeal strengthened Crawford's hold over civil liberties. The court found that the National Committee meeting had been held to "publicly discuss a subject in a locality where in the past its discussion has been the cause of riots, bloodshed and death, a subject which at this time provokes great excitement, bitter feeling and inflamed passions among those who discuss it." Further, the meeting was to be held when "an unusually large number of idle and curious people" were to be present, "ready and willing to be entertained by any attraction which might furnish excitement . . . and in the heat of the argument liable to overstep the bounds of mere verbal polemics." Therefore the mayor had the right to deny the meeting after judging the situation unsafe. This despite the peacefulness of Duquesne's recent past.[87]

Conclusion

The early history of the Duquesne Works, which included two major strikes during its first three years of operation, seemed to foretell turbulent labor relations for the plant. However, Andrew Carnegie's and U.S. Steel's rebuilding of the mill created a deeply fragmented workforce, divided by ethnicity and race and further divided by department and skill. These fissures undermined united working-class action, but they did not abolish the deep-seated workplace grievances steelworkers held. The welfare programs of U.S. Steel and the Duquesne Works ameliorated some of these grievances and created worker dependency on the company. The welfare programs tied skilled workers' economic interests to the corporation, but they also provided services and opportunities for foreign-born and unskilled workers. In addition, immigrant workers could move into higher semiskilled job classifications with better pay. If this did not provide enough protection against unionization, management had other methods at its disposal. The spy system, the Coal and Iron Police, draconian city ordinances against assemblies and rallies, and the city government of Mayor James Crawford all proved effective against the rise of unionism. This elaborate labor strategy, in place by World War I, ensured peace at the Duquesne Works. The Great Steel Strike, which barely touched the mill and its workforce, proved its success. But how long could this labor system last?

2. From Economic Stability to Depression, 1920–34

ELMER MALOY DROPPED OUT of high school in 1911 at fifteen and hired on at the Duquesne Works as a water boy.[1] His father, an Irish Catholic, had been a coal miner and later a steelworker. Young Maloy wanted to learn a skilled trade at the mill, and he soon settled on millwrighting, which entailed repairing and servicing various machinery. He became a millwright's helper, a training position below millwright, but left the mill in 1918 for a stint in the army. When he went to war, the general superintendent told him that he would not be penalized while away and that he would receive any promotions he would have earned if he had stayed. When he returned in August 1919, his foreman did not promote him to millwright as Maloy had expected and instead put him to work again as a millwright's helper.

About the time Maloy reentered the mill, the electrical department hired a new worker who had no steel mill experience. The new man, a relative of a foreman, gained promotion to millwright within three days. The move angered Maloy.

> I had spent eight years then, in the electrical department in the mill. When I didn't get the job, I got peeved and quit. It all came over a fuss. I went to help this guy one day and he was supposed to lay out safety brackets for cranes and do a lot of burning and measuring everything. He didn't know how to burn and the boss said, "Well, you don't have to know how to burn, Maloy knows how to burn." I said, "Yes, but I'm not burning, as a helper, you know. I thought I was helping the millwright, and not having him help me." "Well," he said, "if you don't like the job, why the hell don't you quit?"[2]

Unfortunately for Maloy, he quit just before the 1919 strike. When he returned

to the mill during the third week of the strike to get his job back, management assumed he was a striker. After repeated appeals, the electrical department rehired him, not as a millwright or millwright's helper but as a crane
operator.[3] The job paid within the middle range of semiskilled work at the
mill, and it provided a regular work schedule with fairly safe and agreeable
working conditions. However, the job offered no room for advancement and
it paid less than a millwright. If he wanted to move into higher-paying work,
he would have to transfer to a lesser-paying job and again work his way up.

When the Great Depression struck Duquesne, Maloy's work days became
irregular. Although he was one of the most experienced crane operators in
the mill, he averaged only one or two working days a week from 1932 to 1934.
Before the depression he regularly earned an incentive bonus, but with the
slow production conditions he now went years without earning it. When
operations in the open hearth department nearly ceased, he at times received
weekly paychecks of 5 or 45 cents and actually owed 40 cents one payday
because of deductions for insurance premiums. Sensitive to the issue of discrimination and favoritism, which he had faced earlier in his career, and upset
over the archaic wage structure within the mill, Maloy's anger at the company grew.

Many workers had their careers blocked in the 1920s by the same discrimination and favoritism that Maloy faced. Others found themselves working
exceedingly long hours with few days off, earning low pay, and toiling in hot
and unsafe working conditions. The options for redressing these grievances,
however, remained severely limited. U.S. Steel and Duquesne management
offered no workable procedures for resolving steelworker grievances. Still, the
1920s were a quiet period for labor relations at the mill. Management's open-
shop policies, combined with the lingering fear in the aftermath of the 1919
strike, left little room for workers to challenge management. But calm labor
relations also rested on the stability of the steel industry. Steady work and
steady wage rates provided a trade-off: security for poor working conditions.
Informal promotion structures within the mill, although open to abuse as
in Maloy's case, worked well enough to provide some job advancement and
relieve pressure. Finally, the general prosperity within the overall industry
ensured enough employment opportunities that workers could shop around
for better jobs.

The Great Depression upset this equilibrium. U.S. Steel laid off large numbers of workers and slashed wages and work hours for those who remained.
The security of the 1920s quickly evaporated. Because its earlier labor and
welfare policies now were unworkable, U.S. Steel created new ones early in
the depression to meet the economic emergency. However, the new welfare

and labor policies fell far short of workers' expectations and instead fed a growing anger on the shop floor. Still, workers did not form a united response. Far from providing a leveling or unifying effect, the depression further divided an already fragmented workforce.

Management Supremacy

The 1920s marked a turning point for the Duquesne Works. Rebuilding and expansion had been the watchwords at Duquesne since 1893, but expansion ceased after World War I. Growth in the steel industry shifted geographically to the Chicago region and to the South because of new markets, such as automobile production. Except for minor improvements, the Duquesne's size and scope remained constant; the years of growth and vitality ended and the mill entered its long aging process. Not until World War II did any change in its steelmaking capacity occur, and then the open hearth department added only one furnace. Instead, the improvements the company made in the 1920s were aimed at reducing costs, speeding up production, and modernizing steam and electrical power sources.[4]

The cessation of expansion ushered in the first extended period of industrial regularity at the plant. Employment, which fluctuated throughout the plant's early history because of the construction projects, leveled off at approximately six thousand workers. The town's growth paralleled the mill: after its rapid expansion from 300 residents in 1880 to 9,036 in 1900 and 19,011 in 1920, the town's population increased to only 21,396 in 1930.[5] A steady demand for Duquesne's products also kept the plant financially successful through the decade. "Stock market speculation, wildcat bonds, . . . and scores of other problems which are arresting the attention of nearly the entire country," noted the *Duquesne Times* in early 1929, "seem to make little or no impress upon a growing and prosperous Duquesne. Industry in this city is humming to capacity."[6] The Duquesne Works profited from its connection with the growing automobile industry. The plant produced semifinished bars, which it sold to finishing plants specializing in automobile steel. Duquesne also benefited from a secondary demand for billets used in the construction of pipes for oil lines and for bars used in the construction of highways.[7]

Management at the Duquesne Works continued its successful labor strategies, which had provided it with a strike-free environment during the 1920s. In part this was achieved by repressing all union activity. Workers at Duquesne and other U.S. Steel plants considered it common knowledge that "if you'd even so much as mentioned the word 'union' around the plant, you got fired." A Homestead worker, Charles Bollinger, noted that Carnegie management would fire a worker if it "thought that you'd even dreamt about a union."[8] Duquesne had access to U.S. Steel's elaborate system of spies and informants. At the Pittsburgh offices of Carnegie Steel, management developed files on all suspected unionists and radicals, using the information to track down and blacklist any workers it suspected were subversive. The mill's use of seventy-five uniformed industrial police complemented the company's covert activities. The aftermath of the 1919 strike added to this atmosphere. The historian Robert Asher found that during the 1920s "a mood of terror permeated the steel towns of the United States"; the mood was especially prevalent among newer immigrants.[9]

Outside the mill, management continued its alliance with James Crawford, who won reelection as mayor through the 1920s. The Republicans enjoyed a monopoly on political power in the town, as the Democratic Party withered during the decade and did not even field local candidates in 1929. Republican registration far outstripped the Democrats', largely because mill managers fired workers who registered Democratic. Nevertheless, this did not completely preclude workers from voicing their protests from within the supposed privacy of the voting booth. In the 1924 election Republican Calvin Coolidge received 1,909 votes in Duquesne, while the Democratic, Socialist, and Progressive candidates polled a combined 1,185 votes, with the largest share of 558 votes going to Robert M. La Follette.[10] In addition to its control over political registration, the Republicans' local power emanated from the influence Crawford and the Duquesne Works exerted on the city's racial and ethnic religious leaders, who in turn influenced their followers and flocks. The mill gave $200 for the construction of the Jerusalem Baptist Church, for instance, and provided the electricity for the Polish and Slavic churches; as a private citizen, Crawford donated a new furnace to the Polish church, helped pay for repairs to the Greek Orthodox church, and made a large donation to the Lutherans.[11]

The Duquesne Works also bolstered its political power with the regular election to public office of mill superintendents. Their involvement in local politics became an extension of their mill work. As members of the city council and school board, the superintendents regulated the mill's tax rates, ensured adequate police protection, prevented unwanted groups from meeting in town, and oversaw the public school curriculum. The general superintendent held a council seat for most of the 1920s, joined by the mill's labor department superintendent, Joseph A. Hughes, who served on the council during the 1910s and from 1923 to 1936. The mill also held a virtually perpetual seat on the school board. When one mill superintendent resigned from the board, another immediately filled the vacancy. For those who would rise to the post of general superintendent, holding public office appeared to be a prerequisite for the job. Both men named general superintendent of the Duquesne Works during the 1930s, A. C. Cummins and King H. McLaurin, served on the school board before they were promoted.[12]

The mill continued its extensive welfare programs throughout the 1920s, and U.S. Steel added new programs for its workers. The corporation offered a new group life insurance plan in 1928 and supplemented its housing agenda with a new loan program for workers. Duquesne management still offered its summer recreation programs, English classes for immigrant workers, apprenticeship programs in skilled trades work, and visiting nurses. In addition, the plant expanded its sports leagues.[13]

Labor peace would not have been possible without industrial stability, which provided regular employment, steady wage rates, and a reduction in work hours. Employment remained level after 1923, achieving remarkable stability for an industry known for wide fluctuations. Wage rates also achieved an unparalleled consistency after the war and the deep economic downturn of 1920–21. The hourly wage for common labor at U.S. Steel peaked at 50.6 cents in 1920 but then plummeted to 30 cents in 1921. Three wage increases brought the rate up to 44 cents in 1923, and there it stood until October 1931.[14] In addition, U.S. Steel abolished the twelve-hour day in 1923, although only after public prodding and the intervention of President Warren G. Harding.[15] Indeed, labor strife drastically declined during the 1920s. The steel industry suffered seventy-six strikes in 1919, twenty-five in 1920 and again in 1921, and only two a year in 1926, 1927, and 1928.[16] At Duquesne and other steel mills, managers began exuding a growing confidence. "Closer association of capital and labor in manufacturing industries of the United States," editorialized the trade journal *Iron Trade Review*, "is the keynote of the present trend in employment relations."

> Co-operation is replacing conflict, resulting in benefits that otherwise could not be obtained. Time and experience are strengthening the doctrine of a mutuality of interest, breaking down class lines, and accomplishing an equitable distribution of wealth without disorder. . . .
>   Progress made in this direction is no more striking than the steel industry, singularly free from labor discord; where wage rates have been maintained for years on a uniformly high level, where hours of labor and working conditions have improved.[17]

Skill and Ethnicity on the Shop Floor

Steelworkers did not share the glowing assessment offered by *Iron Trade Review*. They knew that repression and intimidation had bought a large amount of industrial peace. They also harbored grievances about issues that industry spokesmen either considered resolved or failed to mention, including wages and hours, discrimination, and working conditions. Yet these grievances did not affect all steelworkers in the same way. Skill, type of wage compensation, ethnicity, and race all affected the shop floor and the world of work.

At the lowest end of steelworker jobs were unskilled and semiskilled hourly positions. The unskilled primarily included common laborers who were paid by the hour and earned the lowest wages in the mill. Slightly above laborers were various semiskilled hourly workers, such as crane operators, machine tenders, and chippers. What most distinguished these less-skilled hourly workers was their low rate of pay and their exclusion from any incentive or tonnage bonus plans. Eastern and southern European immigrants and blacks filled these jobs.

The experiences of Andy Chervenak illustrate how many unskilled and semiskilled workers, paid hourly wages, adapted to mill conditions in the 1920s. Chervenak began working at the Duquesne Works in 1928, hiring on as a laborer in the open hearth department.[18] Open-hearth laboring jobs, a common entry-level position at the plant, entailed arduous work in unsafe and disagreeable working conditions. Laborers frequently had to lift materials weighing one hundred pounds or more, use pneumatic hammers weighing eighty pounds, and remove slag with six-foot pry bars and sixteen-pound sledge hammers.[19] Metropolitan Life Insurance Co. found that steel laborers had a death rate in the 1920s that was 227 percent higher than the rate for men of comparable age in other occupations.[20] A former Edgar Thomson worker who held the same job described the work Andy Chervenak faced:

> [We repair] a hole in an open-hearth while the furnace is still literally white hot. The men swathe their faces and shoulders in wet sacks, seize bricks and clay, rush up, place a few bricks trying to shield their faces, and then, when they can no longer stand the heat, rush back. Sometimes the outside scaffolding they work on catches fire. I've seen men forced to go from one hot job to another with barely a pause for breath in between. I have worked for several hours on end on top a furnace when it had cooled somewhat, but was still so hot and gassy that you grew sick and faint from the fumes arising. Other hot jobs include working inside the checker chambers of a furnace, cleaning out the old "checkers"—wheeling heavy brick from a hot and gassy chamber into a zero [degree] night—in and out, in and out, all night long. Cleaning out flue dust in a blast furnace oven: literally imprisoned inside amidst a welter of fine red dust that penetrates to the skin through the clothing. . . . Cleaning cinders out of a pipe from the oven to the furnace: ten minutes in on your belly and knees, shovel like hell lying flat on your face for a few minutes; then when you can't stand it any more, crawl out into the zero air, bathed in sweat, and cool off.[21]

After several months as a laborer, Chervenak moved into another unskilled job in the department: oiler and wiper. The work paid only about a penny more an hour, but it provided better working conditions. After nearly a year as an oiler and wiper, Chervenak transferred to the conditioning department and became a chipper.[22] His new job entailed the arduous and hand-swelling work of chipping imperfections from steel blooms and billets with chisels mounted on deafening air hammers. The mill used more than one thousand chippers, divided into crews of five, in the large conditioning yards outside each blooming and bar mill. Chippers earned a dime more per hour than laborers and had the added advantage of somewhat better working conditions. Unlike laborers, chippers did not move throughout their department, working different jobs every day. Nor did they work in the heat and dangerous conditions that laborers often faced. At the Duquesne Works chipping became the province of immigrant workers and their sons, who valued the security and steady working conditions the job provided.[23]

The change in jobs increased Chervenak's pay and perhaps extended his life, but it did not alter his work hours. He worked an eight-hour day with each of his three jobs and had few days off for rest. In his first ten months as an oiler and wiper he averaged one day off every three weeks. When he became a chipper in 1929, his work became somewhat intermittent and he averaged 5½ days of work per week. But to achieve this he frequently worked twenty straight days without a day off. Work actually picked up in 1930 and during one six-month stretch he had only six days off. At one point he worked 111 straight days through the late summer and early fall.[24]

Andy Chervenak's situation typified the conditions faced by many unskilled and semiskilled hourly workers. Entry-level laboring jobs exposed new workers to the lowest pay and worst working conditions, but most could escape these conditions and rise to better-paying or safer jobs. Although this safety valve acted to relieve much discontent, workers still harbored many grievances. Even for semiskilled hourly workers, such as chippers and crane operators, wages were not high enough and the workweek was too long.

The length of the workday and workweek remained a source of irritation for steelworkers in the 1920s, even though U.S. Steel had officially ended the seven-day workweek and twelve-hour day. Hours remained long and days off few. The eight-hour day covered only 60 percent of the Duquesne workforce by 1929, while the other 40 percent worked 8½ to 10½ hours a day. Management also frequently forced workers to work beyond these hours, with no advance warning, and no pay for the extra work hours. Duquesne did not officially use the seven-day workweek, but the number of days some workers labored at the mill without a day off made a mockery of the mill's official six-day workweek. And workers could not refuse the extra day of work without risking being fired.[25]

Management ordered the long workweek and workdays, but low-skilled workers needed the long hours to eke out a living. Steel work tended to be intermittent even in good times. After the initial postwar depression, which extended into 1922, the decade provided unusually steady employment. Still, even in these flush times the timing of orders, the shutdown and rebuilding of furnaces, and seasonal variations created fluctuations in each mill department's employment levels. Without runs of twenty or more straight working days, workers could not make up for the slower periods of three- and four-day workweeks. In addition, many steelworkers needed long hours and long workweeks to make up for their low rate of pay. When U.S. Steel changed the working day from twelve to eight hours in 1923, a reduction of 33 percent, it also raised wages but by only 25 percent. Laborers who had earned $4.80 per day now earned only $4.[26]

For unskilled and many semiskilled hourly workers, wages provided bare subsistence, if that. In 1937 Carroll R. Daugherty, an economics professor at the University of Pittsburgh, and his associates estimated that in 1929 a family of three needed at least $1,420 to achieve a healthy and decent standard of living. The National Industrial Conference Board found in that same year the average unskilled steelworker earned $1,405. Semiskilled workers fared better, earning $1,968, which put them slightly below the earnings necessary to sustain a family of five. Two informal studies of Duquesne steelworkers reported by the Socialist writer Harvey O'Connor revealed even lower earnings. A 1934 sample of thirty-three steelworkers in the Amalgamated, which tended to attract unskilled and semiskilled workers, found their average 1929 earnings to be $1,348. A much larger study in 1935 using pay stubs found that in 1928–29, 62 percent of the 638 men sampled earned less than $1,400.[27]

Low wages and poor working conditions in the lowest-skilled jobs made advancement to better-paying jobs a critical issue. Promotions meant the chance to enter higher-paying tonnage work or to move into a job that saw fewer layoffs. For some, like Milan Tankosich, an immigrant from Bosnia who began working in Duquesne before World War I, the ideal promotion placed him as a crane hooker. The job did not pay much, but Tankosich told an interviewer in 1974 that "I got the job that is good for me, that's why I lived long."[28] Many other steelworkers had been killed or injured. Phillip Bonosky, who grew up in Duquesne as the son of a Lithuanian steelworker, noted, "Our town was full of men with fingerless hands, footless legs, eyes squashed back into their heads."[29]

As with wages and hours, most unskilled and semiskilled hourly workers found the promotion process to be far from adequate. The Duquesne Works, like other steel mills, unofficially used lines of promotion, or job ladders. These informal lines of promotion developed over time in each department (e.g., open hearth or bar mill) and in each shop in each department (e.g., Open Hearth #1 or 10-inch bar mill). A shop floor had several job ladders, some short and leading to dead-end unskilled or semiskilled jobs, and some longer, leading to the highest-paying skilled job.[30] Job ladders, however, contained a glaring weakness for workers. Although mill departments generally practiced promotions based on job sequences, the criteria for promotion remained management's prerogative. Workers mostly favored basing promotions on some form of seniority, but management stressed ability, strength, and experience. Management did not completely discount seniority, but it was not at the top of the list of promotion criteria. According to Elmer Maloy, "It didn't matter if you worked ten years or two months or three days."[31]

Inconsistency, favoritism, and discrimination further undermined the ability of workers to rise through the lines of promotion. This situation derived from U.S. Steel's management structure. Although the corporation established the basic parameters of the labor policies for each mill—specifically, the open shop—it offered little or no guidance on other labor questions, such as layoff and promotion policies, or systematic criteria for judging workers' ability and performance. U.S. Steel lagged decidedly behind other large corporations in the development of personnel policy, still acting like a holding company and offering little centralized direction in labor matters. This forced general superintendents at the plants to develop their own policies. But without guidance and resources, the general superintendents could not develop consistent policies. Nor did they have any incentive to do so. Repression, industrial stability, and a weak labor movement assured labor peace.

Without incentive, general superintendents placed little emphasis on personnel questions. U.S. Steel did not have an industrial relations or personnel department at the corporate, subsidiary, or plant level. Instead, the Duquesne Works had a small employment department, which did not make personnel policy and consisted of only one employment agent, two interpreters, and three clerks. The department's functions included supplying the mill's labor needs and keeping records on six thousand workers. The Duquesne Works did not even coordinate the work of the employment, welfare, and safety departments, each of which remained autonomous.[32] With no personnel department the authority to hire, fire, and promote rested with department superintendents and foremen. This unchecked power of the foreman created what some U.S. Steel executives labeled "the problem of the overzealous official."[33] However, neither U.S. Steel nor the general superintendents sought to rein in lower management. The system worked: production continued unabated and strikes had virtually been abolished.

Unchecked by upper management, foremen often made a mockery of job ladders and traditions within departments. The majority of foremen at Duquesne were U.S. born or from northern or western Europe. Their ethnic background prompted Slavic workers to label them "all-American," or "Johnny Bull," an allusion to the British heritage of many foremen. These labels denoted a strong sense of ethnic division, which formed the basis for charges of discrimination. Slavic workers regularly contended that they were denied promotions based on their ethnicity. Some foremen hired only members of their own ethnic groups for their work crews, and some whose departments were of mixed ethnicity advanced only workers of their own ethnicity or religion. Workers also argued that most foremen advanced their favorites, relatives, or members of their social clubs. And corruption, irrespective of ethnicity, played a part in promotions and work assignments. It was not uncommon for foremen to accept kickbacks for hiring or promoting workers. One labor foreman at Duquesne took payments from more than thirty men working for him. Those laborers received the easiest jobs, while those who did not kick back were given the hardest and dirtiest jobs.[34]

Immigrants from eastern and southern Europe dominated the large ranks of the low-skilled hourly workers through the 1920s and 1930s. They faced some of the worst conditions in the mill, earned low pay, and constantly faced discrimination. Still, they were not the lowest in the pecking order. Of all the groups in the stratified workforce at Duquesne, black workers faced the worst conditions. Management retained blacks at the mill after the war and continued to recruit southern blacks as a fresh source of labor. However, their employment levels fluctuated widely in the 1920s; black turnover remained higher than white turnover until the Great Depression. Despite these fluctuations, African Americans never made up more than 5 to 10 percent of the workforce at Duquesne. Thus they were far less influential than foreign-born workers in regard to both unionization and company labor policies.[35]

The black welfare worker, hired to address the issue of high black turnover, found only limited success at eliminating the problem. Part of the turnover resulted from the company's firing of what it considered "loafers" and "poor Negroes" in the 1920s. At the same time, many black workers did not view their steel jobs as permanent year-round employment. Many remained tied to the land and their families in the South. They periodically quit and returned to the South, only to come back to the mill after a few months or longer and reclaim their jobs. During the high employment of the 1920s this strategy worked. During the 1930s, however, leaving Duquesne meant not getting a job upon their return.[36]

Discrimination also played a key role in turnover, both in welfare programs and on the job. Although the black welfare worker instituted a welfare program paralleling the one for whites, black workers found the two programs far from equal. The mill banned blacks from membership in the Carnegie Library club, thus denying them use of the gymnasium, swimming pool, and recreation and club rooms open to white workers. The Duquesne Works also denied company housing, except for labor camp housing, to black workers. A greater cause of resentment among black workers centered on the shop floor, where the black welfare worker held no authority. It involved the relationship of black workers and their foremen and straw bosses (also known as pushers, or gang leaders). The straw bosses, who did not have management authority, were workers chosen by foremen to lead gangs of laborers. Many straw bosses were immigrants who worked hard and showed a willingness to push their fellow workers to work harder. Newer black workers, sometimes unaccustomed to the work rhythms of the steel mill, clashed with the foremen and straw bosses, who also tended to hold racist beliefs. Foremen and straw bosses also consistently assigned black workers the dirtiest, hardest, and hottest jobs on the laboring crews, work that many foreign-born workers refused to do. On the hottest days of the year blacks could expect to get the hottest jobs. Faced with these conditions, many black workers in the 1920s simply walked away from their jobs.[37]

Like immigrant workers, blacks also endured promotional discrimination. Still, foreign-born workers dominated semiskilled hourly jobs and had made some inroads into the skilled trades and tonnage work. For blacks management maintained a much lower promotional ceiling. During the labor shortage of World War I blacks appeared to be rising into higher-paying jobs; by 1920 this trend was reversed.[38] A sample from the 1920 census manuscript reveals no blacks in skilled, skilled trades, or management jobs. During the 1920s the vast majority languished in unskilled positions. According to one Carnegie official, 90 percent of the blacks at the Duquesne Works were unskilled. Even two highly optimistic 1920s surveys—one by the Pittsburgh Urban League—that overestimated the skill levels of black workers found 70 to 74 percent of Duquesne's black workers held unskilled jobs.[39]

Most blacks at the Duquesne Works worked in the open hearth and blast-furnace departments, which used the highest numbers of common laborers. Within these two departments management did not allow blacks to rise out of the lowest-paying jobs. "I have never been promoted," a black Duquesne worker told an interviewer in 1934. "I am the oldest on my job and have never been advanced and have no chance." A black coworker described the highest unskilled and semiskilled hourly jobs available to blacks: "I have never got any promotion. The highest paying job is cinder pit man in the open hearth, as far as colored are concerned. There is quite a few there. The next highest is furnace tender in the blast furnace department. In general colored have been kicking about the same level. The company just don't want them to go higher."[40] Lack of advancement can be explained in part by the work records of many black workers, who frequently left the mill for periods of time, thus losing seniority. But this cannot explain why after World War I not a single black worker entered semiskilled hourly jobs such as chipper and crane operator in the 1920s, jobs that employed well over one thousand workers throughout the plant and were open to workers with lower seniority. Blacks wanted these jobs for the same reasons the immigrants did: better working conditions and pay. However, management, most probably supported by white workers, kept these jobs off-limits for blacks.[41]

Two other groups at Duquesne experienced different working conditions and fared much better. The first group included semiskilled and skilled tonnage workers. The majority of these workers, especially in the skilled positions, were born in the United States or immigrated from western and northern Europe. Skilled tonnage workers earned the highest wages in the mill, with highly skilled rollers in the blooming and bar mills, for instance, earning two and three times more than the laborers. Semiskilled tonnage jobs, which paid considerably less than the highest-skilled jobs, still paid 20 to 30 cents more per hour than semiskilled hourly jobs.[42]

Tonnage men received either a set amount of money for each ton of steel they and their group produced, or they received a base wage rate plus an incentive bonus for producing anything more than minimum tonnage. Tonnage and incentive pay systems could be used only for jobs in which workers took a direct part in producing a measurable product. Tonnage workers thus worked as a group; for example, an open hearth crew ran a furnace or a rolling crew rolled so many tons of steel into bars. Each job on the crew received a different rate of pay, from semiskilled workers who earned the lowest incentive bonus all the way up to the highest-skilled workers, who were paid solely by the ton and earned the most. Tonnage work excluded laborers, who worked in their own crews, traveled throughout the department, and did not directly take part in one production run. Almost all other unskilled jobs also were excluded, along with chippers. Semiskilled crane operators worked for either hourly or tonnage rates. They earned tonnage rates if they served only one production crew and their product, but they earned hourly rates if they served many crews or did various jobs unrelated to a production run, such as moving scrap.[43]

Tonnage and incentive pay systems served as a unifying force for the tonnage crew, but they divided these crews from hourly workers. Tonnage men, sometimes referred to as "hogs," earned more money by working harder and faster. They frequently began work early, worked through lunch, and stayed beyond the end of their shift. But this forced hourly workers in the same department also to work faster, miss lunch, or work past quitting time. Management rewarded the tonnage men with higher pay for their effort, while the hourly men gained nothing, because the company did not pay overtime for missed lunches or working past quitting time.[44]

The second group of workers that fared better than hourly unskilled and semiskilled workers were skilled tradesmen, such as bricklayers, machinists, millwrights, and pipe fitters. The ethnic composition of the trades more resembled that of the tonnage workers than the low-skilled hourly workers. Like the unskilled, skilled tradesmen worked for hourly wages, but they earned significantly more money, comparable to highly paid semiskilled tonnage workers. Skilled trades work, which frequently involved movement throughout the mill and a high degree of self-direction, could not be paid on an incentive system. The good wages, autonomy, and steady employment involved in skilled trades jobs made them enviable positions. Despite this high status, wages for tradesmen consistently fell below the standard union rates for their crafts.[45]

The work experiences of skilled tradesmen and tonnage men thus differed significantly from those of the unskilled, and even semiskilled, hourly workers. Their wages were higher and their skills provided greater job security. That a majority of these workers also shared their foremen's ethnic background led to further employment advantages. Still, with a management structure that placed all the power over workers' lives with the foreman, all workers found their employment tenuous at times.

Neither did workers have many opportunities to change their situation. U.S. Steel offered no formal mechanism for resolving worker grievances before 1933. Operating as an open shop, and refusing to hold any negotiations with unions, the corporation's policies precluded any form of union grievance procedure. U.S. Steel regarded unions as outside influences that represented only unions and not workers. Summing up this view, Elbert Gary, chairman of the board of U.S. Steel, wrote in 1921, "We do not look with favor upon the request for an interview concerning our employes by a volunteer outsider, representing only himself or his own selfish interests, and who is known to be actually hostile to both the employer and employe, or to the country."[46] Gary considered the proper resolution of grievances to be between the worker, or a committee of workers, and his immediate supervisor. If unresolved, the worker could raise the complaint with higher management, including Gary himself. But upper management rarely overruled foremen, and foremen punished workers who went over their heads. In addition, this system could not address issues such as wages, hours, or seniority, which would affect a whole department, plant, or the entire corporation. Gary's idea of dispute resolution fit with a nineteenth-century small shop, not a twentieth-century corporation employing more than 200,000 workers.[47]

Faced with this archaic system for resolving grievances, workers tended to rely on individual, and not collective, solutions to their problems. Skilled workers benefited most in this environment, because their knowledge of the production process made them more indispensable. Semiskilled workers also held a critical position in the production process. In large-scale steelmaking, semiskilled operatives kept materials flowing continuously in a process that transformed raw materials into iron, iron into steel, and steel into structural shapes. Without their diagnostic and operative skills, thousands of tons of materials could be wasted in an instant. But unlike skilled workers, the power of semiskilled workers lay in their ability to resort to collective action. Individually, semiskilled workers could be easily replaced. Unskilled workers held no bargaining power, as their jobs entailed no built-up knowledge or skill.[48]

Workers faced with low-paying jobs in poor working conditions depended on promotions for changing their situation. However, when a hostile foreman blocked advancement, workers could not resolve the problem through any meaningful administrative process. In these cases workers depended on a series of individual options. Many simply quit and sought employment at other plants. Turnover in the steel industry, especially in the low-skilled positions, remained high during the 1920s as workers floated from mill to mill searching for a favorable situation. Some workers stayed and stood up for what they saw as their rights but ended up being fired. John Smitko worked as an electrician's helper at the Duquesne Works during the early 1920s and refused to work an extra Sunday. He had made plans to attend a special church service that day and become a godfather. His foreman fired him on Monday.[49]

For workers with high seniority quitting or being fired wiped out their chances for a pension. The option of transferring to other mill departments or other Carnegie mills solved this dilemma, because their pensions remained intact. Andy Chervenak had improved his situation by transferring from the open hearth to the conditioning department, where he became a chipper. William J. Smith tried a different approach by transferring within the Carnegie system. He began work at the Edgar Thomson Works in 1920 and transferred to the Duquesne Works in 1925. He transferred to the Clairton Works in 1929, but by the end of the year he had returned to Duquesne with his pension seniority in place. Gyorgy Ilkanics transferred between the Duquesne, Edgar Thomson, and Homestead Works eight times from 1913 to 1931.[50]

Although collective action remained an option for workers, the management of the Duquesne Works stifled any hint of rebellion. The ability of workers to use individual solutions—quitting, transferring, making friends with a foreman—ensured that low pay, long hours, and internal job ladders open to management abuse did not become flash points of conflict. In addition, the different shop-floor conditions faced by workers based on their skill, method of pay, ethnicity, and race further undermined collective action. But these conditions depended largely on sustained industrial production and not the economic conditions of the early 1930s.

U.S. Steel and the Great Depression

The Great Depression brought a near-total collapse of the steel industry. Ironically, 1929 had been an especially good year for steel and, in particular, U.S. Steel, which posted its highest nonwar-year earnings in its history. But as consumer industries and building and construction declined, orders for steel dropped. Industry-wide steel and iron production first declined during the last two months of 1929, finally leveling off by mid-1930. After July 1931, however, the bottom fell out. The rate of operation for blast furnaces, which generally remained higher than 80 percent in 1929, dropped to less than 20 percent in 1932, reaching a low of 12 percent in July. Of the 270 blast furnaces in the United States, only forty-four remained lit in 1932. Steel ingot production dropped from 63 million tons in 1929 to 15 million tons in 1932, the lowest total since 1901.[51]

The depression created massive financial and labor policy dilemmas for U.S. Steel just as it had begun a reorganization of its corporate policies. Gary, who had guided U.S. Steel from its earliest years, died in 1927. Myron C. Taylor then became the head of the corporation. Taylor's efforts at modernizing U.S. Steel's corporate, financial, and sales structures stretched through the 1930s and profoundly altered the corporation's history.[52] In the fields of labor policy and labor relations his actions were no less significant. Taylor forced U.S. Steel to rationalize its management structure and centralize and professionalize its industrial relations policies. However, the depression delayed the implementation of these programs until the mid-1930s and forced Taylor to immediately address and develop corporation-wide policies concerning layoffs, work sharing, and relief. In this fashion U.S. Steel increasingly directed the labor policies of its individual plants but without the benefit of modern management structures, much less an industrial relations department.

Taylor's response to the steel industry's depression-induced tailspin mixed cost-cutting measures and production cuts with a welfare program aimed both at providing relief for U.S. Steel's workers and at keeping the company's workforce intact. "Let it be said of the steel industry that none of its men was forced to call upon the public for help," he vowed in late 1930.[53] Although U.S. Steel dismantled many of its traditional welfare programs as a cost-cutting measure, the corporation's new welfare measures proved equally ambitious.

The major labor problem facing Taylor and U.S. Steel at the beginning of the depression was how to manage its large workforce (225,000 in 1929) in a time of shrinking production. Instead of instituting massive layoffs, Taylor introduced a work-sharing program in late 1929. As the depression deepened, more and more U.S. Steel employees became part-time workers. By the end of 1931, 145,000 worked part time. In the spring of 1933, when U.S. Steel production stood at 9 percent of capacity, the corporation had virtually no full-time workers. Even as late as 1936, 61 percent of its workers still labored part time.[54]

Taylor stressed that he instituted the work-sharing plan as a humanitarian measure aimed at spreading the work as fairly and as equitably as possible. He also sought to spread the program to other corporations through the national Share-the-Work movement, begun in 1932 under the leadership of Walter Teagle of Standard Oil. Taylor believed the Share-the-Work movement was "the most important single contribution to the human side of the depression."[55] In his public addresses on the subject, however, Taylor did not mention that U.S. Steel also instituted large layoffs; one quarter to one third of U.S. Steel's workers lost their jobs between 1929 and 1933. The corporation also used work sharing as a means to continue its control over its workforce. By keeping most of its workforce part time, it was assured of being able to quickly resume production during an economic upturn. Sharing the work also kept its workers from going "soft"; part-time work kept them physically fit.[56] In 1930 U.S. Steel conducted an internal study to determine the economic advantages of work sharing and turned up another unexpected benefit: a greater efficiency in some departments, according to Taylor, "due to the desire of the men to keep their jobs by making a showing."[57]

In order to cut costs and remain competitive during the depression, U.S. Steel cut wages for salaried and hourly workers. Industrial wages held remarkably steady during the first two years after the stock market crash, as industrialists heeded President Herbert Hoover's call to stop any deflationary spiral. But U.S. Steel became the first major employer to break its pledge to Hoover, thus opening the industrial floodgates of wage cuts. The corporation cut the earnings of salaried workers 10 percent to 15 percent in August 1931, then followed with a 10 percent wage cut for production employees in October. In May 1932 wages and salaries were reduced another 15 percent, dropping the hourly common labor rate to 33 cents. Managers and stockholders also found that they were not immune to U.S. Steel's austerity program. The corporation stopped paying bonuses to managers, reduced preferred stock dividends, and canceled common stock dividends for seven years. Stockholders recouped the three years of preferred stock reductions during the next two years.[58]

The depression also led the corporation to take a new direction in its welfare policies. In 1930 it began instituting what would become a three-stage relief program. The first part of the program did not entail corporation money but instead encouraged good-fellowship clubs and other employee welfare organizations to help the poorest workers. Here, Hoover's emphasis on private relief resonated. As the depression deepened, however, the corporation began providing direct relief to its neediest workers. Direct relief, which the workers did not have to repay, included medical care for family members, food, rent, and some direct monetary payments. Used primarily during the first two years of the depression, direct relief cost the corporation $1.3 million. As misery spread in 1932, U.S. Steel switched to a third relief program, which provided loans to its workers. Roughly half the loans went toward food and clothing and the other half toward rent and mortgage payments. By August 1936 U.S. Steel had loaned $8 million to its workers, more than half of which had been repaid.[59]

Myron Taylor frequently spoke with pride of the depression-era policies of U.S. Steel toward its workers. He told the annual gathering of stockholders in 1933 that there was "practically no want among the workers within the Corporation at the present time, so carefully have we distributed the work, such work as there has been, among those in our employ."[60] In 1934 he boasted to the stockholders, "I do not believe there is a brighter page in industrial history than your corporation wrote through this depression in its treatment of its servants."[61] Indeed, U.S. Steel's efforts at providing relief and work for its immense labor force went unmatched in its history. Although U.S. Steel's actions did not derive completely from humanitarian impulses, they were in large part a sincere attempt by Myron Taylor to ameliorate the worst conditions of the depression.

In order for Taylor's policies to achieve their desired aim of relief fairly and evenly distributed, U.S. Steel needed a management structure immune to discrimination and favoritism. But Taylor inherited from Gary an outdated management structure that placed an inordinate amount of authority with foremen, many of whom regularly used their power to further their own agendas. Because U.S. Steel still was lacking personnel departments or well-developed personnel policies to aid in the implementation of Taylor's welfare programs when the depression struck, his assurances of fairness and equality, filtered through the ranks of superintendents and foremen—the men who determined who worked and when—became meaningless. U.S. Steel's benevolence appeared to workers to be mean spirited and stingy.

The Depression Hits Duquesne

The Duquesne Works, like most U.S. Steel plants, suffered serious economic losses and was forced to make sharp production cuts. Duquesne primarily produced blooms, billets, and bars, which were used in building and construction and in fabricating mills for railroad and auto production. The only types of steel production that weathered the depression were lighter flat-rolled products, such as sheets, strip, and tinplate. Duquesne also produced large quantities of specialty steel, which required the plant to run at high capacity to make a profit. With the drop in orders and production the Duquesne Works ran in the red for five straight years, beginning in 1931.[62]

Production at the Duquesne Works remained surprisingly high through October 1930. In November, however, the mill suffered a serious production decline, which was followed by more downturns in 1931 and 1932 and a bottoming out in 1933. The company shut down Open Hearth Shop #1 in February 1931 and left it closed through 1934. Open Hearth Shop #2 remained open but with curtailed production. Of the thirty-two open hearth furnaces at the plant, only two to eight were in operation at any one time early in the depression. In addition, the department often shut down before the end of the week or periodically remained closed for a week. Four of the seven bar mills shut down for at least three years. The blast-furnace department remained idle for most of two years beginning in mid-1931. Blast furnaces were not as easily and as inexpensively blown out and relit as open hearth furnaces; once shut down, a blast furnace generally remained idle for at least a month. The company relit three of the six furnaces in June and July 1933 but by October blew them out once again. Production resumed the following month, but not until October 1935 would three blast furnaces again run at one time. Still, the Duquesne Works made it through the depression better than some Carnegie mills; the Edgar Thomson Works completely shut down for several months during 1932 and 1933.[63]

The management of the Duquesne Works responded to the crisis by implementing Taylor's program for work sharing. However, the sheer magnitude of the downturn forced the company also to implement extensive layoffs. By early 1934 employment, which had stood at six thousand, was fluctuating between three thousand and forty-five hundred.[64] Layoffs allowed workers to keep their pension seniority. Under pension rules, however, a laid-off worker had to work at least one day during any two-year period to remain eligible for his pension. Because many workers faced layoffs of two to four years, the company called in its laid-off workers every two years to work one day for pension purposes. The pension and layoff policy also allowed the company to maintain contact with its original workforce, thus assuring it of experienced workers when the economy picked up. So long as laid-off workers knew they would be rehired, they were less likely to leave the area.[65]

Massive layoffs and work sharing would have taxed any system that sought to distribute work fairly. However, few corporations, U.S. Steel included, had any formal layoff policy in 1929. Carnegie Steel Co. would not even begin to develop one until 1935. Without corporate guidance each plant established its own layoff policy or, in the case of Duquesne, no policy at all. The plant superintendent told workers in 1934, a full three years into the layoff process, that he did not know which considerations to use in determining who should be laid off: experience, family responsibility, length of service, whether the worker lived in town, or other factors.[66]

This lack of guidance effectively left layoff policy and procedure in the hands of department superintendents and foremen. As in the 1920s arbitrary decisions by foremen determined who kept his job. Workers with twenty-five years' seniority found themselves laid off, while men with as few as one or two years' seniority might keep their jobs. Poor company record-keeping procedures, coupled with rigid U.S. Steel policies, robbed a number of laid-off men of their seniority. Although the company called back workers for one day of work every two years, inadequate record keeping by the understaffed employment department sometimes led the company to miss notifying a worker. Bricklayer William J. Smith, laid off on June 19, 1933, and not called back to work until June 28, 1935, missed the two-year period by nine days. U.S. Steel refused to reinstate his service break, thus wiping out his fifteen-year record. The treatment accorded Smith and fifteen other Duquesne workers with similar breaks in their service record did little to build goodwill between management and its workers.[67]

For workers lucky enough to keep their jobs, work sharing meant short days, short workweeks, and short paychecks. Andy Chervenak, the chipper who had worked 111 straight days only months earlier, now found himself with too many idle days. Chervenak's average workweek, which amounted to three and a half days by 1931, dropped to two seven-hour days in 1931 and 1932. During one slow period he spent four months with no work at all. After the two wage cuts his hourly wage sank to less than what he had made when he first hired on as a laborer in the 1920s. Still, Chervenak was lucky;

many who held on to their jobs worked only one day a week. During the worst months a workweek might consist of three hours.[68]

Although the amount of work available varied from department to department, foremen held the ultimate power to determine who worked and for how long. When a few work hours here or there meant keeping a house or feeding a family, workers frequently protested the unfair distribution of working hours. Workers complained in every large department of the mill, from large semiskilled departments (chipping) to skilled trades departments (masonry and the machine shop). Within the machine shop, for instance, some machinists worked 90 percent of full time, while others worked only 30 percent. Even skilled open hearth workers complained of problems with unequal distribution of work. Graft, which prevailed in the 1920s, became more onerous. One foreman in the maintenance department threatened workers with the loss of a workday if they did not buy a $1.25 ticket for the department picnic.[69]

Far from unifying workers, the depression further fragmented the workforce. Despite the hardships all workers faced, layoffs and work sharing hit unskilled and semiskilled hourly workers disproportionately hard. In this large labor pool jobs were easy to learn and workers' skills were similar. Unskilled workers faced either a complete layoff or, at best, only one to two days of work per week. Skilled trades workers fared much better. Despite low production schedules, work remained in the form of maintenance and repairs. Many even worked ten-hour days and five- and six-day weeks until late 1933.[70] Tonnage men faced varying conditions in regard to hours. With a decrease in the number of open hearth furnaces and bar mills, some faced layoffs, whereas others shared the work available. Unlike hourly unskilled workers, tonnage men received favorable treatment from management. When production slowed, foremen placed skilled workers in unskilled jobs, allowing them to fill out their paychecks. In turn, this further depleted work for the unskilled. The favorable treatment accorded tonnage and skilled tradesmen derived from their indispensability to the company. Further, the threat of a skilled labor shortage, which the steel industry predicted would arise when production once again picked up, also enhanced their status.[71]

Unskilled hourly workers also more often faced the foreman's arbitrary use of power. This was most evident in picking workers to fill unskilled and semiskilled jobs. Workers had to report to work each day, even if they averaged only one turn a week. As workers milled about the plant gate, foremen chose the workers they wanted, leaving the rest to return the next day. Workers accused their foremen of making sure "their boys" or "favorites" got the most turns, while the rest of the workers "took pot-luck." The depression had erased all semblance of a job ladder and fairness.[72]

Working conditions also deteriorated during the depression, again affecting unskilled workers more adversely than skilled. Myron Taylor noted that work sharing had benefited the corporation because workers worked harder in order to impress management. But Taylor's distance from the shop floor clouded a more common effect of work sharing—the speedup. Economic pressures during the depression forced the company to cut costs. In addition, with so few jobs available, a foreman expected more work out of his men. A hard-driving management style, combined with workers' fears of losing their jobs, forced workers to labor harder. A Duquesne steelworker told an interviewer, "Push, push, push, alla time, push." Another complained, "Sometimes no can catch breath," while one lamented, "Now I've got no time to eat lunch even." The speedup entailed doubling up, especially among the unskilled, as management eliminated a job and then placed the responsibilities of that job on other workers. According to one worker, "On the blast furnace gang there used to be six men. Now there's only four—same work." Because of the type of work they performed, skilled workers rarely were confronted with such problems. Some semiskilled workers, such as crane operators, did fall victim to the speedup. With slower operations management expected a crane operator to run and maintain more than one crane during the day or to use his crane to do work generally reserved for another crane.[73]

Nowhere did the uneven effects of the depression on unskilled and skilled workers show more clearly than in earnings. Although tonnage workers found their traditional wage structures in disarray, hourly unskilled and semiskilled workers experienced a devastating drop in income. For those who held on to their jobs, fewer working days and hours, coupled with two wage cuts amounting to 25 percent, translated into pitifully small earnings. In all industries wage cuts for the same time period averaged only 13.6 percent.[74] Various surveys by the Duquesne Amalgamated lodge; Harvey O'Connor, a chronicler of steelworkers and their efforts to unionize in this period; and Dr. Carroll Daugherty, the University of Pittsburgh economist, found that unskilled and semiskilled Duquesne steelworkers earned approximately $400 in both 1933 and 1934, or roughly a quarter to a third of their 1929 earnings. In one survey more than 94 percent of respondents said they earned less than $600 in 1934.[75] The cost of living also declined but not enough to keep pace with the drop in earnings. Steelworkers sank into debt. A sample of fifty lower-skilled Duquesne steelworkers in 1933 showed an average debt of $925, with $581 owed for rent or mortgage, $126 for groceries, $76 for taxes, and $142 in miscellaneous debt. "Debts," remarked one worker, "I'm lousy with them."[76]

Semiskilled and skilled tonnage men did better. Although they too faced layoffs and decreased hours, they generally worked more days and had greater overall earnings than the hourly employees. Charles Erickson, a skilled first helper in the open hearth department, kept his job throughout the depression and occasionally still could earn $8 to $9 per day. Because few skilled workers performed his job, he also did not have to share his work with as many workers. Thus, even though his earnings suffered, they remained substantially higher than for part-time unskilled workers.[77]

However, the sharp decline in production wreaked havoc with the pay systems of tonnage workers, creating grievances that hourly workers did not share. Tonnage rates were based on the mill's running at, or near, full capacity. Therefore the rates did not adequately compensate workers when the mill ran at low capacity, such as during the depression. Straight tonnage workers were paid only for how much steel they produced. With no floor on their earnings, they could work a full day, make no steel, and earn no money. Likewise, incentive workers had a low base pay rate—often the common laboring rate—and depended on producing large quantities of steel to earn a sizable incentive bonus. When the depression struck and production dropped, they did not produce enough to earn incentives and only earned their low base rate.

Suddenly, tonnage workers found their earnings fluctuating and dropping. Although straight tonnage men still had high tonnage days, they were frequently sandwiched between low tonnage days. On bad days skilled workers even found themselves earning less than laborers, which hurt not only their wallet but their pride. Workers on incentive pay systems sometimes did not make their incentive bonus for years. Crane operators fell into this category, because the number of furnaces they tended had been cut and they could never move enough steel to earn their bonus. In addition to these problems, tonnage workers did not know from day to day or from week to week how much they might earn, because production levels fluctuated so widely. Tonnage and incentive rates always had been a mystery to many workers, who could not figure out the complicated calculations that determined them. As the depression further upset rates, the connection between work and earnings became more muddied.[78]

Throughout the early years of the depression shop-floor grievances continued to mount. Whether the complaints centered on the amount of work available, its distribution, or low wage and tonnage rates, most steelworkers believed they had been treated unfairly. For unskilled and semiskilled hourly workers the depression ended one of the company's keys to peaceful labor relations—its ability to promote workers, however imperfectly, into better-paying jobs. In addition, the depression more fully exposed the vagaries of the foreman's empire, which rewarded ethnicity, kickbacks, and friendships as much as it rewarded seniority and ability. The desperate scramble for a few working hours each week amplified these problems in the workers' minds each time they received fewer hours of work than a fellow worker. For the poorest workers sharing work meant sharing the misery. The depression also weakened the company's relations with its skilled workers. Some faced difficulties because of favoritism and unfair distribution of work hours, and most found their earnings dropping and their wages falling to less than what they considered fair remuneration for the work they performed. Taylor's humanitarian efforts at work sharing found little support on the shop floor. And as hard times spread, Taylor's relief efforts too would create bitter feelings.

Corporate Relief

Mrs. Krasman described to a reporter the situation her husband, Andrew Krasman, a mill worker, faced:

> It was the depression more than anything else. . . . You see, we have nine children to feed and clothe and my husband works only one, and at most two days [every two weeks]. We own our home and we have a few chickens, but they'll soon be gone. I kill one every time the children get too hungry and we use the mill's donated flour to make soup, because soup is so strengthening. Our children aren't fed right and my husband wasn't fed right. He would come to the table and after dividing what few provisions we had, seldom ate enough himself.
>
> My daughter went to the room for a swimming suit at 1 o'clock and upon returning said her father was seated on the cedar chest. I went to the room about an hour later and upon finding the door locked, asked him to open it. He replied "I'll never open it anymore." I immediately called the neighbors who helped knock down the door. We found him lying on the floor and the room was covered with blood. I think he regretted his act and tried to save himself.[79]

Andrew Krasman's attempt to kill himself by slitting his throat failed and he recovered from his wound in the hospital. But during the depression at least four other mill workers committed suicide.[80]

Suicides stood as a testament to the desperate and bleak conditions Duquesne steelworkers faced: 29 percent had no job by 1934, and another 48 percent worked only part time. Suicides also are evidence that steelworkers continued to rely on individual solutions to their problems. With little or no work in any mill department or in any of the Carnegie mills, unskilled laborers no longer could transfer within the plant or to another plant. And they no longer had the alternatives of quitting or being fired and moving to another mill job. Workers in Monongahela Valley steel towns had no other employment opportunities. Duquesne, like Clairton, Braddock, and Homestead, remained relatively isolated, and workers depended on the mill for almost all blue- and white-collar manufacturing employment. Duquesne had only one other manufacturing establishment, but it employed only about seventy workers. With this limited job market workers had to stay and accept whatever employment or promise of future reemployment the mill offered. The mill's policy of requiring unskilled workers to show up for work every day, even if no work was available, also kept workers from having the time to tramp for other employment. Indeed, the quit rate of the steel industry dropped to one of the lowest in all of manufacturing.[81]

Among blacks and immigrants family and community strategies for surviving the depression also proved limited. Wives and daughters could find little work. In 1930 only seventy-one women held salaried or wage jobs within Duquesne, a number that declined during the decade. Some Duquesne daughters worked in the Squirrel Hill district of Pittsburgh as domestics, and wives took in a little extra money by doing laundry or housework, but the mill remained the primary, or the only, source of income for most steelworker families.

The depth and length of the depression simply overwhelmed both the immigrant and black communities. Although both had built many social, cultural, and economic institutions in Duquesne by 1929, these could not sustain their impoverished members, nor could their impoverished members support these institutions.[82] "I was laid off three years so I quit the Croatian Union," one Duquesne worker remarked. "Couldn't pay the dues."[83] Instead, steelworkers looked to the mill, the Salvation Army, and, to a lesser extent, the city to tide them through the depression. Oral histories, and Duquesne surveys conducted in the 1930s by Harvey O'Connor and by Horace Davis, a communist writer in the 1930s, show that steelworkers, especially immigrants and blacks, overwhelmingly depended on the mill for relief. Their food and loans came primarily from the mill, the city, and the Salvation Army, not the ethnic community.[84]

The city and mill began their relief efforts in late 1930 and early 1931. Following Hoover's and Taylor's emphasis on voluntary relief, mill managers, local businessmen, Mayor Crawford, and the city council instituted private and public relief programs. The city provided employment for local workers in various street and maintenance projects, and local welfare agencies and churches provided aid to families, including food, clothing, and interest-free loans. The Duquesne Businessman's Association gave out food baskets and the Duquesne Republican Club established a children's milk fund.[85] Carnegie Steel provided a small amount of free direct relief (food, clothing, and coal) to its workers but only to the most destitute, including widows of former workers. The mill also provided credits for rents and mortgages for workers in company housing.[86]

This early relief phase ended abruptly in January 1932 when a crisis finally forced the company to take a greater role in welfare efforts. Because the city faced budget shortfalls for 1931, it drastically slashed spending and taxes, which effectively ended all local public works. Crawford and Hughes, the mill's labor department superintendent who also served on the city council, led the entrenchment efforts. With local private relief programs also drying up, the Salvation Army took over the direction of local relief in October 1931. Even money made through fund-raisers in the immigrant community went to the Salvation Army for distribution. By January 1932 those contributions were drying up, and the Salvation Army began to turn away families. As the social and fiscal crisis mounted, U.S. Sen. James Davis, a Pennsylvania Republican, asked the city council whether the federal government should provide aid to the town. The council's response, forcefully argued by Hughes, noted that Duquesne could handle its own problems and needed no outside help.[87] Instead, Hughes soon announced that the Duquesne Works would provide all the relief necessary for Duquesne steelworkers, thus reducing the Salvation Army's caseload by 60 percent.

The plant's relief program, following U.S. Steel directives, centered heavily on deferred loans, not grants of direct relief. The company expanded the use of mortgage and rent credits and added a food distribution program. Once or twice a week the company distributed food baskets filled with meat, cheese, macaroni, flour, and other staples. Management recorded the cost of each basket, and workers repaid the loans through payroll deductions when their hours picked up.[88]

Although the company essentially supported its workforce during the first years of the depression, its efforts did not win its workers' loyalty. Steelworkers frequently complained about the poor quality of the company's food baskets, which they claimed contained spoiled meat and flour infested with maggots. "Sure I got some damned boxes," complained one. "Such rotten bacon it was green."[89] Instead, they wanted direct payments so that they could decide their own diet and buy from their grocer of choice. The dependence on the company for food baskets, often wheeled by workers from the mill to home in children's wagons, was humiliating. Workers also objected that the mill's relief program ultimately made them pay for their own relief, with all rent, mortgage, and food credits deducted from future paychecks. Meanwhile, the mill ensured that workers could not receive county relief, which provided direct grants before 1933. Any steelworker who attempted to seek county relief quickly found his effort blocked. The county routinely denied the steelworkers' applications, because in background checks the Duquesne Works always listed the men as employed, even if they had been laid off or were working only a few hours a week. Only by quitting the mill, and thus losing pension seniority and risking the loss of future mill employment, could a worker in Duquesne receive county relief before the New Deal.[90]

As the Duquesne Works created its unpopular relief program, it cut back on its popular traditional welfare programs. By 1932 the company no longer offered the supervised playground program. It dropped its apprenticeship program and English classes for immigrants in 1932. Mill-sponsored sporting leagues also disappeared as a result of the plant's cost cutting.[91] U.S. Steel further cut benefits unilaterally. It reduced pensions by 5 to 25 percent, cut life insurance benefits from $3,000 to $1,000, and dropped its stock-purchasing plan in 1934, which left many skilled workers holding stock worth a fraction of what they had paid for it. By mid-1932 rumors circulated throughout Monongahela Valley steel towns that the company even might cancel workers' compensation insurance.[92]

Conclusion

Duquesne steelworkers expected more from U.S. Steel than the company delivered, and this would prove to be the lasting legacy of welfare capitalism. Through its programs and promises, welfare capitalism gave workers certain expectations. During the depression those expectations included a livable income, whether from work or relief. The whole thrust of welfare capitalism had been to provide for the needs of employees, whether by building housing, developing pension and insurance benefits, or giving instruction in English. During the depression the workers' needs centered on relief, and Myron Taylor had promised that no steelworker would suffer want. In denying the need for federal relief in the city, Hughes, the plant's labor superintendent and member of the city council, had promised that the Duquesne Works would provide all the relief its workers needed. Work sharing kept as many workers on the U.S. Steel payroll as possible, and calling laid-off workers back for one day of work every two years tied workers to the corporation more tightly than ever. Because U.S. Steel made promises and did not release its hold over its workforce, steelworkers expected something in return. They regarded the company's depression-era programs as an obligation, not a form of goodwill.

In the minds of steelworkers U.S. Steel failed to meet that obligation. In large measure, the mill simply could not provide for its entire workforce. U.S. Steel lost money for many years, and there was not enough work to keep everyone employed, even with work sharing, or sufficient money for relief. The mill's management structure also proved inadequate by providing little guidance and inadequate record keeping and by placing too much power with foremen. When the company attempted to implement work sharing and provide relief, the problems created by these programs at times outweighed the help the company intended to provide. Myron Taylor's efforts to help the worker had backfired. According to Elmer Maloy, the steelworker who had quit in disgust in 1919 only to return, the Duquesne's policies created "a lot of [sore] spots about the company's lack of responsibility for the people that worked for them."[93]

The Duquesne Works' successful labor strategy, built up over decades to ensure a nonunion workforce, stood in shambles by the early 1930s. Management's efforts to create a temporary system based on work sharing and relief loans failed to provide an alternative acceptable to workers. Grievances, which had been kept in check during the 1920s, became aggravated and new ones now arose. Although in the early years of the depression workers were forced to find their own solutions to their problems, the rise of the New Deal would provide steelworkers with new opportunities for collective action. However, the depression did not affect all steelworkers in the same way, thus further dividing workers from each other. As in 1919 the workers' movement during the New Deal would fracture along skill and ethnic lines. Leading one of the first efforts to bring a union to Duquesne would be an unlikely alliance of the mill's most dispossessed workers. Their initial success would demonstrate how the once-supreme open shop in Duquesne had begun to crumble.

3. The Rank-and-File Movement, 1933–35

AT A HEARING BEFORE the New Deal's National Steel Labor Relations Board (NSLRB) in October 1934, a Carnegie Steel lawyer questioned a black steelworker from the Duquesne Works. The NSLRB was created to oversee labor relations in the steel industry, and it held two days of hearings about an Amalgamated organizing campaign at Duquesne. Alluding to the strife that the union claimed existed in the mill, the lawyer asked Fletcher Williamson, "Where is all this unrest you speak of?" Williamson answered as he hit his chest with his fist, "Here in mah heart."[1]

Williamson was born in North Carolina in 1882. He worked in the turpentine fields of Georgia and Florida and during World War I was employed by the Muscle Shoals project in Alabama. During the 1920s he migrated north and settled in Duquesne, where he opened a small storefront church and took a job at the mill. Williamson was angry that blacks had "the sorriest jobs in the Duquesne Mills." "There are no Negro rollers . . . chippers or crane runners," he complained. "The skilled jobs are barred to Negroes in the steel mills." When the depression arrived, he held on to his unskilled job of bundling and loading steel for shipping, a job that paid laborer's wages and provided at most only three days of work each week. When in 1933 the New Deal's National Industrial Recovery Act (NIRA) accorded workers the right to organize unions and engage in collective bargaining, Williamson became one of the first Duquesne workers to join the Amalgamated Association of Iron, Steel, and Tin Workers.[2]

A few thousand other Duquesne workers shared Williamson's unrest and joined the Amalgamated. Like Williamson, the majority had migrated to Duquesne—blacks from the South but mostly immigrants from eastern and southern Europe. They too were unskilled and semiskilled hourly workers, receiving only a few days of work a week. Together they built a remarkable multiracial and multiethnic movement of the mill's poorest and least-skilled workers. Between 1933 and 1935 they forced the impervious U.S. Steel to redefine its labor policies and once again meet face to face with a union. The Duquesne unionists also challenged and threatened federal officials to back up the promises of the New Deal with action. In the process they helped intensify the growing national crisis in labor relations.

The New Deal and Unionization

By November 1932 Duquesne steelworkers were no closer to organizing a union than they had been in the 1920s. Still, they found a way to effect change. In the 1932 presidential election Franklin Roosevelt outpolled Herbert Hoover by a margin of 2 to 1 in the town. By voting for Roosevelt, Duquesne workers helped usher in the New Deal and change the course of labor relations in steel. The New Deal set in motion a series of legal, economic, and political changes that made possible the rise of unionism in the city. Far from instantaneous and complete, these changes flowed directly from New Deal programs and indirectly from the social forces set in motion by the New Deal.

Before the New Deal the outlook for unionism remained bleak. The depression fostered a greater dependence on the company by its workers. Although they complained about the company's relief efforts, workers ultimately looked to the company for food, rent and mortgage credits, and sometimes even clothing. On the shop floor the reduction of work hours and wages tended to increase labor disunity, as each worker tried to figure out how to keep his job and earn more pay. Even if workers had tried to organize, the Amalgamated, the only AFL union with the jurisdiction to represent steelworkers, used all its meager resources defensively, attempting to hold on to its dwindling membership. During the first four years of the depression it made no attempt to expand.

The Communist Party fared little better in Duquesne. Although the party placed an organizer in Duquesne, he did not succeed in establishing a local of the organization's Steel and Metal Workers Industrial Union (SMWIU) before the New Deal. The party had little success with its union in most of Allegheny County, and although it was more successful with miners in southwestern Pennsylvania, the party had difficulty keeping members.[3] The Communists showed better results in their work with the unemployed, building successful Unemployed Councils in McKeesport, Homestead, and Braddock. In Duquesne, however, the Communists' organization was not very visible.[4]

Their failure stemmed from Crawford's control of the town. There is "nothing of the kind going on in this city," reported Police Chief Thomas J. Flynn, whose officers, he noted, kept "an absolute check-up on every available meeting place in the city of Duquesne. . . . It would be next to impossible to carry on un-American agitation without knowledge of the police."[5] In their zeal to stop Communists, Crawford and the police not only denied meeting requests from the International Workers' Order, a fraternal organization associated with the Communist Party, but also frequently refused to give permits for meetings and social affairs to the six local Croatian clubs and societies. Town authorities suspected those organizations of harboring Communists.[6]

The passage of the New Deal's "First One Hundred Days" programs in 1933 profoundly altered these conditions by breaking down corporate paternalism, providing workers with economic stability, and legitimizing labor unions. The Federal Emergency Relief Administration (FERA), which granted relief through federal, state, and county agencies, replaced U.S. Steel's relief programs. FERA provided grants directly to Pennsylvania, which then funneled the money through county agencies in the form of direct payments to unemployed and part-time workers. By November 1934, 64 percent of Duquesne families had enrolled for county relief. When it arrived, U.S. Steel disbanded its relief efforts, arguing that it would be unfair to be taxed twice for relief.[7]

The Home Owners Loan Corp. created a similar change with workers' mortgages. During the 1920s Duquesne's ethnic steelworkers spent much of their earnings to buy homes. By 1933 Duquesne had the highest percentage of home ownership of all the Monongahela Valley steel towns.[8] Phillip Bonosky, a writer, noted that his Lithuanian father "put every dime into a roof over his old age—into a wall between him and the American Poor House."[9] When the depression struck, workers attempted to hold on to their homes, putting much of their meager earnings into their mortgages or using U.S. Steel credits to delay mortgage payments. Most were successful— the city had only thirty-five home foreclosures between 1928 and 1933. By the end of 1934 the New Deal's Home Owners Loan Corp. had removed much of this pressure by insuring more than five hundred Duquesne homes, thus providing relief from foreclosure.[10] The federal program again took U.S. Steel out of the relief business and provided workers with a level of security they had not experienced in the past.

It was the National Industrial Recovery Act, however, that created the legal underpinnings for a renewed union movement in Duquesne. The NIRA, which established the National Recovery Administration (NRA), allowed industries, with government participation and approval, to draft codes of fair competition. The codes established production levels, pricing, and product standards without the threat of antitrust action. The steel industry had a relatively free hand in writing, implementing, and revising its code, essentially ignoring most government suggestions. The historian Jesse Moody, who studied the NRA and the steel industry, concluded that the "Steel Code was industrial self-government without constraint." However, each industry code also had to include two labor provisions: section 7(a), which gave workers the right to organize and bargain collectively, and section 7(b), which called for minimum wage and maximum hour levels. The industry's original proposal in the early summer of 1933 reasserted the industry's open-shop policies and noted that employee representation plans (ERPs), also referred to as company unions, would meet all the collective bargaining requirements of the NRA. Hugh Johnson, the retired brigadier general who headed the NRA, labeled the industry's language inappropriate. Eager to establish the steel code, the industry backed down and inserted standard NRA language in its code, upholding labor's right to organize and bargain collectively. Still, the industry had made its point: it would continue to fight for the open shop.[11]

The Amalgamated at first appeared little interested in meeting this challenge. By 1933 the union had a membership of fewer than five thousand nationally and bargained with only thirteen companies, mostly smaller finishing mills.[12] Its leaders had become hopelessly out of touch with rank-and-file steelworkers and had no intention of building the union. The leaders also did not fully understand the NRA, nor did they even know where to find information about it.[13] The labor journalist Louis Adamic described the Amalgamated's president, Michael F. Tighe, as "a fattish, drooling, loose-lipped, watery-eyed old codger in his late seventies." "A typical old-time trade-union bureaucrat," Adamic wrote, "he is profoundly ignorant of the forces now operating in the world or in the country; . . . [but] deeply experienced in the official trickeries and 'practical trade-union politics' long since perfected by leaders in A.F. of L. affiliates." The Amalgamated's national leaders, he concluded, earned salary and expenses that they "could not conceivably hope to receive in any other racket except by some fluke, and they naturally think a great deal of their positions and want to keep them."[14]

The union did not begin an organizing drive until August 1933, nearly a month and a half after passage of the NIRA. Even then, AFL president William Green had to prod the Amalgamated into launching a membership drive.[15] However, as union organizers entered the field, they quickly found what United Mine Workers' organizers had discovered: workers were highly receptive to unionization. The effect of the NRA had been instantaneous and unforeseen. During August the Amalgamated added fifty-three new lodges and another twenty-four joined in September.[16] The Amalgamated used themes of patriotism and support for Roosevelt and his recovery program to win workers: "Our President has called for a new deal. Are we going to be slackers, or are we going to stand behind him 100 per cent, and help bring about that prosperity of which we have heard so much? There is no better way of bringing it back than by joining our ranks."[17]

Like the United Mine Workers (UMW), the Amalgamated implied that Roosevelt wanted workers to organize: "Under the Industrial Recovery Act, the workers of the steel mills are CHALLENGED BY THE PRESIDENT OF THE UNITED STATES TO BECOME MEMBERS OF A LABOR ORGANI-ZATION."[18] The union also assured workers that they need no longer fear the steel companies, because the NRA protected workers joining a union from discharge.[19] The new lodges paid homage to Roosevelt and the New Deal, choosing names such as "Blue Eagle," "Delano," "Recovery," "New Deal," "NIRA," and "Prosperity." This success provided the union with money to place one hundred organizers in the field.[20]

In Pennsylvania, and particularly southwestern Pennsylvania, two factors facilitated the steel organizing drive: a revitalized labor movement that brought together miners and steelworkers, and the pro-worker public pronouncements and actions of Gov. Gifford Pinchot and his wife, Cornelia.

Passage of the NRA had immediately revived the moribund UMW, and within a week thousands of miners flooded into the union. Problems with writing and approving the NRA's coal code led to a wildcat strike of seventy-five thousand miners in mid-September. The coal operators acceded to most demands of the UMW and signed the coal code, but one problem remained. The management of mines owned by U.S. Steel's Frick Coal Co. refused to sign the agreement or bargain with the union. This led the wildcatting miners to continue their strike, which encompassed the southwestern Pennsylvania counties of Greene, Fayette, and Washington.

To bring additional pressure on the Frick Co., the insurgent miners attempted to shut down U.S. Steel's Clairton plant. Located just south of Duquesne, the Clairton Works produced not only steel but the coke and gas by-products necessary to run the Duquesne, Homestead, and Edgar Thomson plants. For nearly two weeks waves of miners, some driving old jalopies and others marching along county roads, entered Clairton and picketed the plant. A new Amalgamated lodge at the Clairton Works, created in the wake of the NRA, joined the miners in their efforts to shut the plant down. Although they succeeded in stopping steel production, the strikers could not shut down the coke facilities, which the company kept open by housing workers inside the mill and paying them triple wages. As the miners continued picketing, steelworkers struck the mill in Ambridge, Pennsylvania, and the Ohio and West Virginia mills of Weirton Steel, creating a strike movement of nearly 100,000 miners and steelworkers in Ohio, West Virginia, and southwestern Pennsylvania.[21]

Pinchot, a Republican elected in 1930, solidly supported the strikers. Although some state legislators' attempts to abolish the Coal and Iron Police had failed, Pinchot refused to grant any police commissions to companies during the strike, effectively ending the practice. Pinchot even used the state police to stop the violence of deputy sheriffs against striking miners in Fayette County.[22] Pinchot spoke publicly as a friend of labor and a union supporter and castigated the mine and steel owners for their open-shop policies. When miners marched on Clairton, I. Lamont Hughes, the president of Carnegie Steel, wired Pinchot to protest the pickets outside his plant. Pinchot's well-publicized tart reply won him worker plaudits:

> If the Carnegie Steel Company is threatened by striking miners, it has nothing but the blind and brutal conduct of affiliated officials to thank for it. The moment these officials cease to let their willful and antiquated prejudices against organized labor stand in the way of national recovery and sign the coal code the trouble will be over.
> . . . Now that this violence is recoiling upon you, and you are getting a taste of your own medicine you run to me for help.[23]

Pinchot's stand in the Clairton strike won him praise from newly formed Amalgamated lodges in the Monongahela Valley. Responding to their calls for organizing help, he sent his wife, Cornelia, on a speaking tour. Steelworkers and organizers from throughout southwestern Pennsylvania, including Duquesne, requested that Cornelia Pinchot visit their town. Union leader George McBride asked her to come to McKeesport and "remove the fear of the men and, possibly, put a little of that fear into the managers of our plant."[24] When she toured southwestern Pennsylvania in November, hundreds of enthusiastic steelworkers showed up to hear her message. At Duquesne workers filled a meeting hall and spilled out into the street. Her message to the steelworkers mixed encouragement and a strident defense of labor unions with a detailed litany of abuses by the "tyrannical and self-willed business man" and the "Steel Trust."[25] Forty years later a Duquesne steelworker, asked how Roosevelt helped the unions, never mentioned the president: "Ms. Pinchot," he said, "was the one that really started that around here."[26]

The speed at which Amalgamated lodges sprang up has led the historian and activist Staughton Lynd to conclude that workers virtually organized themselves without help from the Amalgamated.[27] Although this might have been true of some mills, it was not the case in Duquesne. Early in its drive the union targeted the Monongahela Valley and the big Carnegie mills. At least two Amalgamated organizers worked in Duquesne during the late summer and early fall, meeting steelworkers in their homes, barbershops, and pool halls. However, Duquesne still lagged behind the nearby McKeesport mills, where numerous union lodges formed in early August.[28] McKeesport unionists immediately challenged Duquesne workers to follow suit:

> Listen, men, can't you hear the President calling you? Will you heed him and march to victory by his side? Or will you be a slacker, and through your unpatriotic action go down to defeat, dragging him with you? How earnestly, tenderly, the President is calling—oh, workers, organize. Must he get down on his knees and plead with you? Or will you be men and help shoulder your own burden?
>
> Are you satisfied to continue being a poodle dog, or donkey for the boss?[29]

Despite passage of the NRA, Mayor Crawford and the Duquesne mill managers were not prepared to step aside and allow unionism to flourish. In addition, the miners' strike caused a heightened level of panic. "We expect the miners to march into McKeesport, Duquesne, and Homestead Pa., within the next couple of days," the secretary of the Amalgamated's McKeesport Lodge 163 wrote to Governor Pinchot on September 29.[30] Responding to the threat, Crawford vowed, "We're not going to stand for any God-damned hoodlums coming into town. We're going to meet them at the bridge and break their God-damned heads."[31] The mayor called Duquesne's religious, business, industrial, and professional leaders to a mass meeting and pledged to keep peace in the town and "protect" steelworkers from the miners. A. C. Cummins, general superintendent of the Duquesne Works, had learned well the strategy of 1919 and placed numerous foremen and skilled workers on guard duty and ordered $1,095 worth of "sickening gas" and tear gas.[32] Calling the miners' strike "a serious threat to the welfare of the Duquesne community," Cummins labeled the miners irresponsible and vowed to keep the mill open as long as the men showed up for work. In a theme he would repeat regularly when labor conflict threatened the mill during the next several years, Cummins noted that a strike would lose valuable business for the mill and upset its fragile, though limited, recovery: "What will happen if we have labor disturbances and production is stopped? Business will not wait for us to get going. Orders will be placed elsewhere and much of it permanently lost to Duquesne. We will face another winter with little or no work for our people; with dire want staring everyone in the face."[33]

The miners never marched beyond Clairton, and by the third week in

October the threat of a larger regionwide coal and steel strike had subsided.[34] However, while tension still hung in the air in early October, the Amalgamated opened a headquarters in Fletcher Williamson's storefront church, establishing the open union presence that had been impossible in 1919. A few weeks later the Amalgamated succeeded in opening a new lodge in Duquesne, housed in the same storefront church: Fort Dukane Lodge No. 187.[35] "We formed a lodge that will be known as 'Fort Dukane,' composed of men employed by the Duquesne Carnegie Steel plant, men who have longed and lived to see dawn the day that they could join a union of their own choosing without awakening in jail with a broken head," the lodge announced. "Brothers, those days are gone, and will never return if we organize and stand 100 per cent behind our great President Roosevelt."[36]

However, the Duquesne unionists quickly learned the limitations of the new political order. For its second meeting the union expected a large turnout and rented the Croatian Hall. Although it was unable to secure a meeting permit from Crawford, the union went ahead with its plans. With hundreds of workers arriving for the union's first large open meeting, the Duquesne police showed up and, under orders from the mayor, informed the lodge that without a permit no meeting could be held. Crawford had been willing to allow the union to hold closed meetings in its small storefront church, a concession that demonstrated how the NRA had begun to "open up" closed steel towns. Nevertheless, Crawford would not give the union free rein; he would confine it to its small meeting hall.[37]

The union immediately appealed to Governor Pinchot and the AFL, asking for "advice and assistance in securing our rights to hold our meetings as guaranteed by the Constitution of our beloved country and under the N.R.A."[38] Pinchot telegraphed Crawford, pointing out that his "action is directly opposed to every American tradition. I ask you to respect the Constitution and let these men act under it."[39] When asked about the telegram by a reporter, however, Crawford answered, "I don't care anything about Pinchot's telegrams."[40] Pinchot realized his powerlessness, telegraphing William Green: "But most unfortunately I have no authority to compel him to obey constitutions of Pennsylvania and the United States. I gladly would if I could. All I can do is to call his attention to what the Constitution provides."[41]

Undeterred, the Fort Dukane Lodge scheduled another large open meeting for November 1 but this time at its storefront headquarters. Again Crawford refused a permit on the ground that it was an open meeting. Buoyed by the belief that they could assert their constitutional rights, the unionists held their meeting in defiance of Crawford. The mayor, facing regionwide publicity for his meeting bans and Pinchot's entreaties, backed down and did not stop the meeting. Between four and five hundred workers attended, although they had to be divided into three shifts to fit into the small building.[42]

The union had battled Crawford to a standoff. The mayor effectively contained the union to its small headquarters, but the union won the right to hold open meetings. The struggle with Crawford highlighted what would become a trademark of the lodge's approach to unionism. It freely sought the aid and intervention of public figures and bureaucracies while threatening to use the strength of its large membership to achieve its ends. The New Deal had made this approach possible. Encouraged to join unions by their governor, and told that the president both wanted them to unionize and would protect them from firings, steelworkers confidently joined a movement they believed would bring them out of the depression and establish justice in the workplace. They asserted their constitutional rights and openly defied Crawford, believing that the dark days of government opposition to labor's rights had been vanquished. "Now is Duquesne in the United States and under the jurisdiction of President Roosevelt, or Mayor Crawford?" their organizer asked.[43]

Fort Dukane

"We didn't seem to have much trouble at all to get the foreign class to fall in line, but the so-called American seemed to have a yellow streak all the way up his back," the Fort Dukane Lodge reported after its first month.[44] The lodge had a distinctive ethnic and racial composition, composed primarily of immigrants from eastern and southern Europe, their sons, and blacks. Many other mills in the Pittsburgh region, such as the Jones & Laughlin South Side plant and the Edgar Thomson Works, also had an immigrant majority.[45] The Fort Dukane Lodge consciously built and sustained its support among these groups, but a deeper reason lay behind why they, and not U.S.-born whites of western and northern European heritage, flocked to the new Amalgamated lodges. By March 1934 Fort Dukane had the active support of more than fourteen hundred workers, or roughly a quarter of the mill's pre-depression workforce. An examination of those supporters, who left behind a petition with names, occupations, and wage rates, reveals their particular character. A sampling of every fifth worker reveals that an overwhelming majority (89 percent) came from the ranks of the hourly unskilled and semiskilled workforce (see table 2). Higher-paid skilled trades and tonnage workers accounted for only 10 percent of the petitioners. The union also found its strongest support among semiskilled chippers, who accounted for 37 percent of all petition signers, followed by unskilled laborers at 13 percent. A

Table 2. Union Support by Skill Level, 1934

Skill	Number	Percentage
Hourly, unskilled/semiskilled	254	89.4
Skilled trades	17	6.0
Tonnage, semiskilled/skilled	12	4.2
Unknown	1	0.4
	284	100.0

Source: Fort Duquesne [*sic*] Lodge No. 187 petition, March 1934, Box 4, File: Carnegie Co. Clairton [*sic*], Pennsylvania Petition, National Steel Labor Relations Board.

breakdown of their wages reveals that 88 percent of the union supporters earned a chipper's hourly wage (54 cents) or less.[46]

If the union's appeal had been based primarily on ethnicity, a larger percentage of its supporters would have come from the skilled trades and tonnage jobs. By 1920 immigrants from eastern and southern Europe had made inroads into these jobs, especially the skilled trades. Instead, the union gave voice to the poorest and most desperate steelworkers: hourly unskilled and semiskilled workers who bore the brunt of the depression's slowdown. Immigrants, their sons, and blacks filled the union ranks precisely because they filled the least-skilled jobs. Unlike skilled workers, who averaged more hours and still made extra tonnage earnings, or skilled trades workers, who worked longer workweeks, low-skilled hourly workers faced either layoffs or one or two workdays per week. This explains the wide support the union received from chippers, who numbered nearly one thousand in 1929 but who by 1933 faced massive layoffs and severely reduced hours. For low-skilled hourly workers at Duquesne and other mills, the New Deal and unionization raised hopes for increased hours and wages.

Eastern and southern European immigrants provided the bulk of the union's ranks. The lodge regularly enlisted men to speak in Croatian, Italian, Russian, and Hungarian at its meetings, and it built close ties with local ethnic fraternal groups. For example, William C. Turner, the president of the Lithuanian Club, regularly spoke at meetings. Croatian fraternal leaders who held membership in the lodge included Vince Poljak, who served as president of the Croatian Fraternal Union No. 6 and as treasurer of Fort Dukane.[47] Like other new Amalgamated lodges in the Monongahela Valley, the Fort Dukane Lodge soon became known derisively as the "Hunky" union.[48] To counter this the lodge officers turned "Hunky" into an inclusive and positive label, devoid of negative ethnic connotations. "The so-called Hunky is the man that has the back bone and is willing to fight for his just dues," wrote

Ray Ruhe, the lodge correspondent for the union journal. "Men, when the truth is known we are all hunkies, or foreigners. All our forefathers were all born in the old country. It doesn't make any difference what nationality or color we are, we all have the same God and need the same necessities of life, so why can't we belong to the s[a]me organization[?]"[49]

The ethnic potpourri within the union was not exceptional. It mirrored the steelworkers' own work, residential, and social worlds. In laboring and chipping gangs ethnic diversity prevailed, as Slovaks, Italians, Croats, Russians, and Czechs worked side by side.[50] Carnegie Steel consciously mixed nationalities and races, because—according to a Homestead employment official—if only one nationality were represented in a gang, "under these conditions they stick together too much."[51] Duquesne's working-class neighborhoods took on similar characteristics. On one block near the mill might reside Magyar, Croatian, Russian, Slovenian, Serb, Greek, and Ruthenian immigrants along with black families. At an early age a Hungarian child might learn also to speak Polish, Russian, and Croatian.[52] This pattern continued into the 1930s, and residents of Monongahela Valley mill towns recalled their neighborhoods as congenial places. Milan Tankosich remembered Duquesne as a place where "people were really close, as though they were one great big family. . . . There was hardly ever any trouble."[53] A black resident of the period found that even the Slavs and blacks "got along together, they mixed together" and would go over to each other's houses.[54] Likewise, the flourishing fraternal organizations did not rigidly distinguish between nationalities. Michael Kerekac, a Czech, and John Smitko, a Slovak, both attended the Russian social club in Duquesne, and Tankosich, a Serb, attended both the Croatian and the Serbian clubs. The Croatian Fraternal Union accepted all nationalities, including the Irish.[55]

The task of holding together this collection of workers would fall in large part to William J. Spang, president of the Fort Dukane Lodge from 1933 to 1936. Spang appeared an unlikely leader of the union movement in Duquesne. His father, a German immigrant, was a foreman at the Duquesne Works who served guard duty during the miners' strike. William Spang at first avoided the mill and worked for the city as a fire fighter, but by 1920 he also hired on at the plant. Unlike many of the other local rank-and-file steelworkers who were becoming union leaders throughout the steel region in 1933, Spang did not have a skilled job. After thirteen years in the mill he had advanced only to a semiskilled job. Furthermore, as the son of a German father and a Scottish-Irish mother, his ethnicity did not match that of his fellow Duquesne unionists, whose heritage was eastern and southern European. However, Spang brought to the union movement an uncommon ability to build and sustain a multiethnic and multiracial alliance. What he did have in common with the other unionists was that he worked only a few days a week and by 1934 faced a layoff.[56]

The rest of the lodge's leadership reflected the membership's eastern and southern European origins. The first officers of the union included Vince Poljak, a Croatian immigrant who served as treasurer; John Miskanic, the Slovak vice president; Henry Budahazi, the Czech recording secretary; and Peter Peletchy, the Russian who served as inside guide. In 1936 an Italian immigrant would replace Spang as president. The union also drew the American-born sons of eastern and southern European immigrants. The sons, who came of age in the 1920s, also filled leadership posts and increasingly played a prominent role in the union. For example, Mike Kovalsky, the son of Slovak immigrants, served as financial secretary, and Andy Olah, the son of Magyar immigrants, eventually replaced Budahazi as recording secretary. Throughout its existence the lodge maintained this mix of leaders.[57]

What most distinguished the new Amalgamated lodge from the union movement of 1919 was its racial dynamics. Whereas only one black supported the strike in 1919, the majority of Duquesne's three hundred black workers joined the Fort Dukane Lodge. This marked a profound shift for the Amalgamated, a union with a long history of hostility toward blacks. However, the change did not emanate from the national leadership. In the middle of its membership upsurge in 1933, the national leaders did not view African Americans as integral to the union effort, and they even implied that blacks should have separate lodges. Instead, the racial changes occurred at the local level, especially in lodges at mills with sizable black workforces.[58]

Fort Dukane's success at recruiting blacks resulted largely from the efforts of Spang and the early black leaders within the lodge. "My sole idea in going into the movement was to get white and colored people together whom capitalist [*sic*] have tried to keep apart," Spang told an interviewer.[59] Although his choice of words reflected his association with the Communist Party in later years, he pushed blacks into leadership posts from the lodge's inception. Initially, the lodge elected only one black officer, a guard. Spang soon lobbied for more black leaders in meetings with small groups of black and white steelworkers. At the lodge's next election in February 1934 the lodge elected a black vice president, Thomas Watson, and two black trustees. When Watson relinquished his vice presidency later that year, Fletcher Williamson replaced him. Williamson, who had offered his church for the lodge's first meetings, had been a strong presence in the lodge since the beginning, opening each meeting with a prayer and regularly giving speeches. Two other black preachers, "Father" Henry Cox and Frank Gore, joined him as speakers, mixing union sentiments with Scripture. The black preachers held a great deal of authority with fellow black workers, and their preaching experience gave them oratorical skills many other workers lacked. At some meetings black unionists gave most of the talks.[60]

The lodge's leadership and membership also forcefully opposed segregation within the lodge and the Amalgamated, further consolidating black support. When the issue of segregation arose in regard to an Amalgamated Pittsburgh District 1 picnic, the Duquesne lodge took the lead in opposing it. The picnic organizers had signed a contract with park management that provided separate dance facilities, but when three black members of the Duquesne lodge objected at the planning meeting, the whole picnic was called off. Upon hearing a report of the incident at the Fort Dukane Lodge meeting, a white member of the lodge spoke in support of the black workers, arguing, "We are all brothers, not only in the lodge room but everywhere; in work, pleasure, and grief." His motion not to participate in segregated picnics won unanimous approval. The Amalgamated's national secretary, Shorty Leonard, however, saw the cancellation as unfortunate and claimed that the blacks responsible for raising the issue were in the pay of the bosses. On another occasion a delegation of Duquesne and McKeesport lodge officers en route to Washington, D.C., walked out of a restaurant when the owner told Fletcher Williamson that he had to eat in the kitchen.[61]

The Fort Dukane leadership kept its diverse and large membership active and cohesive by building a kind of movement culture. The lodge held three events every week: a regular closed business meeting on Monday for members only; a bingo night on Wednesday; and an open meeting on Friday, aimed at drawing in nonmembers and creating a relaxed atmosphere with speeches by members in English and various foreign languages. The lodge also worked to establish labor traditions among its new members, most of whom had never participated in unions. On the Fourth of July the lodge held its own picnic, and on Labor Day the union marched in a parade from Duquesne through McKeesport and into Glassport. Fort Dukane's contingent that day, including workers and their families, was estimated at more than three thousand by the lodge and exceeded the total of all other union marchers—miners, steelworkers, and glassworkers—from all the nearby cities who gathered in Glassport. The lodge also sought to insert itself in traditions once reserved for the Duquesne Works management. On Christmas William Spang dressed up as Santa and distributed candy to hundreds of mill workers' children at the lodge Christmas party. In the past the Carnegie Steel Co., in a ritual dating to at least 1920, had distributed candy to the mill workers' children on Christmas.[62]

The lodge also organized one of the few women's auxiliaries within the Amalgamated. The women of the Fort Dukane Women's Auxiliary No. 2 conducted weekly meetings, raffled quilts, held bingo games, and helped organize social events for the lodge. The auxiliary asked the women of Duquesne, "Will we stand idly by and watch our children and men suffer, as they have in the past, or are we going to join in the fight for our own upliftment and from the starvation period, and get a little of the good things of life?"[63] Affiliation with the Amalgamated also allowed the women to participate beside men in official capacities within the labor movement. The Duquesne auxiliary, which grew to four hundred members, regularly sent delegates to participate in AFL Trades Council meetings in McKeesport, and one of its officers, Betty Sabo, became secretary for the Amalgamated's Pittsburgh District 1. And, like the Fort Dukane Lodge, the women's auxiliary directly confronted racial divisions in its ranks.[64]

The lodge further expanded its members' exposure to the labor movement and forged their union consciousness by presenting talks from other Pittsburgh-area unionists. The sharing of speakers also allowed the lodge to build fraternal ties with other Amalgamated lodges and to nurture a growing regional steelworkers' movement. Spang and Williamson, along with other Duquesne unionists, frequently spoke at other lodges' meetings. Steelworkers from Braddock, McKeesport, and other lodges reciprocated with talks at the Duquesne lodge's Friday meetings. Duquesne also participated in Amalgamated district meetings, which brought together all the Amalgamated lodges in and near Pittsburgh for monthly meetings. Duquesne regularly sent a large contingent to the meetings, hosted some, and became a leading lodge in the Pittsburgh District 1 movement.[65]

The efforts of the Fort Dukane Lodge to build and sustain its membership proved quite successful. By early 1934 the lodge had attracted more than six hundred workers to some of its meetings and had become the largest Amalgamated lodge in the Carnegie system.[66] However, management refused to recognize the union or even meet with its leaders. Fort Dukane could not hold on to its membership indefinitely without offering returns to those who had risked their jobs to join. The promises of the New Deal had raised workers' expectations to great heights, and they joined unions expecting immediate returns. When they received none, they could just as quickly abandon the labor movement. It became crucial for unions to gain recognition and bargaining rights; at the least, they needed to sustain momentum by promising recognition in the future or by providing immediate improvements in employment conditions.[67]

Employee Representation versus Trade Unionism

The NRA not only revitalized the labor movement in steel but also created mechanisms that Amalgamated lodges could use for gaining company recognition. Buoyed by a large but increasingly impatient membership, Fort Dukane worked within the legal and administrative framework of the NRA, attempting to force U.S. Steel to grant recognition. This move appeared suicidal: a union grounded in one plant was trying to secure recognition from a giant corporation with scores of plants and an open-shop labor policy. However, the NRA opened up this very possibility through the emerging policies of its National Labor Board (NLB). Still, the lodge did not depend solely on the federal government. It also worked with other new Amalgamated lodges to create a labor movement led by the rank-and-file. The movement built upon the upsurge in union membership and connected the growing intradistrict organizations centered in Chicago, Pittsburgh, Youngstown, and Wheeling. In early 1934 the confidence of the Fort Dukane unionists was challenged as they confronted the open-shop resolve of U.S. Steel, the limits of the New Deal's commitment to unionization, and the Amalgamated's ability to mount a viable organizing drive.

When the New Deal spurred the upsurge in steel unionism with passage of section 7(a) of the NIRA, neither Roosevelt nor his advisers had a coherent labor policy. The NIRA, having given workers the right to join unions and bargain collectively, remained silent on what exactly collective bargaining entailed. From this void emerged two versions of workplace representation that battled for supremacy: company-sponsored employee representation plans (ERPs) and independent trade unionism.[68] Much of the history of steel unionism in the 1930s would turn on this struggle, and the Fort Dukane Lodge would be the first union to confront U.S. Steel's commitment to ERPs.

ERPs originated in the steel industry in 1904 but did not emerge in larger corporations until John D. Rockefeller, Jr., established the Colorado Fuel and Iron Co. Plan in 1915. Developed by the Canadian politician and industrial relations expert W. L. Mackenzie King for the Rockefeller Foundation, the plan provided a "compromise between industrial autocracy and union recognition," in the words of the historian Stuart Brandes. Premised on the belief that cooperation and not conflict should underlie management-labor relations, the Rockefeller plan provided a procedure for improving working conditions and opening an ongoing dialogue between workers and management. Rockefeller did not win any steel industry converts to the plan until World War I, when some large companies installed ERPs after the National

War Labor Board ordered them to bargain with their workforces. Bethlehem Steel, Youngstown Sheet and Tube, Midvale Steel, and Inland Steel all instituted plans in 1918–19 to meet government directives and sidestep bargaining with trade unions. After the war the interest in ERPs waned with the resurgence of the open shop. By 1932 only seven ERPs survived in the steel industry, down from twenty in 1919.[69]

The survival of the ERP at Bethlehem Steel, the second-largest steel producer in the United States, kept the movement alive. Bethlehem Steel also belonged to the highly secretive and exclusive Special Conference Committee (SCC), a grouping of ten major corporations that included General Motors, Du Pont, International Harvester, General Electric, Goodyear, Jersey Standard, Irving National Bank, Westinghouse, and U.S. Rubber. The group sought to coordinate labor and personnel policies, using the SCC as a clearinghouse. Eight of the ten corporations also used ERPs and found them to be the best way to promote management-labor cooperation and ward off industrial conflict and trade unions.[70] U.S. Steel, however, opposed ERPs and lagged behind the SCC firms' commitment to systematic corporate-wide personnel policies. William Dickson, a former U.S. Steel vice president, contended that Elbert Gary did not see the need for ERPs. Instead, Gary believed that U.S. Steel's welfare policies, combined with the "general good treatment of the workmen, had practically eliminated any danger of labor trouble."[71]

When Congress passed the NIRA in 1933, a mad scramble to create ERPs ensued. In the steel industry the ERP became the solution of choice to meet the new requirements of the law. According to the trade journal *Steel,* ERPs both met the labor provisions of the act and "preserve[d] the open-shop principle." By the end of 1934 the steel industry had at least ninety-three ERPs covering more than 330,000 workers. U.S. Steel quickly joined the movement, borrowing wholesale from the Bethlehem plan and establishing an ERP at each of its plants.[72] The ERPs acted as protective fences, ensuring that any organizing drive by the Amalgamated would be met with "localized contests at every plant."[73] U.S. Steel's ERPs called for the annual election of employee representatives at each plant. The representatives could make requests to management in regard to working conditions, hours of work, wages, and other employment conditions in a process not unlike a grievance procedure. Management paid all expenses incurred under the plan and reserved the right to end the plan at its discretion after the termination of the NRA. The employee representatives, but not the workers themselves, also could terminate the plan by a majority vote.[74]

As employers scurried to create ERPs, and trade unions attempted to organize workers under the NRA, a wave of strikes quickly developed over a

representation battle between ERPs and trade unions. Roosevelt answered
with the formation of the National Labor Board, a tripartite board of public, management, and union members, headed by U.S. Sen. Robert Wagner,
the New York Democrat. The board at first sought to settle disputes through
facilitation and mediation, both in keeping with the voluntary spirit of the
NRA and because the board had no legal standing. As Roosevelt gave the NLB
increasingly greater powers, it began to hand down formal decisions and
build a consistent stance on collective bargaining.

The board's collective bargaining position came to be called the "Reading Formula." It held that in the case of a strike over union recognition, the
striking workers must return to work, the company must rehire all workers,
and the NLB would hold an election to determine who represented the workers for collective bargaining purposes. By early 1934 the board had further
refined the Reading Formula by adding the concept of majority rule. Thus
the winner of a representation election, whether trade union or ERP, held
sole bargaining rights for all workers. Problems arose when companies refused to follow NLB directives. In the highly publicized Weirton Steel case,
the company ignored an NLB order to hold an election and instead fired
union activists and held its own ERP election. Roosevelt at first responded
hesitantly and expanded the board's power only slightly. As the crisis mounted, he finally heeded the board's pleas for more authority and announced the
sweeping Executive Order No. 6580 in February 1934. The order granted the
board the power to conduct representation elections for the purpose of collective bargaining when a "substantial number" of employees requested such
an election, instead of only when a strike situation occurred. Roosevelt gave
the board the power to subpoena company records for election purposes and
granted the board the power to refer noncompliance cases to the U.S. attorney general for prosecution. Further, the president supported the board's
Reading Formula and its recent opinions by incorporating in the executive
order the concept of majority rule.[75]

The changes in federal labor policy directly influenced labor relations at
U.S. Steel and the Duquesne Works. Responding to the board's new powers
and its recent decisions concerning ERPs, Arthur H. Young, a newly hired vice
president in charge of labor relations at U.S. Steel, rewrote the company's ERP
bylaws. The NLB differentiated between valid ERPs and invalid company-
dominated ERPs. A valid plan had to be free of any management coercion,
restraint, and interference. It had to allow workers a mechanism for accepting or rejecting the plan by a majority vote and had to grant workers the right
to elect representatives from outside the plant. Young proposed a series of
changes to the U.S. Steel plan that included these provisions. Before placing

the changes before the corporation's workers, Young gained the NLB's informal approval.[76]

In February 1934 U.S. Steel presented the changes to all its ERPs, which scheduled plantwide elections on the revised plan for later in the month. What management failed to anticipate was that the ERP election fortuitously provided the Fort Dukane Lodge with an issue around which to organize a representation campaign. Fort Dukane, along with some McKeesport steel unionists, sent a delegation of fourteen officers to meet Senator Wagner and protest the ERP election. They argued that the ERP election ballot did not allow workers to vote against the ERP but instead forced workers to vote only for or against the proposed revisions. Whether voting yes or no, the worker in essence endorsed the plan. The delegation left Washington vowing that if U.S. Steel did not recognize the union, they would demand NLB elections at their plants.[77]

From its inception the Fort Dukane Lodge had renounced any involvement in the employee representation plan. The consensus within the Amalgamated had been that involvement in ERPs either represented a selling-out of trade union principles or at best achieved nothing, because the company dominated the plans. Unionists who suggested that the Amalgamated follow a strategy of capturing the ERPs and turning them into trade unions found themselves labeled company stooges.[78] However, by refusing to work within the ERP, the Fort Dukane Lodge conceded the struggle over shop-floor issues to the ERP, which had the authority to raise shop-floor grievances with management.[79] Although the Amalgamated had several well-organized crews, especially in the chipping department, it found itself unable to mount any effective shop-floor protests. More often, Amalgamated members had less control over their jobs than nonunion workers. Management, constrained by the NRA, did not fire union men outright, but it harassed union members on the job. Union men received fewer workdays than nonunion men and faced more layoffs. Jessie Black, a union officer whose foreman called him a "nigger," found that whenever he asked for a shovel or wheelbarrow to do his job, the foreman derisively told him to go ask Amalgamated lodge president William Spang for it.[80]

When U.S. Steel held its ERP election, Fort Dukane sought to demonstrate its power by mounting a boycott. The lodge instructed workers to refuse to vote, and it passed out red, white, and blue ribbons for union members to wear on their lapels. This symbolic act represented changes that resulted from the NRA. The ribbons, tantamount to wearing union buttons, would have met with firings and blacklisting just a year earlier. Nevertheless, management threatened the union supporters. Foremen hounded the men in their crews to vote, threatened to fire the men who did not vote, and warned that if the vote total was too low, the company would shut the plant down. Foremen, white-collar employees, and elected ERP representatives traveled by car throughout the city to bring workers to the mill to vote, including men who had been laid off for years and who suddenly were given a few days of work. Management called chipping crews of 150 off their jobs and told them that if they did not vote the company would replace them with chipping machines. Frank Bodnar, a chipper, said that his foreman told him, "Mr. Leffler, the big boss over the chippers, had 400 chippers too many, and if we did not vote for the Representatives, Mr. Leffler had a good idea how to lay them off." Many Amalgamated workers, however, stood up to their foremen and refused to vote. Joseph Tkach, a chipper, told his foreman, "I don't care to vote and I don't have to vote if I don't want to, for our President says the United States is a free country and we poor workers have the rights to have a little bit of Liberty."[81]

The Amalgamated's efforts proved mildly successful. Although 4,217 workers were eligible to vote, only 2,846 did so. Of those voting, 65 percent favored the revisions, a figure consistent with the other Carnegie Steel Co. mills. U.S. Steel hailed the vote as an endorsement of the ERP, choosing not to mention that at a plant such as Duquesne, only a minority of the eligible voters (44 percent) supported the revisions.[82]

After the election the Fort Dukane Lodge demanded a representation election from the National Labor Board. Backed up by a petition signed by fourteen hundred workers, the lodge asked that the NLB election be between itself and the ERP, be supervised by the NLB, and be conducted off company property. The union handed the petition to the board on March 20, along with forty affidavits showing employer coercion and intimidation during the ERP election. Noting in its petition that if the board did not find the fourteen hundred signatures to be "a substantial number," per Roosevelt's executive order, the lodge would secure more. Except for the Weirton case, which evolved from a strike situation, Duquesne would be the only other large steel mill to seek a representation election before the board. Within Carnegie Steel only the small McDonald Works also filed for an election.[83]

Unfortunately, Fort Dukane could not have submitted the petition at a worse time. Although Roosevelt's February executive order had been a vindication for the board and its conception of collective bargaining, New Deal labor policy was far from decided. Johnson, the head of the NRA, never subscribed to the board's idea of sole bargaining rights, and after the issuance of Executive Order No. 6580 he publicly contradicted the board on this point. On March 25, just five days after Duquesne requested the election, Roosevelt and Johnson undermined the National Labor Board in the settlement of the threatened nationwide auto strike. The settlement established a new Automobile Labor Board, which bypassed the NLB, made no provisions for representation elections, and gave all organized groups of workers, including ERPs, similar collective bargaining rights. Discarding the board's stance on sole bargaining rights, the auto settlement affirmed a pluralist conception of collective bargaining, whereby a plant could contain multiple bargaining units. In essence, this interpretation meant that companies could continue to bargain with their ERPs, even if the ERP had been beaten in an election by a trade union.[84] In the words of two historians of the NLB, the auto settlement struck "a staggering blow to the prestige and authority of the Board."[85]

Caught in the federal crossfire over collective bargaining policy, the Fort Dukane Lodge doggedly stuck to its NLB case. The unionists were unfamiliar with the bureaucratic process and impatient for quick results but confident of the New Deal's commitment to unions and workers. As their case dragged into April with no response, the lodge members became frustrated.[86] Spang telegraphed President Roosevelt, asking whether the lodge had to strike to get the NLB to act.[87] On April 18 Spang told the Federated Press, a small leftist news service, "If the labor board is serious about holding an election, it will send its members here. . . . We're tired of sending delegations to Washington and of the endless run-around we get there. If the labor board doesn't want to come to Duquesne, I think there will be something happening here so interesting in the near future that even Pres. Roosevelt may want to come out."[88]

Unbeknown to Spang, the NLB and U.S. Steel had entered into negotiations in regard to the election request. Arthur H. Young secretly proposed to the board that the corporation again revise its ERP to accommodate the Amalgamated's challenge. U.S. Steel conducted the negotiations informally, because it did not accept the board's legal jurisdiction in the case, nor did it wish to be bound in any way by the board's decision. The negotiations led to an agreement between the board and U.S. Steel, in which the corporation would hold an election at the Duquesne Works on May 15; the election would be observed but not supervised by the NLB; and it would be held within the framework of the ERP. Workers running for ERP office could designate their affiliation (Amalgamated or ERP), and workers would have the opportunity to terminate the employee representation plan.[89] The agreement satisfied both the board and U.S. Steel, because it avoided a representation election that U.S. Steel would have had to challenge in the courts. Neither the board, which was unsure of its constitutionality, nor U.S. Steel, which was unwilling to undermine the NRA, wanted to square off in court. U.S. Steel also seemed confident that the ERP could win the election. The trade journal *Steel* reported that only a few of Duquesne's work crews were well organized. In addition, the Duquesne lodge had a key weakness: although fourteen hundred workers had signed the petition, many were laid off and could not vote in the election.[90]

The Fort Dukane leadership believed differently, confident it could win an election.[91] The lodge was not a party to the negotiations between the board and U.S. Steel and learned of the election plan only after it had been finalized. The board then spent two days in early May trying to sell the election to Duquesne lodge representatives William Spang and Ray Ruhe. L. H. Marshall, the board's vice chair, argued that the Amalgamated should run in the election, take control of the ERP, and abolish it. But Spang and Ruhe refused. They asserted that they could not receive a fair election under the ERP. Instead, they again demanded an NLB-conducted election between the Amalgamated and the ERP. They further demanded that the board publicly order the election that day or "we will announce it ourselves." Unable to move the workers, the board reluctantly ordered an election for Duquesne, with the form and method of procedure for the election to be announced later.[92]

"Brother Spang won the decision and came home a happy man," the Duquesne correspondent reported in the *Amalgamated Journal*.[93] That elation proved short lived. On May 11 Young terminated negotiations with the NLB, arguing that U.S. Steel "refused the right of the board to make such an order." "The company was unwilling to participate in any program," reported an NLB official, "which would in any way indicate its submission to this Board's jurisdiction in the matter."[94] The board spent the next three weeks trying to bring U.S. Steel back into negotiations but failed. On May 31 the board postponed the election indefinitely, though not because of U.S. Steel's actions. The election was put on hold pending the outcome of the larger steel industry-wide struggle over union recognition, which board members knew would undermine their authority once again.[95] As Fort Dukane's National Labor Board case had been winding its way through Washington, a rank-and-file movement within the Amalgamated had been building in the steel towns of the Midwest and East. When the NLB postponed the Duquesne case, the movement was reaching its culmination in a threatened nationwide strike set for the middle of June.

The Rank-and-File Movement

The rank-and-file movement had begun spontaneously in late 1933 because of the growing frustration of the Amalgamated lodges with the national's leadership. The Amalgamated's commitment to organizing steelworkers, which never had been strong, began to wane as early as November 1933. The union's organizing efforts had been funded by the influx of initiation fees and dues, but part-time and unemployed steelworkers, who made up the bulk of the new membership, found the high initiation fee of $3 and the monthly dues of $1 difficult to pay. The new lodges quickly failed to meet their financial obligations to the national union. By the end of 1934, for example, Fort Dukane owed the national union more than $6,000. Instead of reducing the fees and dues, which traditionally had been set high for full-time skilled workers, the national union sharply reduced its organizing staff—from 106 to 15 between September 1933 and May 1934—and complained about the lack of commitment from the new union members.[96] Dissatisfied with the support and guidance provided by the national leadership, the new lodges revived the union's moribund district organizations, elected their own district leaders, and used the organizations as forums to discuss organizational problems. The district meetings, especially from the key steelmaking centers of Chicago, Pittsburgh, Youngstown, and Wheeling, pushed to the forefront a group of young, militant, local leaders, including Duquesne's William Spang.[97]

The district leaders, increasingly concerned that the national officers would allow the momentum of the movement to dissipate, called an interdistrict meeting for March 1934. Held one month before the union's national convention, the meeting attracted 257 rank-and-file delegates from fifty lodges, who were loosely organized around a program of action for the coming convention. The delegates agreed to go back to their lodges and discuss with their memberships how the lodges should gain recognition from their companies. Upon returning to their steel towns, the leaders learned that their memberships supported immediate united action—by striking if necessary—to secure recognition.[98]

At the April Amalgamated convention, in which the national leaders unsuccessfully attempted to unseat the new lodges, the rank-and-filers pushed through a program for union recognition over the objections of the conservative leadership. The rank-and-filers benefited from the advice of four intellectuals—the Socialist author Harvey O'Connor; Stephen Raushenbush, an investigator for the Nye Committee of the U.S. Senate, which was investigating the causes of World War I; Heber Blankenhorn, investigator for the National Labor Board; and Harold Ruttenberg, a University of Pittsburgh graduate student and researcher—who remained anonymous to most steelworkers and the national officers. The Big Four, as they became to be known, preferred not to set a strike date but supported a national organizing drive instead. However, they did not rule out an early summer strike. Although rank-and-file leaders agreed with the strategy in theory, they believed that it would not work. They knew that the national union had botched the first organizing drive and that it had no money to mount another one. Steelworkers had stayed in the movement this long, but if the convention failed to devise an immediate recognition strategy, the rank-and-file leaders believed that the movement would collapse. Instead, the rank-and-filers called for a program in which all lodges would demand recognition from their companies on May 21. If the demands were not met, the Amalgamated would call a strike for June, with no lodges signing an agreement until all lodges had gained recognition. Their demands included union recognition, a six-hour day, five-day week, $1 per hour minimum wage for the unskilled and proportional increases for other workers, and equal rights for black workers. The convention approved the program and elected a Committee of Ten to conduct any negotiations and prepare for a strike.[99]

The rank-and-filers knew they had probably set themselves on a suicide course. Although some mills, such as the Duquesne Works and those in Gary, Youngstown, Monessen (Pennsylvania), and South Chicago, were well organized, large segments of the industry remained virtually unorganized. Within Carnegie Steel both the Edgar Thomson and Homestead lodges lagged behind Fort Dukane in membership, although they were based in larger mills. The Edgar Thomson lodge had only about 450 members, of whom only eighty ever paid initiation dues. The Homestead lodge had trouble even securing meeting permits from the city, and a Duquesne worker was arrested for leafleting at the Homestead plant. The Clairton Works lodge still had not recovered from its disastrous sympathy strike with the miners. However, the rank-and-filers believed they had no alternative.[100]

After the convention the rank-and-file leaders saw their efforts sabotaged by the national leadership. In addition, their inexperience and timidity caused the movement to waste several valuable weeks of organizing time. Unable to depend on the AFL or the Amalgamated for organizing aid, and incapable of mounting the effort themselves, the rank-and-filers turned to the federal government for help. Working closely with the Big Four, they sought to force Roosevelt to intercede before a strike.[101] Clarence Irwin, a leader of the rank-and-filers, noted that "we were trying to force the thing back into Washington by demanding that the President use his power to bring the leaders of the Iron and Steel Institute and the Amalgamated Association together to settle in the public limelight instead of fighting it out with company police in the twilight of the Black Valley, the Mahoning, and the Monongahela."[102] For the next six weeks the rank-and-filers worked their way through the Labor Department, the NRA, the NLB, and the White House, but they could not bring the government to commit to an industry-wide labor-management conference.[103]

At the same time, neither the rank-and-file leaders nor the national officers had organized the weak mills or planned for the actual strike. In addition, the Amalgamated lodges suffered from the same weakness as in 1919: skilled white workers of northern and western European heritage did not support the movement. The union also faced increasingly well-organized and well-armed steel managers who took the threat of a strike seriously and began to stockpile unfinished steel. The Duquesne Works, which refused to accept the lodge's letter requesting recognition on May 21, prepared for the strike in what had become a routine manner. As in the strike of 1919 and the miners' strike of 1933, the mill created a special police force of loyal workers to guard the mill, and it spent $732 for gas munitions to supplement the stock purchased in 1933.[104]

Mayor Crawford lent his support by chairing a mass meeting of what the *Duquesne Times* called "a cross section of the better people of this city." Crawford lashed out at the union for threatening a strike and promised to preserve the city's peace and protect its citizens. Those in attendance passed a resolution declaring the threatened strike "unwarranted, unjustified and vicious," "a blind destructive tendency," and "a vital thrust to the very hearthstone of our community." The resolution passed "unanimously," with Crawford calling only for aye votes and refusing to recognize a contingent of Amalgamated workers. Crawford followed up on his promise to keep the city safe by hiring numerous mill workers as special police officers for the city.[105]

Mill managers took advantage of the ethnic and skill division between the union and nonunion men. In late May a leaflet suddenly appeared throughout Duquesne, distributed in the dead of night and signed a "Group of Steelworkers." The leaflet, which the Amalgamated claimed was the work of mill bosses, labeled the threatened strikers a "bunch of hoodlums, hunkies and a few negroes" who "banded together for their own greed, and are trying to dictate to the management of the Steel Works." The leaflet noted that the strike could be stopped and asked, "Are you willing to go along with us, and run this bunch of trouble-makers out of our community[?]" The leaflet ended with a list of the lodge's leaders that noted their race and nationality.[106]

The mill also put together a large picnic just one week before the threatened strike for the entire maintenance department. More than eight hundred workers and managers from maintenance and key workers from other departments boarded a specially rented train for Idlewild Park. Officially labeled the "gloom chasers" picnic, the event included mushball and boxing matches; three-legged, chicken, and wheelbarrow races; and various other contests throughout the day and evening. I. Lamont Hughes, president of the Carnegie Steel Corp., and L. H. Burnett, a Carnegie vice president, also attended the daylong picnic.[107]

As the steel mills prepared for war, demoralized rank-and-file leaders met with the national officers on June 14 at a reconvened convention. Talk still centered on a strike, but the rank-and-filers knew that a strike would not succeed. Into this void stepped AFL president William Green, who offered the delegates an alternative.Green proposed—with Roosevelt's backing—the creation of an impartial, three-member steel labor board that would investigate and adjust complaints under section 7(a) of the NRA and order and conduct representation elections. In turn, the Amalgamated would call off its threatened strike. The proposal was difficult for the rank-and-filers to accept. First, it committed them to an agreement similar to the auto settlement, which they already had refused to accept when they lobbied Washington in May. Second, the Weirton and Duquesne cases before the NLB had led many steelworkers to believe that the government never would honor their claims for representation elections. Third, the proposal originated not from Green or Roosevelt but instead from consultations between the NRA's Johnson and the steel industry. Steel executives envisioned the steel board as a policing agent for its ERPs.[108] Faced with a choice between Green's proposal and a strike, the rank-and-filers voted for the new steel board. A last-minute loss of nerve, drunkenness, and internal dissension contributed to their decision. More important, the rank-and-file leaders realized the hopelessness of their situation and saw in Green's proposal a way out.[109]

Staughton Lynd has written that the failure of the rank-and-file movement to strike for recognition was the fault of the Big Four and John L. Lewis of the United Mine Workers. Lynd contends that Lewis did not want a strike to threaten his plans to organize the industry, and he had the Big Four dissuade the rank-and-filers from striking. Lynd's evidence rests on an assertion that Ruttenberg made in oral histories of the period. However, no supporting evidence backs Ruttenberg's claims, and others of the Big Four note that they did not influence the rank-and-file leaders not to strike. In addition, Lynd's analysis ignores the realities that the rank-and-filers faced at the time. Lynd offers no analysis of the skill, ethnic, or racial makeup of the rank-and-file movement or an assessment of its strength.[110]

The case of Fort Dukane, the strongest of the Carnegie lodges, and arguably one of the best organized in the rank-and-file movement, demonstrates that even the strongest lodges were extremely weak. The lodge had virtually no support from U.S.-born workers of northern and western European heritage or from skilled workers and skilled tradesmen. Many of the union's strongest supporters were not even working, because they had been laid off. And Duquesne management and the city government were prepared for war. As Harvey O'Connor succinctly summed this situation up in a letter to Lynd in 1972, "Privately not many of the rank and file leaders saw the possibility of much more than a spotty strike with the distinct possibility of a bloody end."[111]

Congress quickly passed Joint Resolution 44 on June 16, authorizing the president to set up NRA labor boards with the authority to investigate and conduct representation elections. On June 28 Roosevelt created the National Steel Labor Relations Board.[112] Thomas Bell wrote in his novel, *Out of This Furnace,* that when a radio announcer read the news bulletin that the Amalgamated had called off the strike in exchange for the NSLRB, a steelworker rose from his bar stool and slowly ripped up his union card. "That's what I think of the union now," he exclaimed.[113] Throughout the steel towns disgusted workers dropped out of the Amalgamated in what Clarence Irwin called "a terrific blow to the rank-and-file movement."[114] In the Amalgamated's Pittsburgh District 1, the rank-and-filers had drawn three hundred to one thousand workers to their meetings before June; only fifty-three attended the first meeting after the strike was canceled. Attendance at Fort Dukane meetings also dropped sharply.[115]

The National Steel Labor Relations Board

The events of June forced the Fort Dukane Lodge to develop a new strategy for achieving recognition. With the creation of the National Steel Labor Relations Board, the National Labor Board ended all involvement in Duquesne's representation case. The rank-and-file movement survived but in a severely weakened state. In the fall some rank-and-filers ran an opposition slate in the election for national officers, but the incumbents overwhelmingly beat them.[116] Despite the settlement, Fort Dukane remained a well-organized lodge, yet it found itself isolated. Within the mill it could not draw the skilled and American-born workers of western and northern European heritage, a weakness that meant it could not pull off a strike. The other Carnegie and U.S. Steel mills remained unevenly organized, with weak lodges in the key Clairton and Homestead mills. This situation, along with the fragility of the rank-and-file movement, dashed any hope of a company-wide or industry-wide strike movement. The unionists' only option was to work within the NRA bureaucracy and demand from the NSLRB the rights promised them by the New Deal.

Following the creation of the NSLRB, the Amalgamated instructed its lodges to demand collective bargaining sessions with their employers. Fort Dukane immediately demanded a session with Duquesne Works management and, in characteristic fashion, voted to strike if it did not receive a reply. When the company stalled, the lodge asked the Amalgamated to file a complaint before the NSLRB.[117] Remarkably, however, Carnegie Steel Co. officials changed their position and agreed to sit down with the union. It marked, in the words of the industry's trade journal *Steel*, "the first time, at least in many years, that the Carnegie Co. has held any kind of parlay with the Amalgamated."[118] The session, held in late July between a lodge committee and Duquesne Works management and Carnegie vice president L. H. Burnett, gave the lodge officers a false sense of how much the company would concede. Vince Poljak, the lodge's treasurer, noted that the Carnegie officials greeted them "as brothers, not as hunkies or hoodlums." Fletcher Williamson said he had "never met a better man than Burnett," who, he said, spoke to the union delegates "as decent as could be expected of any man."[119] The union officers conceded that they had gained only a "few points" and had not discussed wages or hours, but they believed the progress to be ample enough that they did not push the Amalgamated to proceed immediately with their steel board case. However, Cummins, the Duquesne Works general superintendent, later told ERP representatives that just because he had met with the union did not mean "we are dealing or plan to deal in whole or in part" with the union. He also noted that Burnett attended the meeting only so that it would "conform in a legal way" to the NRA.[120]

After the initial meeting the lodge could wrest no further concessions from Carnegie Steel. In the middle of August the lodge once again demanded a steel board election, much to the consternation of the national union's attorney, Charlton Ogburn, who had shelved the lodge's initial request.[121] The national leadership did not want to proceed with the Duquesne case for several reasons. First, the Amalgamated officers refused to put the time or money into helping lodges prepare NSLRB cases. This marked a continuation of its behavior under the NLB, when Fort Dukane had to depend on the Big Four for advice and aid. The national union's lack of cooperation became so pronounced under the NSLRB that Ogburn, who was on loan to the Amalgamated from the AFL, threatened to resign and William Green had to persuade him to stay on.[122] Second, the national leadership did not believe that Duquesne could win a representation election. The Amalgamated wanted to conduct elections only at plants where it had signed up at least 75 percent of the employees, which tended to be only small plants. The Pennsylvania Department of Labor conducted a survey of the mill and informed the national leaders that it believed the Duquesne lodge would lose an election. Privately, others close to the lodge believed the same.[123] Third, Duquesne had not paid dues to the national union since 1933. Ogburn saw this as a sign of weakness that could be a problem if it came out in hearings. The failure to pay dues also angered the national officers, who held Spang, a rank-and-file leader, in low regard.[124]

Despite its reservations the Amalgamated filed for an NSLRB representation election in September.[125] If the Amalgamated had been hesitant about filing the election petition, the NSLRB members felt even more reluctant to take the case. Created to win a truce between the Amalgamated and the steel industry, the board saw its role as mediation, not regulation. Board members also knew from the history of the Duquesne case that U.S. Steel had refused to cooperate with NLB orders and that Fort Dukane had refused to accept the continued existence of the ERP.[126] In an effort to find a middle ground between the corporation and the union, the board ordered two days of hearings in early October.[127]

Instead of leading to a compromise, the hearings highlighted the conflicting visions of collective bargaining held by the two sides. The union charged that "a great spirit of unrest," caused by the ERP, existed at the plant. The ERP did not constitute an agency for collective bargaining, according to the union, but was "a mere plan, a false hope, and [was] designed to lull the employees into a sense of security." It had created "rivalry and bitterness between groups of employees" and impeded the workers' "full right of collective bargaining."[128] The Fort Dukane Lodge, which claimed an exaggerated membership of 2,942 mill workers, again refused to compromise on the issue of full representation rights. When asked by Walter Stacey, one of two board members to attend the hearings, whether the union would accept a written contract that covered only lodge members, Spang turned the offer down. The union wanted an election and majority rule to end the "confusion now existing." Spang then backed his position up with a threat: "Unless we get what we want we have but one weapon left—the strike."[129]

U.S. Steel entered the hearings, as did the Amalgamated, unwilling to change its position on collective bargaining. As it had at the NLB hearings, the corporation refused to recognize the "jurisdiction, power, and authority" of the NSLRB. Although Carnegie and U.S. Steel officials attended the hearings, they did so "informally" so that the facts of the case could be established. I. Lamont Hughes reassured the board that his company would meet and bargain collectively with any employees or their representatives, although he did not commit the company to signing a collective bargaining agreement. Hughes and Young both staunchly defended the ERP as an instrument for collective bargaining, arguing that it represented the vast majority of the workers at the plant. Both men cited the 87 percent participation rate at the last Duquesne ERP election in June as evidence of workers' support for the plan.[130]

During the early part of the hearing, Stacey held out hope for a settlement, noting that the two sides "might not be as far apart as you think."[131] But after two days the lack of common ground became painfully apparent. In addition, the board members showed a growing skepticism of the ERP as a vehicle for collective bargaining. A cross-examination by the union attorney of the chairman of the Duquesne ERP, a skilled open hearth worker named Charles Erickson, exposed glaring inadequacies in the plan. Erickson admitted that he did not understand what collective bargaining meant and that he was not familiar with the rules of the ERP. He further stated that the ERP had never entered into an agreement with management and that all the expenses of the plan were borne by the company, because the ERP did not collect dues. Asked who would pay strike benefits to the men if the ERP struck the plant, Erickson only smiled.[132] Erickson's and Young's testimony led Henry A. Wiley, the other board member present, to tell U.S. Steel officials that "as for collective bargaining, it appears to me your plans have no provisions for it."[133] By the end of the hearings Stacey's hope for a compromise had evaporated. Following a summation by a U.S. Steel attorney of why the corporation opposed a representation election at the plant, Stacey ominously noted, "Power is seldom surrendered; it is always taken."[134]

Two weeks after the hearings U.S. Steel reopened the possibility of a compromise with the Amalgamated. The corporation, worried that the board would grant the Fort Dukane election request, offered the NSLRB a proposal for avoiding an election. Delivered to the board in person by U.S. Steel president W. A. Irwin and Young, the new proposal reasserted U.S. Steel's position that it would bargain with workers and their representatives but in language that was explicitly more accepting of the Amalgamated. The board quickly placed the Duquesne case on hold, unwilling to upset U.S. Steel officials. The Amalgamated's Ogburn immediately rejected U.S. Steel's proposal, but over the next month U.S. Steel and the Amalgamated exchanged seven proposals and counterproposals. As the bargaining intensified, U.S. Steel made a significant concession by agreeing to submit all irreconcilable cases of discrimination in employment, discharge, and promotion to the NSLRB for determination; in essence, the company was recognizing the board's authority in a limited manner. However, U.S. Steel expected a larger concession from the union: pull all election petitions before the NSLRB.[135]

The Amalgamated rejected U.S. Steel's entreaties for three reasons. First, Ogburn would not back down on the issue of majority rule, even though the national officers appeared less committed. *Iron Age* noted that the Amalgamated leadership would have compromised on this issue, as it had at other plants, if not for Ogburn's and the AFL's objection. Second, the union did not accept the corporation's refusal to agree to a signed contract. Third, the Amalgamated would not abandon its right to elections before the NSLRB.

The union had called off the June strike because the government promised the creation of a steel board to conduct such elections. If the Amalgamated abrogated its right to NSLRB elections, the union would make a mockery of the June settlement.[136]

As the negotiations dragged on, confidence in the board among Duquesne unionists plummeted. The lodge had been buoyed by the October hearings, but as October turned into November with no decision, the lodge members were "getting disgusted." As in the NLB case, Fort Dukane once again found itself shut out of negotiations in which it had a stake. Morale among the unionists sank to new lows when a severe slowdown in the industry hit Duquesne hard, dropping production to less than 10 percent of capacity. Both the NRA's labor policy and its recovery program had failed the steelworkers. It looked like another bleak winter in Duquesne.[137]

Unwilling to admit that negotiations had failed, and sensing that a compromise was still possible, the NSLRB called the principal parties together for a conference at the White House with the president and the secretary of labor in December. The steel industry, represented by Myron Taylor and the presidents of Republic Steel and the American Iron and Steel Institute, once again offered to bargain with the Amalgamated for its members only and to recognize the NSLRB in discrimination cases, but the Amalgamated would have to agree not to seek representation elections. Although both the president and secretary of labor pressured the AFL and Amalgamated to accept the agreement, the labor leaders rejected the proposal and again asserted their right to majority rule. Two weeks after the failed conference the NSLRB gave up all hope for a compromise. On December 31 the board ordered a representation election at the Duquesne Works.[138]

The NSLRB gave U.S. Steel seven days to hand over its payroll records, which the board planned to use to establish voter eligibility. Rather than give up the records, the company blocked the election through the U.S. Circuit Court of Appeals. The Duquesne ERP filed the appeal, but the Carnegie Steel Co. paid the retainer for the law firm handling the case and it paid the $505 court deposit. The legal move not only blocked the election but saved U.S. Steel from directly challenging the constitutionality of the board. The ERP suit narrowly took up only the Duquesne case, arguing that holding the election was not in the public interest. The ERP was a proper vehicle for collective bargaining and had achieved an 87 percent participation rate at its last election, the lawyers argued; the steel board should vacate the election order because the plant was not experiencing unrest, and because Carnegie Steel had not refused to bargain with the Amalgamated. The suit stalled the election and once again placed Fort Dukane in NRA limbo. In February the Justice Department decided to delay the Duquesne case until its United Rubber Workers case was concluded—which ensured that it would not be heard until September at the earliest.[139]

For one year the Fort Dukane Lodge had tried to work within the legal framework of the NRA to achieve recognition. The National Labor Board and the National Steel Labor Relations Board, unsure of their authority and unwilling to directly challenge U.S. Steel, both attempted to convince the Fort Dukane Lodge to share collective bargaining with the ERP. Fort Dukane steadfastly refused the offer and adamantly demanded sole representation rights through a federally sponsored election. Twice the union won recognition election orders, but both times the elections were postponed indefinitely. By the time the NSLRB finally had ordered an election at Duquesne, a strong undercurrent of frustration and hostility toward federal labor policy had surfaced within the lodge. When Carnegie Steel blocked the election, Spang and the lodge members began looking for new ways to wage their battle.

The Decline of Fort Dukane

"Slogan of the steel workers is to hell with all labor boards," William Spang wired the columnist Heywood Broun in February 1935. "We can't live on Roosevelt's promises."[140] Spang's telegram marked the distance he and his lodge had traveled since they had first applied for an NLB election. Back in the spring of 1934, the Fort Dukane Lodge had passed a resolution that called Roosevelt's inauguration the day "when our Heavenly Father gifted us with a new leader and showed us the light of a new day."[141] The resolution demonstrated the adoration workers held for Franklin Roosevelt and the early NRA. Black unionists in the lodge viewed Roosevelt as the heir to the legacy of Lincoln. In him they saw a Christlike savior, battling evil for the good of the common man. "He is trying to help those that need help, and that is the working class," said black Duquesne unionist Russel Moore. "[Roosevelt] is a lone man and he is depending on the mass to help him through, as he has done all that he can to give the working man his rights that have so long been denied him, and that if you do not accept it, it is no fault of the President."[142]

The workers' faith in Roosevelt explains much of Fort Dukane's tenacious behavior with NRA labor boards. However, as Fort Dukane unionists worked their way through Washington, D.C., they became less convinced that the NRA was designed to advance workers' rights. As frustration with the NSLRB grew in late 1934, two events occurred that provided a new direction for the lodge. First, the Communist Party abandoned its dual union program, dissolved its Steel and Metal Workers Industrial Union (SMWIU) locals, and sent its members into the Amalgamated. Second, and to some degree fueled by the infusion of Communists into the Amalgamated, the rank-and-file movement shook loose from its doldrums and again attempted to push the national union into an extensive organizing drive. But the effort came too late to rescue the rank-and-file movement and Fort Dukane.

The Communist Party had built a local of the SMWIU in Duquesne, but it never achieved a consistent or large presence in the mill. SMWIU members participated in Amalgamated social events, but generally the two unions abhorred each other.[143] The Communists had been critical of the rank-and-file movement and its handling of the June 1934 strike threat, especially after the rank-and-filers shut the Communists out of the strike planning.[144] The SMWIU charged the rank-and-file leaders with selling out the steelworkers, noting that Spang was a man who talked strike but in the end followed Green and Tighe in a "betrayal" of the workers. Likewise, Spang had little respect for the Communists, noting that their criticisms of the Amalgamated and Roosevelt were comparable to the actions of Judas in the days of Christ.[145]

During the summer of 1934 the Communist Party began a transition in its trade union work that would lead it into the era of the Popular Front. As workers flocked to AFL unions under the NRA, the Communist unions found themselves isolated. In the steel industry the Communist Party's SMWIU led a few disastrous strikes in 1933, but its influence paled beside the newly created Amalgamated lodges. The inability of the party to participate in the 1934 strike movement, and its inability to make inroads at the large steel mills, underscored the Communists' isolation. In addition, the Communists had trouble recruiting SMWIU members into the party, an important function of the union. These problems, coupled with broader changes in the party's political line, led to the dismantling of the SMWIU in November 1934 and the movement of its members into the Amalgamated lodges.[146]

Many rank-and-file leaders, including Spang, welcomed the infusion of Communists into the Amalgamated. The Communists provided money and advice to the cash-strapped rank-and-file leaders, who had been largely on their own since the Big Four had stopped working closely with the movement in June 1934.[147] When the Communists joined the Amalgamated, the rank-and-filers once again began holding large district and interdistrict meetings. In Pittsburgh District 1, Spang replaced Earl Forbeck of McKeesport as president, and Fort Dukane placed two others on the executive board.[148]

The Communists' influence on Spang and other rank-and-filers was most pronounced on the issue of federal labor policy. The Communists viewed the creation of labor boards, especially the NSLRB, as a capitalist strategy designed to delude workers into believing in the neutrality of the federal government's labor policies.[149] After a year of delays with both the NLB and the NSLRB, this view also had been building within the Amalgamated, especially at Duquesne. At an interdistrict Amalgamated meeting on December 30, which marked the first large presence and influence of Communists in the rank-and-file movement, the rank-and-filers finally condemned federal labor boards for doing nothing for steelworkers. The rank-and-filers also agreed to hold a meeting in February 1935, in conjunction with dissident members of the UMW and the Aluminum Workers of America, to launch a massive steel organizing drive.[150]

The day after the December district meeting, the NSLRB ordered the Duquesne representation election, a move that Fort Dukane interpreted as the government's response to the threat of force. The Communist Party's *Daily Worker* noted that the election order was "aimed to sidetrack the growing discontent of the steel workers and to prevent them from striking."[151] Whether Fort Dukane would soften its growing antilabor-board stance after the election announcement became a moot point when the ERP filed its lawsuit and blocked the election. The new delay only confirmed in the eyes of the unionists the futility of labor boards and Roosevelt's labor policy.

Although the Communist presence revitalized the rank-and-file, it terrified the national leadership. Mike Tighe, fearing both Communists and a strong rank-and-file movement, sought to expose the relationship between the two. To derail their momentum Tighe ruled that the February meeting with the mine and aluminum workers to plan an organization drive would be tantamount to dual unionism. The Amalgamated would expel any member or lodge that attended the meeting.[152] Spang, who became a key leader of the effort to mount an organizing drive, responded that the rank-and-filers were "in revolt against Tighe's do-nothing policies," that they did not intend to build another union, and that they instead would democratize the Amalgamated. In response to Tighe's charges that the rank-and-filers were dominated by communists, Spang asked, "Are [our] demands Red? Does fighting for them make us Communists? If so—very well."[153]

The rank-and-filers held their February meeting and promptly felt Tighe's wrath. The national union expelled thirteen lodges immediately and another seven a month later. Included were Fort Dukane and the lodges representing Carnegie's Edgar Thomson and Clairton Works. At its convention two months later the Amalgamated had no lodges from U.S. Steel.[154] The expulsion also quickly ended Duquesne's NSLRB case. Tighe had long been attempting to sabotage Fort Dukane by sending the NSLRB copies of Spang's letters and statements, apparently with no other purpose than to undermine the lodge in the eyes of the board.[155] When he expelled the lodge, Tighe wrote to the NSLRB to cancel the Duquesne election. According to the Amalgamated, no union existed in Duquesne. Both the board and U.S. Circuit Court of Appeals dropped the case in early March, almost one year after the lodge filed its first NLB case.[156]

The expulsion weakened the rank-and-file movement by diverting much of its energy from an organizing drive and toward gaining readmission to the Amalgamated. Following the expulsion, the rank-and-file leaders, including Spang and the Fort Dukane Lodge, spent the next six months suing the union for readmittance and lobbying William Green to rescind the expulsion order.[157] While a majority of the rank-and-filers sought Green's help in the lodge's struggle with Tighe, a smaller group, led by Spang and the Communist Party, pushed for militant organizing and strike preparations. The effect of this effort was to alienate the very AFL leaders from whom they were attempting to gain support.

Expulsion from the Amalgamated had pushed the Duquesne lodge, and especially William Spang, closer to the Communist Party. The Fort Dukane Lodge passed resolutions disavowing the "parties of capitalism," calling for the formation of a labor party, and endorsing the *Daily Worker.* The lodge also set up a youth committee to win over young workers, a structure favored by Communist organizations. Spang spoke at Communist-sponsored events and increasingly followed the party's positions on labor questions in the steel industry.[158] Because of Spang's association with Communists, David Williams, president of the AFL's National Council of Aluminum Workers, speaking for the Aluminum Workers and the AFL, labeled Spang and the rank-and-file "a bunch of Communists acting as agents from Moscow."[159] When Spang appeared at a Communist May Day rally in McKeesport, Pittsburgh-area AFL leaders immediately sought to remove him as vice president of the McKeesport Trade Union Council.[160]

In late March, Spang strongly supported an industry-wide steel strike to be held in conjunction with a UMW strike scheduled for April 1. The UMW did not support the joint strike, but the Communist Party tried to get its supporters in the UMW and the steel industry behind the idea.[161] "Steel workers are organizing rapidly," Spang claimed. "We have decided to disregard all arbitration boards, after all the raw deals union labor has received from them. . . . There is only one way that we can win our demands—by an industry wide strike. That's just what we're building up for now."[162] The United Mine Workers did not strike, and it was extremely doubtful that many rank-and-file steel lodges would have been prepared to strike. It had been less than two months since their February meeting, and the group did not have a well-developed structure to either organize the industry or lead a strike.

Increasingly espousing radical rhetoric but isolated in a fracturing rank-and-file movement, Fort Dukane once more promoted a strike in May. The lodge passed a resolution notifying other Amalgamated lodges to prepare to strike alongside Fort Dukane. The resolution attacked Roosevelt, the NRA, labor boards, the Amalgamated, and the courts, arguing that the lodge had followed these channels for two years, but now the strike remained the lodge's only weapon.[163] Then, on May 27, 450 workers walked out at a subsidiary plant of Republic Steel. The strike soon broadened to include strikers from two other Republic subsidiaries employing thirty-five hundred workers. Although some rank-and-file leaders attempted to spread the strike within Republic and the industry, it gained no support.[164] Fort Duquesne attempted to build on the Republic walkout and mount a plantwide strike, but it too failed dismally. On Memorial Day the lodge sponsored an American Youth Congress demonstration against war and fascism and sent a delegation of two hundred men to march (illegally) in the city's parade. That afternoon Spang announced that a strike would commence at 11 P.M. But about two hundred workers, accompanied by several hundred wives and children, attended a meeting of the lodge that evening and rescinded the strike announcement. Although it appeared a sizable portion of the membership was opposed to any strike, Spang pushed through a motion that only postponed the strike deadline until 3 P.M. the next day, May 31. A lodge committee would present its demands to management, and if they were turned down, the strike would commence.[165]

The Duquesne Works management publicly estimated the union's strength to be exceedingly small, but it and the city council prepared for the worst. Plant managers appointed more than 250 foremen and workers as guards, and the city deputized them. In addition, thirty county deputies were called to Duquesne. Unwilling to wait for a strike, the city ordered the police to arrest Spang for parading without a permit at the Memorial Day parade. Swooping down early in the morning of the planned strike, the police arrested Spang and four other lodge leaders as they slept. The five leaders were arraigned that morning, and police arrested three other leaders who came to the court that day. The men could not meet bail and quickly were taken to the county jail in Pittsburgh. Without the guidance of their leadership the membership did not carry out the strike, a move that saved the lodge that day. Management would have refused the demands, forcing the lodge either to call off its strike and show itself to be quite weak or to launch a strike with its dwindling membership and face certain defeat.[166]

Fort Dukane still did not give up. Spang attempted to push one more strike date, but he called it off when support for the move failed to materialize. The rank-and-file movement was dead. Although in the summer of 1935 the rank-and-filers would win their court case for readmission to the Amalgamated, by that time many lodges were literally shell organizations. In addition, many rank-and-file leaders had been fired from their plants. Spang was laid off in 1934 and did not return to the mill.[167] Duquesne had kept its lodge active longer than most, but the yearlong battle for a representation election and the constant strike threats had depleted the membership.

Unwilling to let the union movement in Duquesne die, the lodge turned to the political arena in one final attempt to gain power and stay active. The Democratic Party in Duquesne had yet to build a strong local organization, despite the growing Democratic vote in national and state elections. During the 1932 presidential election Democratic registration trailed the Republicans' 403 to 3,242, although the Democrats carried the presidential, Senate, and House elections. In 1933 local Democrats failed to match those victories and lost the mayoral and council elections. The election of 1934 followed the 1932 pattern: Democratic registration heavily trailed Republican registration, but Duquesne voted for the Democratic candidates for senator, governor, and lieutenant governor.[168] Workers could express their support for the Democrats only in the privacy of the voting booth, because they still feared retaliation from the steel company if they registered Democratic.

In the city primaries in September 1935 Fort Dukane challenged the status quo. Spang and Williamson ran for city council, and Amalgamated members Anthony Salopek and Stanley Neff vied for two constable positions, all on the Democratic ticket. The entrance of the Amalgamated candidates split the Democratic Party into competing factions, and most Amalgamated candidates were beaten soundly in the primaries. To the surprise of local politicians, however, William Spang won the Democratic council primary. In the general election Spang placed last in a field of four candidates for two council seats, but he still polled 2,489 votes. His effort to unseat Joseph Hughes, the general labor superintendent of the Duquesne Works and a twenty-one-year council incumbent, failed by only 71 votes. The political revolution of the New Deal had yet to blossom in Duquesne. The late entry of the Amalgamated into local politics—at a point when the union stood in absolute decline—coupled with divisions within the Democratic Party spelled defeat for the Democrats and the union. Even if Spang and Williamson had secured council seats, they still would have been a minority on the otherwise all-Republican council. For the moment Mayor Crawford could feel secure. However, he could not have been unaware of the returns from the nearby Carnegie mill towns of Homestead and Braddock, where Democratic victories signified the beginning of the end for local Republican regimes.[169]

Conclusion

Spang's primary triumph marked the last victory for him and the Fort Dukane Lodge. The lodge that had challenged U.S. Steel and influenced New
Deal labor policy now lay in ruins. The rank-and-file union movement in
Duquesne had been the creation of the depression and the New Deal. The
depression had made the working conditions of unskilled and semiskilled
hourly workers intolerable. Still, the frustration and anger building within
the workforce found no outlet until the early years of the New Deal, when
government policies began to break down the near-feudal authority of mill
managers and Mayor Crawford and infused steelworkers with a newfound
courage and belief in their constitutional rights. In this new atmosphere the
Fort Dukane Lodge flourished, however briefly, and brought the poorest
Duquesne workers together in a multiethnic and multiracial union. Meanwhile, tonnage workers and skilled tradesmen were following their own path
toward unionism on the shop floors of the Duquesne Works. They did it with
an organization that the Fort Dukane men detested and despised.

4. The Employee Representation Plan, 1933–36

WHEN THE DUQUESNE WORKS ran at full capacity, skilled heaters earned among the highest wages in the mill, more than $10 per day. Their job came at a critical transition in the production process—after steel had been poured from the open hearth furnaces into huge cast-iron molds and before it entered the blooming mills to be rolled into billets and blooms. From the open hearth department the steel traveled by rail to the heaters' workstation, the soaking pits. A large overhead stripper crane removed the molds, and the soaking-pit crane placed the huge ingots into the pits to be heated by jets of white hot flames fed by natural gas. The heaters regulated the ingots' temperature and determined the precise moment they were ready to be removed and sent into the rolling mills. Customers specified not only the chemical content of the steel but often its particular heating requirements as well. A mistake by the heater could waste tons of steel and delay an order.[1]

These highly skilled workers earned a set amount for every one hundred tons of steel that went through their soaking pits and became finished product. When the depression struck and orders decreased, their work became intermittent and their pay dropped. The company guaranteed them a minimum hourly wage but averaged it over a two-week pay period. That meant that when the heaters' work fluctuated between high and low production days, the average would determine their pay. As the heaters saw it, the company was taking their money, making them pay for their bad days with their good days.

The depression disrupted the heaters' tonnage rates and reduced their earnings but not to the destitution levels experienced by unskilled and semi-skilled hourly workers. Moreover, the heaters looked to the employee representation plan (ERP)—not the Amalgamated—to redress their grievances. The ERP offered workers the right to file requests with management for changes in working conditions, hours, and wages. In November 1933 the heaters and other tonnage men in the rolling department filed a request through their ERP representative to have all tonnage and wage information posted, thus demystifying the complicated procedures used to determine wages. In April 1934 the company granted the request. That same month the heaters filed another request, asking that their steel-watching rate be increased from 55.5 cents to $1 per hour. Steel watching entailed heating cold ingots from storage, a process that could take an entire shift. At full operation heaters watched steel for only one turn on Sunday, when the rolling department did not operate. However, the depression conditions made steel watching a common shift duty throughout the week because operations were so slow. Six months after filing the request, management agreed with the heaters that each steel-watching turn included about two hours when the heater performed his regular duties. Although the company did not grant the large increase sought by the heaters, it did raise the steel-watching wage to 70 cents an hour.[2]

In April 1936 the heaters in the 38-inch blooming mill filed another request, asking that their minimum rate of pay be increased to a "fair" amount. They believed that their minimum rate should be based on each turn (shift) and not on the two-week pay period, so that "part of our earnings for a better turn are [not] taken to pay ourselves to average us over the [two-week] pay."[3] They also wanted a raise that would enable them to earn as much as the heaters in the 40-inch blooming mill. On March 10, 1937, the heaters received both a raise in their tonnage rates to bring them into line with the 40-inch mill and a raise in their hourly minimum rate. In addition, management changed the determination of the minimum rate from pay period to each day, thereby allowing the heaters to keep their earnings from high production days from being averaged with their low production days.[4]

When the Duquesne Works first organized its ERP, it appeared that the plan would accomplish little except keep the Amalgamated at bay and grant only minor concessions to workers. As the ERP matured, however, many workers—especially tonnage workers, such as heaters—used it as a mechanism to correct antiquated wage structures, rein in the arbitrary power of the foreman, and improve overall working and safety conditions. The first ERP representatives tended to be aligned with management, but they soon found themselves replaced by more independent and militant workers who sought to stretch the limits of the plan. Before the formation of the Steel Workers Organizing Committee (SWOC) in June 1936, the ERP already had developed a sophisticated shop-floor bargaining structure and grievance procedure.

While the Amalgamated led unskilled and semiskilled hourly workers, a small group of tonnage and skilled trades workers sought to create an embryonic independent union within the ERP.

Employee Representation

U.S. Steel established individual ERPs in all its mills and mines in June 1933 to keep its open shop intact and meet the minimum requirements of the National Industrial Recovery Act (NIRA) regarding collective bargaining. The manner in which the corporation implemented its ERPs left little doubt that the organizations were neither worker inspired nor worker controlled. At Duquesne and the other U.S. Steel mills management allowed workers no participation in forming the plan and no power or procedure to reject it. Management selected the workers who guided the first elections of ERP representatives, and these early representatives quickly became allies of management in its battles with the Amalgamated. Still, during this initial period under the ERP, even with sharp worker criticism and widespread apathy toward the plan, working conditions improved and a rudimentary form of shop-floor bargaining emerged.

U.S. Steel's ERPs rested on a constitution. The plan called for the annual election of worker representatives, one for every three hundred workers. Workers, through their representatives, could raise requests with management regarding working conditions, hours of work, wages, and other employment conditions. The request procedure, which was similar to a grievance process, provided for a series of appeals. If the request could not be settled in consultation with a foreman, it went to the department superintendent, then to the management representative appointed to oversee the ERP, and then to the general superintendent. If the request still remained unresolved, or if the worker rejected management's decision, he could appeal to the General Joint Committee on Appeals at the plant. On the committee sat equal numbers of employee and management representatives who voted on any request. A further appeal sent the request to the president of Carnegie Steel, and beyond that—and only if both parties agreed—it could be sent to arbitration. The request procedure had obvious weaknesses. Management could reject all requests, and it could deny access to arbitration. Nor could workers strike under the plan. Still, for the first time in its history U.S. Steel offered a device to address workplace grievances and a democratic process for electing worker representatives. Although significantly weaker than a union grievance procedure, the ERP marked a tremendous advance over management's absolute and arbitrary authority of the past.

Other aspects of the plan held similar contradictory advantages and disadvantages for workers. Management paid for the plan, including the wages of representatives while they worked on requests. This provision made the representatives less likely to fight aggressively for worker requests. For some representatives ERP work amounted to a perk, and they did not want to anger management and upset what could amount to paid time off. Management also reserved the right to abolish the plan. The employee representatives, but not the workers themselves, held similar termination rights. Clearly, management did not wish to lock itself into a long-term commitment. Finally, revisions to the plan had to be approved by a two-thirds majority of a joint committee on rules or a simple majority at the plan's annual conference, both of which met with an equal number of management and employee representatives. By establishing a framework in which all committees held equal numbers of employees and management representatives, the two-thirds approval stipulation for all changes to the plan ensured management's control. Despite these problems the plan did provide a forum for workers to debate plant policies with management, something that never had been possible before.[5]

The first elected employee representatives under the plan did not reflect a cross-section of the mill's workforce. In part this was the result of management's actions in implementing it. Management first explained the plan to a small select group of key workers. Management then selected eleven to act as a committee to supervise the first primary and general elections.[6] The men represented each mill department but tended to be highly paid workers. The group included clerical workers, skilled tradesmen, skilled tonnage men, and a salaried engineer.[7] The general election produced a large but unrepresentative slate of candidates. Of the forty-one candidates vying for fourteen positions, no unskilled workers and only four semiskilled hourly workers stood for election. Of the fourteen elected, only one held a semiskilled hourly job. The rest included skilled tonnage men (including some of the highest-paid workers in the mill), skilled tradesmen, clerical workers, and the salaried engineer (see table 3). The representatives also did not reflect the ethnic and racial makeup of the mill's workforce. The group included no blacks (none ever would serve on the ERP), and most had been born in the United States to parents who also were native born or who had been born in western and northern Europe.[8] In addition, the ERP men tended to have close ties with management. At least two eventually became foremen, and another three held jobs that either involved some management responsibilities or that placed them in contact with sensitive management information. The skill and ethnic makeup of the Duquesne representatives, along with their close

Table 3. Characteristics of the First ERP Representatives

Name	Department	Job	Job Type	Birthplace	Parents' Birthplace
Charles Scanlon	Blast	Chief clerk	Clerical	Unknown	Unknown
Charles Erickson	Open hearth	1st Helper	Tonnage	United States	Sweden
Harry Lynch	Open hearth	1st Helper	Tonnage	Unknown	Unknown
Carl Anderson	Rolling mill	Shearman	Tonnage	United States	Sweden
William D. Flannigan	Rolling mill	Heater	Tonnage	United States	United States/Ireland
Joseph Soffa	Rolling mill	Chipper	Hourly	United States	Austria (German)
John J. Kane	Maintenance	Machinist	Skilled trade	Scotland	Scotland
Jeremiah McWilliams	Maintenance	Boilermaker	Skilled Trade	United States	England
Jacob Wise	Bar mill	Heater	Tonnage	United States	United States
Paul R. McCarty	Bar mill	Assistant roller	Tonnage	United States	United States
James Witherspoon	Accounting	Clerk	Clerical	United States	United States
Roy Griffiths	General labor/masonry	Bricklayer	Skilled trade	Unknown	Unknown
William F. Betzner	Shipping/inspection	Unknown	Tonnage	Unknown	Unknown
Daniel S. Tobin	Engineering/metallurgy	Test engineer	Technical/salary	Unknown	Unknown

Source: Inactive voter registration cards, Allegheny County, Pennsylvania, Voter Registration Records, AIS; Duquesne Works payroll ledgers, 1933–37, USSC; U.S. Census, *Fourteenth Census of the United States: 1920, Manuscript Schedules,* vol. 10, Pennsylvania, Allegheny County, reel 1511; Records of the War Department, Office of the Provost Marshall General, Selective Service System, World War I Draft Registration Cards, State of Pennsylvania, County of Allegheny, Local Board #8, Microfilm copy, reel 14, Hillman Library, University of Pittsburgh; *Duquesne Times,* various issues, 1933–59; *U.S. Steel News,* various issues, 1936–60; Obsolete Change of Employment and Rate Cards, Box 4, USSC; DWERP, minutes of meeting, 27 June 1933, NSLRB; Duquesne Works, "Report of Positions Excluded from Representation by the Union Under the Terms of the September 1, 1942 Agreement," 7 Oct. 1942, Box 30, File: Positions Excluded from Union Membership, USSC; Steel Workers Organizing Committee Grievance 27-39-U material, Box 26, USSC; Exhibit 7, Box 21, Grievance File 46-20, USSC; Duquesne Works, "Confidential," booklet, 31 Aug. 1949, Box 28, File S-6(a), USSC.

contact with management, matched the characteristics of most other U.S. Steel ERPs in the Pittsburgh region.[9]

Charles Erickson, elected by his fellow representatives as the first chairman of the Duquesne ERP, exemplified their elite character. Erickson was a second-generation Swedish American and thirty-year veteran of the mill. He was a first helper, the highest-paying nonmanagement job in the open hearth department, and it earned him an average of $1.13 per hour. He also participated in Duquesne politics, serving as a Republican committeeman. Following his service in the ERP, Erickson won promotion to first melter foreman.[10]

A key responsibility of the new representatives involved resolving workers' requests. Management did not limit the issues workers could raise, and during the plan's first year workers brought up ninety-one requests and management settled at least seventy-four wholly or partially in the workers' favor. Many requests made during this initial period support the contemporary labor movement's argument that ERPs did little more than placate workers with minor concessions. Management provided drinking fountains and hot water for washing, fixed holes in roofs, cleaned and fixed toilets, organized a bowling and mushball league, and built benches for lunch breaks. Other requests involving working conditions proved more substantive and offered all workers, including the unskilled and semiskilled, an opportunity to improve their workplace. In the past, poor working conditions, including safety problems, remained unresolved because of the inaction of foremen. However, the ERP request system now drew these conditions to the attention of upper management, which granted workers' requests in an effort to win support for the plan. Before the formation of the Fort Dukane Lodge, for example, chippers made several improvements to their working conditions through the ERP. But they so hated the ERP that after the lodge was formed, the chippers' use of the ERP dropped off considerably.[11]

The ERP also began to address more fundamental worker concerns, including the distribution of work hours and wage and tonnage rates. Before the plan, workers could not stop foremen from distributing work unevenly within a crew and from rewarding some workers with more hours. Through the ERP workers instead demanded from upper management the equal distribution of work hours. Ironically, the whole notion of equal work hours first had been broached by Myron Taylor with his program of work sharing implemented fairly and equitably. But Taylor's promise had not become shop-floor practice, and it became viable only with the formation of the ERP. Through their representatives workers now called on management to honor this promise and bring about workplace justice. If the requests centered on the unequal distribution of hours among what management considered equally qualified workers, such as chippers, it generally granted the requests.[12] Less easily resolved requests involved management's right to assign the most qualified worker to a job. In the machine shop, for instance, management regularly gave some men, whom it deemed better qualified, more working days than others. Management responded to ERP requests by evening out the gross differences, but it still did not distribute hours equally for all machinists. According to John Kane, an ERP representative, management would not back down from its assertion that ability ultimately determined work distribution and that the highest-skilled machinists would receive more work. The question of the distribution of work hours under the ERP thus tended to fall into an uneasy compromise: upper management responded to worker complaints and attempted to equalize work hours at the expense of the foreman's authority, but it also freely used workers where and when it believed they were needed.[13]

Wage requests gave workers another opportunity to improve job conditions that had worsened during the depression. The early wage requests involved no bargaining between management and representative: management simply agreed to the request, rejected it, or imposed a compromise. Foremen, who in the past had much authority for deciding wage rates, lost that power. Now wage requests went directly to management's newly formed Duquesne Works Wage Committee, composed of the assistant general superintendent, ERP management representative, plant industrial engineer, and chief mechanical engineer. As with the distribution of work hours, foremen found that wage requests further diminished their once near-dictatorial authority over the shop floor.

The Wage Committee used many criteria to determine rates. First, an industrial engineer analyzed the job on a point scale (rating skill, responsibility, fatigue, safety, etc.) and assigned a wage based on the total rating. Management then factored in other considerations before changing the wage rate. If the job belonged on a promotional job ladder, management would not raise the pay higher than the next job in the promotion sequence. Management also worried about a ripple effect. When the company considered raising the rates of open hearth and soaking-pit crane operators, for instance, it studied what effect the increase would have on other crane operators in the mill. Management granted the request only after it determined that the rates for other crane jobs did not raise the same wage issues and would not have to be increased. During the depression management had to keep wage hikes to a minimum. The company further compared its wage rates to those of other Carnegie mills, making sure not to raise wages beyond the norm for the region. A final consideration involved the temporary nature of the depression. Management did not want to raise a worker's pay to compensate for low earnings during the depression, if that meant creating wage rates that would be out of proportion during full operations.[14] As with the overall plan, the treatment of wage cases marked a vast improvement over past practices. For the first time workers had a forum to which to appeal their wage and tonnage rate grievances and also rein in their supervisor's authority to reward favored workers with higher wages. However, the new procedure contained glaring weaknesses. Wage requests involved no bargaining, and the multiplicity of conflicting criteria for determining wages did not allow for the establishment of a consistent and objective policy.

Wage requests benefited tonnage workers but not unskilled and semiskilled hourly workers. Until orders picked up, management would not provide more hours, and without profits management would not raise overall wages. In addition, the plant sometimes had hundreds of hourly workers in a single job category. A wage increase for one job, such as chipper, would involve hundreds of workers and large outlays of money, not only at Duquesne but also among all the Carnegie mills that paid similar wage scales. During the first eighteen months of the plan Duquesne granted only one unskilled/semiskilled hourly wage request.[15] Conversely, the ERP worked well for tonnage workers. It proved a useful instrument for restructuring tonnage rates that the depression had exposed as inadequate. Changes were needed, and the ERP provided both management and workers with a forum for addressing these issues. Unlike unskilled jobs, each tonnage job had its own distinct pay system and wage level, and each job employed smaller numbers of workers. A wage hike for a stripper crane operator, for example, involved only six workers.[16]

During the first eighteen months under the plan, tonnage men raised and won several changes in their pay systems. In order to understand why and how their wages varied, tonnage men from the open hearth, bar mills, and blooming mills all demanded that their tonnage rates and totals be posted. Management complied. In the #5 bar mill, which did not provide a minimum wage rate for tonnage workers, management agreed to pay the men at least a laborer's wage when conditions slowed. The tonnage men who worked in the #6 bar mill won a wage increase for rolling small bars, which were becoming a significant portion of production during the depression.[17] Smaller groups of tonnage men also benefited from the ERP. Open hearth crane operators and narrow-gauge train engineers, for example, both won higher minimum wage rates. First and second helpers in the open hearth department, like the heaters in the soaking pits, sought and won higher pay for special work not involved in their regular job. The open hearth superintendent recommended the raise in this and similar cases, because "while these cases would be few in number and cost very small they are more or less the cause of petty discontent."[18]

Skilled tradesmen raised fewer wage requests than tonnage workers. When they did use the request process, it generally was to correct wage rate inequities that had built up over the years. Some tradesmen earned raises from foremen while others had not, thus creating different wage rates for workers doing the same work. This was the case in the newly formed welding department, which grew out of the amalgamation of two older departments. Tradesmen working side by side, performing exactly the same work, had wage rates that varied by as much as 18 cents an hour. They used the ERP to force management to address this issue, which it did by establishing a completely new wage structure for the department. Skilled tradesmen further used the ERP to protect the distribution of what they considered trades work from being distributed to nontradesmen.[19]

The ERP proved advantageous not only for skilled tradesmen and tonnage workers: management also discovered unintended benefits. Wage inequity cases, for example, allowed upper management to restructure department wage scales, thus reducing shop-floor tension caused by foremen-created wage inequities. In essence, the ERP requests invited management to step back from its day-to-day practices and study operating efficiencies. In the newly formed welding department management not only organized a new wage scale but restructured the supervisory force and job-training program.[20] Similarly, a wage request by motor inspectors and electrical millwrights in the rolling department led to a study of all those jobs throughout the plant. As a result, management created one job sequence, a single wage scale, and standard job titles for all the plant's motor inspectors and electrical millwrights.[21]

In addition to restructuring the workplace and alleviating shop-floor tensions, management continued to use the ERP for its original purpose as an antiunion tool. Especially during the first year of operation, Carnegie Steel managers regularly sent the representatives statements concerning the company's interpretations of the NRA labor provisions. They expected the representatives to acquaint their fellow workers with the pronouncements.[22] The representatives also directly helped management in its battles with organized labor. When the miners' strike of October 1933 threatened to spill into Duquesne, A. C. Cummins, the general superintendent, used the ERP as his forum for stating the company's position on the strike. During the threatened Amalgamated strike of 1934, seven of the fourteen employee representatives served on special police duty and guarded the mill. The representatives aided management's attempts to divide the workforce along ethnic lines during the crisis by passing a resolution demanding that management hire only U.S. citizens. Management agreed.[23] Further, mill managers asked the employee representatives to attend the October 1934 hearing of the National Steel Labor Relations Board (NSLRB) that focused on the Fort Dukane Lodge. The representatives testified at the hearing, defending the ERP, discounting any employer coercion in ERP elections, and assuring the NSLRB that no unrest existed in the mill.[24]

Management even found the ERP politically useful in its legislative battles in Washington. When the Wagner Labor Disputes bill came up for consideration in the Senate in 1934, the American Iron and Steel Institute (AISI), the trade association, mobilized its forces to defeat it. Major steel corporation executives testified against the bill, joined by ERP representatives. Charles Erickson testified on behalf of the Duquesne Works ERP, noting that the plan was "responsible for better and closer cooperation between the employees and the Company." He lauded the plan for improving working conditions and for clearing up shop-floor misunderstandings. He then castigated trade unions for protecting the industrial slacker, limiting workers' freedom to choose their representatives, and causing strikes. Showing his disdain for the Fort Dukane Lodge, he said that its leaders were "absolutely unfitted [sic] by education, experience or capability to properly present employee problems." His testimony later became part of an AISI pamphlet defending ERPs against trade unions.[25]

Management in turn helped to bolster the ERP and its representatives. During the June 1934 elections for new representatives the company provided ERP candidates with automobiles and the addresses of workers who had not yet voted. These efforts both helped candidates to amass more individual votes and ensured the high voter turnout that management publicly used to defend the plan. But according to ERP representative John Kane, workers voted not because they necessarily supported the plan but because their foremen told them to vote.[26] Management also attempted to build up public and worker support for the ERPs by giving representatives greater credit for improvements in working conditions than they deserved. A month after the formation of the Duquesne Works ERP, U.S. Steel granted a 15 percent wage increase and raised the rate for common labor from 33 cents to 40 cents an hour. Although the increase was unrelated to the ERP—it stemmed from passage of the NIRA—management stated that the raise had been negotiated with the general subcommittee of employee representatives. Likewise, when Duquesne workers voted on the 1934 revisions of the ERP, management gave much of the credit for the revisions to the ERP representatives. However, U.S.

Steel printed the changes and local management simply provided them to the representatives and suggested that they agree to them.[27]

During this first phase of the ERP, the request system had led to numerous improvements in working conditions, distribution of hours, and wage and tonnage rates. Even unskilled and semiskilled hourly workers, who through the Amalgamated constantly criticized and belittled the ERP, occasionally used the plan to their advantage.[28] However, it offered no help in alleviating the worst conditions facing the unskilled—low wages and too few work hours. For tonnage men the plan proved more effective. As word spread that workers could win pay increases, more and more tonnage workers began using the process to improve their rates.

For all these improvements the ERP depended on management's goodwill and its willingness to make the plan work. As its name implied, the request procedure placed authority in management's hands. Workers requested and management granted or denied those requests; neither workers nor ERP representatives openly challenged denied requests. Thus the plan's appeals process went unused for two years. In large part the request system operated in this fashion because workers feared retribution from their supervisors if they challenged management. But more important, the first representatives did not view their role as management adversaries but as management allies. They accepted the notion of cooperation between management and workers that underlay the plan, and they supported management's efforts to defeat the Amalgamated. However, the ERP soon would take a different course.

The Evolution of Shop-Floor Bargaining

John Kane, an employee representative from the maintenance department, at first did not object to management's manipulation of the plan. But by mid-1934 he found himself increasingly unhappy with the course of the ERP and began challenging management. Still, his challenges were at first timid and he frequently retreated and followed the advice of managers and his fellow representatives. In early 1935, however, he would set in motion a movement that would transform the ERP into a semi-independent, worker-led organization that developed a sophisticated shop-floor bargaining structure.

Kane had emigrated to the United States from Scotland and hired on at the Duquesne Works in 1906 as an apprentice in the machine shop. He secured a machinist position in 1910, which he kept into the 1950s. A remarkable and responsible man, he had only one foot and headed a household that included his younger siblings.[29] Kane was in the small group of men management called to organize the ERP, and he won election as a maintenance department representative in 1933, 1934, and 1935. He went along with the plan at first because, he said, "I had thought that perhaps we might be able to make something out of it."[30] He also accepted management's orchestration of the plan. He freely put his name on the circular announcing the 15 percent wage hike, although he knew he had nothing to do with the raise. "It was a surprise to me," he noted. He also recommended to his fellow workers in the maintenance department that they vote to approve the February 1934 changes to the plan, although he claimed that he "did not understand them" and did not have time to figure them out.[31]

When management used the ERP to shore up its defenses against both the Amalgamated and labor reform in Washington, D.C., Kane objected. He presented a resolution calling for Charles Erickson's resignation from the ERP after Erickson testified against the Wagner Act in Washington. Kane argued that Erickson had no right to speak for the ERP or the workers at the plant. Management opposed the inclusion of the resolution in the ERP minutes, and Kane agreed to draft a milder one that did not mention Erickson and simply banned anyone from speaking publicly on behalf of the ERP unless cleared by the other representatives.[32] When management asked the ERP men to testify in support of the plan at the October 1934 NSLRB meeting, Kane again asserted his independence. Along with a few other representatives suspicious of management's motives, he argued against taking part in the hearing, despite his own opposition to the Amalgamated. Aware that "the average employee did not think much of employee representation," he believed that testifying would put him in "a very unfavorable light with the employees of the plant," because he would be defending the company and not his fellow workers. Kane's motion to keep the ERP men from testifying was defeated 8-6, and he relented and testified himself.[33] Kane had limited options and few allies on the ERP. He also was unwilling to break with management and renounce the ERP, which he still believed could serve workers' interests.

Kane further found himself at odds with management in regard to shop-floor issues. He had raised the machinists' request to equalize their work hours, and he had refused to accept management's solution to the problem. Although he acknowledged that management had improved conditions, Kane still rejected management's right to give some machinists more work based on their ability and experience. Kane also represented the welders' wage inequity request. Ironically, he suggested some of the restructuring solutions for the department that management adopted. However, in one key area their ideas diverged: Kane wanted only objective test results to determine pay rates and to forbid foremen to simply rate the workers based on observation. In both the machinists' and welders' cases, Kane exhibited a level of independence and a willingness to challenge management that the other representatives did not display. This increasingly put him at odds with the philosophical underpinnings of the ERP, which stressed cooperation and a commonality of interest between workers and managers.

In early 1935 Kane sought to unify U.S. Steel's disparate ERPs and begin addressing company-wide issues. He successfully pushed through the Duquesne ERP a resolution supporting the creation of a central committee of employee representatives from each Carnegie Steel mill. The central committee, as Kane envisioned it, would discuss common problems and address issues of a company-wide nature. Similar spontaneous efforts had begun within other U.S. Steel plants at the same time as representatives discussed the creation of district-wide, company-wide, and subsidiary-wide councils. The idea met with stiff resistance from Cummins, the general superintendent, who finally persuaded the group to drop its demand. The central committee movement continued to flourish in Carnegie Steel's Chicago district, although in the Pittsburgh region it died down in the face of management opposition. Still, talk of a central committee resonated on the shop floors of the Duquesne Works. When the ERP held its June 1935 elections, Elmer Maloy decided to join forces with Kane.[34]

Maloy came from a union family—his father was a member of the Knights of Labor and United Mine Workers—but he did not support the Amalgamated. He had no respect for its national leadership and he believed Fort Dukane's president, William Spang, to be irresponsible, a deadbeat, and a "stinker besides." Maloy, like other tonnage workers and skilled tradesmen, looked to the ERP, not the Amalgamated, to improve his wages and working conditions. Maloy had settled into his job as a stripper crane operator after his foreman blocked his efforts to become a millwright. As with other incentive jobs, the depression exposed the inadequate wage structure for strippermen, including its exceedingly low guaranteed minimum rate. Frustrated with his small paychecks, Maloy filed an ERP request for a raise. Management granted an increase of only 6 cents an hour, and his ERP representative, Charles Erickson, accepted the sum without fighting for more. "I was mad as hell," Maloy remembered, "because I didn't want six cents, we were getting fifty-five cents, guaranteed, and I wanted a dollar an hour for the job." He told Erickson, "Who the hell are you, to have the authority to sign away my rights, either it means something, the company union, or it doesn't mean anything." In his anger Maloy decided to run for open hearth representative. He also was inspired by Kane's attempts to bring the ERPs together, a movement Maloy wanted "to try to help." A popular worker, Maloy found that his co-

workers had scrawled his name and employment number in chalk throughout the open hearth department when he announced his candidacy.[35]

The 1935 election proved to be a turning point in the Duquesne Works ERP.
It became a referendum on the course of the ERP: would it follow the conservative promanagement style of representatives such as Charles Erickson,
or would it follow the increasingly independent path of John Kane? In the
open hearth department four men were running for two representative slots:
the incumbents Charles Erickson and Harry Lynch, both skilled first helpers, and two semiskilled tonnage workers, Fred Barker, a second helper, and
Maloy. The election marked a stunning defeat for the more conservative and
highly skilled representatives, as 97 percent of the eligible workforce voted.
Maloy and Barker both polled more than 400 votes to Lynch's 204 and Erickson's 88. Overall, of the eleven representatives seeking reelection, only seven
won.

Still, the new representatives resembled their predecessors. The majority
were native born or of northern or western European heritage, and a majority held tonnage or skilled trades jobs. However, the tonnage men now tended
to be less skilled. The highest-skilled workers in the mill—first helpers, heaters, and rollers—no longer served on the ERP. In the 1935 election two open
hearth department first helpers went down to defeat, and in the rolling mills
a semiskilled crane operator defeated a skilled heater. That workers rejected
the highly skilled and conservative representatives also meant that management's influence over the plan had decreased. Superintendents no longer
could turn to compliant representatives who sat one promotion away from
management.[36]

The passivity the Duquesne Works representatives displayed during the
first years now gave way to a more independent and confrontational style.
They became more sophisticated in the art of bargaining, and workers increasingly pushed them to demand more from management. In the areas of
distribution of working hours, safety, and wage and tonnage rates, the ERP
representatives made significant strides in reducing the arbitrary authority
of the foreman and improving working conditions. At the same time, however, they met the limits of management's willingness both to bargain and
to concede shop-floor authority.

The new group of representatives elected in 1935 quickly exhibited their
militancy, especially in the area of safety and accident prevention. Ironically, their efforts found an ally in upper management. Throughout the early
1930s Duquesne had one of the highest accident rates of all U.S. Steel mills,
perhaps because of its aging facilities. The mill's safety director had proved
unable to enlist either workers or foremen and superintendents in his efforts

to improve safety. Workers hesitated to report unsafe work practices by their fellow workers for fear of being labeled a stool pigeon, and they hesitated to point out unsafe conditions for fear of earning their foreman's wrath. Department superintendents also balked at implementing the safety department's recommendations, because the costs of correcting conditions came out of their operating budget. Upper management, insulated from these day-to-day worries and nervous about the plant's accident record, saw a way to address the problem through the ERP.[37]

After the June 1935 ERP election the representatives became very insistent about safety. Much of the new aggressiveness came from Maloy, who had won election as chair of the ERP's rules committee. He quickly pushed through a new safety plan that called for the rules committee to conduct monthly inspection tours, focusing on whatever areas of the mill the members deemed appropriate. Maloy then worked surreptitiously with the mill's safety director, who coached him on conditions to report. Unable to influence the superintendents to implement his suggestions, the safety director knew that upper management would respond if the issues were brought up by the ERP. The monthly inspection tours turned up numerous suggestions for improving conditions. According to Maloy, management corrected almost every problem and implemented almost every suggestion. In 1937, when he still was a representative, Maloy noted that the safety work of the ERP had made the physical and working conditions of the mill "very much better."

Maloy himself displayed a high degree of aggressiveness in correcting safety conditions. On one safety tour of the mill he encountered an overhead crane ladder that had lost a side rail. Management temporarily fixed the problem by securing a two-by-four to the ladder with telephone wire. Maloy considered the arrangement unsafe and he ripped off the two-by-four and reported the problem. The superintendent then had to call out a repairman on overtime to repair the ladder. Angered, the superintendent threatened to fire Maloy if he ever acted in a similar manner. In June 1936, perhaps in response to complaints from foremen and superintendents about the ERP's aggressiveness, upper management suddenly reversed course. Instead of encouraging ERP men to report unsafe conditions, plant officials now instructed them to report only unsafe worker practices. Unwilling to report fellow workers, the inspection committee quickly became ineffective.[38]

The distribution of work hours continued to be contentious. Nevertheless, the ERP had significantly changed management's approach. By early 1936, although management still firmly argued it had the right to distribute work hours as it saw fit, the equal distribution of work hours clearly had become its de facto policy. In some departments, such as maintenance and general labor, the ERP representatives forced the superintendents to post weekly and yearly totals of the hours each man worked. In the blast-furnace department, when the banking of a furnace upset working schedules, the superintendents consciously rearranged them to reach an equal distribution of hours. Upon inspection the ERP representative agreed that they had achieved "100% equal distribution of time."[39] By forcefully taking up the demand for equal hours, the ERP representatives undercut management's right to manage and helped to further workers' conception of workplace rights. Workers and ERP representatives countered management's position, that merit and ability determined treatment, with their concept of equality. Clearly not all workers held this view, and some did attempt to secure more hours than others; however, equality had become the steadfast position of the ERP representatives on the question of work-hour distribution.

Some ERP representatives further challenged management's right to manage by raising the issue of seniority. Seniority, like the equal distribution of work hours, contravened management's right to use merit to determine working forces. Unlike the fight about the distribution of work hours, however, seniority did not become a consistent ERP issue until 1936. The depression and the timing of the ERP's creation made seniority a secondary concern because the ERP did not exist during the massive layoffs of 1930–32, when seniority would have been a point of contention. Promotion, the key category involving the seniority principle, simply did not exist during the economic slowdown. The superintendent of the open hearth department noted in early 1936 that no one in his department had been promoted since 1929.[40] The Duquesne Works also did not use layoffs as a method to rid the plant of union militants. If that had been the case, the demand for seniority would have been raised in order to force the company to lay off by length of service and not by union sympathy.

Seniority also remained a lesser concern because management consciously used the ERP to promote merit arguments.[41] The American Iron and Steel Institute defended ERPs for giving "free play to individualism" and providing the "opportunity for advancement based upon capacity for leadership, proven intelligence, and production efficiency, and the like." Conversely, the AISI argued that unions supported seniority, which brought "all employees to the same level, independent of ability, energy or initiative."[42] When Erickson testified against the Wagner Disputes Act, he defended the Duquesne Works ERP by noting, "Our men are promoted by merit. . . . We believe that the outside union protects the industrial slacker and has a tendency to prevent the industrious and ambitious workman from procuring his just reward."[43]

The ERP representatives first attempted to push seniority rights in the summer of 1935, when Kane proposed the establishment of a veteran workers' club in the mill. The club, which would include all workers with twenty or more years' seniority, would put on social events such as banquets. However, Kane designed the club primarily to stimulate discussion of seniority and pension rights by workers. A lack of interest from most representatives killed the plan. Elmer Maloy also pushed for seniority rights, and during the plant's biannual joint ERP conference of management and employee representatives in February 1936, he made a forceful presentation for the establishment of seniority as the primary criterion for demotion, layoff, and promotion. Seniority had to prevail, he argued, because superintendents and foremen all had their pets, whom they looked after and promoted before better-qualified workers.[44]

Even with Maloy and Kane, the most stalwart proponents of seniority on the ERP, the concept remained weak. For instance, when the ERP request changed the wage structure for the newly created welding department, Kane proposed that management use an objective test, not seniority, to place workers along the wage scale. Maloy too supported seniority only because of management abuses. In theory, he agreed that merit—not seniority—should decide all promotions, but in the real and arbitrary world of the mill seniority had to prevail. However, he added a caveat. U.S. citizens should gain all promotions over noncitizens. This inconsistent application of seniority flowed largely from Kane's and Maloy's skill and ethnic background. Unskilled and foreign-born workers, who faced the greatest discrimination and who saw the merit system most often abused by management, were the stronger supporters of seniority.[45]

As representatives continued to handle safety and work-hour issues, the greatest and ever-increasing share of the requests they received covered wage and tonnage rates. Like safety and distribution-of-time issues, wage and tonnage requests revealed the independence and assertiveness of the ERP representatives. Amounting to roughly half of all requests by late 1935, wage requests also demonstrated the growing sophistication of the ERP bargaining process. However, wage issues also exposed the growing tension between militant ERP demands and the slow and cumbersome procedures used to resolve them.

As with other ERP bargaining, the success of the workers' requests depended heavily on the representative's aggressiveness. Some representatives still framed workers' requests passively, asking management to address a job's wage rate without making clear demands. But some representatives, in particular Maloy, chose to make strong demands, bargain aggressively, and follow requests through each bargaining stage. Maloy tested the limits of the ERP structure by devoting much of his time to his work as a representative. Aided in part by depression conditions that limited his hours on the job, he often spent twenty to forty hours a week on ERP work. His tenacity became quite well known, and workers throughout the mill often brought their requests to him, not their own area representative. He estimated that at one time he gave assistance in two-thirds of all workers' requests. In addition to his own efforts, he enlisted several men, much like assistant grievancemen or shop stewards, who kept him informed about his department.[46]

His work and the evolution of the bargaining process can be seen in a request for a wage increase by workers in the mold yard. These unskilled workers performed laboring duties and were responsible for cleaning and preparing the huge open hearth ingot molds after the steel had been stripped from them. The work was extremely hot and disagreeable because dipping the hot molds into tar created smoke and fumes. Citing the danger, heat, hard work, and tar smoke, the workers demanded a raise. The case went directly to the Duquesne Works Wage Committee, which rejected it, noting that the plant did not pay extra for hot jobs and that the mold yard crew earned a rate comparable to that commanded by crews in other area mills. Rather than acquiescing, Maloy appealed the case to the ERP management representative, adding to the request the argument that the mold yard work required special skills and that perhaps management had not factored this into its comparison with the valley plants.

R. F. Sanner, the management representative, denied the appeal, arguing that the skill level was comparable. Unwilling to abandon the case, Maloy appealed to Cummins, who brought in Carnegie-Illinois Corp. industrial engineers. The engineers studied the mold yard work at Duquesne and Homestead, where a similar request had been made, and concluded it warranted no wage increase. The committee judged the work to be less dangerous and arduous than regular open hearth laboring jobs, although it recognized the problem with disagreeable fumes. The committee did recommend that a position be created for each shift—mold yard leader—and paid 2.5 more cents per hour, with that man responsible for directing the crew. Using the industrial engineers' conclusions, Cummins denied the workers' appeal. Cummins also promised that the company would change the method of tarring the molds in an effort to reduce the fumes, but he did not mention the creation of the position of mold yard leader.

Still unwilling to concede, Maloy filed an appeal with the ERP's General Joint Committee on Appeals. Maloy countered management's last arguments by again asserting that the skill involved in the work, and the danger, heat, and fumes, made it different from unskilled laboring. He also added the new argument that a wage raise would be advantageous to management, because it would induce workers to stay on the job, thus decreasing the need for job training and ensuring that operations would run smoothly. At the appeals committee meeting management offered a compromise. The mold yard laborers would not receive a raise, but the company would accept the engineers' recommendation of adding a crew leader position. In addition, another worker on the crew who did special duties repairing the railroad cars in which the molds traveled would receive a raise of 1.5 cents per hour. The committee voted on the compromise but rejected it in a tie vote, with the employee representatives voting against management's proposal.[47]

This request illustrates how the ERP request procedure at Duquesne had begun to operate in ways similar to a union grievance procedure. As in a grievance procedure, Maloy walked the case through various appeals levels, adding new arguments to counter management's arguments. Unlike the earlier ERP wage requests, which involved essentially one step, the mold yard case showed how Maloy pushed management through the appeal process. At the joint appeals committee level, the representatives acted as a grievance committee, arguing the case before management. Although the workers ultimately lost and received no added compensation, their working conditions improved because of changes in tarring the molds. Management also went so far as to offer a compromise, to increase the pay of two workers on each crew. That the increases did not take effect resulted from the representative's refusal to accept the compromise. Maloy's resolve also forced Duquesne management to conduct three studies of the mold yard work, one by the Duquesne Works Wage Committee, one by Carnegie-Illinois engineers, and one by management representatives on the eve of the joint appeals case.

The mold yard case also marked a breakthrough for the ERP. Until that point, the joint appeals committee had not functioned, even though it had been written into the plan in 1933. In the past, when management granted all or part of a request, the case ended with the representative's accepting the answer.[48] As Maloy demonstrated in the mold yard case, concessions could be wrung from management throughout the bargaining process. In another wage request, filed by the mold yard tonnage crane operators at the same time as the laborers' case, Maloy was rebuffed by the department superintendent, the management representative, and the general superintendent. On the eve of Maloy's filing with the joint appeals committee, however, the general superintendent reversed himself. After viewing firsthand the crane operators working in the mold yard, he granted them a wage increase.[49] That the appeals process had begun to function pointed to the growing maturity of the

ERP. No one else bothered to push cases personally like Maloy did. He did not fear management, and his self-professed attitude was "I just don't give a damn so I'm going to get what I go after."[50] He was elected in June 1935, and his wage cases did not reach the joint appeals committee stage until the spring of 1936. In essence, the representatives, led by Maloy, learned how to bargain only in early 1936. As a result, they began appealing almost all requests that management rejected.[51]

When representatives began to push management more aggressively in late 1935 and early 1936, weaknesses appeared within the ERP bargaining process. But the representatives remained determined to make the process work. At the same time, upper management also agreed to improve the request process. After requests lingered for long periods at each level, the representatives passed, with management's approval, time limits for each request step.[52] When some wage requests still continued for months, Maloy pushed through the formation of an executive committee of ERP representatives to meet with management. The new committee acted much like a special grievance committee, with the authority to resolve stubborn cases. When department superintendents refused to meet with the committee, the ERP men convinced the general superintendent to order them to attend the meetings.[53] And after the first few joint appeals committee meetings, which ended in deadlocks and showed that neither side had all the facts in the case, both representatives and managers began to discuss new procedures to make the committee work.[54]

As the ERP wage request process became more sophisticated, it continued primarily to benefit tonnage workers. They used the ERP process much more often and experienced a much higher success rate. Although they rarely won exactly what they requested, tonnage men often won a partial raise. Tonnage workers' wage demands also became more complex. Earlier requests often simply sought a "fair wage" or demanded to know why a similar job paid more. Beginning in the last half of 1935, and originating with Maloy in the open hearth department, workers' requests centered on restructuring payment formulas. In part spurred by the new availability of tonnage and wage information that demonstrated why and how their pay varied, workers sought to create new pay formulas that ensured higher wages. Straight tonnage workers, whose earnings fluctuated widely or had decreased significantly during the depression, sometimes asked to be put on a straight hourly wage or a combination of hourly wages plus a tonnage bonus. This did not represent a rejection of the tonnage incentive system, merely a frustration with low earnings derived from depression conditions. In addition, requests also still centered on the low minimum pay rates and the method of averaging minimum rates from a two-week period. Although they rarely used the ERP for wage requests, skilled tradesmen continued to benefit from the ERP by evening out the distribution of work hours and ensuring all trades work was performed by tradesmen.[55]

Unskilled and semiskilled hourly workers continued to find no relief through ERP wage requests. Part of the problem Maloy encountered in the mold yard laborers' case derived from the unskilled nature of their work. To increase the labor rate in that case would have opened up the issue of laborers' pay throughout the corporation. Representatives lost a similar case brought by open hearth general laborers who sought extra pay for work in extremely hot conditions. Carnegie-Illinois engineers studying the problem observed that hot jobs did warrant a higher wage rate and that it was difficult to justify denying the request. The engineers even pondered, months before the formation of Steel Workers Organizing Committee, that perhaps such a rate should be established to "prevent possible labor friction." In the end, however, management rejected the request, because such a move would open a Pandora's box of similar requests.[56] By 1936 this had become one of the major complaints of the ERP representatives: although management granted wage increases to small groups of workers, it never increased wages for large numbers of unskilled workers.[57] Through June 1936 management still had granted only one wage request for a low-skilled hourly job.

By the middle of 1936 the increasing volume of tonnage requests, the large number of wage case appeals, and the number of requests for new payment formulas created a crisis in the ERP. Plant engineers spent almost all their time on studies of various jobs, and appeals forced them to reevaluate their studies or call in Carnegie-Illinois engineers.[58] Delays in answering requests increased. This crisis in wage-request bargaining coincided with management's decision to undercut the representatives' safety inspections. Combined with the continuing battles about work-hour distribution, these issues forced representatives to reexamine the ERP's scope and structure. But management's resistance to ERP demands formed only one impulse behind the representatives' efforts to change the plan. While the Duquesne representatives were becoming more militant in their bargaining, U.S. Steel was seeking to reorganize and rationalize its corporate structure in ways that would have profound effects on the ERP. These efforts at reorganization, coupled with the bargaining experiences of the representatives, would lead to an evolution of the ERP in a more dynamic and independent direction.

Corporate Reorganization

U.S. Steel established its ERPs as individual bargaining units for each plant, separate and isolated from each other. This structure allowed the corporation to achieve two ends: it created smaller bargaining units, which were conducive to management-employee cooperation; and it created separate organizations that could stifle a consolidated union drive. While U.S. Steel was creating decentralized ERPs, however, it was centralizing and rationalizing its management structure. At the corporate level U.S. Steel divided its financial and production functions into separate corporations, a move that allowed for a greater coordination of its subsidiary operations. In addition, U.S. Steel added an industrial relations department to coordinate its labor policy. It merged two of its major subsidiaries, the Carnegie and Illinois Steel Companies and realigned their management structures. The restructuring effort came too late to rescue U.S. Steel from the disastrous implementation of Myron Taylor's early depression relief and work-sharing programs; nevertheless, it offered U.S. Steel the opportunity to stabilize labor relations.

U.S. Steel and its subsidiaries had long needed an overhaul. Elbert Gary had held tight control of the corporation from its inception, but by the 1920s its health was suffering at his hand. The corporation's market share in the steel industry dropped by half between 1901 and 1934, from 66 percent to 33 percent. In addition, profits as a percentage of sales, which had averaged 19.6 percent annually during the first full ten years of operations, declined to 10 percent during the 1920s. U.S. Steel's problems dated to Gary's early policies, which, although successful at the time, became a drag on the corporation by the 1920s. Gary, a banker, had sought to bring stability to the steel industry through stable pricing. This would create regular profits for the industry and U.S. Steel, and it would keep the corporation safe from antitrust actions. U.S. Steel did not act in a monopolistic manner by trying to corner the market; instead, it proved willing to share the steel market with other steelmakers, even at its own expense. The strategy worked by bringing stability to the industry and winning a federal antitrust suit before the Supreme Court. However, Gary accomplished this at a huge cost to the corporation. To stabilize the industry U.S. Steel did not follow aggressive growth policies. It failed to rationalize its organizational and management structures, and it failed to experiment with new technologies. U.S. Steel had become a monolith with outdated production facilities and an archaic corporate structure.[59]

During his ten-year tenure with U.S. Steel that began after Gary's death, Myron Taylor fundamentally changed the character of the corporation. Taylor broke with Gary's outdated management policies by ushering in a more progressive management philosophy. He worked closely with other corporate liberals on the Business Advisory Council, which established regular contacts between the liberal corporate community and the New Deal government.[60] But where his influence was felt most was in his reversal of U.S. Steel's internal corporate policies. Taylor not only restructured finances and consolidated plant operations but realigned the corporation's structure and oversaw a nearly complete turnover of its top management. Although his changes would not bring U.S. Steel back to its undisputed dominance of the first decade of the twentieth century, they stopped the corporation's steady decline. One of his first tasks was to enlist U.S. Steel engineers in a massive study of all its production facilities. Begun in 1928 and completed in 1935, the study focused on the company's market position and obsolete and redundant plants. Its conclusions, which pointed toward a fundamental restructuring of the corporation's production facilities and product lines, led Taylor to enlist an outside engineering firm—Ford, Bacon, and Davis, Inc.—to study the company's properties, methods, efficiencies, sales, personnel and markets. The engineering firm's surveys confirmed many of the recommendations of the earlier study and served as a blueprint for many changes within the corporation, including the rationalization of its corporate structure.[61]

The most important restructuring effort that came out of these studies would not be completed until after the ERP period. Delayed for five years because of the depression and finally implemented in 1938, the restructuring included the incorporation of the U.S. Steel Corp. of Delaware. The U.S. Steel Corp. of New Jersey, formed in 1901, was a holding company, but it also directed many of the policies of its subsidiaries. The criticism of U.S. Steel's top management had been that it did both too much and too little. The structure of the corporation was too decentralized to direct its many operations efficiently, while what guidance U.S. Steel did provide came from a board of directors made up of lawyers and bankers who did not understand the production and sales needs of the thirty subsidiaries. Taylor's creation of the new corporation addressed this structural flaw by separating the financial and long-term planning functions of U.S. Steel—now located in New York in the New Jersey corporation—from the production and sales functions, now centered in the new Delaware corporation. Taylor placed the Delaware corporation's headquarters in Pittsburgh, at the center of U.S. Steel's empire, and staffed it with experienced steel managers.[62]

At the subsidiary level, restructuring occurred earlier and would have an important effect on the company's labor policies during the ERP period. The most important change took place in 1935, when Taylor merged U.S. Steel's largest steelmaking subsidiaries, the Carnegie and Illinois Steel Companies. In 1936 Taylor added the American Sheet and Tin Plate Co. to the new giant subsidiary. For decades the Carnegie and Illinois Steel Companies had produced the same product and sold to similar markets, but their management, production, and sales forces never had been coordinated. At times the two companies competed with each other for sales and even bought steel from

competing companies instead of each other.[63] This merger helped set in
motion key changes in the industrial relations policies within the individual
plants, by realigning and coordinating the management structure between
the corporation, its subsidiary, and the individual plant.

Although the new structural changes provided the opportunity for a more
coordinated industrial relations policy, Taylor needed to commit the corporation to this course. Here again he would bring a new progressive direction
to U.S. Steel. Before the merger of Carnegie and Illinois Steel, Taylor instituted a management realignment program. When Taylor took control of the
corporation in 1928, many of its top managers were old and facing retirement.
Taylor replaced these men with young executives, and in a break with corporate practice he recruited many from outside. From Republic Steel he hired
Benjamin Fairless to head the new Carnegie-Illinois Corp. and later the U.S.
Steel Corp. of Delaware; from the auto industry he brought in Edward R.
Stettinius, Jr., a corporate liberal (who would serve as FDR's last secretary
of state), as chair of the corporation's finance committee. In February 1934
Taylor hired Arthur. H. Young of the Industrial Relations Counselors, a consulting firm, to serve as vice president for industrial and public relations.
Young's hiring signified not only that U.S. Steel saw the need to coordinate
industrial relations within its subsidiaries but that it had hired the man considered the leading authority on ERPs to do it.[64]

Young, the son of a steelworker, had worked his way up from unskilled
laborer to safety and employment supervisor at Illinois Steel's South Chicago plant. In 1918 International Harvester hired him as manager of industrial
relations. There Young wrote the company's works council plan, a type of
employee representation plan, and directed it for six years. He also represented the company on the Special Conference Committee, the secretive national
corporate clearinghouse for labor and personnel policies. As industrial relations director, Young also proved instrumental in centralizing and professionalizing labor policy, establishing an occupational rating plan, and equalizing
wage rates throughout the company's plants.[65] Young left International Harvester in 1924 to become an industrial relations counsel for the law firm of
Curtis, Fosdick, and Belknap. Two years later the industrial relations staff of
the law firm formed a nonprofit consulting firm, the Industrial Relations
Counselors (IRC), headed by Young. Financially supported by John D. Rockefeller, Jr., the IRC researched industrial relations problems and conducted
industrial relations surveys for large corporations. The work of the IRC dove-
tailed with that of the Special Conference Committee, of which Young remained a member, with both groups attempting to extend the use of employee representation plans. Early in the depression IRC personnel also became

active in federal agencies, with Young serving in the U.S. Employment Service and consulting for both the Department of Labor and the National Labor Board. Young brought to U.S. Steel years of practical experience with ERPs and industrial relations, as well as industry and government contacts and a close knowledge of the National Labor Board.[66]

At U.S. Steel, Young would be responsible for both strengthening the ERPs and professionalizing industrial relations. Young's first task, completed in February 1934, was the revision of U.S. Steel's ERP. Although the revisions were set in motion by the Fort Dukane National Labor Board case, they also solidified the ERPs and marked a new stage in their history. Established as a temporary measure to conform to the NRA labor requirements and block any union upsurge, the ERPs now took on a greater permanence and independence. Management could not abolish the plans without seriously undermining whatever improved relations it had established with its workforce, especially skilled workers, and without bringing the corporation under the further scrutiny of the National Labor Board. By democratizing the plans, the revisions also increased worker interest.[67]

The ERP revisions emanated from changing New Deal labor policy, but they fit neatly with Young's long-term commitment to ERPs as a necessary component of successful industrial relations. Young abhorred unions, which he believed disrupted the natural cooperative relationship of management and labor. According to Young, the work relationship throughout history had evolved from one of master and slave to master and servant and now had become one of "associates, jointly interested in a common enterprise for their mutual advantage." As one who had worked his way up in the industry from unskilled worker to corporate vice president, Young also firmly believed that upward mobility further erased divisions between management and labor. Instead of conflict, he saw "industrial mutual self-interest." According to Young, the ERP, composed of workers and managers from the same plant, made this vision workable. It provided a democratic forum for working out problems, ensuring that each side learned what the other thought.[68] Young had worked toward these goals at International Harvester for six years, and with the Industrial Relations Counselors for ten years, and now he sought to instill them in the thinking of U.S. Steel managers and workers.

In addition to strengthening U.S. Steel's ERPs, he presided over the centralization of the company's industrial relations policies. In July 1934 Young formed a department of industrial relations within U.S. Steel, merging into it the old Bureau of Safety, Sanitation, and Welfare. A year later he helped establish personnel departments at the plant level. At Duquesne, Ross Leffler, who had been serving as the plant's ERP management representative, took over as superintendent of personnel. He would fill that job for only a few months before being tapped to become the Pittsburgh district manager of industrial relations for the newly formed Carnegie-Illinois Steel Corp. He would be replaced at Duquesne by Robert Sanner, who also took over as ERP management representative. Thus the ERP served as a school for U.S. Steel managers, training a generation in the field of industrial relations.[69]

For the first time in its history U.S. Steel now had established personnel departments in its plants and linked the superintendents of those departments to the district level of the subsidiary. The new level of coordination allowed Carnegie-Illinois to begin to regularize its industrial relations policies within its mills. In 1936 the company established in Carnegie and Illinois Steel mills company-wide policies regarding layoff and rehiring criteria—merit trumped seniority—and procedures for hiring new workers and instituting departmental transfers. In 1936 it published a pamphlet for workers that listed rules for employees, placing in print for the first time offenses punishable by firing. Although the practice of the various mills at times varied from the established procedures, these efforts marked the first time that Carnegie workers and supervisors worked under a standard set of rules pertaining to employment.[70]

Written industrial relations policies meant a further erosion of the foreman's authority. Indeed, one of Young's major concerns was the professionalization and education of foremen, removing the arbitrary use of authority that caused so many shop-floor conflicts. Young oversaw the creation of personnel departments that increasingly took over hiring and firing functions. At the Carnegie-Illinois plants personnel superintendents now interviewed workers for all skilled positions and supplied unskilled labor, albeit with final approval reserved for superintendents and foremen. The personnel superintendent at Duquesne now took over all hiring functions. Carnegie-Illinois started training classes for foremen and in 1936 published "Instructions to Supervisory Personnel Governing Employee Relationships," which set guidelines for foremen and superintendents, checking much of their former arbitrary control of the workforce. The individual plants, including Duquesne in 1935, also established foremen's clubs, which sought to promote social contacts between foremen but also offered educational lectures from upper management. The key to all this was Young's emphasis on cooperation between management and labor. The instructions to supervisors reiterated cooperation in the preamble and included a section on the ERP, encouraging supervisors to support the plan.[71]

In the space of two years, between 1934 and 1936, Young had helped to redirect more than thirty years of decentralized labor relations within U.S. Steel.

Symbolizing this new direction would be U.S. Steel's admission to the Special Conference Committee in 1934, with Young serving as the corporation's representative.[72] No less important was Young's imprint on U.S. Steel's ERPs. Young impressed upon U.S. Steel management the view that ERPs were permanent mechanisms for resolving shop-floor issues. They no longer served as strictly antiunion tools designed to circumvent New Deal labor legislation. But this new direction for the ERPs in no way ended U.S. Steel's use of the ERP as an antiunion bulwark.

Nor did passage of the National Labor Relations Act, or Wagner Act, in 1935 alter the ERPs' antiunion direction. The Wagner Act's section 8(a)(2) outlawed company domination and support, including financial, in the formation and continuance of labor organizations, such as ERPs.[73] The Wagner Act especially incensed Young, who labeled it "an unpalatable and unrighteous and unjust technique imposed on us by demagogues" that would "make it illegal for free discussion of problems by employee and employer." Just before its passage he vowed that instead of following the new law, he would "rather go to jail or be convicted as a felon and yet be true to the principles of peaceful cooperation in industry."[74] However, the Wagner Act had no immediate effect on U.S. Steel. As it had maintained consistently regarding the National Labor Board and the National Steel Labor Relations Board, U.S. Steel also held the Wagner Act to be unconstitutional. Although some companies responded to the Wagner Act by abolishing their ERPs or setting them up as quasi-independent unions, U.S. Steel did nothing. Until the Supreme Court ruled on its constitutionality, U.S. Steel would ignore the new law.[75]

The changes in U.S. Steel's industrial relations policies seemed to portend a strengthening of the ERP, but they instead exposed a central flaw in the plan. As the ERPs matured from company-dominated, antiunion tools into semi-independent, worker-led organizations, the scope of the ERP representatives' demands broadened correspondingly. At the same time, U.S. Steel's reorganization centralized decision making and removed authority from plant-level superintendents. If the ERPs remained based on a model of plant-level bargaining, how could representatives resolve shop-floor issues, which increasingly encompassed corporate-wide policy, with plant managers who were losing their authority to decide even traditional plant-level issues?

The Central Committee Movement

The increasing centralization at the corporate and subsidiary level of decision making in regard to labor relations led to a similar centralization movement within the ERPs. It was only logical that the employee representatives sought to broaden their bargaining unit, because the individual plant managers were increasingly losing their powers to subsidiary managers. The movement to link the ERPs of nearby plants began hesitantly, and in its infancy the representatives showed a willingness to defer to management requests that stalled and blocked the movement. By mid-1936, however, U.S. Steel found itself on the defensive and losing its influence over the ERP merger movement.

John Kane's first effort at linking up the Carnegie Steel ERPs in early 1935 had melted under management opposition. Still, it helped to inspire Elmer Maloy to become a representative. Following the 1935 election, which produced a more independent base of representatives, Kane introduced an eight-point agenda designed to guide the ERP's demands for the coming year. Many of Kane's demands cut across skill lines and thus were an attempt to broaden the appeal of the ERP beyond its tonnage and skilled trades base. He called for a uniform five-day week throughout U.S. Steel, vacations with pay after ten years' service, the creation of a mutual benefit and relief association, and an increase in pension benefits.[76] What most distinguished his plan was that Carnegie Steel could grant many demands only on a subsidiary-wide basis. With this in mind the agenda also supported the creation of an ERP central committee, composed of two representatives from all the company's plants.

Once again, management objected. This time Ross Leffler, management's ERP representative, pleaded with the representatives not to have Duquesne lead the fight for the central committee. He asked them to consider what effect Kane's proposal would have on the future of the Duquesne Works.[77] This had become a consistent management theme, in which it pointed out that unfavorable publicity could lead to a loss of orders. Cummins had noted during the miners' strike of 1933 that a shutdown of the works would mean a devastating loss of orders from nervous buyers, and workers had been warned in the February 1934 ERP election that a low voter turnout could doom the plant's future. These threats appear not to have been completely idle. The Duquesne Works was an aging plant, with no significant improvements since the 1910s, and none planned for the 1930s. In addition, it had lost money throughout the early 1930s and Carnegie Steel president I. Lamont Hughes had told the representatives in 1933 that he personally saved the plant from closure two or three times. True or not, Duquesne workers knew that U.S. Steel had been conducting studies of its plants with the goal of closing down the inefficient ones.[78]

Management's pleas proved successful and the representatives twice tabled Kane's eight-point program. In the meantime, John Mullen, the ERP chair at Carnegie's Clairton Works, took the lead and invited all Carnegie-Illinois representatives in the Pittsburgh area for a get-together dinner during January 1936 in Pittsburgh. In response, Kane and Maloy withdrew the eight-point plan and substituted a six-point plan, which again called for the creation of a central committee, consolidated some of the earlier proposals, and called for a 15 percent wage hike and seniority rights. Despite pressure from management to drop the proposal, the representatives now unanimously approved it and elected Kane and Maloy to attend the dinner.[79]

The dinner meeting represented just one example of the growing militance and independence shown by ERPs throughout the nation. The NRA's Hugh Johnson had warned industries back in 1933 that the headlong rush to create ERPs could backfire if workers figured out how to turn the management-created plans to their advantage. By 1936 his forecast appeared to be accurate. Within the steel industry Jones & Laughlin, Republic, and Inland Steel all experienced a broadening in the scope of their ERPs' demands. Within U.S. Steel, Duquesne was just one of many large mills that experienced a growing rebellion among its ERP representatives: in May 1935 the Edgar Thomson ERP demanded a 10 percent wage hike and vacations with pay, and in August it demanded that Carnegie Steel cancel all debts that workers owed for company food baskets. Also in August the ERP representatives at the South Chicago plant organized an independent dues-paying union. In September the representatives from American Sheet and Tin Plate held a conference and demanded a 15 percent wage increase and vacations with pay, and the Carnegie-Illinois ERPs in the Chicago and Gary regions formed the Calumet Council, which linked their organizations in a type of central committee. In November the ERP men at the Carnegie-Illinois Gary plant voted 17-17 to abandon the ERP and join the Amalgamated and then passed the same motion in December.[80]

The January 1936 dinner meeting called by Mullen brought together eighty representatives from the nine Pittsburgh district Carnegie-Illinois plants. Carnegie-Illinois Steel officials did not want the meeting to occur, but when they could not head it off, they sought to send observers and pay for the event. Mullen refused to allow corporate officials to attend, noting that many representatives would act as spies for the company anyway. He also had the participants pay for the dinner themselves. Although a sizable minority of the ERP representatives expressed doubts about the central committee idea, a majority voted to return to their plants and elect two representatives to establish the new committee in March. The Duquesne ERP supported the March meeting and again sent Maloy and Kane as its representatives. In the meantime, however, the Mingo Junction and large Homestead Works dropped out of the process, arguing that they did not have the authority to form such a committee. This left just five members—Duquesne, the Edgar Thomson Works, Clairton, Farrell, and the Youngstown mills—to form the Carnegie-Illinois ERP Central Committee. The group decided to push for only two demands: recognition by the company of the central committee as the bargaining agent for the Pittsburgh district of Carnegie-Illinois, and compulsory arbitration. Although the group supported the six-point Duquesne plan, it agreed to put off the other demands until it had won the first two.[81]

The independent movement of the Pittsburgh-region Carnegie-Illinois ERPs exposed two differing visions of the ERP: management's, based on the original plant-level conception of the plan; and the representatives', based on the realities of corporate reorganization. These contrasting views found expression in the Duquesne Works' biannual joint ERP conference of management and employee representatives, also held in February 1936. Speaking at this meeting, Cummins opposed the creation of a central committee, instead hewing closely to one of the original reasons for the plan: to solve problems at the local level. "The closer contact we can maintain with the Local Representative Group without expanding our activity," he explained, "the better the chances of the Plan functioning in a way to accomplish [the] most good." He noted that the representatives had the right to contact whomever they wanted, but he wanted them to attend to their own plant "instead of trying to mix up in the other fellows' problems." K. H. McLaurin, the assistant general superintendent, also opposed the central committee idea but argued that the benevolence of U.S. Steel precluded the need for such a group. Reducing the central committee idea to one of higher wages, he stated that "the Corporation was very much alive to the necessity of maintaining the highest wage scale that business conditions will permit" and that the representatives must understand the corporation's financial limitations.[82]

The employee representatives, however, took a page from the corporation's own book and argued that linking the ERPs was both necessary and natural. They had grasped the implications of U.S. Steel's and Carnegie-Illinois' restructuring efforts and sought to make the ERPs responsive to corporate realities. Joseph Soffa, a chipper, offered this rationale for linkage:

> It is the Company's desire to deprive the men of something upon which they themselves depend upon for existence. "An Organization."
> The headquarters of this great organization [Carnegie-Illinois] is located at Pittsburgh where all Subsidiaries must go for their orders to operate. Regardless of what Subsidiary[,] all of their problems of vital importance are put to the main office at Pittsburgh. The brilliant minds behind this organization then take care of it. The Carnegie-Illinois Steel Corporation is a strong chain of steel mills whose profits or losses of each link is classed together.

If we send two delegates from each plant to a Convention then by collective action we are only following the same principal as the Company has been following since it's [*sic*] incorporation.[83]

Another representative, George Zuzo, noted the necessity of "collective action" between the ERPs if they were to win larger pensions, vacations with pay, and the forty-hour week. "It seems foolish," he argued, "to say we must confine our activities to one Plant, for no General Superintendent is in a position to grant any of these requests."[84]

For some ERP representatives, however, the central committee represented a much more fundamental break with the ERP philosophy. Men such as Maloy and Clairton's Mullen saw that the central committee could be a first step in the formation of an independent union. According to Maloy,

Our original idea in the creation of a central committee was to form an independent union within the United States Steel Corporation under the employee representation plan, if possible with the approval of the management; if not possible, to form it, regardless of the opinion of management, and I saw and men I was associated with saw that we were never going to accomplish anything unless the management wanted it. We would get exactly what they wanted. So we . . . thought that we might be able to create some sort of an independent union free from the domination of the company.[85]

Indeed, the whole proposed structure and purpose of the central committee marked a fundamental break with Arthur H. Young's vision. U.S. Steel had organized the ERP as a joint council, with equal representation and voting power for management and employees. The central committee proponents offered an alternative that would move the plan closer to a trade union conception of bargaining. The central committee was not to be a joint committee with equal numbers of management and employee representatives. Instead, the committee would be composed only of employee representatives who met directly with corporate officials. Their function was not to cooperate with management and reach compromises through an orderly voting process but to serve demands on management and bargain. The central committee representatives also wanted compulsory arbitration. The ERPs contained an arbitration provision, but it could be used only if management agreed. By the end of 1936 no case had gone to this stage.[86] Arbitration never did fit well with the plan, as it was essentially antithetical to Young's belief that management and employees should cooperate and arrive at mutual decisions without a third party. Realizing their powerlessness and aware of management's unwillingness to voluntarily agree to arbitrate, the central committee proponents proposed compulsory arbitration, with the National Labor Relations Board serving as arbitrator. This represented a break with the notion of cooperation, and it exposed the distrust representatives held for management. The representatives wanted arbitration, because, according to Maloy, they needed an outside party to verify management's statements and figures concerning issues such as pay hikes.[87]

The central committee, however, still fell far short of independent unionism. Neither Maloy nor Mullen openly spoke of independent unionism, despite Mullen's desires to transform the ERP into a "bona fide labor organization."[88] The central committee proponents would not have had a majority of representatives in support of such an action. A large number of ERP men did not even support extending the plan beyond the plant level, and for those who did, a majority saw it only as an extension of the plan, not a break with past practice. The Duquesne Works ERP, for instance, still requested that management pay all expenses of the central committee, thus limiting its independence. Further, the central committee would encompass only the Pittsburgh district, and no attempt was made to link it with Chicago.[89]

The halting and incomplete movement of the central committee toward independent unionism reflected in part its general isolation from the broader labor movement. The Amalgamated, both the national organization and the rank-and-file movement, was literally nonexistent, and most ERP men detested it. However, John L. Lewis had formed the Committee for Industrial Organization (CIO) in November 1935 and publicly supported a new drive to organize steelworkers. In early 1936 he tried to push the AFL to support it, but as late as May it was unclear whether the drive would take place. Although Lewis, United Mine Worker officials, and other trade unionists had contact with steelworkers in the ERP and the old rank-and-file movement during early 1936, little coordination occurred between the steel militants and the CIO.[90] John Mullen had the most extensive CIO contacts, but most other central committee representatives remained isolated from CIO circles. Both Maloy and Kane, key leaders in the central committee, did not have such contacts.[91]

Although the creation of the central committee and the boldness of the representatives probably emanated in part from events external to the ERP—the Wagner Act and the CIO—it was more an expression of an internal logic that grew out of the representatives' own experiences with the ERP. Kane first proposed a central committee before passage of the Wagner Act and the formation of the CIO, and Maloy's efforts at transforming the ERP request procedure into a union-like grievance procedure occurred without contact with unionists. Similarly, the central committee, with its incomplete break with corporate ties and failure to encompass other Carnegie-Illinois plants, pointed to the insular experience of representatives and their lack of broader contact with union forces. Even the committee's stance on arbitration pointed to their lack of understanding of the new realities of labor law. The committee looked to the NLRB not to abolish the U.S. Steel's ERPs, nor to order a representation election—strategies an independent union might use—but instead to arbitrate particular bargaining issues between the committee and the corporation. Yet this was a function the NLRB could not perform.

The creation of the central committee, even without its direct ties to the labor movement, put Carnegie-Illinois and U.S. Steel into a bind. At least theoretically, Young did not oppose the centralization of the ERPs. "These movements in the direction of a wider area of collective action," Young argued, "are absolutely inevitable and we don't propose to try to stop them." "We intend," he added, "to go along and by evidencing our sincerity of purpose keep matters from getting beyond the point of reasonable negotiation."[92] However, the company had tried to stop the meeting of the Pittsburgh ERPs, just as it had tried to dissuade its American Sheet and Tin Plate ERPs from meeting. In both cases the groups showed a high level of independence by going ahead with the meetings and by not allowing company observers to attend.

Unsure of what would happen, U.S. Steel and Carnegie-Illinois sought more information about its ERPs and the central committee movement. In early 1936 U.S. Steel hired Young's old company, Industrial Relations Counselors, to study all levels of industrial relations within Carnegie-Illinois. The IRC began the study in February 1936 and paid close attention to the structure and workings of the ERPs.[93] The study marked the new professional approach that U.S. Steel sought to bring to industrial relations. But the corporation also used its older approach to industrial relations. Officials from the H. C. Frick Coal and Coke Co., a U.S. Steel subsidiary, began hiring ERP representatives as spies. An intermediary espionage company, Railway Audit and Inspection, hired ERP representatives, especially leaders in the centralization movement, to report on fellow representatives and the inner workings of the plans. Railway Audit's agents paid the men $50 per month and hid their identity by telling the representatives that they worked for a bonding company hired by U.S. Steel stockholders who wanted to expose the mistreatment of workers. They hired John Mullen and William Garrity, an Edgar Thomson representative, and approached Elmer Maloy and the Chicago ERP leader George Patterson. Maloy declined, but another Duquesne ERP representative, Raymond Ruhe, accepted the offer.[94]

The spy plan backfired on U.S. Steel when two representatives went public with the sordid affair. On April 10 Mullen and Patterson exposed the spy racket in testimony before the U.S. Senate's Education and Labor Subcommittee on Civil Liberties, also known as the La Follette Committee. Mullen had immediately contacted Clinton Golden, a regional director of the National Labor Relations Board, when he first was approached with the spy proposal. He then acted as a double agent, working with the Railway Audit agents and giving them essentially useless information and in turn giving information about his handlers and his spy earnings to Golden. Golden put Mullen, Patterson, and Garrity in touch with the La Follette Committee, and the resulting public hearings caught U.S. Steel off guard.[95]

The exposure by the La Follette Committee proved important for prodding the company to address the demands of the ERP representatives. Three days after the damning testimony, Carnegie-Illinois president Benjamin Fairless finally agreed to meet with the central committee. The ERP men presented their demand for collective bargaining rights, along with a 15 percent wage increase, forty-hour week, and the appointment of an impartial tribunal such as the National Labor Relations Board to arbitrate cases between management and the committee. Fairless in turn questioned whether the committee, particularly Mullen, who no longer worked for Carnegie-Illinois, represented the desires of the workers. By the end of the meeting Fairless had acceded to none of the committee's demands and had rejected outright the idea that Carnegie-Illinois ever would agree to compulsory arbitration. However, he agreed that the committee might gain some form of recognition from the company in the future but only if all the plants (including Mingo and Homestead) were represented. Furthermore, he agreed to contact the two missing ERPs and call the committee within a month.[96]

At this point Fairless again stalled. He did not contact the committee, and the Pittsburgh region's industrial relations director, Ross Leffler, declined an invitation from the group to attend a meeting on May 2, 1936. At that meeting the committee instead pushed ahead with its agenda. It passed resolutions for all the participating plants to hold a referendum and vote on two issues: whether to amend the ERP so that the central committee would "bargain collectively for all the employees of the Pittsburgh-Youngstown District"; and whether the plan should provide for a neutral board of arbitration. Unable to stall the representatives any longer, Leffler asked the ERPs to cancel the referendum, because Fairless was considering the request for the formation of a "general conference." Despite the vagueness of the statement—it did not address bargaining or arbitration, only a conference—the committee delayed its referendum. In early June the central committee again met with Fairless. He announced that he would recognize a committee from the five plants (Homestead and Mingo still refused to participate). He also said that as many representatives as wanted could attend the committee meetings. However, he would not recognize them as speaking or bargaining for the company's workers. Fairless's announcement angered the central committee members, who saw it as complete repudiation of their efforts. As they left, some remarked that if John L. Lewis were present, they would sign up with the CIO.[97]

Conclusion

Two weeks after the Fairless meeting Lewis announced the formation of the Steel Workers Organizing Committee (SWOC). SWOC arrived at a critical juncture in the evolution of U.S. Steel's ERPs and in the shop-floor relations of the Duquesne Works. Offering a well-financed, committed, and professional organizing effort, SWOC marked a break with the failed efforts of the Amalgamated. Most ERP representatives viewed the Amalgamated with hostility, but SWOC's approach to unionization forced them to rethink their stance. SWOC also arrived just as Fairless had alienated the most militant ERP representatives. With SWOC now contesting U.S. Steel for the loyalty of its workforce, the ERP representatives would play a key role in determining the outcome. Could U.S. Steel regain control of the ERP movement or, at least, steer it toward semi-independence as an alternative to SWOC?

The SWOC organizing drive coincided with growing tensions between Duquesne management and the ERP representatives. Management blocked the representatives' ambitious safety and accident-prevention work, and the two sides continued to battle about the distribution of work hours. Wage requests exposed a similar strain within the ERP, especially given the new willingness of the representatives to appeal management decisions and question wage structures. But if these conditions created a growing shop-floor crisis between management and the ERP, and therefore favored a SWOC organizing drive, one historical reality pointed in an opposite direction. The Amalgamated never had been able to unite the unskilled and skilled and the native and foreign born at Duquesne. ERP representatives still were predominantly tonnage and skilled trades workers who had been born in the United States, and they had proved hostile toward the old Fort Dukane Lodge, the bastion of unskilled, immigrant, and black unionism.

5. SWOC and the Rise of Steel Unionism, 1936–37

IN TESTIMONY before the National Labor Relations Board (NLRB) in January 1937, Elmer Maloy revealed publicly for the first time that he had joined the Steel Workers Organizing Committee (SWOC). The hearing focused on SWOC's charges that the Carnegie-Illinois Steel Corp. dominated and manipulated its employee representation plans (ERPs) in violation of the National Labor Relations Act. SWOC argued that the company should dissolve its ERPs, which formed a major obstacle to the union's organizing efforts. In ten days of testimony during December and January, Maloy documented company control of the ERP and management threats directed at representatives.[1]

Maloy acknowledged not only his SWOC membership but that he had been a paid organizer since September 1936. He had recruited ERP representatives from various Carnegie-Illinois mills, along with fellow workers at the Duquesne Works. John Kane, who also testified before the NLRB in December and January, stated that he too had joined SWOC, although not as a paid organizer.[2] SWOC's capture of Duquesne's two leading ERP men was a stunning victory. The defection of these key representatives seemed to spell success for the new union. If SWOC could bring together Fort Dukane and ERP activists in one union, it might break through the rigid skill, ethnic, and racial barriers that had divided Duquesne workers and bedeviled union organizers for decades.

But Maloy's testimony revealed otherwise. He drew a sharp distinction between SWOC and Fort Dukane, and he showed little knowledge of the older union. "There is some sort of an Amalgamated lodge in Duquesne," Maloy told the board, "but I am not a member of that lodge." Asked further about the Fort Dukane Lodge, he replied that he did not know whether it still had a charter from the national union. "I don't know what their standing is," he said, "I have never inquired."[3] This answer came seven months into SWOC's organizing drive and four months after Maloy had joined SWOC as a paid organizer. His responses to NLRB questioning exposed the difficult task SWOC faced in building a union at Duquesne. It first had to win the allegiance of ERP representatives and the membership of the Fort Dukane Lodge, and then it had to unite these bitter rivals in a viable organization. The new union at Duquesne would not be built through the mass movement of workers acting as one, nor from the leadership by one key sector of the mill's workforce. Instead, it would be built slowly and unevenly by two largely separate groups of activists who required strong guidance and funding from SWOC. When SWOC finally granted Duquesne workers a new charter in February 1937, the Fort Dukane and ERP activists would form a new coalition leadership. But unification at the top did not necessarily mean unification within the ranks.

SWOC: A Break with the Past

SWOC's organizing drive marked a fundamental break with the Amalgamated's failed efforts. SWOC avoided the Amalgamated's disastrous policies, which had divided the national leadership from the rank-and-file and the union from key workers in the ERP movement. From the start the differences between the two drives would be striking, and steel industry officials quickly noticed. "The present campaign," L. H. Burnett, a Carnegie-Illinois vice president, told a meeting of the company's general superintendents, "differs from any we have heretofore met, in that it is backed not only by skillful labor leaders and organizers but also by 'plenty of money.'"[4]

The formation of SWOC had been a long time coming. John L. Lewis, president of the United Mine Workers (UMW), had wanted to unionize the steel industry for years in order to shore up his own union. A small but key segment of miners worked in "captive mines" owned by steel companies, and so long as steel remained unorganized, it posed a threat to unionized miners. Lewis actively pushed for steel's organization within the AFL, but he met with stiff resistance from craft leaders who opposed the industrial union advocated by Lewis. Although the AFL conventions in 1934 and 1935 went on record as supporting a drive, Lewis came to accept that nothing would come of it. He believed the Amalgamated was not capable of mounting the drive and that the other AFL craft unions were not willing to support it.[5]

Lewis finally broke with the AFL and formed the Committee for Industrial Organization (CIO) in November 1935. Despite his deep desire to organize steel, Lewis—and the other CIO leaders—believed that the rubber and auto industries would make more logical targets. The problem with steel centered on the Amalgamated. Lewis believed the Amalgamated to be too inept to lead a successful organizing drive. But because he was unsure of what the CIO's future relations with the AFL would be, he did not want to begin a jurisdictional dispute by forming a rival steel union. His solution would be to launch a lengthy campaign, lasting more than six months, to bring the Amalgamated into the CIO fold and give legitimacy to a new steel drive. An agreement signed with the Amalgamated in June 1936 gave the CIO, under the newly created Steel Workers Organizing Committee, complete direction of the organizing drive and any new members. The Amalgamated preserved the right to grant charters and to keep its small pre-SWOC membership. The agreement, however, was more one-sided than it sounded. As the historian Irving Bernstein has written, "For all practical purposes, the Amalgamated Association had passed out of existence."[6]

Lewis cared little for the Amalgamated's structure or traditions. Instead he built SWOC from the ground up. He bypassed the aging, crony-ridden, and incompetent Amalgamated leadership and formed SWOC with well-respected men from both inside and outside the UMW. Leading the new union would be Philip Murray, a UMW vice president who had three decades of union experience and a deep commitment to bettering workers' lives.[7] Lewis also put SWOC on sound financial footing. The Amalgamated had been dependent on workers' dues and fees, which dried up during the depression and left the union chronically poor. By contrast, SWOC arrived with a $500,000 war chest provided by the UMW and a promise of more money from the CIO in the months ahead.[8]

Under Murray's leadership SWOC instituted other changes that distinguished it from the old Amalgamated. Ignoring all semblance of democracy, Murray instituted a top-down structure that gave the national leadership control of all details. Centralized authority gave SWOC the ability to direct and coordinate its organizing campaign more efficiently, thus overcoming the defects in the Amalgamated's decentralized and haphazard organizing work.[9] Murray then put in the field four times as many organizers as the Amalgamated used. More than two hundred organizers spread out to the steel towns of the East, South, and Midwest almost immediately. Another two hundred followed within months.[10]

SWOC further diverged from the Amalgamated in its organizing strategy. Its three-pronged organizing approach sought to win ERP militants to the union and turn the ERPs against the steel companies; to enroll the large population of foreign-born steelworkers; and to use the federal government as an ally in its organizing work. The Amalgamated had belittled the ERP and its representatives, thus cutting off any contact between the union and these key worker militants. SWOC leaders learned from this mistake. They also found themselves beginning the drive just as many ERPs had matured into semi-independent organizations that could not be ignored or ridiculed. By targeting immigrant steelworkers, SWOC continued the practice of the Amalgamated lodges. But SWOC also actively recruited national fraternal and ethnic organizations to aid in its drive, marking a break with the Amalgamated's practice of self-reliance. Finally, SWOC's alignment with the New Deal broke with the Amalgamated's inconsistent relations with the National Recovery Administration (NRA). Instead SWOC would use congressional investigative committees and the new National Labor Relations Board as key elements in its organizing strategy.[11]

Despite the advantages that SWOC held over the Amalgamated, the work of organizing steelworkers into the new union proved slow and difficult. SWOC leaders and organizers might have understood the Amalgamated's mistakes, but they could not erase the conditions that the early New Deal and the Amalgamated had helped to create. Disillusionment, mistrust, and fear, the very conditions that filled the steel towns after the failed 1919 strike, had returned in the wake of the Amalgamated's failure to organize the industry. SWOC also had to overcome federal labor policy failures of the NRA period, which similarly left steelworkers wary of grand government promises. Finally, SWOC had to break down the deep skill and ethnic divisions within the ranks of the steelworkers.

Organizing the Hourly Workers

The workforce of the Duquesne Works appeared likely to be receptive to SWOC's efforts to organize rank-and-file steelworkers. The workers had a history of rank-and-file activism, and Fort Dukane was the strongest Amalgamated lodge in Carnegie-Illinois's Pittsburgh region. The lodge had broken down the city's long history of completely suppressing union activity, and its mobilization of steelworkers in the 1935 election had cracked the city's solid local Republican rule. The lodge had enlisted a majority of the mill's unskilled and semiskilled hourly workers, including large numbers of foreign-born workers, their sons, and African Americans. Yet when SWOC organizers arrived in Duquesne, they quickly found that much of the Fort Dukane Lodge's work and legacy had evaporated. Although SWOC could count on a core of committed militant workers and a large group of workers still receptive to unionism, it found resurrecting unionism a difficult task.

When Lewis finally organized SWOC in June 1936, the economic and political conditions in Duquesne and Pennsylvania were the most advantageous for a drive in years. After five years of severely reduced operations, the Duquesne Works had begun to increase production. The bar mill department, which had shut down half its capacity in 1929, was reopening mills by mid-1936. In August the blast-furnace department had five furnaces in operation—the first time since 1929—and in early 1937 it had all six furnaces lit. By 1937 employment had increased 50 percent over 1935 levels, although most steelworkers still worked part time.[12] It appeared the industry had turned the corner. Operations in the Pittsburgh region, after hovering at 38 percent of capacity in March 1936, increased to 70 percent by August and inched up to 82 percent by January 1937. U.S. Steel especially benefited from the turnaround, with 1936 profits reaching 1920s levels; the number of employees and weekly earnings reached their highest levels since 1930.[13]

In the political arena SWOC faced far more favorable conditions than the Amalgamated had in 1933. Mayor Crawford and mill management still controlled local politics, appearing almost immune to the New Deal arising around them. But the union found it much easier to open a union headquarters in Duquesne and hold meetings, because Fort Dukane members had established those rights in 1933. At the state level Gov. Gifford Pinchot, a Republican, had proved himself to be an ally of labor during the Amalgamated period, but he had been constrained by his more conservative Republican legislature. In 1934 Pennsylvania elected a New Deal Democrat, George Earle, to the governorship, and Thomas Kennedy, secretary-treasurer of the United Mine Workers, as lieutenant governor. But once again a Republican state senate blocked many of their reform efforts. A sweeping Democratic victory in the 1936 general election finally created the first Democratic state senate since 1871 and paved the way for Pennsylvania's "Little New Deal," which reproduced on the state level many of Roosevelt's national programs.[14] The Earle-Kennedy leadership immediately embraced SWOC and provided it with important support. Both Earle and Kennedy spoke at SWOC rallies and protected labor's right to organize. Earle continued Pinchot's policy of refusing to commission Coal and Iron Police and supported legislative efforts to repeal the practice. He also supplied state police protection for SWOC organizers and assured workers that they would receive unemployment relief if fired from their job for union activities.[15]

SWOC found further support through the U.S. Senate's Education and Labor Subcommittee on Civil Liberties, also known as the La Follette Committee. Senate hearings on whether to establish the committee in April 1936 already had exposed U.S. Steel's practice of hiring ERP representatives as spies. Robert M. La Follette, Jr., the Wisconsin Progressive, had won congressional approval for the committee as SWOC was being formed, and the two immediately worked together to expose antiunion company practices, including the hundreds of dollars the Duquesne Works had spent on munitions in the 1933 miners strike and the threatened Amalgamated strike in 1934.[16] The National Labor Relations Board, on the other hand, at first offered the SWOC campaign little help. After passage in 1935, the NLRB's enabling legislation, the Wagner Act, had come under immediate attack from American corporations and its constitutionality remained unresolved. SWOC, unsure whether the Wagner Act would survive a court test, launched its campaign with few references to the law and no immediate plans to use it in its campaign against U.S. Steel. This would soon change.[17]

SWOC began its organizing drive by designating U.S. Steel as its prime target because of its size and distinction as the industry's trendsetter. In addition, SWOC was concerned that the recent activism of U.S. Steel's ERPs might lead them to develop independent of the union. SWOC thus concentrated much of its energy on the largest U.S. Steel subsidiaries, especially Carnegie-Illinois, but also National Tube and American Steel and Wire. SWOC quickly chose the Pittsburgh and Chicago regions as its focal points. Within the Pittsburgh area the Duquesne, Homestead, Edgar Thomson, Clairton, and National Tube Works in McKeesport became the key organizing centers.[18] SWOC kicked off the drive in the Pittsburgh region in June and July with rallies in McKeesport, Duquesne, Homestead, and Clairton. Featuring SWOC officials and local and state political figures, the rallies attracted crowds of five hundred to two thousand. However, UMW members planted in the crowds outnumbered steelworkers at most rallies. Because of the small steelworker turnout, SWOC abandoned this strategy by September, fearful of exposing its weakness. Indeed, U.S. Steel officials tracked the poor attendance at the meetings and knew of SWOC's reliance on miners to pack them.[19] Company officials filmed the Duquesne rally from the second-story window of a nearby building.[20]

George Powers, one of many Communist organizers hired by SWOC, established SWOC's McKeesport district, which included the Duquesne Works. Powers was a Russian immigrant and had been a Communist since the early 1920s. He had served as an organizer for textile workers in the South and for the Steel and Metal Workers Industrial Union in Baltimore. SWOC officials turned to the Communists for quick help in learning the steel industry. The Communists had both years of organizing experience and strong links to steelworker fraternal and ethnic organizations. The Communists also complied with SWOC wishes. As part of their Popular Front strategy, the Com-

munists directed much of their work toward building CIO unions, and
SWOC kept them under tight rein. Except for Lee Pressman, general counsel for SWOC, Communists and those close to the party did not gain national
leadership posts, and few would serve as district directors. Once Powers set
up the McKeesport district office and began the organizing drive, SWOC
placed James Grecula, a veteran UMW official and non-Communist, in
charge of the office and the organizing staff.[21]

To facilitate its organizing drive in Duquesne, SWOC secured the help of
three interrelated organizations: the Fort Dukane Lodge; ethnic and fraternal lodges; and the Communist Party. After its expulsion from the Amalgamated in February 1935, Fort Dukane won a court order giving it the right to
rejoin the Amalgamated the following summer. However, the lodge could not
meet its financial obligation—more than $6,000 in back dues and fees—and
would not be readmitted until April 1936. Fort Dukane was a shell of its
former self, having become, in the words of Harold Ruttenberg, "a lodge of
unemployed." When its leaders sought reinstatement to the Amalgamated,
they specifically asked for their old charter, because a new charter would deny
membership to the lodge's large numbers of unemployed. Throughout the
country the once-active rank-and-file lodges either had dissolved or had
become skeleton organizations with just a handful of committed members.
In addition, many of the rank-and-file leaders found themselves laid off or
fired by 1936, thus weakening their influence.[22]

Fort Dukane also suffered through a contentious change of leadership.
Citing William Spang's "high-handed methods" and the way he projected
himself "into the foreground of labor movements for selfish motives," the
lodge removed him as president. Fletcher Williamson also lost his vice presidency. The lodge leadership no longer included blacks, but it kept its strong
immigrant character.[23] Despite its weakened condition, the lodge continued
to meet and remained connected with the various remnants of the rank-and-
file movement. As with the other lodges, Fort Dukane spent the first half of
1936 waiting for the CIO to launch the new organizing drive. When Lewis
courted the old Amalgamated, Fort Dukane and the other lodges pleaded
with him to begin the drive before the enthusiasm that greeted the formation of the CIO in November 1935 died away.[24]

The old Fort Dukane Lodge would provide SWOC with its core membership. In addition, it supplied leaders for the organizing drive. Salvatore Falvo, an Italian immigrant and semiskilled hourly worker who replaced Spang
as lodge president, became a SWOC staffer and organizer in the mill. Numerous other Fort Dukane activists also made the transition to SWOC and helped
the drive as volunteer organizers.[25] Many of these volunteer Fort Dukane

organizers were also leaders in Duquesne's ethnic and fraternal clubs. Falvo, for instance, was active in Duquesne's Italian community.[26] Some also belonged to the Communist Party, which proved especially valuable to SWOC. Communists in small steel towns held much influence in ethnic and fraternal organizations. They possessed organizational and leadership skills, had grown up in these towns, and were fully integrated into the local working-class culture. The International Workers' Order (IWO), led at the national level by Communists, reinforced the local Communist leadership. The IWO served as an umbrella organization for many local fraternal and ethnic clubs and organizations.[27] In Duquesne the Croatian Fraternal Union (CFU), an IWO affiliate, provided SWOC with many worker activists. The CFU had at least two chapters in Duquesne, and many of its leaders, including Vince Poljak, Ivan Yuran, and Anthony Salopek, had been active in the Fort Dukane Lodge and continued working with SWOC. The city of Duquesne banned IWO social affairs, but ethnic groups could join together in other ways, such as through the Slavonic and Allied League of Duquesne, which included Croatian, Lithuanian, Russian, Serbian, Slovak, Polish, and Carpatho-Russian organizations.[28]

Salopek personified this interplay of Communist, ethnic, and labor activism. A second-generation Croatian American, Salopek had spent his entire life in Duquesne. In 1925 he hired on at the Duquesne Steel Works as an unskilled laborer. A year later he was promoted to a semiskilled hourly job as a lever operator in the rolling mill, a job he still held in 1936. Salopek joined the Communist Party some time in the late 1920s or early 1930s. Although he kept his membership a secret, many of his coworkers knew his political views. He also was active in the CFU and the Fort Dukane Lodge. He did not hold a leadership position in the Amalgamated lodge, but he had been arrested, along with its leaders, on the day of the abortive June 1935 strike. A few months later Salopek joined Spang and other Fort Dukane unionists on the upstart Democratic primary slate for city office. Salopek ran for constable in the city's heavily immigrant First Ward but was defeated.[29]

When SWOC's George Powers began organizing the Duquesne Works, he looked to Salopek for help. Both were Communists with ties to various ethnic communities. Salopek provided Powers with key contacts in the CFU, other ethnic organizations, and the old Fort Dukane Lodge, and among Communists in Duquesne. In addition, he could introduce Powers to ERP representatives whom he had come to know during his years in the town and mill. On the basis of his organizing work, Salopek would become secretary-treasurer of SWOC's Mill Organizing Committee.[30]

A similar pattern of organizing occurred with black workers. SWOC built on the pioneering work of the Fort Dukane Lodge, which had broken down racial barriers, enrolled a majority of the mill's black workers in the union, and elevated blacks to leadership positions. Fletcher Williamson, John McLaurin, and "Father" Henry Cox, all activists and frequent speakers at the old Fort Dukane Lodge meetings, helped organize black workers for SWOC. Williamson was also either a member of, or at least closely aligned with, the Communist Party in Duquesne. James "Mac" McCullough, another volunteer black organizer from the mill, also belonged to the party.[31]

SWOC reinforced these ties to the ethnic communities nationally by allying with the IWO and major black organizations. In October SWOC and the IWO organized the Fraternal Orders Conference in Pittsburgh, which drew more than five hundred delegates from seventeen national and more than 240 local fraternal organizations with a combined membership of nearly 600,000. The conference endorsed SWOC and called on all fraternal organizations to support the union drive by encouraging their members to join the union.[32] SWOC held a similar conference with black leaders in February 1937. SWOC consistently advocated racial equality, a stand derived largely from the heavy United Mine Worker influence on the union and the need to avoid the racial divisions that had helped undermine the 1919 strike. SWOC's backing of black workers and its hiring of black organizers won it the support of many black organizations and leaders in the Pittsburgh region.[33]

Despite the intensity and skill of the organizing drive, SWOC initially experienced only limited success. By September it had signed up only fifteen thousand workers throughout the industry, most of whom were former Amalgamated members. The largest steel mills had only a few hundred workers enrolled. Publicly, however, SWOC claimed more than fifty thousand members.[34] Philip Murray, the SWOC president, defended the slow pace of the drive by placing the organizational work of the union in perspective. Since June, according to Murray, SWOC had passed through two of three necessary organizing stages. The first encompassed setting up the union, hiring organizers, and making initial contacts in the mills. The second centered on getting SWOC's message across to steelworkers through rallies, leaflets, and the press. Now SWOC would enter the third and critical stage, Murray proclaimed, by "signing up members, establishing lodges, and disciplining an army of 500,000 steel workers to secure collective bargaining in the steel industry."[35]

But Murray and the other SWOC leaders also knew that the drive had not progressed as they had expected. Steelworkers were afraid to join the union. "We found the men in the steel mills," averred Murray, "shot through with fear—fear of the boss, fear of the job."[36] David McDonald, SWOC secretary-treasurer, added that workers feared the union and were "apprehensive about dictatorship," a holdover from the Amalgamated days.[37] Clinton Golden, director of the northeast region of SWOC, concluded that "this organizing job has been undertaken in an industry that has exercised unlimited power over its employees for over 50 years, and that nullification of such unbridled control cannot be instituted in 90 days."[38]

Edward Wieck, an investigator for the Russell Sage Foundation, reached similar conclusions. In the late summer and early fall of 1936 he traveled through scores of steel towns, including Duquesne. A year earlier John Fitch, a contributor to *Survey Graphic*, a progressive monthly, had found the National Recovery Administration had generated openness and a lack of fear. Now, both had disappeared. "The NRA is absolutely dead now," wrote Wieck, "none of its influences are left—it might have been two decades ago as far as having any influence on the situation today." Wieck found steelworkers to be afraid "to take it on the chin again" and hesitant to join SWOC, which had yet to "prove its worth." Ironically, the improving economic conditions reinforced this fear. According to Wieck, workers who had had so little for so long wanted "to get as much as they can before the spurt is over" and feared they would jeopardize their jobs if they supported SWOC.[39]

SWOC attempted to assuage these fears with a conservative message. Mindful of both the disastrous and repeated strike threats by the rank-and-file movement and the desire of workers to maintain employment during the economic upturn, SWOC emphasized that it neither wanted nor encouraged strikes. SWOC portrayed itself as a responsible union seeking workers' collective bargaining rights through peaceful means. Much of the SWOC message centered on bread-and-butter issues, such as wage hikes and longer vacations. But SWOC also emphasized the theme of industrial democracy. Organizers emphasized workers' rights as citizens, both on and off the job. In their communities workers had political rights that SWOC would help them claim. This argument worked best in steel towns such as Aliquippa, which workers labeled "Little Siberia," and Duquesne, which still was under conservative Republican rule. SWOC also emphasized workers' rights on the job: safe working conditions, a grievance procedure, and protection against arbitrary firing.[40]

SWOC further sought to overcome workers' resistance by making membership free. At the start of its organizing drive SWOC waived the initiation fee, instead allowing the first month's dues to count as the fee. Dues were set at $1 per month, marking a drastic drop from the Amalgamated's structure of high dues and fees. However, workers who signed membership cards still often failed to pay their first month's dues. Bolstered by money from the UMW and the CIO, SWOC took the added step in November of waiving all dues until February.[41]

Perhaps SWOC's most effective strategy was its work in the November general election. From September to November 1936 SWOC identified itself with Roosevelt and the New Deal, portraying the election as good versus evil. The *Amalgamated Journal* described the political contest graphically: "Stripped to the bone, it was a titanic struggle between the old and the new, between reaction and progressivism, between abuses of capitalism on the one hand and the masses of workers and common people on the other, between the strong who would grab everything within reach and the 'weak' who became tired of exploitation—yes, a conflict between $ interests and human welfare, nothing more. It's as basically simple as that."[42] Claiming "a vote for the New Deal was a vote for collective bargaining and the S.W.O.C.," the union spent much of its organizing time and efforts in securing workers' support for Roosevelt's reelection and the election of local and state New Dealers.[43] In Duquesne, as in other steel towns, Roosevelt won by a landslide. Although Republican registration still outnumbered Democratic (4,267 to 3,123), Roosevelt carried 71 percent of the vote, marking a significant increase over his 60 percent in 1932.[44] Immediately after the election SWOC flooded steel towns with leaflets announcing, "You beat the Steel Barons at the Polls. YOU Re-elected Roosevelt. You must now win in the mills, on the job. Organize Your Union. . . . The re-election of Roosevelt means four more years of political freedom. But your political freedom is worth nothing, unless you have industrial democracy and economic freedom to support it."[45]

Murray would report that SWOC membership, which he claimed reached 82,000 by the beginning of November, was increasing by 2,300 per day since the election. Through the end of 1936 news stories portrayed the union as making giant strides in organizing the industry. The *New Republic*, for example, reported that 4,100 of Homestead's 10,000 workers had signed up, while SWOC itself boasted of 4,600 at the plant. At the end of November Pittsburgh's *Post-Gazette* estimated SWOC's membership to be 125,000, fully one quarter of the steel industry.[46] But public estimates and SWOC announcements masked the real course of the organizing campaign. "Contrary to union propaganda—some of which I helped to write," acknowledged David McDonald, "the steelworkers did not fall all over themselves to sign a pledge card with SWOC. . . . Only Murray and I knew how thin the tally was, although Lewis would insist on the truth whenever I visited Washington, then would shake his head in wonderment at the lack of progress."[47]

Internal membership figures reveal that SWOC was indeed much smaller than estimated. In the McKeesport district—which included Duquesne; the National Tube Works at McKeesport, Versailles, and Christy Park; McKeesport Tin Plate; Firth Sterling Steel Co.; Pittsburgh Steel Foundry Co.; Cop-

perweld Steel Co.; and the Carnegie-Illinois Wood Works—SWOC membership reached only 1,578 by the end of November. It broke 3,000 only in late
January 1937 in a district that had more than 17,000 workers. The Duquesne
Works, the largest of the mills, did not have a membership greater than 1,300
by the first week in February, although SWOC labeled it "one of the best
organized mills along the Monongahela." Figures for Carnegie-Illinois and
U.S. Steel matched these dismal totals. At the beginning of February SWOC
privately claimed only 6,800 of the 47,000 Carnegie-Illinois workers in the
Pittsburgh district, and 23,000 of U.S. Steel's 130,000 workers. But even these
figures fail to reveal SWOC's weaknesses. With initiation fees and dues payments suspended, one could join SWOC merely by signing a card. Of the
McKeesport District's 3,353 members in February, only 617 had paid any dues,
thus leaving as an open question the depth of workers' commitment to
unionism. Furthermore, although the sheer numbers of SWOC enrollees
increased, SWOC membership as a percentage of steelworker employment
did not rise as fast. Many gains that the union registered in early 1937 were
simply a reflection of the overall growth in steelworker employment because
of steadily rising production.[48]

SWOC's strategy for organizing rank-and-file steelworkers built directly
upon the breakthroughs of the rank-and-file period. Because Fort Dukane
had been a union of low-skilled immigrants and black workers, SWOC's limited success at recruiting new members assured the union of the continued
allegiance of most of these early unionists. By February 1937 SWOC had
signed up the old Fort Dukane membership. Breaking down the lingering
fear of the NRA and the Amalgamated period had been a slow and arduous
process. According to Milan Tankosich, who waited before signing up, "When
I find out for sure everything alright, then I join."[49] But what of the U.S.-born
white workers, skilled trades, and tonnage workers who had refused to join
the old Amalgamated and instead looked to the ERP? To win these workers
SWOC would have to confront the ERP and break down its hold on the shop
floor.

SWOC and the ERPs

Many of those who would assume national leadership positions within
SWOC had kept a wary eye on the ERPs for years. As early as May 1935 Lewis
himself had expressed fear that the ERPs, not some rival radical organization, would thwart the AFL in its efforts to organize steel.[50] Another who kept
a watch was Clinton Golden, a regional NLRB official and future director of
SWOC's northeastern region. Through his work with the NLRB he had be-

come acquainted with some key ERP representatives, including John Mullen of Clairton and George Patterson of the South Works in Chicago.

Golden became convinced that the CIO had to address these organizations quickly or face an even stronger ERP movement. What most concerned him was the possibility that U.S. Steel could strengthen the base of antiunion sentiment within the ERP. In May 1936, one month before both SWOC's formation and the annual industry-wide ERP elections, Golden warned against delaying organizational contact with the ERPs. He noted that steel companies could retain control of ERPs by firing and blacklisting militant representatives and "then later . . . grant . . . a few concessions to the 'loyal' company union representatives which they in turn will distribute to their followers."[51] Noting that some ERP militants were growing impatient with the CIO, Golden urged that the union make immediate contact with the ERP leaders and provide guidance to them. With ERP elections scheduled the next month he pushed for an organized effort to get union advocates elected to the ERPs, instead of allowing company loyalists to control the organizations.[52] The CIO proved unable to act on Golden's pleas, although it did print and distribute stickers reading "WE WANT JOHN L. LEWIS" for the June ERP elections. Independent of the CIO, a movement sprang up that was both spontaneous and Communist-led to elect former Amalgamated militants to the ERPs. Amalgamated leaders at the Edgar Thomson Works and the McKeesport Tin Plate Co. won ERP positions, along with scores at U.S. Steel's Gary and South Chicago Works.[53]

When SWOC arrived in June, its leadership already planned to make the ERPs a strategic target. That SWOC would make U.S. Steel's ERPs one of its highest organizing priorities revealed not only the strength of the ERPs but also the leadership capabilities of many employee representatives on the shop floor. As much as SWOC leaders criticized the ERPs as company dominated, they understood the ERPs' appeal.[54] "We realized," Philip Murray wrote, "that many of the employe representatives, perhaps the majority, were men honestly interested in doing a good job under The Plan. . . . To denounce them as company agents or stooges would be both untruthful and poor strategy."[55] SWOC could not continue the AFL policy of ignoring and boycotting the ERPs and "calling company union representatives names," Murray said.[56] Instead SWOC "catered to them with a view to swinging them over" to the union and turning them against the ERPs.[57]

When SWOC began its ERP campaign, it had little contact with Duquesne ERP representatives. United Mine Worker officials had approached Elmer Maloy before SWOC's formation, and he and John Kane both had contact with John Mullen of Clairton. However, it appears that Kane's and Maloy's contact with future SWOC organizers was minimal at best.[58] Likewise, the movement to elect Amalgamated members as ERP representatives found little support at Duquesne. Only two Fort Dukane Lodge members, Ivan Yuran and Raymond Ruhe, ran for office in June 1936. Only Ruhe was elected, and he already sat on the ERP, having won a special election in 1935. Unlike other Fort Dukane activists, Ruhe had U.S.-born parents and he held a tonnage job. He remained in the Fort Dukane Lodge, although some members accused him of being a company man; the hatred of the ERP by Fort Dukane activists remained strong.[59]

The Duquesne ERP election of 1936 instead demonstrated that the plan remained strong and largely immune to the labor movement building around it. Elmer Maloy ran for reelection on a platform of "higher wages and higher pensions" and time and a half for all Sunday work. He had no connections with the CIO or SWOC at the time and won an overwhelming majority of the open hearth votes; he was named on almost every ballot. Kane, frustrated by the lack of progress in the ERP, did not run for reelection and actively campaigned against his own nomination. Despite his efforts, maintenance department workers gave him enough primary votes to place him in the general election, where he came only a few votes short of rewinning his seat. Overall, the pattern established at Duquesne during the 1935 elections continued, with skilled tradesmen and lesser skilled tonnage men of northern and western European heritage holding a majority of ERP positions (see table 4).[60]

In its efforts to win over ERP representatives SWOC initially could secure the allegiance of only Ruhe, who was still a member of the Amalgamated.[61] Maloy and Kane proved more reticent. They had met with management intransigence at two levels within the ERP: on the shop floor, and regionally in their attempts to form the central committee of Carnegie-Illinois ERPs. Although Kane had quit the Duquesne ERP, he remained active in the central committee movement, which sought to bargain with Carnegie-Illinois over company-wide issues. When SWOC entered the picture, neither man had reached the point of abandoning the ERP. Both believed it could work, and both held a deep disdain for the Amalgamated. Nonetheless, as their central committee efforts soon appeared to be getting nowhere, both rethought their positions.

Key to their reevaluation would be a general conference of Pittsburgh-area employee representatives held in August. Just before SWOC was formed, Benjamin Fairless, president of Carnegie-Illinois, had turned down the central committee's demand to be recognized as the regional bargaining agent for Carnegie-Illinois workers. Threatened now by the steel organizing drive, Carnegie-Illinois officials announced in early July that the company would

Table 4. Characteristics of the ERP Representatives Elected in June 1936

Name	Department	Job	Job Type	Birthplace	Parents' Birthplace
Joseph Budday	Blast	Tuyereman	Hourly	United States	United States
Elmer Maloy	Open hearth	Craneman	Tonnage	United States	United States/England
John Dynoske	Open hearth	Unknown	Tonnage	Unknown	Unknown
George Zuzo	Rolling mill	Craneman	Hourly	Austro-Hungary (Czech)	Austro-Hungary (Czech)
Raymond Ruhe	Rolling mill	Manipulator	Tonnage	United States	United States
Joseph Soffa	Chipping	Chipper	Hourly	United States	Austria (German)
George E. Simon	Chipping	Chipper	Hourly	United States	United States
Ed. J. Minnick	Maintenance	Repairman	Skilled trade	United States	Unknown
Ernest Fries	Maintenance	Pipefitter	Skilled trade	United States	Germany
William F. Bowers	Bar mill	Unknown	Tonnage	United States	United States
William J. Smith	Bar mill	Unknown	Unknown	Unknown	Unknown
William F. Betzner	Bar mill	Unknown	Tonnage	Unknown	Unknown
Albert R. Giese	Accounting	Timetaker	Clerical	United States	United States
Roy Griffiths	General labor/masonry	Bricklayer	Skilled trade	Unknown	Unknown
Rex Meighen	Chemical labs/shipping	Unknown	Unknown	Unknown	Unknown

Source: Inactive voter registration cards, Allegheny County, Pennsylvania, Voter Registration Records, AIS; Duquesne Works payroll ledgers, 1933–37, USSC; U.S. Census, *Fourteenth Census of the United States: 1920, Manuscript Schedules*, vol. 10, Pennsylvania, Allegheny County, reel 1511; Records of the War Department, Office of the Provost Marshall General, Selective Service System, World War I Draft Registration Cards, State of Pennsylvania, County of Allegheny, Local Board #8, Microfilm copy, reel 14, Hillman Library, University of Pittsburgh; *Duquesne Times*, various issues, 1933–59; *U.S. Steel News*, various issues, 1936–60; Obsolete Change of Employment and Rate Cards, Box 4, USSC; DWERP, minutes of meeting, 27 June 1933, NSLRB; Duquesne Works, "Report of Positions Excluded from Representation by the Union Under the Terms of the September 1, 1942 Agreement," 7 Oct. 1942, Box 30, File: Positions Excluded from Union Membership, USSC; Steel Workers Organizing Committee Grievance 27–39-U material, Box 26, USSC; Exhibit 7, Box 21, Grievance File 46-20, USSC; Duquesne Works, "Confidential," booklet, 31 Aug. 1949, Box 28, File S-6(a), USSC.

hold periodic nonbinding conferences with employee representatives in the Pittsburgh-Youngstown region. The announcement was far from what the central committee advocates wanted, but it marked a step forward. On August 12 the company convened the Pittsburgh District General Conference, attended by Carnegie-Illinois officials and two management and employee representatives from each of nine Carnegie-Illinois mills. The Duquesne ERP sent Maloy and Kane, who were elected vice chairman and secretary, respectively, of the employee side of the organization.[62]

At the conference, which was chaired by L. H. Burnett, the Carnegie vice president, the representatives raised the central committee issue. Fred Bohne of Youngstown, chairman of the employee representatives, argued that the representatives' demand was designed "to get the Company['s] recognition of collective bargaining." They were not satisfied with nonbinding conferences. Burnett expressed skepticism that it would lead to any improvements, noting that, although a central committee would allow representatives a "degree of uniformity" in their requests, the "present machinery" was adequate. Maloy responded that the central committee would help management by ironing out problems with corporate policies before they were implemented. He then pointed to several recent examples, including the establishment of overtime pay. The company's new policy ignored ERP requests for a forty-hour week and extra pay for weekend work and instead established a forty-eight-hour week and no extra pay for Saturday or Sunday work. Bohne noted that the new policy "was like throwing a match in a powder keg" and that "one hundred organizers for John L. Lewis could not have done as much good for the outside cause [SWOC] as this did." The question of overtime pay, along with other problem policies, Maloy argued, could have been resolved more satisfactorily for workers and caused less shop-floor resentment if the ERP had been able to discuss it with management.[63]

Burnett allowed the central committee resolution to come to an informal and nonbinding vote. With many management representatives abstaining, the central committee motion passed. Burnett then ruled that the representatives should take the resolution back to their plant bodies for approval, although many plants at the meeting—Duquesne, Farrell, Youngstown, Edgar Thomson, and Clairton—already had voted for a central committee. Only after each plant approved the new proposal, Burnett ruled, would Carnegie-Illinois management decide whether to support the proposal.[64]

When the one-day conference ended, the representatives found themselves at a crossroads. The conference had marked a step forward in their campaign to address company-wide issues with management, but their demand for corporate recognition of the central committee had stalled once again. The

representatives had tried several ways to sell management on the idea, arguing that it would improve labor-management relations, save the company
from implementing disastrous policies, and stifle the SWOC organizing drive.
Still, management refused to grant company-wide bargaining powers to the
representatives. If ever there had been a time for Carnegie-Illinois to counter
the SWOC organizing drive by granting its ERPs expanded powers, it had
been at this conference. By continuing to stall, management lost credibility
with key representatives and handed SWOC a golden opportunity.

As a result of the conference, both Maloy and Kane moved toward SWOC.
Kane would not sign up with the union until late December 1936, but by the
end of August he was starting to take consistently pro-SWOC positions that
left little doubt of his true sympathies.[65] Maloy already had been in contact
with SWOC officials by August, and he later would claim that he had been
an early supporter of the union. Maloy remembered that although he did not
officially join the union until September, he "already had committed . . . long
before that." According to Maloy, Philip Murray knew of his union support
and personally told him not to join and jeopardize his position in the ERP:
"'You can be more effective,' he said, 'if you stay out of the union itself. You
can go ahead and do any kind of organizing you want, but don't you personally sign.'"[66]

Others close to SWOC in the period remember a different story. According to William Theis, an early SWOC activist at Clairton, "Elmer Maloy was
one of the boys who did not join SWOC and who did not join with Johnny
Mullen [in June 1936] with[out] capitulating, if you want to call it that, and
going into the union." Theis claimed that Maloy believed that "utopia lay and
the future lay in the ERP, and we could still make something out of it."[67]
Robert R. R. Brooks, who chronicled the early rise of SWOC, also found that
during the summer of 1936 Maloy "was still working on the theory that the
E.R.P. could be made to work. . . . As the summer wore on, he became convinced that he would eventually have to throw in his lot with the union."[68]

If the failure of the central committee alone did not convince Maloy to join
SWOC, the union offered a further inducement. Harold Ruttenberg, SWOC's
research director and codirector of the ERP campaign, noted that some ERP
representatives—a distinct minority—"had to be paid cash and given guar-
antees of jobs" to join SWOC, while the "majority came over on sheer con-
viction." "A man like Elmer Maloy," he argued, "had to be paid cold cash
because he was not willing to take a chance."[69] Although he did not join the
union until September 13, Maloy was put on the SWOC staff as a paid organizer on September 1. Duquesne Communist Phillip Bonosky remembered
that Maloy got more than a cash inducement to join the union. The Com-

munist Party, according to Bonosky, promised Maloy that if he joined, it would support him for the local's presidency and for mayor of Duquesne.[70]

Even after Maloy and Kane began taking more pro-SWOC stances, they still did not abandon the ERP. Maloy continued as an employee representative at the mill, and both he and Kane worked for corporate recognition of the central committee. For Maloy to attack the ERP would have cost him any future support of representatives who still supported the plan but who were critical of management. Of Duquesne's fifteen employee representatives, only Maloy and Ruhe favored SWOC. Maloy thus found himself walking a tightrope. He continued his militant shop-floor ERP work and his pushing for a central committee, while he increased his criticism of management and openly defended SWOC as preferable to the ERP. In this way he still could lead the other Duquesne representatives to confront management policies, all the while hiding his SWOC membership and the full extent of his support for the union.

Carnegie-Illinois, realizing that it was losing many of its key ERP representatives, finally decided to address the central committee issue. However, the way in which the company proceeded did little to win the representatives' confidence. Ross Leffler, director of industrial relations for the Carnegie-Illinois Pittsburgh District, told Fred Bohne, the leader of the emerging anti-SWOC faction of ERP representatives, to draft a proposal for a joint management-employee council for the Pittsburgh-Youngstown district. Although anti-SWOC, Bohne believed that the ERP could develop into an "effective collective bargaining instrument."[71] The purpose of the joint council would be to negotiate company-wide issues. With management's help and no participation of pro-SWOC representatives, Bohne developed a plan for a joint council on September 25. The plan represented a large step back from a central committee: it did not include arbitration and gave the employee representatives little autonomy.[72]

The Duquesne ERP representatives, upset by the timidity of Bohne's proposal, rejected it, labeling it a "plaything for the Management." They further called for Bohne's removal as chairman of the effort to gain a central committee. The Edgar Thomson Works's ERP and even Bohne's own Youngstown ERP also rejected the new plan.[73] Concerned too, especially in the light of the Bohne proposal, that management would never approve a central committee, the Duquesne ERP unanimously passed a resolution calling for an October 18 meeting of all Pittsburgh-region representatives, regardless of corporate affiliation. The representatives hoped to form an organization that would discuss common problems and raise common industry-wide demands. Unbeknown to the Duquesne representatives, Maloy was pushing this resolution as part of a SWOC strategy to bring together broader groups of representatives in regional councils. The meeting call made no reference to SWOC, but SWOC organizers quickly began working surreptitiously to bring 125 representatives, including most of the Duquesne ERP, to Pittsburgh. SWOC secretly orchestrated the meeting, set the agenda, and planted resolutions with pro-SWOC delegates. Out of the meeting came a permanent organization, the Pittsburgh Joint Representatives' Council, and a call to hold a debate between Arthur H. Young and Philip Murray.[74]

SWOC could be pleased with the work of Maloy and the Duquesne Works ERP, but it actually gained little. Although Maloy had been trying to build SWOC, his fellow representatives instead wanted to build ERP independence. The Duquesne ERP rejected Bohne's proposal for a joint council of ERPs because it did not meet its long-standing objective to form an independent ERP bargaining committee. And hardly any Duquesne representatives intended the call for a regional meeting in October to work to SWOC's advantage. Had they known of SWOC's manipulation, they probably would have condemned the proceeding and boycotted it.

After most ERPs rejected Bohne's joint council plan, Bohne and Carnegie-Illinois officials quickly acknowledged their error. They now called a conference and invited two representatives from each plant to draft a new joint council plan. The representatives, led by Maloy, drafted a new plan that included arbitration and gave the representatives broader independence than under Bohne's plan. Management, led by Leffler and Young, rejected the draft and then forced the representatives to accept a management version of the joint council. Aware that the alternative was no collective bargaining, the representatives reluctantly accepted it in October. The proposal created the Pittsburgh District General Council (PDGC), a regional bargaining council that reproduced the structure of the plant-level ERP. Thus management could vote as a bloc, veto all employee proposals, and limit all access to arbitration.[75] In a revealing statement to employee representatives, Young told the men that he was "the father of the employee representation plan" and that he would have to approve any changes to it.[76]

When the PDGC first met in early November, the pro-SWOC forces pulled off a major coup by electing Elmer Maloy chairman of the employee side of the organization. This, after he had called Carnegie-Illinois' recognition of the council "mere lip-service" and severely criticized the new body. Management helped secure Maloy's election through a tactical blunder, by including at the last minute representatives from its sheet and tin division. The move was aimed at diluting the pro-SWOC representatives' power, but it appeared to the representatives as heavy-handed manipulation. Angered, the representatives elected the militant Maloy. Upon hearing of Maloy's victory, Ross Leffler replied in astonishment, "My God, fellows, I am disappointed! That's terrible—a vote like that. Maloy will have to go."[77] For the next three months Maloy indeed had to fight off repeated attempts by ERP representatives, acting in conjunction with Carnegie-Illinois officials, to recall him from office.[78] Despite his pro-SWOC sympathies, Maloy did not undermine efforts by the PDGC to expand workers' rights under the ERP. Minutes of PDGC meetings show that Maloy supported efforts by the group to win seniority rights, pay hikes, and better pensions and overtime pay. Maloy also defended his work as an employee representative when the other representatives sought to remove him, noting that he "had done as much as any man present to push forward their organization." Even those who wanted to remove him had to acknowledge that he was one of the best representatives at securing advances for workers on the shop floor.[79]

Ironically, neither Maloy nor SWOC inflicted the heaviest damage to the PDGC. U.S. Steel and Carnegie-Illinois did that. Management had repeatedly shown little political savvy in dealing with the ERP representatives who sought centralization. But nothing to this point compared to its handling of the wage hike issue, which showed that management still did not accept centralized bargaining with the ERP. Calls for a wage hike had begun in late 1935, when the Homestead ERP called a $5 minimum day, a demand for which SWOC later would take credit.[80] By July 1936 U.S. Steel officials found that "requests for an increase in wages were becoming insistent."[81] Both pro-SWOC and anti-SWOC representatives called for a wage hike, with both sides uniting on the $5 demand. Myron Taylor secretly appointed a committee of U.S. Steel officials, including Arthur H. Young, to study the wage issue. The committee agreed in mid-October that a wage hike, for less than the representatives' demands, was desirable. In addition, the committee sought to tie this and future raises and wage cuts to the cost of living by having the ERP representatives sign a contract with management. The agreement would protect the company against another economic decline, and it would enable management to claim that it was bargaining collectively with the ERPs.[82]

In a hollow attempt at bargaining, Carnegie-Illinois instructed its mills' general superintendents to meet with their ERPs regarding the wage question. Duquesne representatives gave management their demand of a $5 minimum per day for laborers and a $1.24 daily raise for all other workers. Management attempted to get the representatives to ask for a significantly smaller 10 percent raise. For eight hours the representatives refused management's entreaties, arguing that unless management opened its books, their demand would remain the same. The following day managers at each Carnegie-Illinois plant presented their ERPs with the contract drawn up by Young's U.S. Steel committee. Its 10 percent raise lifted the daily common labor rate to $4.20 and tied that raise and future wages to the cost of living. Thus, if the cost of living declined by a set percentage, Carnegie-Illinois would cut workers' wages.[83]

The Duquesne Works ERP representatives immediately attacked the company proposal. They unanimously passed a resolution accepting the 10 percent wage increase but rejecting the rest of the proposal. The resolution condemned the raise "as very inadequate" and stated that the representatives reserved "the right to request a further increase in the near future." The representatives argued that they had "no right under the Plan to sign any agreement or even verbally agree to accept future increases or reduction[s] in wages, and that such authority rests solely with the employees." If they did sign the agreement, the representatives would be "assuming that the present wage is adequate for the present cost of living, . . . denying everything we have stated in the past year."[84] Duquesne would be the first mill to reject the agreement, and it promptly felt the wrath of Carnegie's Benjamin Fairless.

Duquesne's general superintendent, K. H. McLaurin, met with Fairless and then called together the ERP representatives and asked that they change their resolution. "Mr. Fairless told me to convey to you," reported McLaurin, "that he feels it is most unfair and a most unreasonable resolution, as well as a black-eye to the representative body of the Carnegie-Illinois Steel Corporation." McLaurin then raised the oft-used argument that the resolution would cost the mill business:

> For the best interests of the plant and the community I believe you could modify your statement. . . . On Monday I said the Plant was in a bad position and for the interest of all the men in the Plant you should do everything possible to minimize the bad affects [sic] of this particular resolution. Our costs are bad, and for a long time the Plant has been in a bad shape, so I am going to ask you to do everything possible to protect the best interests of the plant. Gentlemen, it is up to you.

He further revealed that "customers have made inquiries as to what labor troubles we have had and whether we could handle their business safely." To this, representative Ernest Fries told McLaurin, "I would hate to think that this gang who has tried to keep down labor trouble would be the ones responsible for starting any uprising." Despite the pressure, Fries and his fellow representatives refused to reconsider their resolution.[85]

Duquesne remained among the few plants that criticized the agreement. Most ERPs either signed the agreement or passed resolutions accepting the contract in principle. Only the Edgar Thomson Works followed Duquesne by passing an identical resolution.[86] Fairless responded by playing hardball. He announced that the mills that did not accept the agreement might not get the raise. Noting that the decision would come from U.S. Steel headquarters, he told the press, "I do not know whether those failing to sign will get the increase."[87] The representatives took the threat seriously, agonizing over their obligations to the men they represented. However, most Duquesne representatives reported that workers on the shop floor instructed them to take the wage hike but to agree to nothing else. A few petitions emerged in support of the wage proposal, drawn up by management and distributed by salaried personnel, but they did not gain many signatures.[88] In the meantime SWOC sent Maloy to Washington, D.C., to gain the secretary of labor's opinion of the agreement. After Frances Perkins publicized her informal opinion that the ERP representatives had no authority to sign the agreement for their fellow workers, U.S. Steel backed down and announced that the raise would go into effect at all its mills.[89]

U.S. Steel's handling of the wage issue seriously undermined its efforts to build up its ERPs against SWOC. Representatives had urged management to grant the pay hike back in the summer, but by waiting until November the raise had become identified as SWOC's demand. In addition, the way in which management attempted to push through the wage hike left in doubt the viability of the PDGC and management's commitment to centralized bargaining. Duquesne representatives criticized management for presenting the wage proposal to the individual plants and not to the PDGC. The move not only made a mockery of the centralized bargaining structure but served to play one mill off against another. Demanded Duquesne ERP representative George Zuzo: "Why didn't the company place this matter before [the PDGC] so each plant would have been working on the same basis?"[90] Fairless's announcement that U.S. Steel would decide the fate of the plants not signing the agreement also undermined the PDGC. "If we could not get information from the President of the company [Fairless], and he had no authority to act for the corporation," asked Maloy, "how in the world could we ever deal collectively on any question, because we couldn't deal with the U.S. Steel Corporation ?"[91]

Despite management's mishandling of the wage issue, the ERP men did not abandon the plan or the PDGC. Duquesne ERP representatives had stood up to management on the wage issue but not out of any support for SWOC. Most defended their actions by stating that they were doing what they believed their fellow workers wanted. Consider Peter Simon's comments during a Duquesne ERP meeting that discussed the wage contract: "Ever since I have been employed by this Company I have strived for peace and harmony. How are we going to get it? Our constituents say do not sign it. After their placing confidence in me I think I should be gentleman enough to stick with them. We want to do what is right."[92] Maloy had led the representatives through the wage agreement controversy, but he still had to lie about the extent of his SWOC connections. When he took his trip to Washington to see the secretary of labor at SWOC's expense, he told his fellow representatives that he paid for the trip himself.[93] Management had blundered severely in its handling of the wage issue, but SWOC once again could not use the event, especially at the Duquesne Works, to win over more representatives. The ERPs were tested and once again survived.

The wage controversy demonstrated that pro-SWOC, anti-SWOC, and neutral ERP representatives could unite on a common agenda. They all held almost identical wage demands and opposed management's handling of the issue. Except for the Homestead representatives, all believed the issue should have been resolved through the PDGC. Herein lay SWOC's dilemma. It had worked within the ERPs to capture the sympathies of the representatives, but it no longer appeared to be making gains. It also risked building up the PDGC as an independent organization. Only management's blunders and continued refusal to commit itself to bargaining with the council saved the union. SWOC now needed to make a strategic shift in its ERP work, and the NLRB provided the opportunity.

SWOC and the NLRB

The industrial relations scholar Raymond Hogler argues that labor law "played at best a minor part in the SWOC organizing campaign" and had little bearing on the outcome of the steel drive. Following in the path of critical legal scholars, he seeks to downplay the importance of the Wagner Act and instead elevate the importance of rank-and-file militancy. The campaign to organize U.S. Steel took place before the Supreme Court handed down its decision on the constitutionality of the Wagner Act, and the NLRB enforced no orders against the company. Instead, Hogler notes, the work of representatives such as Elmer Maloy was what undermined the ERPs. To reach such a conclusion, however, Hogler ignores entirely the unfair labor practices case that SWOC would bring before the NLRB in November 1936.[94] Granted, U.S. Steel refused to recognize the constitutionality of the NLRB, and the board never ruled on SWOC's charges, and the board did not order any form of representation election at U.S. Steel. Still, the case had a major influence on the organizing drive. It provided SWOC with a forum for publicly attacking the ERPs, and the case formally split the ERP representatives into irreconcilable camps. The NLRB case weakened the ERP and wreaked havoc with Young's blueprints for the future of industrial relations. Even as employers challenged the constitutionality of the Wagner Act in late 1936 and early 1937, the new law furthered the growth of the labor movement.

SWOC filed its charges of unfair labor practices against Carnegie-Illinois and U.S. Steel with the National Labor Relations Board on November 27. The union accused the corporations of several Wagner Act violations, including interfering with the rights of workers to join unions, coercion of employee representatives, and dominating and manipulating their ERPs. Carnegie-Illinois officials responded by arguing that the National Labor Relations Act was unconstitutional, that the company would honor its commitment to the ERPs, and that the ERPs "have proved the best [means] devised for the settlement of all questions between employees and management."[95] SWOC could not use the NLRB to order a representation election at U.S. Steel, because it did not have the membership to win an election at most of the corporation's mills. In addition, because the NLRB was still in legal limbo, it could not enforce any order against U.S. Steel anyway. However, SWOC could file the charges and use the board's hearings to gain publicity.

The hearings brought scores of ERP representatives to Washington, D.C., for testimony from December 1936 through February 1937. Among them were Maloy and Kane. The two spent numerous days testifying about the Duquesne ERP, the central committee, and the Pittsburgh District General Council. Their testimony, reported in all the Pittsburgh newspapers, proved damning to the ERP and U.S. Steel and upheld SWOC's charges of manipulation and coercion. Maloy and Kane recalled for the NLRB the many management threats to close the mill if an ERP vote did not turn out a certain way, the free use of cars during elections and management's tracking of who did and did not vote, and the agreements for general raises and revisions to the plan that the representatives had no role in negotiating. Both men also detailed their central committee work, citing Carnegie-Illinois' refusal to bargain with the group and its granting of minor concessions once SWOC formed. Maloy also recounted the history of the PDGC, including management's attempts to remove him as chair and its bypassing of the council during the November wage controversy. Maloy and Kane, along with many other representatives from Carnegie-Illinois mills, effectively exposed the worst aspects of management's use of the ERPs as antiunion tools. If workers and even employee representatives were previously unaware of these events, the hearings and resulting publicity ensured that they now knew.[96]

The hearings also changed Maloy's and Kane's public relationship with the

ERP and SWOC. Before the NLRB case the two had taken openly pro-SWOC positions, but Kane had not yet joined the union and Maloy hid his membership. Their testimony ended all pretexts of nonunion affiliation. Kane publicly joined SWOC, and Maloy, still chairman of the PDGC and the Duquesne Works ERP, now openly stated that he wanted to destroy the representation plan, which he considered a farce. His January testimony, in which he acknowledged he was a paid organizer for SWOC, was widely covered in the trade journals and Pittsburgh-area newspapers. Anti-SWOC representatives labeled him a double agent and published a leaflet entitled "Maloy Unmasked."[97] Maloy's public attacks on the ERP finally led to his removal as chairman of the PDGC. In a meeting stacked with ERP representatives who had not been attending regularly, the PDGC recalled Maloy, resolving that "no man can work for the best interests of a cause in which he does not believe."[98]

The NLRB case served to force the ERP representatives to openly identify themselves as pro-SWOC or pro-ERP; the middle ground had evaporated. By splitting the representatives, SWOC had weakened any chance that management could build up the PDGC, because the two sides no longer could meet and discuss common agendas. But this did not mean that the movement to build a company-wide ERP bargaining committee died. Those loyal to the ERP formed the Defense Committee of Employee Representatives, which held numerous meetings and employed a publicity agent and lawyer. To counter SWOC it emphasized that the ERP collected no dues and would not call strikes.[99] Carnegie-Illinois aided the defense committee by paying for the time representatives lost from work while attending meetings and presumably by paying for the lawyer and publicity agent. Further, Benjamin Fairless acceded to the defense committee's demand that he recognize a "little Supreme Court" of employee representatives. The four-man court, which included Joseph Budday of the Duquesne Works, traveled from plant to plant and had the authority to resolve long-standing ERP requests. Fairless assured the representatives that he would "cooperate in every possible way . . . and should any unsatisfactory conditions be found to exist, immediate steps will be taken to correct them." In February the defense committee met with Carnegie-Illinois officials about another wage hike, which it argued must be granted to defeat SWOC.[100]

The split between the pro-SWOC and anti-SWOC representatives similarly extended to the Duquesne Works. Maloy had been able to lead his fellow representatives against management through November, but once his real allegiance and intentions became clear, he no longer could achieve much support in the Duquesne Works ERP. When Maloy and Kane began their testimony before the NLRB, the other representatives immediately attempted to distance themselves from the two. In addition, at least four Duquesne ERP representatives joined the defense committee. Maloy's and Kane's failure to win over the loyalties of the Duquesne ERP representatives became clear with the outcome of a January 7 vote among the Duquesne representatives. A resolution opposing Lewis and the CIO carried 8 to 4.[101]

SWOC clearly had put U.S. Steel's management in a quandary. The NLRB case dampened public and worker support for the ERPs and split the ERP representatives into two well-defined sides. The case added to U.S. Steel's troubles in two other ways. First, the public scrutiny meant that the company no longer could revise and even strengthen the ERPs. Because management was already facing NLRB charges of manipulating the plans, it could not direct the course of the ERPs as it once had. Second, U.S. Steel officials could not be certain that the NLRB hearings would have no future legal ramifications. The hearings had gone badly for U.S. Steel, and if the Supreme Court ruled the Wagner Act was constitutional, the NLRB could order the destruction of the ERPs. U.S. Steel also had to be concerned for its ERPs on the shop floor, although not because of any SWOC offensive. Instead, corporate reorganization was changing the ERP bargaining structure.

Wage Restructuring and the ERP

When Myron Taylor began his ambitious reorganization of U.S. Steel, he sought to revise an antiquated management structure that made no sense for such a huge corporation. He also sought to instill modern management techniques in place of the decentralized and haphazard systems that had evolved over the years. Of prime concern would be the installation of cost controls and standardized wage rates. Without standardized wage rates between jobs and plants, the corporation could not compare and judge the cost effectiveness of its various mills and departments. But the project would be an immense undertaking. Carnegie-Illinois' twenty-eight mills alone had more than eleven thousand different wage rates.[102]

Cost controls were not the corporation's only concern. What U.S. Steel executive Edward R. Stettinius, Jr., called the "glaring inconsistencies and inequalities in the wage rate structure" also created much worker discontent.[103] Both intraplant and interplant wage inequities had been at the core of many ERP wage requests. Bottom makers in Duquesne's 38-inch blooming mill, for example, complained that they earned as much as 20 cents less per hour than bottom makers in the 40-inch blooming mill; and soaking pit crane operators earned 83 cents an hour at one mill but 92.1 cents at another.[104] ERP representatives, who increasingly expanded their contacts with representatives at other plants, made the inevitable interplant comparisons. For workers these were issues of fairness and workplace justice as well as higher pay. To correct wage inequities, however, meant installing new methods and procedures for setting wage rates. And this meant weakening the authority of plant-level managers and changing the bargaining process that had arisen under the ERP.

To institute its wage rationalization program, Carnegie-Illinois changed its method of setting wage rates. But like the procedures for establishing wages at the plant-level, the new methods were far from objective. Whereas Duquesne managers formerly had discretion in revising rates, the new method placed final wage authority with Carnegie-Illinois' Pittsburgh district manager of operations. Similarly, the plant-level wage committee, which studied wage rate cases and conducted engineering studies for the plant superintendent, was complemented with an interplant wage committee at the district level. Recommendations from the general superintendent and the plant wage committee, which had the closest contacts with the ERP representatives, were now only one factor in establishing wage rates. Consider a wage request by mechanical millwrights in the sintering plant who worked for 68 cents per hour and sought a raise. The Duquesne Works Wage Committee recommended an hourly rate of 71.5 cents, while the district wage committee recommended 73 cents an hour to bring the job into line with area mills. Duquesne's general superintendent then sought the higher of the two rates. However, the manager of operations noted that all the company could allow at the time was 71 cents, a figure below both recommended rates.[105] This process took place repeatedly in wage request cases, with Duquesne management seeking to pay the higher rate of the two recommended by the plant wage committee and the district wage committee, and with Pittsburgh usually granting the lower of the two or an even lower rate.[106]

The erosion of plant-level decision-making authority was also revealed in a wage case covering 170 Duquesne laborers. Mostly black and foreign born, they earned 1.5 cents less per hour than the common unskilled laborer's rate. In November 1936 they filed a request to bring their rate into line with that of other unskilled laborers. Aware of the union drive, R. F. Sanner, Duquesne's personnel director, argued that to "equalize the labor rate would certainly increase the employees [sic] faith and confidence in Management, and would settle a problem which has been brought to our attention on many occasions." The general superintendent also supported the raise, writing to Pittsburgh officials that the lower rate was "a source of continual argument and disagreement" and that it was "difficult to avoid dissatisfaction under these circumstances." After two months Pittsburgh officials finally responded, noting that this was a "company wide matter," and "so, strictly speaking, your group is out of order pending answer to this."[107] Thus the new procedures weakened the power of plant managers and effectively shut the ERP out of the final bargaining stage.

A second result of the cost control and wage rationalization program entailed engineering evaluations of whole operating departments. These massive engineering studies were designed to analyze costs, establish individual job rates, and save money.[108] Again, the engineering studies stemmed in part from the workings of the ERP, which had exposed the antiquated wage structures of numerous jobs. At Duquesne the program was implemented first in the open hearth department, because Maloy had filed so many wage requests on its employees' behalf. In June 1936 Maloy and the general superintendent signed a moratorium on any new open hearth requests, pending completion of the engineering study. Wage bargaining in the department ceased, except for consultations between the engineers and the ERP representatives regarding general payment methods. The engineers completed their time studies at the end of August, but the final results were not completed until late December.[109]

Maloy criticized the results of the study. He complained that most of the final wage adjustments "are not as important as they would be made to appear, because the men have not obtained anywhere what I asked for them under the original request, and I had no say in the amount that would be granted to any of the employees under the set-up." Still, he had to agree that for many workers in the department, the new wage structure offered "substantial increases."[110] Maloy's criticisms touched on problems that employee representatives had with the new methods for determining wages. ERP representatives, accustomed to bargaining directly with management on wage issues, now found themselves with less of a role. Engineers and subsidiary managers made determinations that seemingly completely bypassed anything they might have had to say. Maloy expressed this alienation, at once wanting to take credit for the new open hearth wage structure while acknowledging he had little to do with it. Asked if this was the largest wage case he had ever tackled, he replied, "I think it is the biggest one [departmental wage increase] that has ever been made anywhere under the Carnegie Illinois Steel Company. Of course, I have nothing to do with the arranging for the amounts that are paid."[111]

Nevertheless, the ERP and Maloy did have a major influence on the open hearth study. And far from being inadequate, it addressed many of the concerns of tonnage workers. The ERP representatives, led by Maloy, had raised the numerous wage requests that set the wage study in motion. They also discussed general payment methods with engineers. In comparing the issues raised in the original ERP requests with the final results of the study, it is clear that management responded to the key demands raised by workers and the ERP representatives. The representatives had asked for minimum guaranteed rates on many tonnage jobs, higher minimum guaranteed rates on others, and a change in the time period used to calculate tonnage rates.[112] The new wage structure announced by the Duquesne Works for its open hearth department addressed many of these concerns. It added minimum guaranteed rates to straight tonnage jobs and raised all minimum guaranteed rates, so that even in the worst economic circumstances, tonnage workers would earn at least 80 percent of their normal tonnage earnings. Maloy later would take credit for this and considered it an immense accomplishment. Management did not change the determination for guaranteed rates from pay period to daily—it would, however, in other departments—but the higher minimum rates accomplished the same ends.[113]

What is perhaps more remarkable was management's responsiveness to workers' concerns about the new wage structure. Open Hearth Shop #1 accepted the new rates. However, because of stepped-up production schedules, it quickly became apparent that in Open Hearth Shop #2, the new rates represented a pay cut. Management responded immediately by reinstituting the old rates in Open Hearth Shop #2 and again studying the wage structure.[114] The open hearth study would serve as a model for other large operating departments at the Duquesne Works, including the blooming and bar mills.[115]

The engineering surveys would have a mixed effect on the ERPs. They severely weakened the type of shop-floor bargaining structure that had evolved during 1935 and early 1936. Both the surveys and the concern for regional wage structures tended to remove both ERP representatives and plant managers from the bargaining process. As the open hearth survey showed, ERP representatives still affected the new wage structures but not in the direct way to which they had become accustomed. What damaged the corporation's relationship with the ERP most was management's refusal to involve the ERP more directly in the reorganization. This mirrored management's handling of the November wage rate case and its whole relationship to the central committee movement and the PDGC. Management consistently spoke of its bargaining relationship with the ERP, but it proved continually unwilling to actually bargain. Management viewed the ERP as a distinctly junior partner, not the bargaining agent for its employees. The corporation still remained imbued with its autocratic past. Likewise, the whole wage rationalization program represented the evolutionary state of U.S. Steel policies, which combined new rational and progressive management directions with an older arbitrary management style of imposing decisions.

However, these shop-floor changes did not destroy or fatally wound the ERP, especially from the perspective of the tonnage worker. After all, the ERP process and the militant bargaining of ERP representatives had helped alert corporate officials to the inadequacies of its tonnage wage structure. Tonnage workers would directly associate the ERP with the new open hearth wage structure, which addressed many of their concerns. Although the blooming and bar mill surveys would drag into mid-1937, management responded to ERP requests and instituted daily minimum guaranteed rates in those departments even before the the engineering studies were finished. Like the open hearth workers, blooming mill tonnage workers won minimum rates guaranteed at more than 80 percent of their regular tonnage earnings.[116] For tonnage workers the ERP process still largely worked, albeit quite slowly. In addition, the quickening pace of steel production, which increased overall earnings, ameliorated many wage issues that the ERP had failed to resolve.

Tonnage workers also continued to support the ERP because SWOC did not offer a strong alternative. Much of SWOC's ERP strategy had been aimed at winning over the ERP representatives. But when the union signed up a representative, it brought only one worker into its organization. According to the SWOC organizer Meyer Bernstein, "Our maneuverings with the ERPs were more feint than anything else. Once in a while ERP men would come over to us, but they didn't necessarily bring any membership with them. . . . We got the top men of the Jones and Laughlin Aliquippa employee representation plan to come over to the union. That was all very well, but we still had to organize the employees one by one."[117] SWOC simply failed at the task of organizing tonnage workers who followed the ERP. SWOC attacked the organization they supported and appeared to have little understanding of their distinct needs. SWOC's newspaper, *Steel Labor,* rarely addressed their wage concerns and, when it did, dealt only with overall earnings. It never addressed such issues as daily minimum rates, guaranteed minimum rates, or tonnage rates, the very issues that determined overall earnings and that deeply mattered to these workers. At times the paper even confused skilled and semiskilled workers; for example, it said that hourly crane operators making 57.5 cents an hour were skilled workers.[118]

None of the contemporary SWOC memos, analyses, and summaries of the union's work with the ERPs ever addressed skill or wage structure issues.[119] Harold Ruttenberg, who codirected SWOC's ERP work, lacked a concise understanding of issues critical to skilled workers. In a memo to John Brophy, director of the CIO, that detailed steelworkers' grievances, Ruttenberg echoed the contemporary radical critique of tonnage and incentive pay systems, dismissing them as "instruments of the speed-up."[120] However, skilled and semiskilled workers did not object to these wage systems, only to problems in how the rates were determined. Under the ERP many hourly Duquesne workers actually asked to be put on tonnage pay in order to increase their earnings.

Nearly six months into the steel campaign, Ruttenberg acknowledged that SWOC did not adequately address skilled workers. In a November 1936 memo to all staff representatives, Ruttenberg noted that "certain of our field representatives have been criticized by steel workers themselves because they gave the impression in their speeches that the great bulk of steel workers are common laborers." Ruttenberg went on to explain that 24 percent of steelworkers were skilled, and that "54% of steel workers are semi-skilled or skilled workers, receiving $5.00 a day or more." Despite this recognition, the SWOC organizing strategy did not change.[121]

SWOC and the Unification of Leadership

For six months SWOC had been conducting two largely unrelated campaigns at Duquesne: one to organize the largely unskilled workforce of immigrants and blacks, and the other to win over employee representatives and then destroy the ERP. In both campaigns SWOC depended heavily on activists from the mill's two worker organizations, especially Anthony Salopek from the Fort Dukane Lodge and Elmer Maloy from the ERP. Although both were now members of SWOC, their organizing work did not intersect. That would have to change if SWOC were to build a union at Duquesne. By bringing together these two sides of the campaign, SWOC also could then take stock of its progress in overcoming the deep divisions between workers on the shop floor. At the end of 1936 management handed SWOC an issue that would help unite its two campaigns.

After eleven years in the mill, and ten years in his current job, management fired Anthony Salopek in December 1936. It was an unusual move, because U.S. Steel generally had refrained from firing union activists during the SWOC drive. For all its weaknesses federal labor policy during the New Deal era diminished the outright firing and blacklisting of steel unionists. The official reason for Salopek's dismissal was a vague "unsatisfactory services," but he immediately concluded that his organizing work lay behind it. His foreman had told him nothing was wrong with his work. A year earlier Salopek probably would have avoided the ERP; now he went straight to Elmer Maloy with his grievance. The two had entered the labor movement from opposite and opposing camps, but they both found themselves working as organizers—one paid, the other volunteer—for SWOC.

Maloy called together the other employee representatives for a special meeting to allow Salopek to explain his situation. The group decided to take the case up with management during a joint meeting, a request management failed to honor. In the meantime, management told the ERP that Salopek had been fired for talking too much on the job with Raymond Ruhe, presumably about SWOC. But Ruhe was both a member of SWOC and an ERP representative. Management had fired Salopek, in essence, for exercising his basic ERP right to speak with an employee representative. The explanation galvanized the representatives. Although most opposed Salopek's politics and his union activities, they could not agree with firing him on vague and shifting charges, especially when these may have had everything to do with his ERP rights. Maloy publicized the firing by pointedly bringing it up in his testimony before the NLRB in Washington, D.C. Stung by the publicity and faced with a determined group of employee representatives, management reinstated Salopek without explanation one week later.[122]

Salopek's efforts to regain his job through the ERP held symbolic importance. It marked the beginning of the unification of key Duquesne activists, workers who had been divided since 1933 between the Fort Dukane Lodge and the ERP. More broadly, it pointed to a conscious effort by these activists to break down the persistent skill and ethnic divisions in the workforce. Maloy's efforts to get Salopek's job back marked the start of a political alliance between two union leaders who could not have come from more different backgrounds. Salopek was Croatian, an hourly wage worker, and a Fort Dukane activist; Maloy was Irish, a tonnage worker, and an ERP representative. Salopek was a Communist and active in the ethnic fraternal orders; Maloy was a leader in the Veterans of Foreign Wars and the American Legion.

SWOC both formalized this coalition and further attempted to break down the deep divisions within the mill by appointing a mill organizing committee in early 1937 composed of both ERP and Fort Dukane activists. The dual organizing campaign—working with the ERP and the old Fort Dukane Lodge—had existed for more than six months and it was time to unite the two into one organization. SWOC appointed Maloy president; Kane secretary; Salopek financial secretary; and Ruhe treasurer.[123] Both Salopek and Ruhe had come from the Fort Dukane Lodge, and Ruhe, Maloy, and Kane had all served in the ERP. On February 20 SWOC formally granted Duquesne workers a charter, establishing SWOC Local 1256.[124] Elections for officers were held two weeks later, and the makeup of the new leadership represented a remarkable cross-section of the mill's diverse activists, bringing together blacks and whites, the native and foreign born, tonnage and hourly workers, and ERP and Fort Dukane supporters (see table 5).

Table 5. Characteristics of the First SWOC Local 1256 Officers

Name	Office	Former Organization	Job Type	Birthplace	Parents' Birthplace
Elmer Maloy	President	ERP	Tonnage	United States	United States/England
Robert Boyle	Vice president	Unknown[1]	Unknown	Unknown	Unknown
John J. Kane	Secretary	ERP	Skilled trade	Scotland	Scotland
Anthony Salopek	Financial secretary	Fort Dukane	Hourly	United States	Croatia
Raymond Ruhe	Treasurer	ERP/Fort Dukane	Tonnage	United States	United States
Fletcher Williamson	Guide	Fort Dukane	Hourly	United States (Black)	United States (Black)
Henry Cox	Guard	Fort Dukane	Hourly	United States (Black)	United States (Black)
Mike Rak	Guard	Fort Dukane	Unknown	Russia	Russia
Rex Meighan	Trustee	ERP	Unknown	Unknown	Unknown
[?] Clarke	Trustee	Unknown[1]	Unknown	Unknown	Unknown
[?] Watson	Trustee	Unknown[1]	Unknown	Unknown	Unknown

Source: Inactive voter registration cards, Allegheny County, Pennsylvania, Voter Registration Records, AIS; Duquesne Works payroll ledgers, 1933–37, USSC; U.S. Census, *Fourteenth Census of the United States: 1920, Manuscript Schedules,* vol. 10, Pennsylvania, Allegheny County, reel 1511; Records of the War Department, Office of the Provost Marshall General, Selective Service System, World War I Draft Registration Cards, State of Pennsylvania, County of Allegheny, Local Board #8, Microfilm copy, reel 14, Hillman Library, University of Pittsburgh; *Duquesne Times,* various issues, 1933–59; *U.S. Steel News,* various issues, 1936–60; Obsolete Change of Employment and Rate Cards, Box 4, USSC; DWERP, minutes of meeting, 27 June 1933, NSLRB; Duquesne Works, "Report of Positions Excluded from Representation by the Union Under the Terms of the September 1, 1942 Agreement," 7 Oct. 1942, Box 30, File: Positions Excluded from Union Membership, USSC; Steel Workers Organizing Committee Grievance 27-39-U material, Box 26, USSC; Exhibit 7, Box 21, Grievance File 46-20, USSC; Duquesne Works, "Confidential," booklet, 31 Aug. 1949, Box 28, File S-6(a), USSC.

1. These men were not ERP representatives, but whether they belonged to the Fort Dukane Lodge is unknown.

Bringing together the union activists in one organization was one thing, but unifying the ranks was quite another. Local 1256 had approximately thirteen hundred members in a workforce of six thousand, and only a handful paid dues. In most respects the membership mirrored the old Fort Dukane Lodge. Local 1256 again drew large numbers of black workers, in large part because of the past organizing efforts of the Fort Dukane Lodge and the support SWOC received from black union activists. The core of the union's membership again came from the low-skilled workforce that had migrated from southern and eastern Europe, as well as their sons.[125]

Despite their different ethnic and racial backgrounds, immigrants, their sons, and blacks joined the union for the same reasons: they were low-skilled hourly workers. In SWOC they saw the potential for higher wages and "better benefits." Without a union Michael Kerekac was "working hard and not getting paid enough." They also saw the union as an opportunity to achieve workplace justice. Frank Takach, a Hungarian American, found that the union "got the Hunkies doing all the jobs" and not just low-skilled work. And workplace justice was largely secured with seniority, a common reason many workers stated for becoming SWOC supporters. Perhaps more than anything, SWOC meant security. Years later an interviewer asked Wilbur Collins, a black janitor, why he joined the union. "Well," Collins replied, "for protection." "If anything happened," Homer Brown noted, "you would have the union for you." Remembering the arbitrary authority exercised by foremen in years past, Kerekac found that, with the union, "I was more safe on the job."[126]

Nevertheless, the past still haunted the union. As with the Great Steel Strike of 1919 and the rank-and-file movement of 1933–35, tonnage workers and skilled tradesmen remained outside the union. This meant that the ethnic division remained, with the native and foreign born of northern and western Europe heritage—Germans, Scots, Irish, and English—choosing the nonunion path. The organization that addressed their grievances—the employee representation plan—still functioned, and two-thirds of its representatives continued to support the plan and spurn the union. Despite a well-orchestrated attack by SWOC, the ERP was the only organization with a shop-floor presence and bargaining power at the mill. At the district level the defense committee and the "little Supreme Court" kept alive the demand for collective bargaining. Although it was weakened by the SWOC campaign, the ERP still could evolve into an independent union.

After nine months of organizing in Duquesne, the union still had not met its goals. SWOC had serious weaknesses. The conditions at Duquesne were not unique; other Carnegie-Illinois mills in the Pittsburgh region experienced similar problems. The Edgar Thomson local, organized in February, listed only 783 members. It too could not win the support of the skilled workforce. The giant Homestead Works, despite SWOC's flying squadron efforts to sign up members at the gate and its highly exaggerated claims of four thousand members at the mill, remained largely unorganized. It too failed to win over the skilled. A local would not be established at the mill until late March, about the time SWOC finally formed one at the Clairton Works.[127] Both a national steel strike and an NLRB election were beyond SWOC's reach. "There is no question that we could not have filed a petition through the National Labor Relations Board or any other kind of machinery asking for an election," claimed Lee Pressman, SWOC's general counsel. "We could not have won an election for collective bargaining on the basis of our own membership or the results of the organizing campaign to date."[128] At the end of February 1937 conditions for steel unionism at Carnegie-Illinois were not favorable.

Recognition

"Then the miracle," is how David McDonald described U.S. Steel's decision to recognize SWOC.[129] During January and February 1937 John L. Lewis had been meeting secretly with Myron Taylor. By the end of February the two had reached an accord that formed the basis for a collective bargaining agreement. Only then did Lewis inform Philip Murray, a day before the rest of the country began to learn the news. On March 2 Murray and Benjamin Fairless signed a preliminary agreement that recognized SWOC as the bargaining agent for its members at Carnegie-Illinois. The company also agreed to the $5 day and overtime after eight hours. Approximately two weeks later the two sides signed a final agreement that established procedures for dealing with such issues as grievances, layoffs, promotions, and vacations.[130] U.S. Steel's decision to recognize SWOC could not have come at a more advantageous time. SWOC had not signed a majority of workers in any of the large Pittsburgh-area mills. And it still faced a concerted opposition on the shop floor from the company's ERPs. Perhaps not a miracle but a fortuitous event indeed.

Taylor's decision to change the course of steel history stunned the country; however, it was a decision that he had been coming to for many months. In the summer of 1936, while traveling in Italy, he reconsidered U.S. Steel's labor policies in light of the rise of the CIO and SWOC. Taylor devised a new corporate labor policy based on this reassessment:

> The Company recognizes the right of its employees to bargain collectively through representatives freely chosen by them without dictation, coercion or intimidation in any form or from any source. It will negotiate and contract with the representatives of any group of its employees so chosen and with any or-

ganization as the representatives of its members subject to the recognition of the principle that the right to work is not dependent on membership or non-membership in any organization and subject to the right of every employee freely to bargain in such manner and through such representatives, if any, as he chooses.[131]

The historians Melvyn Dubofsky and Warren Van Tine have argued that Taylor "never altered company labor policy in principle" and that the new labor policy amounted to the open-shop policy of Elbert Gary.[132] But this ignores both the evolution of U.S. Steel's labor policy early in the New Deal and the important shift that marked Taylor's new formula. Under Gary's open-shop policy the company theoretically allowed workers to belong to unions, but it refused to recognize or bargain with any union. The Amalgamated's rank-and-file movement and the New Deal already had forced a revision of that policy. Duquesne managers met with Fort Dukane Lodge members, and the union's case before National Steel Labor Relations Board prodded U.S. Steel into agreeing to bargain with the Amalgamated.

Taylor's new policy built upon that shift in the corporation's labor policy, stated during the December 1935 White House summit of Roosevelt, Perkins, U.S. Steel, and the Amalgamated when U.S. Steel offered to bargain with the Amalgamated for its members only and to recognize the NSLRB in discrimination cases, if the Amalgamated agreed not to seek representation elections. Roosevelt's efforts to mediate the dispute broke down over several points, in particular U.S. Steel's refusal to recognize the Amalgamated as the sole bargaining agent and its refusal to sign a collective bargaining agreement. Under his new policy Taylor continued to refuse to cede sole bargaining rights to the union. However, he made a huge concession by agreeing to sign a contract. Had Taylor not made this concession, Lewis and Murray could not have come to an agreement with Taylor and U.S. Steel. Given SWOC's weaknesses at most Carnegie-Illinois mills, the union needed contractual recognition. The union could use the symbolism of contractual recognition to build its membership, and a contract would give the union authority on the shop floor that it could not otherwise assert.

Many factors led Taylor both to develop his new labor policy and to put it into practice. During the summer of 1936 U.S. Steel finally had begun to recover from the depression. By early 1937 profits and production levels had reached predepression levels. U.S. Steel also stood to increase its orders through an export agreement with Great Britain. With the economic tide turning Taylor did not want a disruption in production. To many the General Motors sit-down strike in January and February, combined with SWOC's continued commitment to organize the steel industry, made a steel strike appear inevitable. Taylor believed, correctly, that most U.S. Steel workers did not belong to the union. But as the auto strike demonstrated, a militant minority could disrupt production and bring a corporation to the bargaining table. The new political environment also favored workers. Roosevelt had remained aloof from the auto strike, and a pro–New Deal governor in Michigan had refused to side with General Motors. In Pennsylvania the New Deal governor George H. Earle, Jr., appeared to harbor the same convictions. Unlike his fellow steel managers, Taylor was not an opponent of the New Deal, and he did not relish the thought of a confrontation with Roosevelt. In addition, public sympathy for the corporation was low because of the damning revelations that continued to emanate from the National Labor Relations Board and the La Follette Committee hearings.[133]

ERPs added to Taylor's considerations. Many historians have assumed that by early 1937 the ERPs were in a state of near collapse, toppled by the weight of their own contradictions and SWOC's campaign. Frederick Harbison notes that the ERP was "most shaky" by February and recounts a Carnegie-Illinois official's telling him that it "was on its way out."[134] Robert R. R. Brooks similarly notes that by then the ERP "was obviously cracking up."[135] But the ERP was far from dead. The ERP defense committee and the little Supreme Court demonstrated that many ERP representatives still chose to bargain with Carnegie-Illinois through the ERP structure. At Duquesne two-thirds of the representatives remained loyal to the plan, and tonnage workers continued to use it on the shop floor. Carnegie-Illinois also could count on support for the ERPs from at least two other large mills in the region—Homestead and Youngstown—along with scores of its smaller mills. SWOC had disrupted and weakened U.S. Steel's ERPs, but it did not capture or destroy them.[136]

Despite the ERPs' vitality, corporate managers had lost faith in them.[137] After all, a function of the ERPs was to form individual "protective fences" against unionism, but SWOC had penetrated the barrier. Corporate reorganization also made plant-level bargaining, which formed the basis for employee representation, untenable. If employee representation still was to fend off SWOC, it needed to be revised and strengthened. U.S. Steel could have built up its ERPs in 1936 by allowing them greater centralized bargaining power, but it proved unwilling to do this, fearful of the independence of ERP representatives. By early 1937 numerous factors were working against giving the ERPs greater power. First, managers could not revise the plan during the highly publicized NLRB hearings without once again raising the specter of corporate manipulation. Second, revisions would be met with a barrage of criticism from SWOC, leaving little maneuvering room for the ERP representatives and management. Third, no one agreed about how to change employee representation. U.S. Steel commissioned the Industrial Relations

Counselors (IRC) in early 1936 to study the company's labor relations and the ERPs. In mid-November the IRC issued its report, which included extensive proposals for overhauling the ERPs. The report then went to the corporation's engineering consultants, Ford, Bacon, and Davis, for evaluation. Ford, Bacon, and Davis issued a critique of the report, objecting to many of the IRC's proposals. In addition, Ford, Bacon, and Davis proposed its own set of revisions for the ERPs.[138]

Taylor also had to consider the NLRB case against the company and its ERPs. The board had exposed the corporation's manipulation and coercion of representatives under the plan. If the Supreme Court declared the Wagner Act constitutional, U.S. Steel faced an NLRB order. Consider the analysis of Nathan Miller, U.S. Steel's general counsel, less than one year after the company signed the collective bargaining agreement:

> If we had gone to a conclusion [of the NLRB case] with the Wagner Act sustained, we would have had an order of the Board so drastic that without the slightest doubt we would have the closed shop in the steel industry today and the C.I.O. would most certainly have been recognized as the exclusive bargaining agent—if nothing happened. But something did happen. We did not get any order, and it is due to the fact that something happened that we didn't: Mr. Taylor concluded the famous "Taylor-Lewis agreement."[139]

Taylor's decision thus made legal, economic, and political sense. It also recognized that however successful the ERPs had been, they no longer could serve as the centerpiece of U.S. Steel's labor policies. Despite all his doubts about whether the ERPs could stand up to SWOC, Taylor did not abandon them. The contract with SWOC allowed the union to bargain only for its own members, not all steelworkers. The corporation then made clear that it also would continue to bargain with its ERPs.[140] Indeed, when Taylor asked subsidiary officers whether they would recognize and bargain with SWOC, he explicitly stated that it would be on terms "in accord with the practice established with the employee representative groups."[141] Taylor thus ensured a smoother corporate transition into the union era by building on U.S. Steel's industrial relations practices with its ERPs. By continuing to recognize the ERPs, he also satisfied the shop-floor needs of key segments of the workforce and limited SWOC's authority by bargaining with a competing organization.

Conclusion

When U.S. Steel and SWOC signed their collective bargaining agreement, the long nonunion era came to an end for workers in Duquesne. Unlike the efforts of skilled workers in 1889 and 1901, and unskilled workers in 1919 and

1934–35, SWOC finally had created a union leadership based on a cross-section of the mill's workforce. By bringing together activists from the Fort Dukane Lodge and the ERP—leaders of the unskilled and skilled, hourly and tonnage, black and white, native and foreign born—SWOC had accomplished what no other union movement had done. SWOC did it by spending huge sums of money, forming a highly centralized national leadership structure, mobilizing scores of organizers, and carefully using the New Deal. This is what it took to bring a union to Duquesne. Yet SWOC was still unable to sign up a majority of the workforce or win a majority of the ERP activists. The nonunion era had ended, but whether it would become anything more than a painful memory in steelworkers' lives remained to be seen.

6. Consolidating the Union, 1937–41

STEELWORKERS OPENED THE UNION ERA in a festive mood. A few days after the signing of the recognition agreement on March 2, Local 1256 held an auto parade through the streets of Duquesne. The next night the union organized a mass meeting at the Croatian Hall. More than eight hundred workers jammed into the building to hear speeches by Elmer Maloy, John Kane, Anthony Salopek, and others. During the jubilant celebration steelworkers asserted that Duquesne soon would be a "100% union town."[1] According to records of the Steel Workers Organizing Committee (SWOC), that prediction appeared to have been no exaggeration. The local began with 1,300 members in February and claimed 3,687 by August. Unlike Fort Dukane, Local 1256 would not be alone in its ascendancy. SWOC's McKeesport District membership quadrupled in four months, from 3,100 in February to more than 13,300 in June. Nationwide, SWOC organized 300,000 workers in six hundred locals by May 1.[2]

Amid the euphoric celebration several troubling issues remained. Duquesne's membership had risen, but skilled tonnage workers largely remained outside the union. The employee representation plan (ERP) continued to function, and workers also could bargain individually with management. In addition, raids by the rival American Federation of Labor (AFL) were a possibility. SWOC claimed a majority of the workforce by May, but because many did not pay dues, the majority was only on paper. Its membership had been built up during an economic upsurge and was untested by strike. How ephemeral were these numbers? If the economy faltered once again, how would the membership react? The union also had no political power. Mayor James Crawford and the Republican city council still could restrict and harass the new union. SWOC itself had yet to become established in the industry. It signed 114 contracts by May, but except for U.S. Steel and Wheeling Steel, it had no agreements with other large companies.[3]

If the union were to become rooted at the Duquesne Works, it had to meet the needs of both hourly and tonnage workers. SWOC and Local 1256 already had shown their ability to unite the warring leaderships of the Fort Dukane Lodge and the ERP but not yet their constituencies. The Fort Dukane Lodge had done little for tonnage workers. Instead, it organized unskilled and semi-skilled hourly workers, whose needs centered on raising the laboring rate, increasing work hours, and breaking down the arbitrary authority of the foreman. It had built a highly politicized mass movement—with almost no shop-floor presence—of the mill's poorest workers. The ERP, in contrast, dominated bargaining on the shop floor but addressed primarily the needs of skilled trades and tonnage workers. Although supported by these higher-paid workers, the ERP had never mobilized them as the Fort Dukane Lodge had done with its membership.

SWOC Local 1256 spent the years from 1937 to 1941 building a union upon the foundations of the ERP and the Fort Dukane Lodge. From the ERP it took much of its shop-floor bargaining structure. It continued to provide for tonnage workers' wage needs, but it expanded its shop-floor protection to more effectively include issues critical to low-skilled hourly workers. Conversely, the local continued the political emphasis of the Fort Dukane Lodge, forcing skilled workers to accept unionism as something more than a shop-floor bargaining mechanism. Although SWOC had been the top-down creation of John L. Lewis and Philip Murray, at the local level steel unionism would be the amalgamation of rank-and-file unionism and the ERP.

Hard Times and a Crisis in Unionism

In the older historiography of the Committee for Industrial Organization (CIO), U.S. Steel's contract signing with SWOC serves as a literary end point. Discussion of U.S. Steel ceases and the narrative moves on to the union's drive to organize the rest of the larger steelmakers, known as Little Steel. Missing is the history of the tenuous nature of unionism at U.S. Steel plants.[4] After the March contract signing, SWOC continued its organizing and union-building work at U.S. Steel. Nevertheless, SWOC's success was not a foregone conclusion. The key Homestead and Clairton Works did not even have a functioning local until late March. At Duquesne economic and political conditions weakened the union, while U.S. Steel's decision to continue to recognize its ERPs undermined the union's shop-floor authority. In many respects the union found itself weaker by December 1937 than it had been when U.S. Steel granted recognition in March.

When he announced the contract agreement with SWOC, Carnegie president Benjamin Fairless noted that the status of the ERPs remained unchanged: "[The ERP] will continue as the spokesman for those of the employees who prefer that method of collective bargaining which has proven so mutually satisfactory throughout its experience."[5] Philip Murray, in turn, declared that the agreement with Carnegie Steel marked "the end of employee-representative plans in the steel industry."[6] But during the next seven weeks U.S. Steel continually made it clear that it had not abandoned its ERPs. At the plant level the corporation continued the ERP request process and accorded the ERP equal status with SWOC in all collective bargaining issues. Unionists would claim the ERP received preferential treatment.[7] Fairless also encouraged centralization of the ERPs. He met numerous times with the little Supreme Court of employee representatives and advised the group to build itself up. The little Supreme Court originally had sought to mediate only long-standing ERP requests, but Fairless now agreed to recognize the group as the central bargaining agent for employees supporting the ERP. The ERP representatives immediately raised several wage and hours demands with Fairless. After signing the preliminary March 2 agreement with SWOC, Fairless entered negotiations with the little Supreme Court. The result was a 10-cent per hour raise for all semiskilled and skilled employees and a promise not to hire new workers, thereby giving the present workforce more hours. By the time SWOC and Carnegie Steel completed their March 17 agreement, the little Supreme Court already had won many of the demands on which SWOC settled. Fairless probably used this maneuver to gain bargaining leverage over SWOC, but it still marked a coup for the ERP.[8]

The ERP representatives not only upstaged SWOC at the bargaining table but made a concerted attempt to organize themselves into a rival independent union. During negotiations with Benjamin Fairless the little Supreme Court sent a telegram to AFL president William Green seeking his advice on what direction to take the ERPs. Green declined to work with the group, citing the AFL's long-standing opposition to company unions. He then held open the possibility of meeting with the ERP representatives if they became independent. The representatives telegraphed John Frey, an AFL vice president and president of the federation's Metal Trades Department, for help. Frey met with the representatives in Pittsburgh, but his plan for dividing steel plants into craft jurisdictions met with immediate disapproval from the little Supreme Court. The structural form of the ERP always had been industrial, even though it appealed primarily to higher-skilled and craft workers. That is, the ERP theoretically represented all the workers at a steel mill, not just one segment of the workforce. By the end of March the little Supreme Court had established plans for launching an independent union, the American Union of Steel Workers. Dues would be fixed at 25 cents per month, much lower than SWOC's $1, and the ERP representatives would serve as organizers. In Carnegie-Illinois' Chicago District a similar independent union drive by employee representatives had begun as the Steel Independent Labor Organization.[9]

The ERPs continued to function at the plant level. Meanwhile, SWOC had some success in sabotaging Duquesne's ERP. During the SWOC organizing drive—from June 1936 though February 1937—SWOC supporters never attempted to overload the ERP process with requests. Even when management finalized the Open Hearth Shop #1 survey in December 1936, introduced new rates, and then reintroduced the old rates in Open Hearth Shop #2, SWOC appealed few individual rates. The contract with Carnegie-Illinois, coupled with the simultaneous announcement of a new rate structure in the blooming mill in March 1937, changed that strategy. Raymond Ruhe, who was both an ERP representative and an officer in SWOC Local 1256, filed a flurry of appeals aimed at challenging the new rates and discrediting the ERP. The strategy forced management to deny request after request.[10] A week after filing the appeals, SWOC members abruptly resigned from the ERP on order from the national union. The resignations left the ERP short staffed just as SWOC had stirred up turmoil.[11]

Still, SWOC again succeeded only in disrupting the ERP without destroying it. The appeals did discredit the ERP and the company to an extent, as management imperiously refused to reconsider or bargain over the new rates. But the majority of the appeals—twelve of sixteen—were filed by hourly unskilled and semiskilled workers, those workers who traditionally had been hostile to the ERP. Only two tonnage workers filed appeals. Considering that the company had reviewed and/or revised the rates of nearly one thousand workers, sixteen appeals is a small number.[12] The resignation of the SWOC representatives similarly demonstrated SWOC's limited appeal. Only five of the fifteen employee representatives resigned. Districtwide, the little Supreme Court could claim that only twenty-four of the nearly two hundred representatives had heeded the union call to quit.[13]

The U.S. Supreme Court and Carnegie-Illinois, not SWOC, finally destroyed the Duquesne Works ERP. In its decision in *NLRB v. Jones & Laughlin* (1937) the Supreme Court in April upheld the constitutionality of the Wagner Act, which made company dominance and support of employee representation plans illegal. Carnegie-Illinois immediately responded by entering into an agreement with the NLRB, whereby the company would discontinue financial support of its ERPs, deny them the use of company property for meetings, and end all recognition of ERP representatives as collective bargaining agents. By quickly signing this agreement, one that appeared to go further than required by the Wagner Act, the company revealed its eagerness to end the NLRB suit that SWOC had brought against it in 1936. Now that the Wagner Act had been found constitutional, the company had every right to fear a negative decision from the NLRB. The agreement with the NLRB led to the dismissal of the suit, thus ending any threat of an NLRB directive that might have helped SWOC achieve sole bargaining rights for all employees. By choosing to end recognition, the company also doomed the independent union movement of employee representatives. SWOC now faced no organized shop-floor competition.[14]

Nevertheless, it did not follow that Local 1256 now stood in a position of strength on the shop floor. SWOC had yet to win over tonnage workers and skilled tradesmen, the traditional supporters of the ERP. SWOC also bargained for its members only, which left open the possibility of AFL raids and, more important, allowed individual workers to bargain with the company without the union. Through at least 1942 nonunion workers filed independent grievances with the company, without SWOC representation. This allowed for a continued grievance procedure for nonunionists, including tonnage workers, who could bypass SWOC in their efforts to improve wage and tonnage rates.[15]

Membership and dues collection figures revealed additional union weaknesses. Duquesne, like other Carnegie-Illinois mills, experienced an initial membership surge accompanied by high dues collections after the contract signing. By the end of the summer of 1937, however, that enthusiasm had worn off. Although SWOC once counted the Duquesne local's membership at more than three thousand, by early fall it had only about one thousand members, mostly low-skilled immigrants and blacks. Dues and initiation payments similarly declined. From April to August monthly union contributions dropped from $2,000 to $1,000. This decline occurred during a peak production period. Steel output and employment levels were the highest since 1929. In the Pittsburgh district steel plants operated, on average, at more than 80 percent of capacity from March through July, reaching 95 percent in the first week in August.[16]

The growing crisis at Duquesne extended to the rest of the union. By the end of the summer SWOC had yet to organize even half of U.S. Steel's employees. The failure to expand the membership, coupled with the 50 percent drop in dues paying, left the union in a financial crisis that necessitated the continued borrowing of money to meet expenses.[17] Moreover, the union failed in its bid to organize the so-called Little Steel companies. SWOC did win a contract with Jones & Laughlin but not the other large steel firms. SWOC called a strike against Republic, Youngstown, and Inland in May 1937 and Bethlehem in June. This Little Steel strike, which resulted in the massacre of the steelworkers by police in Chicago, ended in July with no contract at any of the companies.[18] Industry analysts took stock of SWOC's weaknesses. The *Daily Metal Trade Review* editorialized that there was "considerable basis for believing" that SWOC had a smaller membership in U.S. Steel by the summer than it had in March.[19]

Local 1256's tenuous hold on the shop floor and small membership was matched by the union's lack of political power in the community. Mayor Crawford still wielded political control of Duquesne. Prominent Republicans, many of whom held management positions in the mill, continued to dominate the city council and school board.[20] This posed a continued threat for the union, which faced the same kind of harassment that the Fort Dukane Lodge had suffered. Duquesne police arrested Louis Capone, a SWOC organizer signing up new members, for soliciting money without a permit. However, SWOC did not charge initiation or membership dues at that time. A few days later the charges were dropped without explanation. The union also experienced difficulty in renting buildings for meetings and found itself beholden to Crawford and the city in even minor matters, such as permission to hand out SWOC's newspaper, *Steel Labor*, at the plant gates.[21]

Yet the worst days for SWOC and Local 1256 were still ahead. The deep economic downturn of 1937–38, dubbed the "Roosevelt recession," hit the steel industry hard in late 1937 and lasted well into 1939. Between September and December the industry suffered its sharpest production decline in history. The Pittsburgh district, which had been working at more than 90 percent of capacity in August, bottomed out at 17 percent in mid-December. Production remained below 30 percent of capacity through much of 1938, reverting nearly to 1931–34 levels. Production in the Pittsburgh district would not reach the level of 80 percent of capacity again until September 1939. U.S. Steel, which had begun turning a profit in 1935 after three years of deficits, once again lost money in 1938 and suspended common stock dividends.[22]

The recession wreaked havoc at Duquesne, recreating the economic conditions of the early depression years. The open hearth department literally ground to a halt for two years. From late 1937 through most of 1938 the mill operated only about four of its thirty-two furnaces. Not until September 1939 would management finally light half the furnaces. The blast-furnace department faced a similar fate. Between 1937 and 1939 most of the six furnaces remained unlit, and the sintering plant was shut down for two years.[23]

Steelworkers once again faced the painful conditions of 1931–34. Most workers found their hours drastically cut or faced a lengthy layoff. Again, low-skilled hourly workers were the hardest hit. In the city of Duquesne, unemployed laborers outnumbered both unemployed semiskilled and skilled workers 3 to 1. Likewise, partially employed laborers outnumbered the partially employed semiskilled and skilled by 2 to 1. John Schorr, who had twenty-one years' seniority at the mill, worked at an hourly job as a stocker-bin lever and door operator in the open hearth. Through the first eight months of 1937 he averaged twenty days of employment per month. For two years, beginning in September 1937, he averaged only seven workdays a month. Still, he found work. Andy Chervenak, the chipper who worked 111 straight days in 1930 but received only two days of work per week in 1931–32, now found himself unemployed. He and one thousand other Duquesne workers were laid off in 1937, and two years later they still did not have work.[24]

The poor economic conditions compounded the union's problems. The local's membership centered on low-skilled immigrant and black workers, who faced the shortest work hours and greatest number of layoffs. SWOC did not require unemployed workers to pay the monthly dues of $1 and dues payments dropped sharply. By the beginning of 1938 dues payments dipped below $300 per month. In May 1938 the union brought in less than $100, and through most of 1939 dues payments stayed below $1,000 per month. But dues payments illustrated only one aspect of the situation. Enthusiasm for the union also waned. When the local held elections in June 1938, traditionally the largest membership meeting of the year, only fifty-four members voted.[25]

Large U.S. Steel locals appeared headed the way of the old rank-and-file lodges, which had withered in 1934–35. SWOC estimated that in December 1937, even before the full effects of the economic downturn had been registered, 28 percent of steelworkers recently had been laid off, while another 57 percent worked only part time. Throughout U.S. Steel the poor economic conditions translated into a shrinking union membership. Carnegie-Illinois' McDonald Works, which had twenty-nine hundred employees, had only fifty dues-paying members by late 1937, and at its larger sister plant, the Ohio Works, only thirty-eight of fifty-six hundred workers paid dues. Membership at the Homestead Works dropped to three hundred and the local needed SWOC to pay its office bills. Many of the big locals, remarked the steel union chronicler Frederick Harbison, had "dwindled away" into "skeleton groups of officers and ardent union men."[26]

The Union and Tonnage Bargaining

Local 1256's survival and success depended mostly on how well it met the shop-floor needs of the mill's workforce. The grievance process—how effectively it worked and whether it represented all workers—became a key determinant of the union's future. But the shop-floor bargaining structure did not have to be created anew; instead, it built upon and borrowed from the old ERP structure. This worked to the union's advantage in its quest to win over skilled tonnage workers. Their concerns still revolved around tonnage rates and issues, which the ERP had improved. The union soon learned, however, that defending the economic interests of the skilled tonnage workers at times meant sacrificing the interests of other workers.

Although SWOC had criticized the ERP during its organizing campaign, it incorporated many ERP practices and policies in union contract provisions and grievance procedures. The national union contract codified many of the labor policies the company instituted during the ERP era. U.S. Steel's vacation and pension plans remained the same, as did its handling of health and safety issues. Seniority remained a local issue to be decided at the plant level. The guidelines for promotion, demotion, and layoff spelled out in the union contract simply reproduced company policies enunciated in 1936 and agreed upon by various ERP bodies.[27] When Taylor had assured U.S. Steel's subsidiary presidents that the corporation's recognition of SWOC would mark a continuation of its labor policies during the ERP years, he was true to his word.

The grievance procedure used by SWOC at each of the U.S. Steel mills was as much the ERP procedure as anything else. The new SWOC grievance procedure mirrored the request stages of the ERP but added one critical improvement. Binding arbitration, a long-standing demand of ERP militants, now capped the procedure. However, Carnegie-Illinois effectively stalled the arbitration process by refusing to agree to various arbitrators. For three years no grievances went to arbitration, thus marking no immediate improvement over the ERP.[28] In numerous other ways SWOC built upon the ERP's shop-floor bargaining process. The new grievance forms, for example, combined various CIO union forms with the ERP forms. When SWOC formed its grievance boundaries in the Duquesne and Clairton mills, it simply reproduced the old ERP boundaries. Yet departments of more than one thousand workers that formerly had three representatives under the ERP now had only one grievanceman. By reducing the number of representatives, or grievancemen, from fifteen to six, the density of representation actually declined under SWOC. The reduction reflected both management's desire to limit representation and the union's ability to compensate only a small number of griev-ancemen for their lost work hours.[29]

The movement of former employee representatives into union grievance positions marked the greatest continuity between the ERP and SWOC shop-floor bargaining. It happened not just at Duquesne but at many U.S. Steel mills. Elmer Maloy, who had built his reputation as a tenacious and skillful ERP bargainer, ended his mill career as a stripper crane operator and became SWOC's national grievance officer. Five of Duquesne's first six union griev-ancemen had been employee representatives, and when elections were held for new officers in June 1937, three of the six grievancemen had ERP back-grounds. The former ERP men also dominated the local's presidency. Ma-loy, John Kane, and Ernest Fries, all former ERP chairmen, held the union's top position for its first seven years. Continuing a pattern set early in 1937, however, they would be joined in grievance work and in the local's offices by former Fort Dukane activists.[30]

The first grievance committee meetings with management illustrated the continuity of shop-floor representation between the ERP and SWOC. The union and management men all knew each other well. John Kane, now the maintenance department grievanceman, had been meeting with these same management personnel about shop-floor issues for four years. These early grievance meetings had an air of informality, often focusing on how each side would proceed on various types of cases. Consider the following exchange between Maloy; K. H. McLaurin, the plant superintendent; and R. F. Sanner, the superintendent of personnel, on the posting of tonnage rates, a demand first won under the ERP:

> Elmer Maloy: There used to be a schedule of rates posted in the Open Hearth on what the tonnage men made per hour. Now we do not have this and no one knows what they made.
> K. H. McLaurin: We always posted the tonnage rates.
> R. F. Sanner: I was talking to [ERP representative] Dynoske and he tells me the men objected to others knowing what they made, particularly when earn-ings are high as at present.
> Maloy: Would it not be possible to put up the tonnage rate and also the aver-age hourly rate?
> McLaurin: We have no objection to posting these rates. Do you feel that the majority of the men like to see everyone's earnings posted?
> Maloy: Frankly they would, as none of the men objected who are working around me, as I have heard no complaints.[31]

The continuity from the ERP to SWOC would seem to portend the con-tinued use of the shop-floor bargaining process by tonnage workers seeking greater earnings. Yet during the early SWOC years tonnage wage cases were rare. In 1937–38 the union defended only one tonnage grievance. This would be only one of two grievances filed by tonnage workers in the open hearth department between 1937 and 1941. They filed few wage rate grievances, because they did not initially support the union. Instead, most of the union's early grievances centered on work schedules, seniority, and rehiring laid-off workers, issues central to low-skilled workers. But the paucity of wage rate grievances also reflected the ERP's past success. It had tackled most of the worst wage rate disparities and had helped install new wage scales in the open hearth and blooming mills.

The recession also wreaked havoc with the grievance process. The small number of union grievances filed in 1937—fifteen—dropped to only three during all of 1938, reflecting the near shutdown of mill operations. That same year the union's grievance meetings with management declined from monthly to bimonthly, because neither side had enough issues to raise. The Homestead Works experienced a similar decline in the exercise of its grievance procedure.[32] Beginning in 1939, however, Duquesne and other SWOC locals consciously attempted to rebuild their locals through the militant handling of grievances.[33] But how could they rebuild if the higher-skilled tonnage workers continued to avoid the union and its grievance process? Management provided the answer when it introduced new wage scales in three bar mills in 1939. Now tonnage workers looked to the union for their defense.

The revision of the bar mill wage scales had begun under the ERP, after tonnage men made numerous individual and group wage requests. Management then developed new departmental wage scales that it believed ended various wage inequities. The new wage plans also converted many straight tonnage positions into hourly-plus-tonnage positions, provided higher guaranteed minimum rates, and moved more hourly workers to tonnage earnings. All were policies the company had begun under the ERP and sought to continue as part of its wage rationalization and cost control efforts. Under the ERP, management had unilaterally instituted new wage scales in the open hearth and blooming mill departments. Under SWOC, however, the two sides agreed to put the new bar mill wage plans into effect for three months, at which point each side had the right to accept the plan as a whole or go back to the old wage scale.

The new wage plans went into effect separately in the three bar mills during 1939. At the end of the three-month trial workers in one mill had lost a combined $1,576 in wages compared to what their old wage plan would have paid. Management studied the issue and realized that it had failed to take into account how equipment limited the production of bars of certain sizes. This was a problem that plagued all new wage scales and tonnage programs. Rates established using one year's production schedules were put into effect a year later when the product mix had changed, thus throwing off production projections. Although management addressed the issue by adjusting for the new product mix, the bar mill workers became adamant in their demand to return to the old wage scale.[34]

SWOC took the bar mill grievance, which emanated from the highest-skilled workers—rollers, assistant rollers, and heaters. Their earnings had suffered, and even management's fine-tuning of the incentive plan still led to a wage decline for these particular workers, whom management considered overpaid. The union maintained that the new wage scale amounted to a wage cut, that the old scale should be reinstated, and that workers who lost earnings during the trial period should be compensated. To back up its stance the union secured a petition with these demands, signed by 115 of the 134 workers in the mill. Management granted the grievance, returned to the old wage scale, and paid back wages. SWOC immediately heralded the victory in *Steel Labor:* "Blocked in its efforts to cut wages at its Duquesne plant, U.S. Steel Corp. is paying out $12,000 in back wages." The article stressed that highly skilled and highly paid rollers, assistant rollers, and heaters had their tonnage rates restored. The victory coincided with an organizing drive at the mill, and the local consciously used it to build its membership.[35]

But *Steel Labor* failed to mention information that made this seemingly simple story of a union's successful efforts to eliminate wage cuts much more complex. Indeed, the union's efforts at defending the rollers and heaters blocked lower-paid workers from benefiting under the new wage scale. SWOC's grievance settlement with the company included a clause—not mentioned by *Steel Labor*—that forced fifty-one workers who made more money under the new scale to reimburse the company for those totals through payroll deductions. For the majority of workers in the department (69 of 134), the new wage scale had paid more than the old one. Perhaps wages would have gone even higher after management learned from the trial period and tinkered with the rates. According to its original calculations, management all along assumed that the new wage scale would cost the company $3,685 more in wages each year. The union's demand to return to the old rates actually saved the company money.[36]

SWOC might have won the allegiance of the highest-skilled bar mill workers, much as the ERP had done, but it did so at a large cost. Approximately six months after the settlement a committee of six bar mill employees approached management with an independent (nonunion) grievance for wage adjustments for low-paid positions. They claimed to represent—and the department superintendent concurred—ninety-six of the mill's workers, or all but the highest-skilled positions. They noted that the union petition aimed at throwing the new scale out had been "signed by a great number who did not desire to do so but had to under pressure."[37] Through 1941 numerous grievances that SWOC filed on behalf of individuals similarly attempted to raise the lower rates in the mill. Like the independent grievance, they would be denied by management, revealing the stalemate the union and company had arrived at concerning wage adjustments.[38] Management restudied its wage scale plan for the bar mill and arrived at new rates in late 1940. However, without the union's agreement to accept both wage cuts and wage hikes, the company refused to install the wage scale.[39] The highest-skilled bar mill employees had defended their tonnage rates with the union's help; they did so at the expense of raises for lower-skilled tonnage and hourly workers.

Local 1256, following the lead of the national union, had taken a stand against wage cuts of any kind.[40] The corporation, on the other hand, believed that abolishing wage inequalities between jobs and plants, a goal the union shared, meant both lowering and raising individual rates. "It becomes apparent," the company argued, "that if we adopt a method of correcting wage inequalities that will only raise the low rates, we shall suffer competitively."[41] This is what its bar mill wage scale had meant to do: both lower and raise rates that were out of line and still provide greater overall earnings for the workers in the department. Consider this exchange between the grievance committee and management on a similar wage scale in another department that both raised and lowered rates:

> Management: If we continue to bring all rates up and none down we will never arrive at a balanced wage structure which you have been harping to me about for the past years.
> Union: There is truth in that. This is no time for us to consider anything like this. . . .
> Management: Then we will continue to complain about inequalities in rate structures?
> Union: That is right. You want me to admit that some of these jobs are being paid too much?
> Management: Yes, on the same basis we are raising some of the jobs.[42]

Management and the union faced similar circumstances in the two other bar mills. Newly installed wage scales in both of these mills during a trial period showed lower earnings for the highest-skilled workers and overall wage hikes for less-skilled workers, both tonnage and hourly. In both mills Local 1256 attempted to reject the new wage scales as a way to defend the highest-skilled workers. However, the local could not rally the workers in these departments as it had done in the first mill. The majority of workers made more money under the new scale and they supported it. In one of the two mills the union could not get a majority of workers to its meetings on the issue, and many nonunion workers contemplated joining the union just to force it to accept the new wage scale. SWOC's national leaders finally stepped in and forced the local to bargain with the company over the rates. The new wage scales were adopted in both mills, leading to wage hikes for most workers. The local also secured higher rates for the highest-skilled tonnage workers than management originally intended under the new scales, though not as high as under the old wage plan.[43]

When the same issues arose in the blooming mills, the local again attempted to block the introduction of new wage scales and this time tried to ban the trial period. At issue for the union was the possibility that the highest-paid tonnage workers would see smaller paychecks and that a number of hourly jobs were being switched to tonnage-type earnings.[44] The union feared a speedup with more workers on tonnage rates. Again, the union misjudged the strong desires of lower-paid workers for higher wages in whatever form. Between 1937 and 1941 hourly workers frequently filed grievances to have their jobs converted to tonnage positions. During 1941, with production steadily climbing because of the war in Europe, these grievances proliferated as hourly workers saw tonnage workers making higher and higher earnings.[45]

Again the local succumbed to pressure from workers and the national union. Several blooming mill employees who had not paid their union dues for six months even approached management and asked how they could attend a union meeting and urge installation of the new scale. The national union finally stepped in and forced the local to allow the wage scale trial period to take place. "[A] bunch of rattle brains [who] had rejected the plan were passing up an opportunity," complained a national officer about the local's grievance committee.[46] After the trial period ended, management withdrew most of the wage scale at the union's request and instituted back pay for workers—a minority—who had lost money during the trial. However, both sides agreed to retain "those parts of the plans which cover the employees formerly on straight hourly rates and who now benefit by participation in the incentive earnings plan." The union could not stop the strong desire of hourly workers to make more money on tonnage plans.[47]

Local 1256 found it difficult to reconcile the needs of hourly, semiskilled tonnage, and skilled tonnage workers in departments that had a significant mix of workers. The union at first attempted to protect the tonnage plans of the highest-skilled workers, who had supported the ERP and initially had

remained outside SWOC but who now found in the union a strong advo-
cate for their interests. By defending their interests, the union did not always
support the interests and wishes of the majority of workers. The union ultimately found itself pressured by both lower-paid workers and the national
union to allow wage gains for the broadest grouping of workers, sometimes
at the expense of the highest-paid workers. Even under SWOC, shop-floor
divisions based on skill and compensation systems continued to deeply frag-
ment the workforce and weaken the union.

The Union and Hourly Unskilled Bargaining

Despite the bar and blooming mill cases, the union proved a strong advo-
cate for unskilled and semiskilled hourly workers from 1937 to 1941. Hourly
workers generally had shunned the ERP, except for minor working-condi-
tion requests and occasional, though unsuccessful, wage rate requests. They
now used SWOC to win higher wages, to defend those wages when the economy collapsed, to rearrange part-time work schedules so workers would be
eligible for unemployment benefits, and to defend themselves against the
foreman's arbitrary authority by ensuring the equal distribution of work
hours and layoffs by seniority. For the hourly workers, much more than for
skilled workers, the union meant assurances of workplace justice.

The initial contract between SWOC and Carnegie-Illinois provided perhaps the greatest boost for unskilled workers. Raising the common laboring
rate to $5 per day achieved what the ERP could never gain, a basic raise in
the lower-skilled rates that matched the demands of worker militants. SWOC
consolidated its support among the unskilled when it then took one of its
strongest stands in defending that $5 day against a company-wide wage cut
in 1938. Although all workers would have been affected adversely, a wage reduction affected the lowest-paid workers inordinately, and they also experienced the greatest reduction of work hours because of the recession. The
union successfully negotiated a wage freeze during its February 1938 contract
negotiations with U.S. Steel, but company pressure on the union to accept a
wage cut continued. Hit hard by the economic slump, U.S. Steel lowered
prices in the summer and seriously contemplated a 10-cent wage reduction
in the hourly base wage rate. For common laborers that would have amounted to a 16 percent cut in pay.[48] The union refused to countenance the reduction, and company officials "were thought ready to involve the termination
clause of the [collective bargaining] agreement."[49] In the end, the union's
hard line stalled the wage cut until an improvement in economic conditions
and White House pressure on U.S. Steel eased the crisis. Throughout 1938 the
union would use its successful anti–wage cut stance in its organizing efforts.[50]

The union was far less successful in blocking management's plant-level efforts to change the traditional pay structure of large groups of semiskilled hourly workers, especially chippers and scarfers. Despite its lack of success, however, the union still provided opportunities for these workers to seek improvements in their new pay structures. As part of its cost control program, Carnegie-Illinois had been devising incentive programs to be applied throughout the Pittsburgh region. Because most mills already had incentive programs for chippers and scarfers, Duquesne found it necessary to institute such programs. Although many workers who labored alongside tonnage workers preferred to be put on incentive plans, departments with large numbers of semiskilled hourly workers, such as chippers and scarfers, generally resisted incentive plans. Chippers, the core membership of the Fort Dukane Lodge, objected to an incentive plan because they believed it would lead to a speedup, wage cuts, and the laying off of older, slower workers. Scarfers, who also removed imperfections from steel but used oxyacetylene torches, not pneumatic chipping tools, to do so, also feared a speedup. But Duquesne's management was determined to introduce the incentive rates.

Unlike its practice in setting the bar and blooming mill wage scales, management did not allow the workers or the union a voice in accepting or rejecting the incentive plan. The other wage scales had included wage cuts, which required the union's involvement under the contract; however, the chipping and scarfing plan made the workers' current hourly rate the new minimum rate on the incentive plan. Because no wage cut was involved, and no contract provision at the time governed the institution of incentive plans, management had complete authority to implement it. The union defended grievances by both the scarfers and chippers in an effort to block the incentive plan but to no avail. Even wildcat strikes by the scarfers failed to move management.

Despite the defeat, the chippers and scarfers successfully used the grievance procedure to improve the new incentive plans. The chippers won grievances aimed at securing better working conditions, which not only improved safety but also allowed for higher earnings under the incentive plan. Similarly, the scarfers secured better working conditions through grievances. In addition, they won an agreement by management to reorganize the work area to make it more conducive to higher production and thus higher earnings. Ironically, the scarfers, who at first opposed the incentive plan, eventually forced management to include their department's hourly crane operators in the incentive plan. The scarfers reasoned that once in the incentive plan, the crane operators would move more materials more quickly, which then would allow the scarfers to increase their production and earnings. The union had proved ineffective at stopping these incentive plans, but once instituted, the union aided workers by forcing management to reorganize working conditions for higher incentive earnings.[51]

During 1937–39 the number of available work hours was a far more critical shop-floor issue than the incentive plans. With reduced production low-skilled workers such as laborers, scarfers, and chippers found only a few days of work per week. This meant that the equal distribution of work hours, a demand won earlier by the ERP, once again became a prominent issue. SWOC simply continued the work of maintaining the equal distribution of work hours that the ERP had championed. Because management already had faced this issue, it was not a hotly contested point between management and the union. More than anything, the local served as a watchdog, pointing out company deviations from policy.[52]

The union proved more effective than the ERP when it won a rearrangement of working schedules for unemployment benefits. Under management's work-sharing program, part-time workers could not receive unemployment benefits because they worked each week, albeit for only a day or two. Local 1256 proposed in 1938 that management rearrange workers' schedules so that they could combine all their work hours for two weeks into just one week and then have the next week off. They would then be eligible for unemployment benefits every other week. Duquesne management acceded to the demand. A year later management also rearranged working schedules for chippers at the union's request, again so workers would gain unemployment benefits.[53] The practice was ended when economic conditions improved, but when employment dipped in 1940, the union again requested this type of schedule. Management now refused—subsidiary officials forced plant managers to end the practice in an effort to reduce unemployment compensation costs in Pennsylvania.[54]

The recession of 1937–39 also brought to the fore the issue of seniority in determining who would be laid off. When the depression hit Duquesne in 1930, the company had no layoff procedure and instead allowed foremen to direct the process. This had produced much hostility and bitterness toward the corporation among low-skilled workers. The Duquesne Works ERP had remained weak on the seniority issue; many higher-skilled ERP representatives agreed with management's arguments of merit over seniority. Still, U.S. Steel, pushed by ERP militants in its various facilities, had moved to a general policy of accepting seniority as a determinant for layoff but only if physical fitness, ability, and family status (marital status and number of dependents) of the workers were similar. Like many other company policies, the SWOC collective bargaining agreement merely codified this understanding. Yet implementation of this policy was left to management and the union at the plant level.[55]

In most instances the corporation now used seniority to determine lay-offs. This was especially true when it was dealing with large groups of work-ers of similar abilities, such as chippers or scarfers. Even among skilled posi-tions, however, management had come to accept a correlation between ability and seniority. Remarkably, few seniority grievances were filed at Duquesne over layoffs or recall to work during the economic upheaval of 1937–39.[56] In addition to agreeing to the seniority principle for layoffs, the two sides agreed to apply seniority within departmental units to determine who would be laid off. This meant that within the rolling department, for example, the 38-inch and 40-inch blooming mills each formed separate seniority units, as did each of the three bar mills. The company steadfastly opposed plantwide seniori-ty, because "it would be extremely difficult to make increases and decreases in forces entirely on the basis of Plant service as it would result in continu-ally shifting the forces from one Department to another and make the main-tenance of a trained organization in any unit almost impossible." Skills learned in the rolling mill were not transferable to the blast-furnace depart-ment, for example. Workers and the union also opposed plantwide seniori-ty for determining layoffs because it increased the risk of being bumped out of a department. The amount of work available varied greatly by department, which meant that workers' jobs would be constantly threatened and contin-ually reshuffled.[57]

Seniority for promotion was not as critical an issue during this period, simply because few workers were promoted during the economic downturn. However, seniority for promotion, as with layoffs, worked to the benefit of the unskilled under SWOC. As with layoffs, the union and management had to determine at what level seniority should prevail in promotions. For low-skilled jobs, unit or department seniority generally prevailed. In such cases management rarely resorted to its contractual right to promote workers based on ability, not seniority. Again the union filed few grievances about promo-tion of a less senior employee. When the union raised legitimate cases of seniority violations, management quickly reversed itself. Despite the lack of promotions, and despite management's contractual right to use ability over seniority in promotion, the union protected low-skilled workers from lan-guishing in low-paying jobs. The arbitrary power of the foreman, which first began to erode during the ERP era, continued to decline.[58]

The union provided much-needed shop-floor protection for unskilled and semiskilled hourly workers. It defended their basic wage rate against cuts in 1938, improved working conditions, and stood constant vigil against viola-tions of seniority and division of work hours. But what about black work-ers, who had been kept at the bottom of the job ladder and faced the worst forms of discrimination in the 1920s and 1930s? By defending the basic shop-floor interests of unskilled workers, the union defended black workers. The equal distribution of work hours meant blacks were not discriminated against by receiving fewer hours. By raising the common laboring wage rate, and defending it against reductions, the union elevated and protected the wages of most black workers, who worked at, or slightly above, the common laboring rate.

The union's defense of seniority further extended basic shop-floor protections to black workers. In the area of layoffs, seniority within departmental units protected blacks' jobs. Far from working to the detriment of black workers, narrower seniority units for layoffs offered protection. Determining layoff seniority within a department meant that higher-skilled white workers from other departments whom management wanted to keep employed could not bump blacks out of their jobs. This had been a practice early in the depression, but SWOC ended it. This especially protected blacks within the departments where they were concentrated: blast furnace and open hearth.

Seniority for promotions proved more complicated. Many studies of black steelworkers have stressed how seniority systems are racially biased. That is, the determination of particular units of seniority—whether by department or by plant—combined with job ladders that led either to high-paying tonnage jobs or dead-end hourly jobs, left blacks in the least-skilled jobs. Blacks found themselves hired into jobs that led nowhere, and narrow seniority units meant they could not bid for jobs in other departments in the plant. Studies of these practices thus stress that determining seniority by department, and not by plant, was a key factor in racial discrimination.[59] In fact, seniority systems and racism were intertwined in both northern and southern steel mills, and seniority systems became an obstacle for black advancement to higher-paying work and to jobs with better working conditions. But was this a result of a deliberate abuse of seniority principles by management and/or white workers from the early days of the SWOC contract? At Duquesne, and by implication other northern mills, the answer appears to be no.

First, seniority was not the most important criterion for promotion but came third after ability and physical fitness. Management would not agree to seniority as the sole criterion for promotion, and SWOC could not win this demand. Thus the promotional system in the early years of the contract was primarily management's creation, a formalizing of the practice that prevailed in the ERP period. Because it was a weak union, SWOC had to accept what it was offered. Likewise, SWOC had no power to broaden seniority units to make them plantwide. As I discussed earlier, management adamantly refused to consider plantwide seniority because of the production disruptions it would cause. Similarly, most workers did not want senior employees from other departments to be able to take jobs in their departments. The lack of plantwide seniority thus had no relation to racial considerations.[60]

Second, as a criterion for promotion, seniority was used in conjunction with the job ladders, or lines of promotion, that had long existed in the mill. These lines of promotion predated the employment of blacks and were not racially motivated in their formation. If their origins lay in discrimination, it was as a way to block the advancement of eastern and southern European workers. Further, the demand for using seniority to determine promotions along these job ladders was at first not a racial issue at all. It was a demand that emanated primarily from southern and eastern European workers who wanted the same promotions that U.S.-born workers could earn but that management denied them. Early in the SWOC era seniority and job ladders were not meant to keep blacks from being promoted but were meant to end discrimination. As a result, blacks fully supported the early promotional system in conjunction with seniority. For numerous black workers, seniority was a key reason for joining SWOC. Sylvester Grinage, a black worker whose brother would become a leader in Local 1256, joined SWOC because "certain practices [were] going that I didn't feel were fair, and with the union[,] men were treated fairer and blacks were given better opportunities to advance."[61]

Despite the possibility of advancement for many blacks, decided limitations existed from the earliest days of SWOC. By 1941 still no blacks held semiskilled incentive jobs, such as running cranes, chipping, and scarfing.[62] Nor could blacks make any inroads in the skilled trades, which remained white. Here management bears a large responsibility for not promoting blacks out of labor pools and into crane jobs and for not bringing them into apprenticeship programs. After all, management ultimately decided who gained entrance to these jobs and the various job ladders by promoting out of the common laboring pools, which constituted the entry-level jobs at the mill. By citing ability and fitness clauses over seniority, management effectively blocked black advancement by arguing blacks were not qualified for these jobs.

However, the union and white workers also bear responsibility. There is no evidence that Local 1256 ever made black advancement to these jobs a priority or raised this demand even mildly in grievance meetings with management. This silent collusion of white workers and their union would become explicit during World War II. Facing a severe labor shortage at the end of 1942, management sought to elevate a few blacks to crane positions. Some white crane operators at first refused to train the black workers. Local 1256 responded by filing a grievance citing management's creation of "an intolerable condition" (the promotion of blacks), a "condition that has never existed in this plant before."[63] In this case management held firm and African Americans moved into crane positions.

Despite the lack of advancement, the Duquesne Works would prove to be one the most advanced of the region's mills on issues of race. Blacks held numerous leadership positions within the local from the 1930s through the 1950s. They included Fletcher Williamson, guide and trustee; James Grinage, vice president and chair of the grievance committee; and Carl Dickerson, treasurer, recording secretary, and chair of the grievance committee.[64] In 1951 Grinage would assert that the "the lot of the colored employee was much better at Duquesne Works than it was anywhere else in the valley."[65]

SWOC became entrenched on the shop floor by using the grievance process and the national contract to defend the sometimes separate, even conflicting, interests of both unskilled and skilled workers. Nevertheless, the union could not depend on its shop-floor efforts alone to build and sustain unionism in Duquesne. This had been how the ERP representatives envisioned unionism, but it proved too limiting. It did nothing to address workers' or the union's lack of political power and rights within the community. Nor did it address the continued absence of New Deal relief programs in Duquesne that caused continued misery among the mill's poorest workers during the Roosevelt recession. Local 1256 had to become more than a simple bargaining agent enforcing the union contract. It had to broaden its vision of unionism into areas pioneered by the old Fort Dukane Lodge.

Unionism and Duquesne Politics

While Local 1256 was setting its roots deep in the shop floor, it also expanded into the political arena, seeking to meet steelworkers' needs that were not addressed within the collective bargaining agreement. Resurrecting the political activism of the Fort Dukane Lodge, Local 1256 attempted to dethrone the Crawford–Duquesne Works Republican machine and provide for workers' economic needs during the economic slump of 1937–40. Some union leaders did not fully support these efforts; they believed that unions and politics should not mix. Despite the doubts, the political initiatives expanded the boundaries of the union's scope and activities. But the local quickly met the limits of its reform efforts as well as the limits of its internal political cohesiveness.

SWOC locals faced continuing political repression, despite their success at securing a collective bargaining agreement. Mayor Crawford still held the authority to decide where the local could meet and whether it could hand out leaflets. Workers had secured the machinery to ensure justice on the shop floor;

they now needed to secure their political liberties outside the mill. Buoyed by continued Democratic successes at the national and state levels in 1936, and boosted by successful organizing drives and the SWOC contract signing, steelworkers, glassworkers, electrical workers, and miners organized political campaigns in western Pennsylvania in 1937 to unseat local Republican rule. William Spang and Fort Dukane had attempted this in 1935 but fell short. Although Spang's effort may have been premature, his near-election to the city council demonstrated that Duquesne Republicans were not invincible.

Elmer Maloy, president of Local 1256, decided to run for mayor in 1937. He later noted that he just decided to do it one day "because I was mad at Jim Crawford and the Chief of Police." The two had denied the local a meeting permit.[66] The Communists claimed that Maloy had in fact decided to run for mayor before he joined SWOC and that the party's promise of support helped him decide to join the union. It is also likely that SWOC president Philip Murray approached him to run, as Murray had done with John Mullen in Clairton.[67] Whatever the source of Maloy's motivation, his candidacy reverberated throughout Local 1256 and the city.

Maloy's candidacy was not universally endorsed by the local's leadership. During the primary, and despite motions from the floor during meetings to endorse labor candidates, the local did not formally endorse Maloy. Both John Kane and Ernest Fries—former ERP chairmen, now Local 1256 officers—expressed reservations. Grounded in the ERP's shop-floor bargaining history, they were reticent to see the union expand into politics. Fries questioned the CIO's participation in politics, suggesting "the time was inopportune: inasmuch as the organization wasn't built up sufficiently."[68] After Maloy won the Democratic primary, however, the local immediately endorsed him and provided his campaign with $200. Nevertheless, doubts about mixing politics and unionism continued. Kane, holding Maloy to an earlier promise, presented him with an undated form announcing his resignation as mayor. Maloy signed the document, which was "to be used in the event of President Maloy not living within the ideals of the C.I.O. when and if he occupies the position of Mayor of Duquesne." In addition, Maloy found it necessary to promise the local that he considered the $200 a loan that would be repaid after the election.[69] Upriver in Clairton, Mullen faced similar skepticism from unionists who did not believe SWOC should enter politics.[70]

Duquesne's Democratic Party proved even less receptive to Maloy's candidacy. Nonexistent in 1929, it only slowly had built itself up through the early 1930s. Despite the New Deal, it had no success in mayoral or city council races. The political mobilization of the Fort Dukane Lodge in 1935 had helped increase the party's registration, but the Democrats refused to endorse the unionists, even after Spang won the primary. Maloy's candidacy would have a similar effect. His mobilization of union voters ensured the Democratic Party of its first lead over Republican registration totals in the city's history. For many workers Fort Dukane had broken the fear of registering Democratic in 1935, and Maloy consolidated those gains among a broader segment of Duquesne's working class. Maloy himself did not leave the Republican Party until 1936.[71]

Maloy faced a five-way race in the Democratic primary. His main opposition came from Frank Kopriver, who owned a small business, and Michael Kowallis, a lawyer. Kowallis had been a Democrat for years, but Kopriver had been elected to the city council in 1933 as a Republican. By 1936 he had become an opponent of Mayor Crawford's fiscal conservatism. Kopriver switched parties in 1937 and ran as a friend of the workingman. Both Kowallis and Kopriver had strong support from the city Democratic Committee, but the chairman was Maloy's cousin and supporter. Cognizant that Maloy would fail to gain the committee's endorsement if it came to a vote, the chairman refused to call any meetings of the committee until after the primary. However, the county Democratic Committee, which held authority over the city Democratic Committee, endorsed Kowallis, thus forcing the Duquesne Democrats to follow suit. In addition, splinter groups, such as the Roosevelt Democrats and the Regular Democrats, made their own endorsements, although none for Maloy. Throughout the Monongahela Valley labor candidates divided local Democratic organizations.[72]

Maloy won the primary, beating both Kowallis and Kopriver by less than 100 votes. He now faced R. W. Schreiber, a Republican businessman, in the general election. Perhaps because Crawford saw his party crumbling around him and because he refused to be beaten by a union man, he had declined the Republican nomination. The city Democratic Committee now endorsed Maloy, but it did not work actively for him. Kowallis threw his support to Maloy on election eve, but Kopriver refused to give his endorsement.[73] Also refusing to endorse Maloy was former Fort Dukane Lodge president William Spang, who endorsed Kopriver in the primary and the Republican Schreiber in the November election. "I have no quarrel now with Mr. Crawford," Spang claimed. In addition, Maloy's candidacy received almost no coverage in the pages of the *Duquesne Times*.[74]

Even without active city Democratic Party aid, Maloy ran a formidable political campaign. The national SWOC leadership and the CIO's state political organization, the Labor's Non-Partisan League (LNPL) of Pennsylvania, endorsed Maloy, but they too offered little financial or organizational help. Maloy received no money from SWOC, mostly because "money was very scarce," according to Tom Murray, a national union official.[75] The union had yet to organize Little Steel, and its U.S. Steel membership dues collections were dropping. Maloy instead created his own organization—the Labor Campaign Committee—with the aid of SWOC unionists and the Communist Party. Anthony Salopek, Duquesne's leading Communist, served as Maloy's campaign chairman, thus continuing the alliance they had forged during the SWOC organizing drive. For the Communist Party this marked a successful application of its Popular Front program, which called for forming alliances with progressive forces in trade unions and in politics. Staffing the campaign were mostly low-skilled immigrants and black workers. Especially active were men such as Salopek; Wallace Carroll, a chipper; and Henry Cox, a black unskilled laborer.[76] According to Maloy, "These people that worked for us were a whole indiscriminate group of Croations [*sic*], Serbians, Hungarians, and colored, just a mixture of everything, and they were real workers. Nobody could bribe them; they didn't get paid. . . . They even contributed money . . . to run the campaign. . . . They lost work, they laid off, they went to every meeting, they campaigned door-to-door, they did the most efficient job."[77]

Maloy ran as a "Roosevelt Democrat" representing the interests of workers, who "needed a real friend in the Mayor's office." At one of two rallies he held at the Croatian Hall, he pledged never to allow strikebreakers in the city or the use of vigilantes against workers. Further, he promised to go through the ordinance book and "rid it of laws which were not for the welfare of the workingman." Ridiculing a Republican pledge to keep the streets clean, Maloy asked at a rally whether the GOP promise referred to the antiloitering ordinance, which allowed the police to arrest men standing on the street corner. He also lashed out at Crawford for wasting money by accepting high bids for city jobs and for unrealistic assessments that set the taxes of small property owners too high. But mostly he criticized Crawford and the Republican Party for not bringing the New Deal to Duquesne. "If there's grass in the streets here it's because Mayor Crawford would never allow them to be fixed with the aid of WPA funds," he argued. "Thousands of dollars that could have been spent with local merchants," he continued, "has gone elsewhere." In addition, Maloy criticized the Duquesne police force for driving workers away from the polls and promised a shake-up of that department. Schreiber ran on a probusiness platform. His "business administration," he argued, would lower taxes, keep a close watch on municipal spending, and approve only those projects that would benefit all citizens.[78]

On election day the union leader defeated the businessman, 2,959 to 2,614.[79] Four and a half years after Franklin Roosevelt proclaimed, "The only thing we have to fear is fear itself," Maloy declared, "I believe this election is a mandate to the people to be no longer dominated by fear that the mills will close if the Republican party is no longer in power."[80] Maloy's victory rested squarely on his working-class support. He carried the heavily working-class First and Third Wards but lost to Schreiber in the city's middle-class Second Ward. Maloy's strongest showing came from the First Ward's First District, known as "Below the Tracks." Bounded by the Monongahela River and the railroad tracks on two sides, and the upper and lower Duquesne Works on the other two sides, this poorest section of the city was filled with low-skilled immigrant and black workers. Here Maloy defeated his Republican rival 2 to 1. Overall he carried six of the city's twelve voting districts, the same six in which Spang did best in his 1935 city council campaign.[81] Overall, the Democrats won nine of ten offices, handing the Republicans a stunning defeat. On the city council, on which the mayor sat and voted, Maloy would be surrounded by two new Democratic councilmen and Kopriver, who held his council seat after his primary defeat by Maloy. Against the four Democrats would be the lone Republican on the council, J. H. Hughes, a Duquesne Works superintendent.[82] Throughout western Pennsylvania, SWOC and other CIO and AFL unionists won numerous political campaigns, including mayoral elections in Clairton, Monessen, and New Kensington; city council elections in Brackenridge, Port Vue, Glassport, and Versailles; and burgess elections in Ambridge, Rankin, Brackenridge, and Versailles. Labor-endorsed candidates also won mayoral and council elections in Aliquippa, Arnold, Donora, East Pittsburgh, Homestead, and Pittsburgh.[83]

"Today is a new birth for the city of Duquesne," Anthony Salopek declared from the audience during the first city council meeting under Mayor Maloy, "a day in which the people will at last have their constitutional rights. We needed young blood in the city and now we have it. Not so long ago eight members of our labor group were locked up downstairs when the city did not belong to the people. The new Council will give the city back to the people, where it belongs."[84] Maloy did not disappoint his union supporters. In two quick strokes he demoted the chief of police, Thomas Flynn, to the rank of patrol officer and elevated his brother, William Maloy, a twenty-year veteran, to the rank of chief. As chief, Flynn had arrested striking steelworkers in 1919, thrown the Amalgamated leadership in jail during the aborted 1935 strike, and harassed SWOC organizers. A few miles away in Clairton another new SWOC mayor, John Mullen, also replaced the chief of police as one of his first acts. Maloy also ended all restrictions on the union's handing out leaflets at the plant gates and won city council support for union-sponsored events.[85] Maloy's reform efforts extended to municipal employees. The new council fired the Crawford-appointed Civil Service Commission. Further, Maloy led council efforts that raised municipal workers' pay and instituted the eight-hour day and forty-hour week, ending the twelve-hour day for city workers. Duquesne also encouraged its municipal workers to join the CIO's Municipal Workers of America. Maloy personally presided over the ceremony welcoming them into the CIO and promised not to dismiss any CIO employee. He also signed the first municipal collective bargaining agreement in the state. In the 1938 Duquesne Labor Day Parade the union mayor, flanked by members of the fire and police departments, marched with SWOC Local 1256, the Municipal Workers of America, and the Croatian Citizens' Club, symbolizing the profound political change that had occurred.[86]

Maloy's new administration had the greatest effect on workers' lives by providing economic relief. When he took office in January 1938, the renewed depression had decimated employment at the mill. Crawford had done nothing, refusing even to allow a relief office to be established in the city. On his first day as the new mayor Maloy opened a relief office at union headquarters and personally spent the day signing up workers for relief payments. Federal money began flowing into Duquesne. Crawford's administration had not encouraged Works Progress Administration (WPA) projects. Although the old council approved a few small projects in July 1936, they were subsequently killed by politics and not reinstituted for six months.[87] "At least $600,000 worth of WPA work could have been brought here but the old council passed it up," Maloy complained.[88] Under the new administration the city approved numerous WPA projects, which provided work for unemployed steelworkers and their families. With WPA money the city paved its dirt streets; installed sewerage, including in black sections of town; employed women in sewing projects; hired white-collar workers to index city documents; started an adult education center, which provided classes for blacks to obtain high school credits; and built and renovated school buildings. When WPA workers unearthed a coal seam while building a street, the city suspended work for three days so that WPA workers and unemployed steelworkers could put in their winter's supply.[89] The New Deal had finally arrived in Duquesne.

Local 1256 worked closely with Maloy in relief efforts. SWOC's national leadership had responded to the economic downturn by directing its locals to set up relief committees to aid unemployed and underemployed steelworkers.[90] In December Local 1256 established a relief committee whose structure mirrored the voting wards and districts of the city. When Maloy set up a relief office at the local, the union already had targeted the workers most in need. The citywide structure of the relief committee then gave it clout with the city council. The relief committee also acted as an intermediary between unemployed workers and the Pennsylvania Department of Public Assistance, by representing workers who were not satisfied with their relief payments. The local kept its membership informed of changes in federal and state relief and unemployment compensation laws, and it frequently invited state unemployment officials to speak at its meetings. By helping workers to obtain relief and unemployment benefits, the local made itself indispensable for low-skilled workers.[91]

Maloy and Local 1256 worked closely with other political organizations in the relief effort. In March 1938 Maloy's Labor Campaign Committee officially dissolved and became a local affiliate of the Labor's Non-Partisan League, although its membership did not change. The LNPL became the political arm of Local 1256, with Maloy as president and other Local 1256 members filling in the other elected positions. At that point Local 1256's relief committee, organized along political districts, and the LNPL essentially became the same organization.[92] Separate from the LNPL was the Workers' Alliance, which began nationally as a Socialist organization but by the mid-1930s had come under Communist Party influence after the party merged its Unemployed Councils into the alliance. The Duquesne Workers' Alliance worked alongside Local 1256 and even held its meetings at the local's hall. It organized WPA workers into a union and, like Local 1256, pressured the city council for more WPA projects and represented unemployed workers before state agencies.[93] The cooperation between these groups would be demonstrated in March 1938, when the Workers' Alliance, Local 1256, and the LNPL held a mass meeting of a thousand workers, chaired by Maloy, demanding more federal and state aid for the unemployed.[94]

One chronicler of the 1937 elections of SWOC unionists to positions of local political power, Eric Leif Davin, has argued that they "suggested a possibility of radicalism in the late 1930s of perhaps far-reaching implications." Davin does not explore or delineate what that radicalism would have meant in practice. But Davin does make clear the fundamental reason that radicalism failed to blossom: the national union leadership never provided the local political efforts with a "direction towards more fundamental change." This is an ironic claim, because Davin and other labor historians of the rank-and-file school, such as Staughton Lynd, blame those same national union leaders for subverting and undermining local political radicalism. Here he blames them for not guiding it.[95]

Instead, Duquesne demonstrates how short-lived and politically limited the gains from the election of 1937 ultimately proved to be. Maloy held office through 1945, having won reelection in 1941. However, his and Local 1256's political power would be checked before the end of his first year as mayor. In less than a year the Republicans effectively retook control of Duquesne politics. When Maloy began his term as mayor in 1938, the Democrats held a 4-to-1 advantage on the city council. Although the three Democratic councilmen had pledged to guarantee free speech, protect labor's right to picket, and to support Roosevelt, they had not agreed to follow all of Maloy's or Local 1256's programs. In the early fall Kopriver, who never supported Maloy, returned to the Republican fold. In December he secured the support of Dr. Francis Madden, a conservative Democratic council member. Political opportunism, not a strong commitment to labor or the New Deal, appeared to have been their guiding political philosophy in the election of 1937. And once the economic downturn took firm hold, cost cutting and retrenchment became the mantra of Kopriver and Madden. Along with Hughes, the Republican council member who was a mill superintendent, the three now formed a solid council majority, blocking Maloy and Democratic council member Milan Babic, who represented the Slavic community.

The Republicans consolidated their hold on the city council in the election of 1939. They attacked Maloy's city spending record during a time of reduced taxes and middle-class calls for fiscal conservatism. Kopriver won reelection as a Republican, and Hughes, who had decided to retire, was replaced by another Republican mill superintendent. The 3-2 conservative majority held firm.[96] The Republicans scored additional triumphs. During the 1939 election campaign they outregistered the Democrats, 4,800 to 4,200. In addition, two salaried Duquesne Works officials won election to the school board, handily defeating their Democratic opponents, including Ernest Fries, the Local 1256 officer.[97] Despite the organized presence of Labor's Non-Partisan League, Local 1256 had little success in the political arena beyond Maloy. The Democratic Party remained divided, and in 1938, even Mayor Maloy could not win chairmanship of the City Democratic Club. Although three unionists won positions as city Democratic committeemen in 1938, all had lost their positions by 1940. Labor and the Democratic Party were not one and the same in Duquesne.[98]

The new anti-Maloy city council majority did not recreate the antilabor politics that dominated the Crawford administrations. That era had passed. Organized labor had become a political reality that the city council members had to accept. Indeed, the Republican Kopriver even unabashedly criticized Maloy for not doing enough for the workingman. However, the new conservative council majority blocked, and in some cases reversed, the fiscal programs and reforms of the Maloy administration. Cutting city spending during the Roosevelt recession was their overriding concern. WPA projects came under greater scrutiny, which led to the cancellation of some. In November 1938 the council also voted to forgo greater portions of WPA funding in favor of relief from the state Department of Public Assistance, a program that paid lower wages. Maloy and Babic, backed by Local 1256 and the Workers' Alliance, vehemently opposed the move but were powerless to stop it. Further, the council majority also reversed some of Maloy's municipal reforms. They laid off fire fighters and police officers and abolished the forty-hour week for the fire department.[99] In 1941 Maloy won reelection by defeating Kopriver, 3,365 to 3,213. But he still could count on the support of only one Democrat against three Republicans on the city council.[100]

Local 1256 had been able to secure Maloy's election, but it could not unite its ranks to secure a broader labor victory, even a broader Democratic Party victory. An alternative labor party was not even a possibility. Not a single Duquesne labor or Communist leader, including Maloy and Salopek, ever broached the idea. Abandoning the Democratic Party would have meant cutting the union political leaders off from even the limited financial funding they received from the Democrats. It is also hard to imagine that conservative and even moderate Democratic mill workers would have followed such a venture. Local 1256 had trouble mobilizing its ranks in the Democratic Party, not because workers wanted a more independent or radical alternative but because so many either remained in, or switched registration to, the Republican Party.

Skilled tonnage workers, for example, had ample reason to stay in the Republican Party. Because of their incomes they had more in common with the middle class in Duquesne than the town's partially employed laborers. Those who considered moving into management positions one day also found registering as a Republican to be advantageous. Some former ERP representatives, for example, such as Charles Erickson and Joseph Budday, did not become Democrats. But neither did several officers of Local 1256 and men who would become officers and who were of voting age in the late 1930s. A future sixteen-year grievanceman in the electrical furnace department did not leave the Republicans until 1955; another future grievanceman and former Fort Dukane officer who voted Democratic from 1936 to 1938 joined the Republicans in 1939; and a future financial secretary, later president of Local 1256, did not register as a Democrat until 1948. Union membership, even future union leadership, did not equate with Democratic Party membership.[101]

Although national SWOC leaders did not offer much guidance to the local political efforts, it would not have made much difference, given local political conditions. The national union also was weak financially in this period and had to borrow money simply to meet payroll. Resources were spread too thin, not just at U.S. Steel but at all the Little Steel companies, to adequately organize, lead, and fund political campaigns in dozens of steel towns in numerous states.

Despite the lack of political cohesiveness among steelworkers in Duquesne and the short-lived Democratic dominance of the city council, Local 1256's plunge into local politics accomplished much. By overthrowing Crawford's rule, the union secured the civil liberties it needed to operate without legal harassment. It could meet anywhere in town, hold rallies, and freely distribute information. It is hard to underestimate the importance of these seemingly simple functions for the survival of a local union. By electing Maloy as mayor, the local also assured its membership's access to New Deal economic programs. During the recession of 1937–39 this meant basic survival for many steelworker families. Acting as a liaison between the membership and New Deal programs, the local instilled in its membership the notion of the union as an economic and political necessity for the working class. The ERP vision of unionism as solely a collective bargaining instrument no longer held.

Communism and Politics

Political divisions within the local extended beyond simple Democratic-Republican lines. A serious schism arose between Communist and non-Communist leaders within the Left-Progressive alliance from 1939 to 1941. During the Popular Front period, 1936–39, Communists helped organize the mill, worked to bring Elmer Maloy into the union, and supported his mayoral bid. In 1939, however, the Communist Party changed its foreign policy line and took a leftward turn in its political work. This caused the Left-Progressive alliance to break apart just as Maloy was becoming isolated on the city council. The political rupture affected not only Duquesne politics but also the politics of Local 1256. It demonstrated that any hopes for a long-lasting political realignment in Duquesne would always be tenuous at best.

The Popular Front alliance became strained in August 1939, when the Communist Party changed its political line following the signing of the German-Soviet Nonaggression Pact. The party now labeled the war in Europe an imperialist struggle and criticized President Roosevelt for drawing the United States into the fray.[102] The increasing likelihood that the United States would enter the war, coupled with the reaction to the change in the party's political line, unleashed what the historian Maurice Isserman has called the "most ferocious and concerted anti-radical campaign since the Palmer raids of 1920."[103] Its long-term effect would be to form "much of the administrative and legal groundwork of the 'McCarthy Era.'"[104] Leading this anti-Communist crusade would be the House Committee on Un-American Activities, or Dies Committee. In Pennsylvania, Dies Committee investigators illegally broke into the Philadelphia Communist Party offices and seized documents. The committee also raided the Pittsburgh offices of the party in March 1940, seized literature, and subpoenaed the western Pennsylvania party leaders James Dolson and George Powers to appear at its hearings. Powers, who helped organize the local at the Duquesne Works, refused to name names for the committee and was cited for contempt of Congress.[105]

The nonaggression pact also forced the party to distance itself from Roosevelt and to follow a more independent political path. The Communists at first hoped to build a third party movement with John L. Lewis, but by the spring of 1940 they were advancing their own party for various offices on the November ballot. This required a massive state-by-state campaign to gather qualifying petitions.[106] But the petition drive opened party members up to further physical assaults and legal persecution. In many states, such as Illinois, Communists were beaten by mobs, while in others they were jailed. By November the party had qualified for the ballot in twenty-two states but was ruled off in another fifteen after completing all ballot requirements.[107]

The effort to undermine and harass the party's petition campaign in the Pittsburgh region began in earnest in June 1940. That month the *Pittsburgh Press* published the names and addresses of all area residents who had signed the Communists' petition. The paper then offered to print the names of all who claimed either that they had not signed the petition or that they were tricked into signing it. The Dies Committee followed with a letter to each petition signer that held out an opportunity for a similar repudiation. These efforts led more than sixteen hundred residents to disclaim their actions.[108] Most repudiated their signatures out of fear. With their names in the papers many faced harassment and a loss of employment. In McKeesport a mill worker claimed he was threatened with the loss of his job by a city detective. In nearby Glassport the city council voted to label the eighty-one signers of the petition in that town as members of the "fifth column." In Weirton, West Virginia, the American Legion worked closely with local authorities to secure the arrest of local petition signers. WPA workers throughout the state were dropped from the payroll for signing.[109]

After so many repudiated their signatures, the Allegheny County district attorney convened a special grand jury in June to investigate whether the petitioners had engaged in any criminal conduct. The Allegheny County Grand Jury heard as many as four hundred witnesses a day for three weeks before handing up forty-three indictments on charges of perjury, conspiracy, and/or obtaining signatures under false pretense. Many of those indicted were western Pennsylvania Communist leaders and candidates for public office. Indicted Duquesne residents included Anthony Salopek, for alleged-ly obtaining signatures under false pretext, and Mack McCullough, a mill worker and Communist accused of conspiracy and perjury. The district at-torney's case was built not only on grand jury testimony but also from a seem-ingly unusual source: affidavits collected by Mayor Elmer Maloy at the Du-quesne City Hall.[110]

The *Pittsburgh Press*'s list of petition signers included the names of sev-enty-five Duquesne residents, which the *Duquesne Times* dutifully reprint-ed. Following the actions of the *Pittsburgh Press* and the Dies Committee, Maloy sent each petition signer a card announcing that city hall would be open one evening for petition signers to come in and repudiate their signa-ture. Maloy announced that this would stop any "fifth column" movement in Duquesne. Approximately two-thirds of the Duquesne petition signers came forward to sign affidavits and deny that they knowingly signed the petition. Many argued that their names were forged, while others claimed that they thought they were signing a petition in support of the Democratic Par-ty or to keep the United States out of the war.[111] The signers identified Salo-pek, along with McCullough and an immigrant mill worker, Yeager Masro-pian, as the circulators of the petition. Salopek immediately acknowledged signing the petition, because he noted, "[I] believe in the right of minority candidates to be on the ballot." However, he denied circulating the petition. He then defended his past political work and attacked Maloy, signaling an end to their political alliance. "I fought for civil rights when others didn't dare to," Salopek said. "I actively helped to build the SWOC when others were in company unions. The people of Duquesne will not be intimidated by war hysteria coming from irresponsibles."[112]

The transformation of Maloy from a Communist ally to anti-Communist derived largely from his two leadership positions: mayor and national SWOC officer. As mayor Maloy had to appeal to an electorate broader than the union membership. In addition, he found himself surrounded by a conservative majority on the city council that did not hesitate to use the Communist is-sue for political gain.[113] Supporting the rights of Communists would not help him win reelection in 1941. Maloy also had chosen not to run for another term as president of Local 1256 in 1940. Thus he no longer needed to ally himself with Salopek within the local. Maloy had worked with Salopek and the Com-munists to build the union, win the local's presidency, and secure election as mayor. That alliance became a political liability when the Communists changed their political line and moved leftward.

As a full-time national grievanceman for SWOC, Maloy further found it politically expedient to conform to the political positions of the national union leadership. It was clear in 1940 that the leadership did not want Communists in its ranks. SWOC president Philip Murray was still in the final process of firing the last of the Communist organizers whom he hired in 1936–37. In addition, the pages of the union's newspaper, *Steel Labor*, carried numerous articles approving of anti-Communist resolutions by the United Auto Workers and the CIO.[114] Still, the national union would not challenge locals directly on the issue of electing Communists to leadership posts. SWOC has been portrayed as a strictly top-down organization, but locals held considerable leeway to direct their own affairs. They controlled the election of their own officers, although national representatives at times intervened, but mostly in the form of handpicking workers to run against Communist officers.[115]

A local's right to elect Communists, however, also implied the right to ban them. Some locals took the opportunity handed them by the 1940 petition campaign to clean out Communist leaders and members. The six thousand–member Jones & Laughlin local at Hazelwood suspended eighteen members who signed the petition. The men had to be cleared before an "anti-Fifth Column organization of war veterans" or face expulsion from the local. At least six other SWOC locals in the Pittsburgh region formed similar committees. The national union appeared to condone such actions when *Steel Labor* printed a letter from the Jones & Laughlin local favorably describing its "committee against all foreign 'isms'" and its efforts to root out Communists.[116]

Maloy attempted a similar purge at Local 1256, but he faced formidable opposition from the rank-and-file. Salopek was a highly respected union man, especially among the low-skilled immigrants and black workers who made up the core of the union's membership. They also generally followed Salopek's political positions. During the Popular Front period Local 1256 had contacts with Communist-led organizations, including the People's Congress for Peace and Democracy, the Pennsylvania Workers School, the International Labor Defense, and the Workers' Alliance. In addition, the local frequently passed resolutions concerning the Spanish Civil War, fascism, and the French Popular Front, all introduced by Salopek and sponsored by the American League for Peace and Democracy, which was pro-Communist.[117] Before the petition uproar Salopek's influence in the local had not suffered during the Communist Party's initial abandonment of the Popular Front in August 1939. When Salopek changed his political line and introduced resolutions to the local opposing both war loans to foreign countries and increased expenditures for "armaments at the expense of work relief for the unemployed and aid for youth and farmers," the membership still approved them. When the June 1940 election for the local's officers was held just days after the *Pittsburgh*

Press printed Salopek's name as a petition signer, he received the highest vote count of any officer. Numerous other nominees, including Fletcher Williamson, the former Fort Dukane vice president, also won election after their names appeared as petition signers. And replacing Maloy as president of the local was Ernest Fries, another former ERP chairman who now was a political ally of Salopek's.[118]

After Salopek's arrest in July, Maloy pushed for his removal from office in the local. Maloy told area reporters, "I'm not going to defend any Communist. The SWOC has no place for workers of the Communist Party."[119] He also predicted that Salopek's arrest would lead to an "immediate housecleaning" in which the local would expel Salopek and three other "undesirables."[120] At a July meeting of the local Maloy retreated from his public position of kicking the Communists out of the union. Instead, he introduced a resolution declaring Salopek's position as financial secretary vacant. Maloy claimed that Salopek had used the union hall for "purposes detrimental to the SWOC" and that his "unfavorable publicity" was "causing much dissatisfaction among our members and is thereby hurting our advancements." The local's membership defeated Maloy's resolution by a wide margin.[121] Salopek concluded from the vote that any "attempt to control the political activities of trade unionists is Hitlerism, and American workers won't stand for that."[122] The local not only failed to go along with Maloy but expressed dissatisfaction with his public airing of the issue. Concerned that its internal struggles had gained too much publicity, the local voted to allow only its publicity agent to speak to the press.[123]

Maloy's attack coincided with another management effort to remove Salopek from the mill. On June 21, while the grand jury was hearing testimony, the Duquesne Works suspended Salopek for five days for a violation of work rules. Management claimed that Salopek had performed his job improperly, causing a number of steel bars to be wasted. The local immediately filed a grievance and aggressively defended Salopek, arguing that the company was unfairly discriminating against him. Salopek was issued a second work rules violation slip in July and faced immediate firing. A few years earlier Salopek had successfully defended his job by appealing to Maloy and the ERP when threatened by management. Maloy now almost appeared to be acting in conjunction with management, attempting to remove Salopek from union office while management tried to fire him. By August, however, the union and company had agreed to a settlement and Salopek returned to work.[124]

A mass trial for twenty-eight of the openly Communist Pittsburgh-area petition circulators began in September 1940. Guilty verdicts were returned for all twenty-eight in early 1941, and sentences ranged from two months in jail for Duquesne's Mack McCullough to two years for George Powers. Other Communist Party political candidates and district leaders received at least one-year sentences.[125] Anthony Salopek and six other trade unionists who did not openly acknowledge Communist membership were tried in the summer of 1941. Salopek now admitted that he had circulated the Communist petition. He explained that because he had no reason to hide the petition's objectives, he clearly stated the purpose of the petition to the signers. Under cross-examination two of the five witnesses against Salopek admitted they could not remember what Salopek had told them, and defense attorneys also showed that the repudiations by the other signers had arisen from fear and intimidation. Salopek was found not guilty, although the judge still ordered him to pay court costs.[126]

The combined effects of the trial and the Communist Party's political line during the nonaggression pact years finally weakened Salopek's support in the union. A few weeks after he was acquitted of the petition charges, he lost his first election as financial secretary. His political ally, Ernest Fries, lost the presidency to John Kane, another former ERP chairman-turned-SWOC-president and an ardent anti-Communist.[127] Ironically, two days after Salopek was defeated, Germany invaded the Soviet Union and the Communist Party quickly changed its political line again. A defender of the Left-Progressive coalition once more, Salopek reversed course and joined Maloy's mayoral reelection campaign. The timing was good, and aided by the tireless but discreet efforts of the Communists, Maloy held off his Republican opponent.[128]

Political divisions based on communism would continue within the union despite the reversal of the Communist Party line. The 1942 union elections for local officers saw the institution of political slates. In that election Fries, Salopek, and their allies regained their respective offices, defeating the anti-Communist slate. Maloy's SWOC work increasingly took him away from the local, and John Kane would take his place as the standard-bearer of anticommunism. The Communists were instrumental in building the union and securing union representation in town politics. Nevertheless, their presence also created another lasting division within the labor movement.[129]

Strategies for Building a Dues-Paying Membership

Local 1256 built up its membership in numerous ways. It protected workers' shop-floor rights through the grievance procedure, won economic benefits and job protection in collective bargaining agreements, and secured unemployment relief through its involvement in local politics. But not all workers joined the union. Of those who did, many did not always pay their dues.

This did not demonstrate an inability of the union to meet workers' needs but an ambivalence toward unionism within the rank-and-file. Even workers who successfully used the grievance process to secure raises or improve working conditions often lapsed into nonpayment of dues. Between 1937 and 1941 SWOC experimented with different techniques for building and sustaining a regular dues-paying membership. Mixing positive inducements, negative incentives, and outright coercion, Local 1256 still had trouble keeping even half the mill's workforce in the union at any one time.

The union consciously used the grievance process to build its flagging membership. Key grievances were used to rally workers into joining the union, thus providing a united front against management. The machine shop and boiler shop reported "100 percent" union membership in 1941 when several of their grievances wound their way through the grievance process. The machinists remained fully unionized into 1942 after an attempt by management to introduce incentive rates galvanized them into protecting their hourly rates.[130] But the union's success with the machinists did not always extend to other workers. In the first bar mill case, discussed earlier, the union had to pressure workers into signing its grievance petition, and many workers in the department, dissatisfied with the outcome, then sought to bypass the union by filing independent (nonunion) grievances. When the union satisfactorily settled a scarfers' grievance, its membership in that department then declined. This prompted the president to denounce workers who got "what they want on their grievance case" and then did not pay dues.[131] The successful prosecution of grievances did not ensure a consistent dues-paying membership.

The union also attempted to coerce workers to join and pay dues by withholding the grievance machinery from nonmembers and union men who failed to pay dues. The union did not use this method consistently until after SWOC weathered the Roosevelt recession and became more secure on the shop floor. The danger in refusing to extend the grievance process to workers whose dues were in arrears, especially in the union's early years when it was weakest, was that it encouraged management to break the contract and build up shop-floor precedents. More confident of their position in late 1940, some SWOC locals, including Duquesne, refused to defend grievances from workers who had not been members for three months. Nonmembers thus were forced to join the union, pay dues for three months, and only then have their grievances processed.[132] Again, the maneuver did not ensure that workers would join the union. Not coincidentally, the number of independent (nonunion) grievances at Duquesne increased the month the union instituted its policy.[133]

Carnegie-Illinois policies regarding dues collections and solicitations further constrained the union's ability to build its membership. The company recognized SWOC as the bargaining agent for its members only, and it did not want to encourage further union membership. It refused to allow solicitation for membership during working hours on plant property, and it printed disciplinary forms for management to use in case unionists were caught signing up members. The form for the third and final violation notified the worker that his "services will no longer be required." The company also made clear that the contract provided only for a limited number of grievancemen, who had the authority to raise grievances but not solicit membership or collect dues. U.S. Steel further refused to recognize shop stewards, who in some industries both filed grievances and collected dues on plant property.[134]

Local 1256 did elect shop stewards, although they sought no grievance authority and did not openly solicit dues on plant property. As for the Carnegie-Illinois policy against solicitation, the stewards were, in the words of Elmer Maloy, "to obey the ruling unless they were sure of not being seen."[135] The union depended primarily on workers to come to the union hall to pay their dues. When the economy bottomed out in late 1937 and 1938, the local could do little to collect dues or sign up new members. Dues were suspended for unemployed members, and the local took a defensive stance and did not recruit aggressively.[136]

By the end of 1938 the economic emergency had eased and SWOC desperately needed money. The national union, in addition to local union leaders and grievancemen, ideally wanted a dues checkoff mechanism, whereby workers' union dues would be deducted from their paychecks each month and forwarded to the union. U.S. Steel adamantly refused this demand. The union instead settled on two courses of action to raise more dues: the installation of a formal dues committeeman structure in each plant, and the employment of dues pickets at plant gates. The national leadership preferred the use of dues committeemen, but the combination of the financial crisis and U.S. Steel's continued refusal to allow open dues collections on the shop floor forced the national to condone dues pickets, which militant local leaders pushed.[137]

National SWOC officers at first encouraged locals to deepen their commitment to in-plant dues collections in late 1938 and early 1939. By the summer of 1939 the national had established an elaborate dues collection apparatus based on a modified shop-steward model. Instead of stewards, each local was to appoint or elect a dues committeeman who would be responsible for collecting dues from twenty-five workers. The committeemen would have no grievance authority, and by changing the name from *steward* to *com-*

mitteeman, SWOC in part hoped to lessen U.S. Steel's opposition to the move.[138] However, this system had two problems. First, it was difficult for a union to find enough volunteer committeemen. The Duquesne Works would have required approximately two hundred, but the local secured at most only thirty to forty committeemen at any one time. In addition, the position was marked by high turnover.[139] Second, the functioning of the committeeman structure depended on U.S. Steel's approval. However, the corporation refused to officially recognize the committeemen, thus forcing them to collect dues very discreetly.[140]

Frustrated by poor dues collections, SWOC locals began using dues pickets. The locals threw single-day picket lines around a plant or a particular department's entry gate. Union officers, stewards, and muscular and tough union supporters stopped workers before they entered the plant. Each worker then had four options: produce his paid-up dues booklet to gain entrance; join the union or pay back dues and then gain entrance; not go to work; or attempt to pass through the picket and risk a beating. Dues pickets sprang up throughout the Monongahela Valley, and each mill regularly sent pickets to support the efforts at other mills. Committeemen and union supporters gathered in Braddock one month, Homestead the next, then Duquesne.[141] The dues pickets quickly disrupted production and caused labor shortages. Management found itself forced to cancel orders, call in extra workers the next day, or pay overtime. By mid-1939 U.S. Steel had decided to choose the lesser of two evils. Management agreed informally to recognize the dues committeeman structure but with one committeeman for every thirty-five workers. It also allowed, although not in writing, the solicitation of dues on the shop floor, provided it did not disrupt production. The dues pickets had forced U.S. Steel to the bargaining table. Yet even after the agreement SWOC locals still occasionally used dues pickets to build up faltering memberships.[142]

Dues pickets helped win the dues committeeman structure for SWOC, but how effective was it for building and sustaining a regular dues-paying membership? Anecdotal accounts of SWOC dues pickets describe that locals brought in $10,000 in one night but offer no sense of the technique's long-term effectiveness.[143] Duquesne's experiences with dues pickets, however, shows much less success and reveals other union weaknesses. Dues collections at Duquesne had not topped $250 in any one month during all of 1938. The union then held its first dues picket in January 1939, but it brought in only $386. By April dues collections had again fallen below $200 and did not break $250 through September. A dues picket in November proved much more successful, bringing in almost $2,400. However, the picket came just after a well-organized membership drive, the installation of the dues com-

mitteeman structure, and a temporary reduction in initiation fees, all of
which already had boosted the dues collections the month before. Two other dues pickets in January and October 1940 netted the local only $368 and
$409, respectively. Membership figures reveal a similar pattern, that dues
pickets had no long-lasting effect.[144]

The Duquesne dues picket in October 1940 also showed that the union did
not always have control of the situation. That picket began in the evening after
five busloads of steelworkers and miners from nearby towns arrived. More
than five hundred pickets blocked the entrances to the mill and began checking dues cards. As with all other dues pickets, the Duquesne local needed
outside help. Despite its efforts to seal the plant, the union could not stop
hundreds of men from entering untouched via railroad tracks. After a few
minor skirmishes at the main gate, a group of fifteen club-wielding blacks—
"young punks," according to Maloy—started a fight with the union men. The
attackers, none of them steelworkers, were joined by more than two thousand bystanders who threw pieces of brick. According to Edward Wadeck, a
unionist who came to Duquesne that night to help out, "[We] got the Hell
beat out of us." The outnumbered steelworkers retreated to the union hall.
There they were held virtual prisoners—with plenty of beer, soda, and sand-
wiches—by the large mob. Maloy, acting as mayor, called out the fire department, which connected hoses in case they needed to be turned on the crowd.
For his actions Maloy would lose control of the fire department after the
Republican city council used the incident to reduce the mayor's authority.
The standoff continued for a few hours until the crowd slowly dispersed and
the unionists left in small groups. The use of strong-arm tactics could work
in the short run to raise money for a cash-strapped local, but it could not
build and sustain a membership.[145]

Conclusion

SWOC Local 1256 protected the shop-floor interests of workers by defending their seniority and promotion rights, checking the arbitrary power of the
foreman, and winning wage increases. It protected the civil liberties of workers in the community, assuring them of their right to register and vote as they
saw fit. It provided workers with economic relief through the New Deal because of the local's participation in the political process. If these services did
not compel workers to join the local, the union also used a variety of organizing drives and dues-collecting strategies to encourage membership. Still,
the local had great difficulty sustaining its membership. By the summer of
1941, with war production removing the last vestiges of the depression, the

Duquesne Works once again reached its 1920s workforce levels. A large membership drive by the union in the late summer raised the local's membership to 4,265, but one month later 1,208 were removed from the rolls for not paying their dues. Through the end of 1941 only slightly more than half the workforce belonged to the union.[146] Five years after the creation of SWOC, the union had become rooted in the shop floor and in town, but it was far from a unified and enthusiastic mass movement of all the mill's workers.

Conclusion

THE NATIONAL LABOR RELATIONS BOARD (NLRB) held a representation election to determine sole bargaining rights at all U.S. Steel plants in May 1942. The corporation had refused to cede this right to SWOC through contract negotiations, thus forcing the union to petition the NLRB for the election. A strong vote for SWOC in the NLRB election would then strengthen the union's hand that year in seeking two other contract provisions that U.S. Steel adamantly opposed, the union shop and dues checkoff. Under a union shop all workers had to join the union in order to remain employed. The dues checkoff meant that monthly union dues were deducted automatically from workers' paychecks and forwarded to the union by the company. These rights, SWOC officials believed, would solve the union's chronic dues and membership fluctuations.[1]

"The bigger the majority the better the contract," Philip Murray said of the election that was to precede the collective bargaining.[2] Duquesne's Local 1256 spent the months leading up to the vote in a massive organizing campaign. The union handed out thousands of leaflets, drove sound trucks throughout the town, and provided dues committeemen with monetary incentives for signing up delinquent members. An organizing committee visited the homes of nonmembers, and union members in the conditioning department refused to work with any man who did not join and pay his dues. On election day 96 percent of all Duquesne workers who voted cast their ballots for SWOC. In U.S. Steel mills across the country workers overwhelmingly followed suit. At Carnegie-Illinois mills 93 percent of the voters chose SWOC, marking the successful culmination of the organizing drive that had begun in June 1936.[3]

Despite these impressive tallies, the election was not an accurate reflection of worker support for unionism. Duquesne's workforce did not suddenly become united, nor did workers remain within the union. Of all workers eligible to vote in the NLRB election at Duquesne, 76 percent cast their ballots for SWOC. One in 4 workers either did not bother to vote or voted against the union. Granted, a clear majority favored SWOC. Nevertheless, many workers still refused either to support the union in an election or to join and pay monthly dues. Of the roughly fifty-six hundred employees eligible for union membership, thirty-five hundred (63 percent) were in the union at the beginning of 1942. The massive membership drive raised that total by only 424 before the May election date. During the next month membership quickly fell to 3,072, or just 54 percent of the eligible workforce. The monthly $1 dues payments, which should have equaled the number of union workers, hovered at about $2,000 per month.[4] After five years of unionism at Duquesne barely half the workforce remained organized during any one month.

Despite its wide margin of victory in the NLRB election, the union did not win its contract demand for a union shop in 1942. World War II interrupted the regular collective bargaining procedures between management and the union; instead, the newly created National War Labor Board (NWLB) determined the new contract. Cognizant both of the union's sacrifice in agreeing to a no-strike pledge for the war's duration, and of the disruption the war would have on union membership, the NWLB provided SWOC with a union security clause and the dues checkoff. Instead of granting the union shop, the board had maintenance of membership written into U.S. Steel's collective bargaining agreement. Maintenance of membership provided that all workers who joined the union had to remain in good standing and pay dues through a payroll checkoff for the life of the contract. Workers still could opt out of joining the union, and even union members had fifteen days during which they could leave the union when each contract was negotiated. Still, maintenance of membership assured the union that its dues and membership would not fluctuate so wildly from month to month and that it would not have to hound members to pay up. Indeed, the union's enrollment increased dramatically during and after the war. U.S. Steel forcefully opposed both contract provisions, and if not for the NWLB order, it is highly doubtful the union could have won any kind of union security clause in 1942.[5]

The labor historian Nelson Lichtenstein has argued that CIO unions took a cautious path on the eve of World War II. Instead of relying on rank-and-file activism, they turned instead to the federal government for help in consolidating unionism in mass production industries. In exchange for a no-strike pledge CIO leaders accepted "a government-sponsored union security guarantee designed to increase their internal bureaucratic nature." Maintenance of membership, according to Lichtenstein, was an antidemocratic maneuver, imposed on workers by union bureaucrats, that stifled rank-and-file militancy.[6] Lichtenstein argues that in the long run, despite the vast increases in labor's numbers during the war, the NWLB weakened labor by weakening potential rank-and-file militancy. Duquesne reveals otherwise. The NWLB and maintenance of membership were critical influences on the future of unionism but for a very different reason. Instead of weakening the union, maintenance of membership artificially strengthened an inconsistent and fragmented rank-and-file and masked the internal weaknesses of the union.

To understand labor's weakened position in recent years, it is necessary to understand that from its inception mass-production unionism was never as strong as it might have seemed. The working class was highly fragmented not only before the 1930s but also during and after that critical decade. The building and rebuilding of the giant Duquesne Works in its early decades created a workforce deeply divided by skill as well as by space and time. The unskilled laborer working night shift in the open hearth department understood work very differently than the skilled roller on the day shift in one of the bar mills. Added to this, wage systems, based on hourly, incentive, or straight tonnage, meant that the economic and shop-floor interests of the workers further diverged. Layered onto this were ethnic, and by World War I, racial divisions. These remained through the 1920s, only to harden during the Great Depression. Although the depression affected all workers adversely, low-skilled hourly workers suffered the most. In addition, hourly and tonnage payment systems now created a greater gulf. Unskilled and semiskilled hourly workers most needed a raise in the common laboring rate, whereas incentive and tonnage workers needed revisions in the ways their rates were calculated. Ethnic and racial differences similarly became more stark, as U.S.-born white foremen tended to reward workers of similar background and to discriminate against immigrants and blacks.

Plant managers and local political elites further deepened these divisions between workers throughout the mill's history. U.S. Steel consciously divided workers by ethnicity within work crews and departments. It also promoted only people from certain ethnic groups to the highest-paying jobs or into management positions. During the Great Depression U.S.-born workers and those of northern and western European heritage found more favorable treatment from foremen, whereas workers of southern and eastern European backgrounds and blacks found the least favorable treatment. This favoritism also heightened during times of labor conflict. In 1919 and again in 1934 mill managers and Duquesne's mayor consciously sought to divide workers along ethnic and skill lines and to repress any hint of united labor action.

The early New Deal, far from creating a culture of unity among workers, further deepened the divisions among them. The NRA fostered two competing versions of workplace representation—employee representation under the employee representation plan and trade unionism under the Amalgamated's Fort Dukane Lodge. Because the higher-skilled workers preferred the ERP and the union appealed to lower-skilled hourly workers, federal policy institutionalized for the first time the long-standing skill and ethnic divisions at Duquesne. Although the NRA also provided mechanisms for workers to achieve collective bargaining rights, both the NRA and the Amalgamated's national leadership proved incapable of adequately defending workers' rights. Neither proved strong enough to help a fragmented workforce overcome the powerful open-shop policies of U.S. Steel.

Only with the rise of the CIO, and a strong centralized national steel union, did this become possible. Even then, changes in labor law—the National Labor Relations Act—were necessary to help defeat ERPs. Still, the best SWOC could achieve after a year of organizing and operating under a collective bargaining agreement was a union of half the workforce. By early 1938 SWOC Local 1256 could not even claim that many members. Four years later membership again climbed to the halfway mark but not without coaxing and threats. The differing shop-floor interests of the skilled and unskilled continued to divide the workforce. As the union quickly learned, in order to keep the skilled tonnage workers content, it sometimes had to sacrifice raises for lower-skilled hourly workers and vice versa. And although Duquesne had relatively favorable race relations compared to other area mills, in part owing to the inclusion of black workers during the Amalgamated and SWOC periods, the exclusion of blacks from particular higher-paying jobs led to simmering racial conflict. Fragmentation also was evident in politics when workers could not unify to gain effective Democratic Party control of municipal government for even as long as a year.

For these reasons maintenance of membership and the dues checkoff were essential for the local's survival. The amount of time, energy, and money spent confronting workers for dues each month, and during special registration drives, could have been better spent on confronting the company on shop-floor issues. It even can be argued that the dues checkoff did not lead to a lessening of contact between the union leadership and the rank-and-file but only to a decrease in threats and hostile demands by union leaders for dues from the rank-and-file.

If it had been unable to maintain membership, the union would have had difficult times both during and after World War II, because divisions between workers continued to erupt with regularity. The war created a social dislocation on the shop floor as veteran workers who went to war were replaced by a much different workforce—younger, and often female and black. Gender, not an issue of contention between workers before the war, suddenly became a divisive issue in 1942. The hiring of more than seven hundred women workers at the mill not only reconstituted social relations on the shop floor but also forced Local 1256 to integrate these workers in a union setting that was overtly hostile to women's employment.[7] The war also heightened racial tensions. Duquesne was not beset with hate strikes, but grievances by black workers demanding promotion increased, as did white opposition to black advancement. After the war, increased black militancy and white intransigence divided the union and membership further. By 1950 separate election slates for the local's annual election carried the informal headings of "white" and "colored."[8] The resurgence of the Communist issue after the war also divided Local 1256 politically. In 1948 the union brought Anthony Salopek up on charges of distributing materials detrimental to the union and its leadership. Convicted after a trial that deeply divided the membership, Salopek was expelled from the union he had spent years building.[9]

As social and political divisions increased, divisions based on the production process and management payment systems actually tended to decrease. Greater numbers of workers found themselves on incentive and tonnage payment systems, and greater mobility through seniority-based promotion meant that hourly workers now stood a much greater chance of eventually moving into these jobs. Skill divisions clearly did not evaporate, however, and by the end of the 1950s skilled tradesmen mounted struggles against management—including wildcat strikes—about issues that did not involve the majority of other workers.[10]

Maintenance of membership allowed Local 1256 greater stability and time to fight for shop-floor issues. It essentially forced a divided workforce to act as one, and it forced workers to remain in the union who otherwise would have drifted away. But maintenance of membership and the dues checkoff also provided an inflated view of the union's real strength. Large memberships obscured the lack of spontaneous union support on the shop floor. Even when the union successfully defended workers' interests, those same workers did not necessarily remain active members. Fragmentation and apathy were just as much a part of steel unionism at the Duquesne Works as were unity and militancy.

Notes

Abbreviations for Archives, Record Groups, and Oral History Collections

AIS	Archives of Industrial Society, Hillman Library, University of Pittsburgh
ALUA	Archives of Labor and Urban Affairs, Wayne State University, Detroit
BVLH	Beaver Valley Labor History Society Records, UE/Labor Archives, Archives of Industrial Society, Hillman Library, University of Pittsburgh
CIO-USWA	CIO National and International Unions, United Steel Workers of America Records, Department of Archives and Manuscripts, The Catholic University of America, Washington, D.C.
CPIN	Cornelia Pinchot Papers, Library of Congress
CSG	Clinton S. Golden Paper, Historical Collections and Labor Archives, The Pennsylvania State University, State College
DJS	David J. Saposs Papers, State Historical Society of Wisconsin, Madison
GPIN	Gifford Pinchot Papers, Library of Congress
HAOHP	Homestead Album Oral History Project, Archives of Industrial Society, Hillman Library, University of Pittsburgh
HCLA	Historical Collections and Labor Archives, The Pennsylvania State University, State College
HEB	Heber Blankenhorn Collection, Archives of Labor and Urban Affairs, Wayne State University, Detroit
HJR	Harold J. Ruttenberg Papers, Historical Collections and Labor Archives, The Pennsylvania State University, State College
HOC	Harvey O'Connor Collection, Archives of Labor and Urban Affairs, Wayne State University, Detroit
KPE	Katherine Pollack Ellickson Collection, Archives of Labor and Urban Affairs, Wayne State University, Detroit

L-1256   United Steelworkers of America, Local 1256 Records, Historical Collec-
                tions and Labor Archives, The Pennsylvania State University, State Col-
                lege
LOC   Library of Congress, Washington, D.C.
MCD   David J. McDonald Papers, Historical Collections and Labor Archives,
                The Pennsylvania State University, State College
MCM   John McManigal Collection, UE/Labor Archives, Archives of Industrial
                Society, Hillman Library, University of Pittsburgh, Pittsburgh
MHV   Mary Heaton Vorse Collection, Archives of Labor and Urban Affairs,
                Wayne State University, Detroit
NA   National Archives, Washington, D.C.
NLRB-Exhibits   Records of the National Labor Relations Board, Administrative Divi-
                sion, Files and Dockets Sections, Transcripts and Exhibits, Washing-
                ton National Records Center, Suitland, Md.
NLRB-Miller   Records of the National Labor Relations Board, Pre–Wagner Act Re-
                cords, National Labor Board: Records of the Executive Director, Jessie
                I. Miller, National Archives, Washington, D.C.
NSLRB   Records of the National Steel Labor Relations Board, National Archives,
                Washington, D.C.
POHP   Pittsburgh Oral History Project, Pennsylvania Historical and Museum
                Commission, Pennsylvania State Archives, Harrisburg
STET   Edward R. Stettinius, Jr., Papers, Manuscript Division, Special Collec-
                tions, University of Virginia Library, Charlottesville
T-BL   Tri-Boro Lodge #186 (Braddock, Pa.) Papers, Historical Collections and
                Labor Archives, The Pennsylvania State University, State College
UE/L   UE/Labor Archives, Archives of Industrial Society, Hillman Library,
                University of Pittsburgh
ULP   Urban League of Pittsburgh Records, Archives of Industrial Society,
                Hillman Library, University of Pittsburgh
USAOHP   United Steelworkers of America Oral History Project, Historical Collec-
                tions and Labor Archives, Pennsylvania State University, State College
USSC   U.S. Steel Corp. (Duquesne Works) Payroll Ledgers and Records of the
                Personnel Division, UE/Labor Archives, Archives of Industrial Society,
                Hillman Library, University of Pittsburgh

Introduction

1. See, for example, Elmer Maloy, interview by Don Kennedy, 7 Nov. 1967, transcript;
John J. Mullen, interview by Alice Hoffman, Feb. 1966, transcript; George Patterson, interview by Alice Hoffman, 2 Feb. 1969, transcript, all in United Steelworkers of America
Oral History Project, Historical Collections and Labor Archives, Pennsylvania State University, State College.

2. For recent works on technology and/or management see Thomas J. Misa, *A Nation
of Steel: The Making of Modern America, 1865–1925* (Baltimore: Johns Hopkins University
Press, 1995); Jonathan Hugo Rees, "Managing the Mills: Labor Policy in the American Steel
Industry, 1892–1937" (Ph.D. diss., University of Wisconsin, Madison, 1997).

Works that focus on black workers and racial issues include Robert J. Norrell, "Caste in Steel: Jim Crow Careers in Birmingham, Alabama," *Journal of American History* 73 (Dec. 1986): 669–94; Dennis C. Dickerson, *Out of the Crucible: Black Steelworkers in Western Pennsylvania, 1875–1980* (Albany: State University of New York Press, 1986); Peter Gottlieb, *Making Their Own Way: Southern Blacks' Migration to Pittsburgh, 1916–30* (Urbana: University of Illinois Press, 1987); John Hinshaw, "Dialectic of Division: Race and Power Among Western Pennsylvania Steelworkers, 1937–1975" (Ph.D. diss., Carnegie Mellon University, 1995); John Hinshaw and Judith Modell, "Perceiving Racism: Homestead from Depression to Deindustrialization," *Pennsylvania History* 62 (winter 1995): 17–52; Henry M. McKiven, Jr., *Iron and Steel: Class, Race, and Community in Birmingham, Alabama, 1875–1920* (Chapel Hill: University of North Carolina Press, 1995); Bruce Nelson, "'CIO Meant One Thing for the Whites and Another Thing for Us': Steelworkers and Civil Rights, 1936–1974," in *Southern Labor in Transition, 1940–1995,* ed. Robert H. Zieger (Knoxville: University of Tennessee Press, 1997); Ruth Needleman, "Diplomats and Rabble-Rousers: Black Leadership in Northwest Indiana's Steel Mills, Local Unions, and Communities," paper presented at the annual meeting of the Organization of American Historians, 1998; Judith Stein, *Running Steel, Running America: Race, Economic Policy, and the Decline of Liberalism* (Chapel Hill: University of North Carolina Press, 1998).

For community and ethnic studies see John Bodnar, *Steelton: Immigration and Industrialization, 1870–1940* (Pittsburgh: University of Pittsburgh Press, 1977); Frank H. Serene, "Immigrant Steelworkers in the Monongahela Valley: Their Communities and the Development of a Labor Class Consciousness" (Ph.D. diss., University of Pittsburgh, 1979); Ewa Morawska, *For Bread with Butter: The Life-Worlds of East Central Europeans in Johnstown, Pennsylvania, 1890–1940* (Cambridge: Cambridge University Press, 1985); Curtis Miner, *Homestead: The Story of a Steel Town* (Pittsburgh: Historical Society of Western Pennsylvania, 1989); Lizabeth Cohen, *Making a New Deal: Industrial Workers in Chicago, 1919–1939* (Cambridge: Oxford University Press, 1990); William Serrin, *Homestead: The Glory and Tragedy of an American Steel Town* (New York: Times Books, 1992).

Women and gender also have become recent focuses. See Elizabeth Jones, "Women Steelworkers During WWII and the Korean War," paper presented at the annual meeting of the Pennsylvania Historical Association, Oct. 1995; Karen Olson, "The Transformation of Gender in a Steelmaking Community: An Ethnographic and Historical Study of Sparrow's Point, Maryland" (Ph.D. diss., University of Maryland, College Park, 1994); Jim Rose, "'The Problem Every Supervisor Dreads': Women Workers at the U.S. Steel Duquesne Works During World War II," *Labor History* 36 (winter 1995): 24–51.

3. For essays that address shop floor issues or take a shop floor perspective but in the World War II and postwar eras, see Mark McColloch, "Consolidating Industrial Citizenship: The USWA at War and Peace, 1939–46," in *Forging a Union of Steel: Philip Murray, SWOC, and the United Steelworkers,* ed. Paul F. Clark, Peter Gottlieb, and Donald Kennedy (Ithaca: ILR Press, 1987), 45–86; Victor J. Forberger, "'My Mind Is Made Up—Don't Confuse Me with the Facts': Labor Relations in U.S. Steel, The Duquesne Works from 1955 to 1965" (senior honors thesis, Carnegie Mellon University, 9 May 1988); Victor J. Forberger, "Craftsmen and Contractual Relations at the Duquesne Steel Works, 1950s and 1960s," unpublished manuscript, 30 Nov. 1992, copy in author's possession. A recent dissertation that covers shop floor issues in the 1930s is James Carl Kollros, "Creating a Steel Workers

Notes to Pages 5–7

Union in the Calumet Region, 1933 to 1945" (Ph.D. diss., University of Illinois, Chicago, 1999).

4. Gary Gerstle, *Working-Class Americanism: The Politics of Labor in a Textile City, 1914–1960* (Cambridge: Cambridge University Press, 1989); Cohen, *Making a New Deal*.

5. Staughton Lynd, "'We Are All Leaders': The Alternative Unionism of the 1930s," paper presented at the North American Labor History Conference, Detroit, 1992; Staughton Lynd, *"We Are All Leaders": The Alternative Unionism of the Early 1930s* (Urbana: University of Illinois Press, 1996). For this approach to the history of steelworkers, see Staughton Lynd, "The Possibility of Radicalism in the Early 1930s: The Case of Steel," *Radical America* 6 (Nov.–Dec. 1972): 37–64; Philip W. Nyden, *Steelworkers Rank and File: The Political Economy of a Union Reform Movement* (New York: Praeger, 1984); Eric Leif Davin, "The Littlest New Deal: SWOC Takes Power in Steeltown—A Possibility of Radicalism in the Late 1930s," unpublished paper, no date, copy in author's possession.

6. For largely positive academic accounts see Carroll E. French, *The Shop Committee in the United States* (Baltimore: Johns Hopkins University Press, 1922); Ben M. Selekman, *Employes' Representation in Steel Works* (New York: Russell Sage Foundation, 1924); Ernest Richmond Burton, *Employee Representation* (Baltimore: Williams and Wilkens, 1926). The National Industrial Conference Board (NICB) published many reports and statistical surveys of ERPs for industry and the public during the 1920s and 1930s. See, for example, NICB, *Works Councils in the United States* (Boston: NICB, 1919); NICB, *A Works Council Manual* (Boston: NICB, 1920); NICB, *Collective Bargaining Through Employee Representation* (New York: NICB, 1933). The American Iron and Steel Institute (AISI) published several glowing descriptions of its ERPs. See AISI, *Employee Representation in the Iron and Steel Industry* (New York: AISI, 1934); AISI, *Collective Bargaining in the Steel Industry* (New York: AISI, June 1934); AISI, *The Men Who Make Steel* (New York: AISI, May 1936)

7. For critiques of ERPs from the Left, see Robert W. Dunn, *Company Unions: Employers' 'Industrial Democracy'* (New York: Vanguard, 1927); Harvey O'Connor, *Steel-Dictator* (New York: John Day, 1935); Lincoln Fairley, *The Company Union in Plan and Practice* (Affiliated Schools for Workers pamphlet, 1936). For the American Federation of Labor's views on ERPs during the 1930s, see Louis Adamic, "Company Unions and the A.F. of L.," *Nation,* 18 July 1934; *American Federationist* 40 (Sept. 1933): 950–52; *American Federationist* 41 (Feb. 1934): 130–32; *American Federationist* 42 (May 1935): 469–71.

8. Daniel Nelson, "The Company Union Movement, 1900–1937: A Reexamination," *Business History Review* 56 (autumn 1982): 335–57. Recent studies have addressed the evolutionary capabilities of ERPs. See Sanford M. Jacoby, *Modern Manners: Welfare Capitalism Since the New Deal* (Princeton: Princeton University Press, 1997); David Fairris, "From Exit to Voice in Shopfloor Governance: The Case of Company Unions," *Business History Review* 69 (winter 1995): 493–529.

9. Robert R. R. Brooks, *As Steel Goes, . . . Unionism in a Basic Industry* (New Haven: Yale University Press, 1940); Walter Galenson, *The CIO Challenge to the AFL: A History of the American Labor Movement, 1935–1941* (Cambridge: Harvard University Press, 1960); Irving Bernstein, *The Turbulent Years: A History of the American Worker, 1933–1941* (Boston: Houghton Mifflin, 1970). The most nuanced account of steel's ERPs is Carroll R. Daugherty, Melvin G. de Chazeau, and Samuel S. Stratton, *The Economics of the Iron and Steel Industry* 2 vols. (New York: McGraw-Hill, 1937).

10. Frederick Harbison, "Labor Relations in the Iron and Steel Industry, 1936–1939" (Ph.D. diss., Princeton University, 1940); Annemarie Draham, "Unlikely Allies Fight for Unionization: Homestead, Pa., 1933–1946" (master's thesis, Indiana University of Pennsylvania, 1984); Joel Sabadasz, "Understanding Workers: Labor Relations in Steel from 1930 to 1941 in the Southeastern Monongahela Valley," unpublished manuscript, no date, copy in author's possession.

11. In this voluminous literature see, for example, Thomas Geoghegan, *Which Side Are You On? Trying to Be for Labor When It's Flat on Its Back* (New York: Farrar, Straus and Giroux, 1991); Sheldon Friedman, Richard W. Hurd, Rudolph A. Oswald, and Ronald L. Seeber, eds., *Restoring the Promise of American Labor Law* (Ithaca, N.Y.: ILR Press, 1994). Conversely, what the Wagner Act meant for organizing the steel industry has been downplayed. A study that attempts to measure the effect of labor law on the rise of SWOC does not even mention that SWOC filed charges of unfair labor practices against U.S. Steel in 1936 and that the National Labor Relations Board conducted months of highly publicized hearings on the case. See Raymond Hogler, "Worker Participation, Employer Anti-Unionism, and Labor Law: The Case of the Steel Industry, 1918–1937," *Hofstra Labor Law Journal* 7 (fall 1989): 1–69.

12. Karl E. Klare, "Judicial Deradicalization of the Wagner Act and the Origins of Modern Legal Consciousness, 1937–1941," *Minnesota Law Review* 62 (March 1978): 265–339; Karl E. Klare, "Labor Law as Ideology: Toward a New Historiography of Collective Bargaining Law," *Industrial Relations Law Review* 4, no. 3 (1981): 450–82; Christopher L. Tomlins, *The State and the Unions: Labor Relations, Law, and the Organized Labor Movement in America, 1880–1960* (Cambridge: Cambridge University Press, 1985).

13. David Brody, "Labor Elections: Good For Workers?" *Dissent* (summer 1997): 71–77.

14. For a recent study of Pennsylvania coal miners that offers a similar approach, see Mildred Allen Beik, *The Miners of Windber: The Struggles of New Immigrants for Unionization, 1890s-1930s* (University Park: Pennsylvania State University Press, 1996).

Chapter 1: The Steel Strike of 1919

1. For sensational press coverage in the Pittsburgh region, see *(McKeesport) Daily News,* 22 Sept. 1919; *Pittsburgh Dispatch,* 24 Sept. 1919; *Pittsburgh Press,* 24 Sept. 1919.

2. *Iron Age,* 25 Sept. 1919, pp. 885, 887; "Father Kazinci," *Survey,* 7 Feb. 1920, p. 550; Interchurch World Movement, *Public Opinion and the Steel Strike* (New York: Harcourt Brace, 1921), 178; David Brody, *Labor in Crisis: The Steel Strike of 1919* (New York: Harper and Row, 1965), 112–13, 148; William Z. Foster, *The Great Steel Strike and Its Lessons* (New York: Huebsch, 1920), 100.

3. *Iron Age,* 2 Oct. 1919, p. 920; *Iron Age,* 16 Oct. 1919, p. B; *Daily News,* 26 Sept. 1919; *Pittsburgh Sun,* 23 Sept. 1919; Foster, *Great Steel Strike,* 100, 103, 224–25; National Committee for Organizing Iron and Steel Workers (NCOISW), mimeographed report for 6 Oct. 1919, Box 121, File: Steel—*Strike News*—1919, Mary Heaton Vorse Collection (MHV), Archives of Labor and Urban Affairs, Wayne State University, Detroit; Pennsylvania State Police, "Steel Workers Strike—1919," Box 10, File 1, Records of the Pennsylvania State Police, Pennsylvania State Archives, Harrisburg.

4. U.S. Congress, Senate, Committee on Education and Labor, *Investigation of Strike in Steel Industries,* 66th Cong., 1st sess., 1919, pt. 2: 501–2, 532; *Duquesne Times,* 10 Oct. 1919.

5. Senate, *Investigation of Strike,* pt. 2: 502–3, 505, 511.

6. Charles A. Gulick, Jr., *Labor Policy of the United States Steel Corporation* (New York: Columbia University Press, 1924), 185.

7. *Duquesne, Pennsylvania: Industrial, Historical Supplement to the Observer* (Duquesne, Pa.: Filcer and Blair, 1902), n.p.; James Howard Bridge, *The Inside History of the Carnegie Steel Company* (1903; reprint, New York: Arno, 1972), 174–75.

8. Paul Krause, *The Battle for Homestead, 1880–1892: Politics, Culture, and Steel* (Pittsburgh: University of Pittsburgh Press, 1992), 70–77, 155–92.

9. Bridge, *Inside History,* 175–78; Irwin Marcus, "The Duquesne Lockout of 1889: Prelude to Homestead in 1892," unpublished paper delivered at Homestead Centennial Conference, Pennsylvania State University, University Park, 1992, p. 5; John Ingham, *Making Iron and Steel: Independent Mills in Pittsburgh, 1820–1920* (Columbus: Ohio State University Press, 1991), 70.

10. Bridge, *Inside History,* 176–80; Ingham, *Making Iron and Steel,* 71; Herbert N. Casson, *The Romance of Steel: The Story of a Thousand Millionaires* (New York: Barnes, 1907), 114–15; Marcus, "Duquesne Lockout of 1889," pp. 5–11.

11. Bridge, *Inside History,* 179.

12. On the expansion of the Duquesne Works, see Bridge, *Inside History,* 180–83; *Duquesne, Pennsylvania,* n.p.; Joel Sabadasz, "Duquesne Works: Overview History," unpublished manuscript, summer 1991, pp. 3–8, copy in author's possession; W. Paul Strassmann, *Risk and Technological Innovation: American Manufacturing Methods During the Nineteenth Century* (Ithaca: Cornell University Press, 1959), 44; "Brief History of Duquesne Works," in U.S. Steel, "American Iron and Steel Institute Manufacturing Problems Committee Visit to Homestead District Works and Duquesne Works," 18 March 1958, pp. 8–9, Box 36, U.S. Steel Corp. (Duquesne Works) Payroll Ledgers and Records of the Personnel Division (USSC), 1904–80, UE/Labor Archives, Archives of Industrial Society (AIS), Hillman Library, University of Pittsburgh, Pittsburgh.

13. Bridge, *Inside History,* 180–83, 309–10; Casson, *Romance of Steel,* 115–16; Strassmann, *Risk and Technological Innovation,* 43; James M. Swank, "The Manufacture of Iron and Steel Rails in Western Pennsylvania," *Pennsylvania Magazine of History and Biography* 23 (1904): 10; Sabadasz, "Duquesne Works," pp. 3–4.

14. *Duquesne, Pennsylvania,* n.p.

15. Sabadasz, "Duquesne Works," pp. 4–5; Edward Sherwood Meade, "The Genesis of the United States Steel Corporation," *Quarterly Journal of Economics* 15 (Aug. 1901): 536–38; William T. Hogan, *Economic History of the Iron and Steel Industry in the United States* (Lexington, Mass.: Lexington, 1971), vol. 2: 463–73; Thomas J. Misa, *A Nation of Steel: The Making of Modern America, 1865–1925* (Baltimore: Johns Hopkins University Press, 1995), 167–69.

16. Hogan, *Economic History of Iron and Steel,* vol. 2: 481–521.

17. U.S. Steel Corp., *Annual Report,* 1902–16 (New York: U.S. Steel); A. M. Blair, *Duquesne's Silver Jubilee* (Duquesne, Pa.: n.p., 1916), 18; Sabadasz, "Duquesne Works," pp. 5–8; *Iron Trade Review,* 6 Jan. 1916, pp. 62–64.

18. Marcus, "Duquesne Lockout of 1889," p. 5; U.S. Congress, Senate, U.S. Immigration Commission, *Reports of the Immigration Commission: Immigrants in Industries, Part 2: Iron and Steel Manufacturing,* 61st Cong., 2d sess., 1911, S. Doc. 633, serial 5669, vol. 1: 242–43. The report does not list Duquesne by name, identifying it only as "Plant No. 4."

19. *Duquesne Times,* 13 Oct. and 24 Nov. 1911; Senate, *Investigation of Strike,* pt. 2: 501.

20. U.S. Census, *Tenth Census of the United States: 1880,* vol. 1: *Population* (Washington, D.C.: U.S. Government Printing Office, 1883), 895; U.S. Census, *Thirteenth Census of the United States: 1910,* vol. 7: *Reports by States* (Washington, D.C.: U.S. Government Printing Office, 1914), 740; Senate, *Investigation of Strike,* pt. 2: 531; Immigration Commission, *Reports of the Immigration Commission,* vol. 1: 242–43.

21. Jim Rose, "'The Problem Every Supervisor Dreads': Women Workers at the U.S. Steel Duquesne Works During World War II," *Labor History* 36 (winter 1995): 24–51.

22. Senate, *Investigation of Strike,* pt. 2: 531; U.S. Census, *Fourteenth Census of the United States: 1920, Manuscript Schedules,* vol. 10, Pennsylvania, Allegheny County, National Archives microfilm reel 1511.

23. Abram Lincoln Harris, Jr., "The New Negro Worker in Pittsburgh" (master's thesis, University of Pittsburgh, 1924), 45; Ida DeAugustine Reid, "The Negro in the Major Industries and Building Trades of Pittsburgh" (master's thesis, University of Pittsburgh, 1925), 10; Senate, *Investigation of Strike,* pt. 2: 531–32.

24. Senate, *Investigation of Strike,* pt. 2: 531–32. Northern and western European workers at the Duquesne Works were Germans, British, French, Belgians, Swedes, and Norwegians. Forty-eight percent of the U.S.-born steelworkers had one or more foreign-born parents. Of this group, 63 percent had northern and western European backgrounds. These conclusions are derived from a sampling of the 1920 census manuscript schedule for Duquesne. The sampling technique entailed selecting every fifth steelworker (blue and white collar) from Duquesne in the 1920 manuscript census. The overall sample included 1,007 men and 14 women. In addition to any problems evident in this sort of sampling, especially incorrect data listed by the census taker, not all workers lived in Duquesne, although approximately 84 percent did in 1919, and some steelworkers counted in this sample worked at other steel mills in the area. See U.S. Census, *Fourteenth Census: 1920, Manuscript Schedules.*

25. John A. Fitch, *The Steel Workers* (1911; reprint, Pittsburgh: University of Pittsburgh Press, 1989), 349; David Brody, *Steelworkers in America: The Non-Union Era* (New York: Harper and Row, 1960), 107–8; U.S. Immigration Commission, *Reports of the Immigration Commission,* vol. 1: 281. For sampling of crane positions, see *Fourteenth Census: 1920, Manuscript Schedules.*

26. John Hovanec, interview by Jim Barrett, 14 June 1976, transcript, p. 4, Homestead Album Oral History Project, AIS.

27. Senate, *Investigation of Strike,* pt. 2: 531.

28. Michael Nuwer, "From Batch to Flow: Production Technology and Work-Force Skills in the Steel Industry, 1880–1920," *Technology and Culture* 29 (Oct. 1988): 833; Carroll R. Daugherty, Melvin G. de Chazeau, and Samuel S. Stratton, *The Economics of the Iron and Steel Industry* (New York: McGraw-Hill, 1937), vol. 1: 143; Curtis Miner, *Homestead: The Story of a Steel Town* (Pittsburgh: Historical Society of Western Pennsylvania, 1989), 15–16.

29. Nuwer, "From Batch to Flow," 833; *Iron Trade Review,* 25 Sept. 1919, p. 817.

30. Miscellaneous maps, Box 34, File P-5(b); and Box 10, File P-4(a), USSC.

31. John Patterson, interviewed by Mary Senior, and Edward Rawlings, interviewed by David J. Saposs, undated typed notes, Box 26, File 7, David J. Saposs Papers (DJS), State Historical Society of Wisconsin, Madison.

32. Marcus, "Duquesne Lockout of 1889," pp. 5–11, 15–16; Leon Wolff, *Lockout: The Story of the Homestead Strike of 1892: A Study of Violence, Unionism, and the Carnegie Empire* (New York: Harper and Row, 1965), 152, 192, 195; Krause, *Battle for Homestead,* 32; Arthur G. Burgoyne, *Homestead* (1893; reprint, New York: Augustus M. Kelley, 1971), 176–77.

33. Gerald Eggert, *Steelmasters and Labor Reform, 1886–1923* (Pittsburgh: University of Pittsburgh Press, 1981), 34.

34. Brody, *Steelworkers in America,* 60–68; John A. Garraty, "The United States Steel Corporation Versus Labor: The Early Years," *Labor History* 1 (winter 1960): 8–14.

35. *Pittsburgh Dispatch,* 1, 2, 3, 4, 5 Sept. 1901; *Independent,* 5 Sept. 1901, p. 2071; *Iron Age,* 5 Sept. 1901, p. 37.

36. *Pittsburgh Dispatch,* 2 Sept. 1901.

37. Ibid.; Jeremiah Patrick Shalloo, *Private Police: With Special Reference to Pennsylvania* (Philadelphia: American Academy of Political and Social Science, 1933), 59–64.

38. Brody, *Steelworkers in America,* 71–73, 80–85, 175–76; Fitch, *Steel Workers,* 214–19; *Duquesne Times,* 24 May 1907.

39. Brody, *Steelworkers in America,* 80–124.

40. For discussions of U.S. Steel's welfare capitalist policies before World War I, see Brody, *Steelworkers in America,* 147–79; Garraty, "The United States Steel Corporation Versus Labor," 18–38; Eggert, *Steelmasters and Labor Reform,* 33–76; Gulick, *Labor Policy,* 138–84.

41. Garraty, "The United States Steel Corporation Versus Labor," 18–20, 37–38.

42. Brody, *Steelworkers in America,* 96, 106; Frank Huff Serene, "Immigrant Steelworkers in the Monongahela Valley: Their Communities and the Development of a Labor Class Consciousness" (Ph.D. diss., University of Pittsburgh, 1979), 58–65.

43. John Bodnar, "Immigration, Kinship, and the Rise of Working-Class Realism in Industrial America," *Journal of Social History* 14 (fall 1980): 45–63.

44. The 1920 census sample showed that 14 percent of southern and eastern European immigrant workers had purchased homes in 1920. For U.S.-born workers, the figure stood at 6 percent.

45. Senate, *Investigation of Strike,* pt. 2: 511, 531.

46. Gulick, *Labor Policy,* 141–42.

47. John Bodnar, *Workers' World: Kinship, Community, and Protest in an Industrial Society, 1900–1940* (Baltimore: Johns Hopkins University Press, 1982), 136; Interchurch World Movement, *Report on the Steel Strike of 1919* (New York: Harcourt, Brace, 1920), 132–241; U.S. Immigration Commission, *Reports of the Immigration Commission,* vol. 1: 281–82.

48. *Pittsburgh Gazette Times,* 11 Jan. 1914; *Iron Age,* 20 Jan. 1916, p. 193.

49. *Pittsburgh Gazette Times,* 11 Jan. 1914; *Iron Age,* 20 Jan. 1916, p. 193; Blair, *Duquesne's Silver Jubilee,* 23; *(Duquesne) Times-Observer,* 8 Oct. 1915.

50. Unidentified newspaper clipping on library dedication, in Duquesne clipping file, Carnegie Library of Pittsburgh; *Duquesne Times,* 17 May 1929; Paul L. Krause, "Patronage and Philanthropy in Industrial America: Andrew Carnegie and the Free Library in Braddock, Pa.," *Western Pennsylvania Historical Magazine* 71 (April 1988): 127–45; Curtis Miner, "The 'Deserted Parthenon': Class, Culture, and the Carnegie Library of Homestead, 1898–1937," *Pennsylvania History* 52 (April 1990): 107–35. Carnegie began donating

libraries while he owned Carnegie Steel, but he continued to build them throughout the world after he sold the company. In Carnegie Steel towns, mill officials controlled the boards that oversaw the libraries.

51. *Pittsburgh Gazette Times,* 11 Jan. 1914; Gulick, *Labor Policy,* 143; Blair, *Duquesne's Silver Jubilee,* 23.

52. U.S. Steel, Bureau of Safety, Sanitation, and Welfare, *Bulletin* 4 (Nov. 1913): 8.

53. Serene, "Immigrant Steelworkers in the Monongahela Valley," 112–13.

54. Ibid., 119, 124; U.S. Steel, *Bulletin,* 64; *Iron Age,* 20 Jan. 1916, p. 195; *Times-Observer,* 16 May 1913; Gerd Korman, "Americanization at the Factory Gate," *Industrial and Labor Relations Review* 18 (April 1965): 402–3, 413.

55. *Times-Observer,* 16 May 1913; *Iron Age,* 20 Jan. 1916, pp. 193–96; Serene, "Immigrant Steelworkers in the Monongahela Valley," 111; U.S. Steel, *Bulletin,* 64.

56. *Iron Age,* 20 Jan. 1916, pp. 194–96; *Times-Observer,* 16 May 1913; Blair, *Duquesne's Silver Jubilee,* 23; *Pittsburgh Gazette Times,* 11 Jan. 1914.

57. Dennis C. Dickerson, *Out of the Crucible: Black Steelworkers in Western Pennsylvania, 1875–1980* (Albany: State University of New York Press, 1986), 101–17; Reid, "The Negro in Major Industries," 21–29; "Welfare Activities at Duquesne," (1936), Box 11, File W-2(a), USSC; various minutes of monthly Pittsburgh-area welfare workers' meetings in Box 7, Files 334 and 335, Urban League of Pittsburgh Papers (ULP), AIS.

58. *Duquesne, Pennsylvania,* n.p.; Karen Cowles, "The Industrialization of Duquesne and the Circulation of Elites, 1891–1933," *Western Pennsylvania Historical Magazine* 62 (Jan. 1979): 3; Ingham, *Making Iron and Steel,* 180; Blair, *Duquesne's Silver Jubilee,* 18.

59. *Duquesne, Pennsylvania,* n.p.; Thomas Cushing, *History of Allegheny County, Pennsylvania* (Chicago: Warner, 1889), pt. 2, 76; Cowles, "Industrialization of Duquesne," 4, 7, 9–13; *Duquesne Observer,* 6 Jan. 1905.

60. Cowles, "Industrialization of Duquesne," 10–11, 13–14; *Duquesne Observer,* 27 Jan. 1905, 24 Feb. 1905, 12 and 19 Jan. 1906, and 2, 9, and 16 Feb. 1906; *Duquesne Times,* 24 Feb. 1905.

61. Cowles, "Industrialization of Duquesne," 14; *Duquesne Times* 24 Jan. 1908; *Duquesne Observer,* 8 Nov. 1912.

62. *Duquesne Observer,* 12 Feb. 1909, 6 Oct. 1911; Cowles, "Industrialization of Duquesne," 14.

63. My analysis of the 1919 steel strike rests heavily on Interchurch World Movement, *Report on the Steel Strike;* and Brody, *Labor in Crisis.*

64. John Patterson and Edward Rawlings interviews, DJS; Thomas Bell, *Out of This Furnace* (Pittsburgh: University of Pittsburgh Press, 1976), 48.

65. Interchurch World Movement, *Report on the Steel Strike,* 44–84; Brody, *Steelworkers in America,* 235–36; Eggert, *Steelmasters and Labor Reform,* 47–55.

66. Interchurch World Movement, *Report on the Steel Strike,* 85–118; Brody, *Labor in Crisis,* 70–71.

67. Brody, *Labor in Crisis,* 48, 71–72; Interchurch World Movement, *Public Opinion and the Steel Strike,* 240.

68. Brody, *Labor in Crisis,* 50–69. By 1919 the Amalgamated had added tin workers to its jurisdiction.

69. Senate, *Investigation of Strike,* pt. 2: 501–2; *Duquesne Times,* 10 Oct. 1919.

70. Senate, *Investigation of Strike,* pt. 2: 532; Brody, *Labor in Crisis,* 157–58; Robert Asher, "Painful Memories: The Historical Consciousness of Steelworkers and the Steel Strike of 1919," *Pennsylvania History* 45 (Jan. 1978): 61–86.

71. Senate, *Investigation of Strike,* pt. 2: 532; minutes of the Welfare Workers' Conference, 26 Sept. 1919, Box 7, File 334, ULP.

72. Interchurch World Movement, *Report on the Steel Strike,* 179; Brody, *Labor in Crisis,* 132, 157; Serene, "Immigrant Steelworkers in the Monongahela Valley," 210–11; Senate, *Investigation of Strike,* pt. 2: 532.

73. S. Adele Shaw, "Closed Towns," *Survey* 43 (8 Nov. 1919): 60, 62–64.

74. Ibid., 61; Senate, *Investigation of Strike,* pt. 2: 619. A copy of the city ordinance is reprinted in NCOISW, "A Judicial Curiosity" [1920], Box 120, File: Steel—clippings, leaflets . . . , MHV.

75. Testimony of J. G. Brown, Interchurch (World Movement) Commission, 21 Nov. 1919, 106, Box 26, File 13, DJS.

76. Senate, *Investigation of Strike,* pt. 2: 814; *Duquesne Times,* 12 Sept. 1919.

77. Foster, *Great Steel Strike,* 61–62; Shaw, "Closed Towns," 60.

78. Senate, *Investigation of Strike,* pt. 2: 508.

79. Brody, *Steelworkers in America,* 148, 252; Interchurch World Movement, *Public Opinion and the Steel Strike,* 170; Shaw, "Closed Towns," 61.

80. Duquesne City Council minutes, 8 and 15 Sept. 1919, microfilm copy of Duquesne Borough and City Council Minutes, reel 5075, Hillman Library, University of Pittsburgh; *Duquesne Times,* 26 Sept. 1919; Brody, *Labor in Crisis,* 149; Duquesne payroll ledger, Sept. 1919, USSC; Senate, *Investigation of Strike,* pt. 1: 301; "Substations Doing Patrol Work Incidental to Steelworkers' Strike in 1919" [1920], Box 10, File 1, Pennsylvania State Police records.

81. *Duquesne Times,* 26 Sept. 1919; Senate, *Investigation of Strike,* pt. 1: 809–10.

82. Interchurch World Movement, *Public Opinion and the Steel Strike,* 188–89, 195.

83. Brody, *Labor in Crisis,* 162–84.

84. Duquesne City Council minutes, 16 Feb. 1920.

85. Mimeographed reports of the NCOISW, 24 April and 12 May 1920, Box 121, File: Steel—*Strike News,* 1919, MHV.

86. Ibid.; Foster, *Great Steel Strike,* 64; undated, unidentified newspaper clipping, Duquesne clipping file, Carnegie Library of Pittsburgh; Duquesne City Council minutes, 10 May 1920.

87. NCOISW, "Steel Trust Victims Appeal Heard," mimeographed leaflet, n.d., Box 121, File: Steel—*Strike News,* 1919, MHV. The court's decision—*Commonwealth of Pennsylvania, City of Duquesne vs. Bozo Damich,* County Court of Allegheny County, Pa., Docket No. 477, 1920—is reproduced in NCOISW, "A Judicial Curiosity," Box 120, File: Steel—clippings, leaflets . . . , MHV.

Chapter 2: From Economic Stability to Depression, 1920–34

1. The following biographical and work information on Elmer Maloy is collected from Elmer Maloy, interview by Don Kennedy, 7 Nov. 1967, transcript, United Steelworkers of America Oral History Project (USAOHP), Historical Collections and Labor Archives (HCLA), The Pennsylvania State University, State College; Elmer Maloy testimony, NLRB

Case C-142, 17 Dec. 1936, pp. 66–67, and 11 Jan. 1937, pp. 568–94, *U.S. Steel Corp. and Carnegie-Illinois Steel Corp. vs. Steel Workers Organizing Committee and Amalgamated Ass'n of Iron, Steel and Tin Workers,* Box 110, National Labor Relations Board Records (RG 25), Administrative Division, Files and Dockets Section, Transcripts and Exhibits, Washington National Records Center, Suitland, Md.; miscellaneous undated and unidentified newspaper clippings in the personal papers of Elmer Maloy, in the possession of Joan Striegel; Robert R. R. Brooks, *As Steel Goes, . . . Unionism in a Basic Industry* (New Haven: Yale University Press, 1940), 84; *Who's Who in Labor* (New York: Dryden Press, 1946).

2. Maloy interview, p. 4.

3. Ibid., p. 1; Harold Ruttenberg, "Comments (with Some Illustrations) on Outline," in "Notes and Ideas [for his planned manuscript, 'America's Steelworkers']," 12 Aug. 1942, Box 9, Harold J. Ruttenberg Papers (HJR), HCLA. Contradicting Maloy's account is Brooks's assertion that Maloy "took part" in the strike. See Brooks, *As Steel Goes,* 84.

4. William T. Hogan, *Economic History of the Iron and Steel Industry in the United States* (Lexington, Mass.: Lexington Books, 1971), vol. 3: 811, 878–81; U.S. Steel Corp., *Annual Report,* 1920–30 (New York: U.S. Steel); Joel Sabadasz, "Duquesne Works: Overview History," unpublished manuscript, summer 1991, pp. 13–14.

5. Pennsylvania, Department of Labor and Industry, *Industrial Directory of the Commonwealth of Pennsylvania,* 1922, 1925 (Harrisburg: Commonwealth of Pennsylvania); *Duquesne Times,* 29 Nov. 1929; Harvey O'Connor, notes from interview of Duquesne employment supervisor, 1929, Box 25, File: Steel Labor, Archives of Labor and Urban Affairs, Harvey O'Connor Collection (HOC), Wayne State University, Detroit; U.S. Census, *Tenth Census of the United States: 1880,* vol. 1: *Population* (Washington, D.C.: U.S. Government Printing Office, 1883), 321; U.S. Census, *Twelfth Census of the United States: 1900,* vol. 1: *Population,* pt. 1 (Washington, D.C.: U.S. Government Printing Office, 1902), 330; U.S. Census, *Fourteenth Census of the United States: 1920,* vol. 3: *Population* (Washington, D.C.: U.S. Government Printing Office, 1922), 869; U.S. Census, *Fifteenth Census of the United States: 1930,* vol. 3: *Population,* pt. 2 (Washington, D.C.: U.S. Government Printing Office, 1932), 668.

6. *Duquesne Times,* 15 Feb. 1929.

7. Hogan, *Economic History of Iron and Steel,* vol. 3: 878–80, 897.

8. Maloy interview, p. 6; Charles Bollinger, interview by Alice Hoffman, July 1966, transcript, p. 2, USAOHP.

9. Horace B. Davis, "The Spy System in the Steel Industry," *Common Sense* 2 (July 1933): 20–22; Jessie Lloyd, "'No Company Union at U.S. Steel'—Boss Says So," Federated Press, 21 Oct. 1935, Box 25, File: Spies, HOC; *Duquesne Times,* 3 July 1931; Robert Asher, "Painful Memories: The Historical Consciousness of Steelworkers and the Steel Strike of 1919," *Pennsylvania History* 45 (Jan. 1978): 84–85.

10. *Duquesne Times,* 20 Sept. 1929; *Pennsylvania Manual* (Harrisburg: Commonwealth of Pennsylvania, 1925). A similar situation occurred in the 1910s when Socialist Party registration lagged behind Democratic and Republican registration, but during elections Socialists had strong support from workers and outpolled the Democrats. See *Duquesne Times,* 11 Nov. 1910; Michael Nash, *Conflict and Accommodation: Coal Miners, Steel Workers, and Socialism, 1890–1920* (Westport, Conn.: Greenwood, 1982), 116–17.

11. Maloy interview, p. 6; *(McKeesport) Daily News,* 30 June 1934; Harvey O'Connor,

Steel-Dictator (New York: John Day, 1935), 8, 271; Phillip Bonosky, "When Freedom Came for a Look in in [*sic*] One Steel Town," copy of typescript in possession of author.

12. O'Connor, *Steel-Dictator,* 272; *Duquesne Times,* 1 Jan. 1929, 22 March 1929, 26 Aug. 1932, 5 May 1933, 18 Oct. 1935, 8 Nov. 1935, 31 July 1936.

13. U.S. Steel Corp., *Annual Report,* 1933 (New York: U.S. Steel), 11; Duquesne Works payroll ledgers, 1920–29, U.S. Steel Corp. (Duquesne Works) Payroll Ledgers and Records of the Personnel Division (USSC), 1904–80, UE/Labor Archives, Archives of Industrial Society (AIS), Hillman Library, University of Pittsburgh; *Duquesne Times,* 27 Sept. and 13 Dec. 1929. For the work of visiting nurses, see various reports in Box 11, File W-2(a), USSC.

14. "Stability of Employment in the Iron and Steel Industry," *Monthly Labor Review* 27 (Nov. 1928): 1–3; *Steel,* 24 Sept. 1931, p. 17. The common labor rate referred to the lowest wage held by unskilled laborers. At the Duquesne Works, laborers who worked turn labor—rotating between day, evening, and night shifts—earned 6 cents more per hour than common laborers. Turn laborers also outnumbered common laborers in the mill. See "Tabulation of Common and Turn Labor Rates," in Duquesne Works Employee Representation Plan (DWERP) request 4-50, Box 26, USSC.

15. Charles Hill, "Fighting the Twelve-Hour Day in the American Steel Industry," *Labor History* 15 (winter 1974): 19–35.

16. Hogan, *Economic History of Iron and Steel,* vol. 3: 861.

17. *Iron Trade Review,* 5 Jan. 1928, pp. 13–14.

18. Work record of Andy Chervenak, 1928–37, Box 5, File S-2(a), USSC.

19. For responsibilities of open hearth laborers, see Charles Rumford Walker, *Steel: Diary of a Furnace Worker* (Boston: Atlantic Monthly Press, 1922), 16–80; Whiting Williams, *What's on the Worker's Mind: By One Who Put on Overalls to Find Out* (New York: Scribner's, 1920), 13–38; and Paul Peters, "Notes from My Notes While Working at the Braddock U.S. Steel Plant," typewritten notes, undated [1933?], Box 274, File: Steel, Cornelia Pinchot Papers, Library of Congress (LOC), Washington, D.C. Descriptions of Duquesne open hearth and unskilled work are found in Open Hearth Department, descriptions of "jobs women cannot perform," no date, and "Bricklayer Helper Detailed Job Description," Box 32, File W-3(a), USSC.

20. Horace B. Davis, *Labor and Steel* (New York: International Publishers, 1933), 37.

21. Peters, "Notes . . . While Working at Braddock," p. 2.

22. Chervenak's work record. The wage differential between laborer and oiler and wiper is found in H. G. R. Bennett to K. H. McLaurin, 29 March 1937, in DWERP request 4-86, Box 26, USSC.

23. Maloy testimony, NLRB Case, 18 Dec. 1936, p. 273; Michael Kerekac, interview by Linda Nyden, 9 July 1974, Pittsburgh Oral History Project (POHP), Pennsylvania Historical and Museum Commission, Pennsylvania State Archives, Harrisburg; Phillip Bonosky, typewritten "semiautobiography," 101–2, partial copy in author's possession; "Special Allowance for Employees Working on Special Police Duty," in the October entry of the Duquesne Works payroll ledger for 1935, USSC; "Tabulation of Common and Turn Labor Rates."

24. Work record of Andy Chervenak. See also, "Record of Time Worked by Michal Milenki . . . (8/1/23 to 2/14/33)," Box 26, Grievance File 42-40-U, USSC.

25. O'Connor, notes from interview of Duquesne employment supervisor; Maloy interview, pp. 2–3; John Smitko, interview by Carl Romanek, 24 June 1974, POHP.

26. Carroll R. Daugherty, Melvin G. de Chazeau, and Samuel S. Stratton, *The Economics of the Iron and Steel Industry* (New York: McGraw-Hill, 1937), vol. 1: 165–66; "Tabulation of Common and Turn Labor Rates."

27. Daugherty, de Chazeau, and Stratton, *Economics of the Iron and Steel Industry,* vol. 1: 155; M. Ada Beney, *Wages, Hours, and Employment in the United States, 1914–1936* (New York: National Industrial Conference Board, 1936), 114; "The Duquesne Situation" [1934], Box 23, File: Duquesne Works–Carnegie Steel Corp. (DW-CSC), HOC; O'Connor, *Steel-Dictator,* 6.

28. Milan Tankosich, interview by Peter Gottlieb, 16 Aug. 1974, transcript, p. 5, POHP.

29. Phillip Bonosky, "The Life and Death of a Steel Worker," *Masses and Mainstream* 5 (April 1952): 17.

30. For steel industry job ladders see Katherine Stone, "The Origins of Job Structures in the Steel Industry," *Review of Radical Political Economics* 6 (summer 1974): 69–70, 73–75; Sanford Jacoby, *Employing Bureaucracy: Managers, Unions, and the Transformation of Work in American Industry, 1900–1945* (New York: Columbia University Press, 1985), 93–97; Judith Stein, *Running Steel, Running America: Race, Economic Policy, and the Decline of Liberalism* (Chapel Hill: University of North Carolina Press, 1998), 45–46. For Duquesne's promotional practices see DWERP requests 96-5 and 98-7, Box 26, and Duquesne Works, "Present and Proposed Promotional Sequences," Feb. 1947, Box 32, Folder S-3(b), both in USSC.

31. Maloy interview, p. 4.

32. "The U.S. Steel Corporation: III," *Fortune* 13 (May 1936): 138, 141; Duquesne Works payroll ledgers, 1920–30.

33. "U.S. Steel Corporation: III," 138.

34. Ibid., 141; Daugherty, de Chazeau, and Stratton, *Economics of the Iron and Steel Industry,* vol. 1: 177; Maloy interview, pp. 4–5; Tankosich interview, p. 5; Kerekac interview; John Hovanec, interview by Jim Barrett, 14 June 1976, transcript, p. 5, Homestead Album Oral History Project (HAOHP), AIS; Smitko interview; comments by Elmer Maloy, in DWERP, Fifth Joint Conference, transcript, p. 22, Box 26, USSC.

35. Black employment ranged from 455 workers in November 1919 to 569 in 1920, 252 in 1921, 720 in 1925, and 302 in 1934. See minutes of welfare workers' conference, 12 Nov. 1919, Box 7, File 334, Urban League of Pittsburgh Papers (ULP), AIS; Ida DeAugustine Reid, "The Negro in the Major Industries and Building Trades of Pittsburgh" (master's thesis, University of Pittsburgh, 1925), 8, 10; F. Alden Wilson, "Occupational Status of the Negro in the Iron and Steel Industry, Pittsburgh and Environs," unpublished paper, 23 May 1934, p. 47, Box 10, File 469, ULP.

36. J. W. Knapp, "An Experiment with Negro Labor," *Opportunity* 1 (Feb. 1923): 19–20; Wilson, "Occupational Status of the Negro," p. 45; Reid, "The Negro in Major Industries," 21. Quotations are from Knapp.

37. Philip Klein, *A Social Study of Pittsburgh: Community Problems and Social Services of Allegheny County* (New York: Columbia University Press, 1938), 275, 284; Peter Gottlieb, *Making Their Own Way: Southern Blacks' Migration to Pittsburgh, 1916–30* (Urbana: University of Illinois Press, 1987), 135–36, 193; minutes of Negro industrial welfare work-

ers' meeting, 23 May [1921], Box 7, File 334, ULP; Reid, "The Negro in Major Industries," 26–29; Horace R. Cayton and George S. Mitchell, *Black Workers and the New Unions* (Chapel Hill: University of North Carolina Press, 1939), 31–33.

38. Minutes of welfare workers' conference, 29 Oct. 1919, Box 7, File 344, ULP. A sample from the 1920 census reveals only two self-described semiskilled black workers out of eighty-three. For sampling methodology see chap. 1, note 24.

39. Daugherty, de Chazeau, and Stratton, *Economics of the Iron and Steel Industry,* vol. 1: 132; Reid, "The Negro in Major Industries," 13; Wilson, "Occupational Status of the Negro," pp. 7, 23, 52.

40. Cayton and Mitchell, *Black Workers and the New Unions,* 34.

41. Ibid., 26, 34; *Daily Worker,* 16 May 1935; Albert Carter, interview by George Mason, 22 July 1934, POHP; Kerekac interview; Nate Jones, interview by Jack Bergstresser, 16 July 1991, Steel Industry Heritage Corp., Homestead, Pa.

42. Daugherty, de Chazeau, and Stratton, *Economics of the Iron and Steel Industry,* vol. 1: 143–45. In October 1935, for instance, skilled rollers and heaters at Duquesne earned $1.185 to $1.597 per hour, while laborers earned 48.5 cents.

43. The various tonnage and incentive plans at Duquesne can be traced through documents related to grievances filed under the employee representation plan and Steel Worker Organizing Committee (United Steelworkers of America) in the USSC records. The Duquesne Works became more aggressive later in the 1930s by extending incentive systems to larger groups of workers in each department. In 1938 the plant installed a chipper incentive system. See Box 26, Grievance 21-39-U, USSC.

44. Maloy interview, p. 1; Williams, *What's on the Worker's Mind,* 43, 55; Daugherty, de Chazeau, and Stratton, *Economics of the Iron and Steel Industry,* vol. 1: 143.

45. "The U.S. Steel Corporation: III," 136; Peters, "Notes . . . While Working at Braddock," p. 1. No black would be hired in the skilled trades until well after World War II.

46. Gary is quoted in U.S. Steel Corp., *Principles and Policies of the U.S. Steel Corporation* (1921), excerpted in a memorandum from Jacob Karro to David J. Saposs, 2 Feb. 1937, Box 25, File 1, David J. Saposs Papers, State Historical Society of Wisconsin, Madison.

47. David Harvey Kelly, "Labor Relations in the Steel Industry: Management's Ideas, Proposals, and Programs, 1920 to 1950" (Ph.D. diss., Indiana University, 1976), 22–23; "The U.S. Steel Corporation: III," 134.

48. Michael Nuwer, "From Batch to Flow: Production Technology and Work-Force Skills in the Steel Industry, 1880–1920," *Technology and Culture* 29 (Oct. 1988): 828–38.

49. Smitko interview.

50. Various work records attached to grievances 4-37-U, and 35-39-U, Box 26, USSC; K. H. McLaurin to L. H. Burnett, 26 July 1939; and James H. Knapp to J. R. Ellwood, 14 June 1948, both in Box 2, File S-3(a), USSC.

51. Hogan, *Economic History of Iron and Steel,* vol. 3: 1119–20, 1134; *Steel,* 7 May 1931, p. 29, and 10 Dec. 1934, p. 25.

52. "The U.S. Steel Corporation: III," 180, 182, 184, 186, 188.

53. Quoted in Davis, *Labor and Steel,* 103.

54. *Iron Age,* 19 April 1934, p. 33; Myron C. Taylor, remarks at Share-the-Work Movement Luncheon, 2 Dec. 1932, Box 7, Myron C. Taylor Papers, LOC; *Steel,* 30 April 1931, p. 26, and 27 March 1933, p. 51; Davis, *Labor and Steel,* 93; "The U.S. Steel Corporation: III," 94.

55. Taylor, remarks at Share-the-Work Movement Luncheon; Myron Taylor, address at annual meeting of stockholders of U.S. Steel, 17 April 1933, Box 7, Taylor Papers; Myron Taylor, *Ten Years of Steel* (New York: U.S. Steel, 1938), 25–26; *Iron Trade Review,* 2 Oct. 1930, p. 24.

56. Douglas A. Fisher, *Steel Serves the Nation, 1901–1951: The Fifty Year Story of United States Steel* (New York: U.S. Steel, 1951), 226; testimony of James A. Farrell, in U.S. Congress, Senate, Committee on Manufactures, *Establishment of National Economic Council,* 72d Cong., 1st sess., 1931, pt. 1: 342; Davis, *Labor and Steel,* 101; Daugherty, de Chazeau, and Stratton, *Economics of the Iron and Steel Industry,* vol. 1: 169.

57. Taylor, remarks at Share-the-Work Luncheon.

58. *Steel,* 6 Aug. 1931, p. 23, 24 Sept. 1931, p. 17, 9 May 1932, p. 18, and 24 April 1933; Fisher, *Steel Serves the Nation,* 225.

59. Myron C. Taylor, "A Few Observations on Employment," transcript of New York radio talk, 27 Jan. 1931, Box 7, Taylor Papers; "The U.S. Steel Corporation: III," 147; *Pittsburgh Press,* 7 Aug. 1935; *Iron Age,* 19 April 1934, p. 33; *(Pittsburgh) Post-Gazette,* 10 Dec. 1932; Davis, *Labor and Steel,* 107; resolution of U.S. Steel Finance Committee meeting, 6 Oct. 1936, Box 37, Edward R. Stettinius, Jr. Papers, File: Finance Committee Resolutions, Oct.–Nov. 1936, Manuscript Division, Special Collections, University of Virginia Library, Charlottesville.

60. Annual meeting of stockholders of U.S. Steel, 1933.

61. *Iron Age,* 19 April 1934, p. 33.

62. *Steel,* 18 March 1935, p. 24; Hogan, *Economic History of Iron and Steel,* vol. 3: 1119; Maloy testimony, NLRB Case, 18 Dec. 1936, p. 273; DWERP, minutes of meeting, 23 Oct. 1933, Records of the National Recovery Administration (RG 9), Records of the National Steel Labor Relations Board (NSLRB), Box 4, National Archives, Washington, D.C.; DWERP, Fifth Joint Conference, p. 27.

63. Chervenak work record; Milenki work record; DWERP request 156-65, Box 26, USSC; Maloy interview, p. 7; *Duquesne Times,* 24 April 1931, 25 Aug. 1933, 18 Oct. 1935; *Daily Worker,* 26 Feb. 1933, 13 Nov. 1934, 18 Feb. 1935; *Amalgamated Journal,* 20 Dec. 1934; DWERP, minutes of meeting, 20 Feb. 1934, Box 4, NSLRB; *Post-Gazette,* 14 June 1933; *Steel,* 19 June 1933, p. 14, 26 June 1933, p. 17, 10 July 1933, p. 16, 7 Aug. 1933, p. 15, 4 Sept. 1933, p. 17, 9 Oct. 1933, p. 15, and 6 Nov. 1933, p. 16; Farrell testimony, p. 344.

64. *Amalgamated Journal,* 20 Dec. 1934; DWERP, Fifth Joint Conference, p. 24; *Daily Worker,* 18 Feb. 1935.

65. R. W. Graham to E. H. Gott, 8 Nov. 1954, Box 3, File S-3(g); K. H. McLaurin to L. H. Burnett, 26 July 1939, Box 2, File S-3(a), both in USSC.

66. Jacoby, *Employing Bureaucracy,* 218; William C. Oberg to A. C. Cummins, 20 Dec. 1935, Box 3, File S-3(f), USSC; DWERP, minutes of meeting, 27 Aug. 1934, Box 4, NSLRB; DWERP, Fifth Joint Conference, pp. 5, 7.

67. "The U.S. Steel Corporation: III," 138, 141; Daugherty, de Chazeau, and Stratton, *Economics of the Iron and Steel Industry,* vol. 1: 177; O'Connor, *Steel-Dictator,* 264; R. W. Graham to E. H. Gott, 8 Nov. 1954, Box 3, File S-3(g), USSC; K. H. McLaurin to L. H. Burnett, 26 July 1939, Box 2, File S-3(a), USSC.

68. Chervenak work record; *Steel,* 24 Sept. 1931, p. 17, and 9 May 1932, p. 18; *Amalgamated Journal,* 20 Dec. 1934; DWERP, Fifth Joint Conference, 25; Kerekac interview; Tan-

kosich interview, p. 8; questionnaires of Duquesne workers by Horace Davis [1932], Box 42, File: Interviews, HOC.

69. DWERP, minutes of meetings, 26 March 1934, 18 May 1934, and 25 June 1934; DWERP requests 8, 11, 18, 58, 80, 82, 84, 90, 105-14, 116-25, and 118-27, all in Box 4, NSLRB; O'Connor, *Steel Dictator,* 264–65.

70. DWERP, minutes of meeting, 11 Sept. 1933; DWERP request 11, both in Box 4, NSLRB.

71. Robert Ruck, "Origins of the Seniority System in Steel," unpublished paper, 1977, in the author's possession; testimony of Charles Erickson, in U.S. Congress, Senate, Committee on Education and Labor, *To Create a National Labor Board,* 73d Cong., 2d sess., 1934, pt. 3: 876, 879; *Steel,* 22 Jan. 1934, p. 11.

72. Maloy interview, p. 7; Kerekac interview; Bollinger interview, p. 2; John Bodnar, *Workers' World: Kinship, Community, and Protest in an Industrial Society, 1900–1940* (Baltimore: Johns Hopkins University Press, 1982), 147; interview by Peter Gottlieb of a person who stipulated anonymity, 9 June 1976, Southern Blacks' Migration to Pittsburgh Oral History Project, AIS.

73. DWERP requests 4-19, 4-26, 4-30, 4-38, 159-68, 175-9, 179-13, and 211-45, Box 26, USSC; *Daily Worker,* 18 Feb. 1935. The workers are quoted in O'Connor, *Steel Dictator,* 264–67.

74. *Steel,* 4 July 1932, p. 14.

75. The various surveys are reported in "The U.S. Steel Corporation: III," 142; *Nation,* 30 May 1934, p. 604; Jessie Lloyd, "Steel Looks After Its Own," *Social Work Today* 1 (May–June 1934): 7; O'Connor, *Steel-Dictator,* 5–6; Rose Stein, "Steel Lines Up for Battle," *New Republic* 74 (20 June 1934): 146; Harvey O'Connor, "The Second Battle of Duquesne," p. 11, and Harvey O'Connor, "The Duquesne Situation," typewritten summary of 1934 survey, both in Box 23, File: DW-CSC, HOC.

76. "Cost of Living in the Pittsburgh District from the U.S. Dept. of Labor Statistics Bulletin R-396," reproduced in Box 4, File 6, HJR; Lloyd, "Steel Looks After Its Own," 7; O'Connor, *Steel-Dictator,* 270.

77. Erickson testimony, pp. 876, 879; DWERP request 192-26, Box 26, USSC.

78. For the effects of the depression on tonnage and incentive earnings, see DWERP requests 63, 67, 98-7, 161-70, 179-13, 193-27, 209-43, 214-48, and 4-83; DWERP, Sixth Joint Conference, transcript, 2 June 1936, p. 7; and Grievance 1-37-U, all in Box 26, USSC.

79. *Duquesne Times,* 1 July 1932.

80. *Duquesne Times,* 1 Sept. 1931, 17 Nov. 1933, 6 Sept. 1935, and 22 Nov. 1935.

81. Klein, *Social Study of Pittsburgh,* 160; Davis, *Labor and Steel,* 95; R. B. Sayor and A. E. Warne, *Duquesne, Pennsylvania* (State College: Bureau of Business Research, Penn State College, 1953), 9; "Labor Turn-over," *Monthly Labor Review* 38 (June 1934): 1393.

82. *Duquesne Times,* 2 Oct. 1931 and 28 July 1933; Tankosich interview; Harvey O'Connor, typed notes from survey of Duquesne mill workers, Box 23, File: DW-CSC, HOC; Dennis C. Dickerson, *Out of the Crucible: Black Steelworkers in Western Pennsylvania, 1875–1980* (Albany: State University of New York Press, 1986), 125–29; Lizabeth Cohen, *Making a New Deal: Industrial Workers in Chicago, 1919–1939* (Cambridge: Cambridge University Press, 1990), 214–49.

83. O'Connor, *Steel-Dictator,* 272.

84. See, for instance, Tankosich interview, p. 10; Kerekac interview; Horace Davis questionnaires of Duquesne steelworkers; O'Connor, *Steel-Dictator,* 269–70.

85. *Duquesne Times,* 21 March 1930, 10 and 31 Oct. 1930, 7 and 26 Nov. 1930, 2 and 16 Jan. 1931, and 27 March 1931.

86. See various welfare reports from the Duquesne Works' visiting nurse for September and October 1931 in Box 11, File W-2(a), USSC.

87. *Duquesne Times,* 23 and 30 Oct. 1931, 20 Nov. 1931, 22 Jan. 1932, 12 and 19 Feb. 1932, 22 April 1932, 24 June 1932, and 21 Oct. 1932.

88. *Duquesne Times,* 29 Jan. and 3 June 1932; Maloy interview, pp. 7–8; O'Connor, *Steel-Dictator,* 269–70; Tankosich interview, 10; Kerekac interview; Lloyd, "Steel Looks After Its Own," 7; Phillip Bonosky, "Pittsburgh Experiment," *Masses and Mainstream* 3 (Aug. 1950): 30; George Powers, *Cradle of Steel Unionism: Monongahela Valley, PA* (East Chicago, Ind.: Figueroa, 1972), 33.

89. O'Connor, *Steel-Dictator,* 269.

90. Powers, *Cradle of Steel Unionism,* 33; Maloy interview, 7; Bonosky, "Life and Death of a Steel Worker," 18; Lloyd, "Steel Looks After Its Own," 7–8; Davis, *Labor and Steel,* 103; R. Stein, "Steel Lines Up," 146.

91. Duquesne Works payroll ledgers, 1929–32; A. C. Cummins to W. C. Oberg, 22 April 1936, Box 10, File P-4(a), USSC; DWERP, minutes of meeting, 20 Sept. 1933, Box 4, NSLRB; *Duquesne Times,* 27 Sept. 1929; "Welfare Activities at Duquesne Works" [1936], Box 11, File W-2(a), USSC.

92. *Steel,* 24 April 1933, p. 16; *Duquesne Times,* 17 June and 26 Aug. 1932.

93. Maloy interview, p. 8.

Chapter 3: The Rank-and-File Movement, 1933–35

1. Harvey O'Connor, "The Second Battle of Duquesne," typewritten manuscript, p. 1, Box 23, File: Duquesne Works, Carnegie Steel Co. (DW-CSC), Harvey O'Connor Collection (HOC), Archives of Labor and Urban Affairs (ALUA), Wayne State University, Detroit.

2. Inactive voter registration card for Fletcher Williamson, Allegheny County, Voter Registration Records, Archives of Industrial Society (AIS), Hillman Library, University of Pittsburgh; George Powers, *Cradle of Steel Unionism: Monongahela Valley, PA* (East Chicago, Ind.: Figueroa, 1972), 42; Clinton Golden and Harold J. Ruttenberg, *The Dynamics of Industrial Democracy* (New York: Harper, 1942), 18–19; *Pittsburgh Courier,* 4 June 1960. Quotes are from *Daily Worker,* 16 May 1935.

3. J. C. Pegram, "Third Corps Area Summary of the Subversive Situation as of August 1, 1932," p. 3, in *U.S. Military Intelligence Reports: Surveillance of Radicals in the United States, 1917–1945* (Frederick, Md.: University Publications of America, 1984), microfilm reel 27, frame 0482; J. Rapaport, "Will the Comrades Explain?" *Party Organizer* 5 (July 1932): 22–23; "Problems Faced in Building Organization in a Steel Town," *Party Organizer* 6 (Feb. 1933): 16–18; "Facts and Material on Organizational Status, Problems, and Organizational Tasks of the Party," *Party Organizer* 7 (May–June 1934): 9–10.

4. *(Pittsburgh) Post-Gazette,* 13 April 1933; Powers, *Cradle of Steel Unionism,* 34–41; Annemarie Draham, "Unlikely Allies Fight for Unionization: Homestead, Pa., 1933–1946" (master's thesis, Indiana University of Pennsylvania, 1984), 49–53; *Daily Worker,* 26 Dec.

1933; Ray Tucker, interview by Kim Coberly, 27 July 1983, in *Crashin' Out: Hard Times in McKeesport* (McKeesport, Pa.: McKeesport Oral History Project, Mon Valley Unemployed Council, 1983), 44–45.

5. *Duquesne Times,* 28 March 1930.

6. Unidentified newspaper clipping, Box 22, File: DW-CSC, HOC; *Duquesne Times,* 12 June 1931.

7. Philip Klein, *A Social Study of Pittsburgh: Community Problems and Social Services of Allegheny County* (New York: Columbia University Press, 1938), 438; Ralph Carr Fetcher, Katharine A. Biehl, and Joseph L. Zarefsky, *Direct and Work Relief and Federal Work Programs in Allegheny County, 1920–1941* (Pittsburgh: Bureau of Social Research, Federation of Social Agencies of Pittsburgh and Allegheny County, 1942), 5, 10; Myron Taylor, *Ten Years of Steel* (New York: U.S. Steel, 1938), 27.

8. Harvey O'Connor, typed notes from survey of Duquesne mill workers, Box 23, File DW-CSC, HOC; Harvey O'Connor, *Steel-Dictator* (New York: John Day, 1935), 7; Duquesne Works Employee Representation Plan (DWERP), minutes of meeting, 27 Aug. 1934, Box 4, Records of the National Recovery Administration (RG 9), Records of the National Steel Labor Relations Board (NSLRB), National Archives (NA), Washington, D.C.

9. Phillip Bonosky, "The Life and Death of a Steelworker," *Masses and Mainstream* 5 (April 1952): 18.

10. *Real Estate Statistics for Allegheny County, Pennsylvania* (Pittsburgh: Bureau of Business Research, University of Pittsburgh, 1936), 47, 93.

11. Jesse C. Moody, Jr., "The Steel Industry and the National Recovery Administration: An Experiment in Industrial Self-Government" (Ph.D. diss., University of Oklahoma, 1965), 120–22, 325.

12. Carroll R. Daugherty, Melvin G. de Chazeau, and Samuel S. Stratton, *The Economics of the Iron and Steel Industry* (New York: McGraw-Hill, 1937), vol. 2: 944.

13. See, for instance, copies of letters from Amalgamated president Mike Tighe to William Green, in Daugherty, de Chazeau, and Stratton, *Economics of the Iron and Steel Industry,* vol. 2: 950–52.

14. Louis Adamic, "The Steel Strike Collapses," *Nation,* 4 July 1934, p. 9.

15. [Harold Ruttenberg], "Steel Labor, the NIRA, and the Amalgamated Association" [1934], typewritten manuscript, p. 1, Box 2, File 10, Heber Blankenhorn Collection (HEB), ALUA; O'Connor, *Steel-Dictator,* 185, 187.

16. Melvyn Dubofsky and Warren Van Tine, *John L. Lewis: A Biography* (Urbana: University of Illinois Press, 1986), 134; Edward A. Wieck, "The Steel Workers Under the NRA," 3 Aug. 1936, typewritten manuscript, p. 83, Box 5, File: Steelworkers Under the NRA, Edward A. Wieck Collection, ALUA.

17. *Amalgamated Journal,* 16 Aug. 1933.

18. Amalgamated leaflet, no date, Box 22, File: Amalgamated Association of Iron Steel and Tin Workers (AAISTW), HOC.

19. *Amalgamated Journal,* 16 Aug. 1933.

20. Ruttenberg, "Steel Labor," p. 1; Horace R. Cayton and George S. Mitchell, *Black Workers and the New Unions* (Chapel Hill: University of North Carolina Press, 1939), 125.

21. Dubofsky and Van Tine, *John L. Lewis,* 131–42; Joel Sabadasz, "Understanding Workers: Labor Relations in Steel from 1930 to 1941 in the Southeastern Monongahela Valley,"

unpublished paper, no date, pp. 3–12; Gene and Frank DiCola, interview by Alice Hoff-
man, August 1968, United Steelworkers of America Oral History Project (USAOHP),
Historical Collections and Labor Archives (HCLA), The Pennsylvania State University,
State College; John J. Mullen, interview by Alice Hoffman, February 1966, USAOHP; *Post-
Gazette,* 26 Sept.–12 Oct. 1933; *(McKeesport) Daily News,* 26 Sept.–6 Oct. 1933.

22. Jeremiah Patrick Shalloo, *Private Police: With Special Reference to Pennsylvania* (Philadelphia: American Academy of Political and Social Science, 1933), 64. Pinchot is quoted
in *Post-Gazette,* 27 Sept. 1933.

23. *(Pittsburgh) Sun-Telegraph,* 26 Sept. 1933.

24. Guy Battles to Gifford Pinchot, 29 Sept. 1933, Box 2523, File: Strikes 1933 Iron and
Steel, Gifford Pinchot Papers (GPIN), Library of Congress (LOC); E. A. Long to Cornelia Pinchot, 13 Oct. 1933; Joe Bissell to C. Pinchot, 20 Oct. 1933; George McBride to C. Pinchot, 8 Nov. 1933; and Louie Smolinski to C. Pinchot, 17 Oct. 1933, all in Box 274, File: Steel,
Cornelia Pinchot Papers (CPIN), LOC.

25. *Amalgamated Journal,* 30 Nov. 1933. Various versions of her speeches to steelworkers are found in Box 274, File: Steel, CPIN.

26. John Yuhos, interview by Jim Barrett, 4 June 1976, transcript, p. 7, Homestead Album Oral History Project (HAOHP), AIS.

27. Staughton Lynd, "The Possibility of Radicalism in the Early 1930s: The Case of Steel,"
Radical America 6 (Nov.–Dec. 1972): 39; Staughton Lynd, ed., "Personal Histories of the
Early CIO," *Radical America* 5 (May–June 1971): 53.

28. *Amalgamated Journal,* 27 July 1933; O'Connor, *Steel-Dictator,* 3; DWERP, minutes
of meeting, 29 Sept. 1933, Box 4, NSLRB; *Post-Gazette,* 7 Aug. 1933.

29. *Amalgamated Journal,* 10 Aug. 1933.

30. Guy Battles to G. Pinchot, 29 Sept. 1933.

31. O'Connor, *Steel-Dictator,* 3–4.

32. *Daily News,* 9 Oct. 1933; Duquesne Works payroll ledger, Oct. 1933, U.S. Steel Corp.
(Duquesne Works) Payroll Ledgers and Records of the Personnel Division (USSC), 1904–
80, UE/Labor Archives (UE/L), AIS; U.S. Congress, Senate, Committee on Education and
Labor, *Violations of Free Speech and Rights of Labor,* 77th Cong., 1st sess., 1939, S. Rept. 6,
pt. 3: 208.

33. "Remarks of General Superintendent A. C. Cummins to the Employees' Representatives October 5th, 1933, in Reference to the Labor Situation in Western Pennsylvania,"
Box 110, National Labor Relations Board Records (RG 25), Administrative Division, Files
and Dockets Section, Transcripts and Exhibits (NLRB-Exhibits), Washington National
Records Center, Suitland, Md.

34. Dubofsky and Van Tine, *John L. Lewis,* 142; *Post-Gazette,* 9 Oct. 1933.

35. E. A. Long to C. Pinchot, 13 Oct. 1933; *Amalgamated Journal,* 26 Oct. 1933; Powers,
Cradle of Steel Unionism, 42.

36. *Amalgamated Journal,* 2 Nov. 1933.

37. *Amalgamated Journal,* 9 Nov. 1933; William J. Spang and Henry Budahazi to G. Pinchot, 28 Oct. 1933, Box 2522, File: Strikes 1933 Duquesne, GPIN; E. A. Long to C. Pinchot,
13 Oct. 1933. For an assessment of the changes found in steel towns after passage of the
NRA, see John A. Fitch, "A Man Can Talk in Homestead," *Survey Graphic* 25 (Feb. 1936):
71–76, 118–20.

38. Spang and Budahazi to G. Pinchot, 28 Oct. 1933; Spang and Budahazi to William Green, 28 Oct. 1933, *American Federation of Labor Records: Samuel Gompers Era* (Sanford, N.J.: Microfilming Corp. of America, 1979), microfilm reel 38, frame 2528.

39. G. Pinchot to James S. Crawford, 1 Nov. 1933, Box 2522, File: Strikes 1933 Duquesne, GPIN.

40. *Post-Gazette,* 2 Nov. 1933.

41. G. Pinchot to Green, 1 Nov. 1933, *American Federation of Labor Records,* microfilm reel 38, frame 2527.

42. *Post-Gazette,* 2 Nov. 1933; *Daily News,* 2 Nov. 1933.

43. *Amalgamated Journal,* 9 Nov. 1933.

44. *Amalgamated Journal,* 21 Dec. 1933.

45. Sam Bielich, interview by Marilyn Petroff, 22 Oct. 1976, transcript, p. 14, Ethnic Fraternal Organizations Oral History Project (EFOOHP), AIS; John Bodnar, *Workers' World: Kinship, Community, and Protest in an Industrial Society, 1900–1940* (Baltimore: Johns Hopkins University Press, 1982), 139; John Chorry, interview by Alice Hoffman, Oct. 1966, transcript, pp. 7–8, USAOHP.

46. Fort Duquesne [*sic*] Lodge No. 187 petition, March 1934, Box 4, File: Carnegie Co. Clairton [*sic*], Pennsylvania Petition, NSLRB. In the sample of 284 petition signers, 104 were chippers, 37 were laborers, and 250 earned 54 cents an hour or less. For supporting evidence of the skill composition of the Duquesne lodge, see Elmer Maloy, interview by Don Kennedy, 7 Nov. 1967, transcript, p. 26, USAOHP; O'Connor, "Second Battle of Duquesne"; Charles Bollinger, interview by Alice Hoffman, July 1966, transcript, p. 9, USAOHP.

47. For foreign-language speakers see *Amalgamated Journal,* 30 Nov. 1933, 7 June 1934, and 2 Aug. 1934. For ethnic fraternal ties see *Amalgamated Journal,* 9 Nov. 1933, 11, 18, and 25 Jan. 1934, 15 and 22 Feb. 1934; *Duquesne Times,* 24 March 1933.

48. Maloy interview, p. 26; Bodnar, *Workers' World,* 139; *Amalgamated Journal,* 21 Dec. 1933 and 24 May 1934.

49. *Amalgamated Journal,* 21 Dec. 1933.

50. Michael Kerekac, interview by Linda Nyden, 9 July 1974, Pittsburgh Oral History Project (POHP), Pennsylvania Historical and Museum Commission, Pennsylvania State Archives, Harrisburg; Milan Tankosich, interview by Peter Gottlieb, 16 Aug. 1974, transcript, p. 5, POHP.

51. F. Alden Wilson, "Occupational Status of the Negro in the Iron and Steel Industry, Pittsburgh, and Environs," unpublished paper, 23 May 1934, 44, Box 10, File 469, Urban League of Pittsburgh Papers, AIS.

52. See, for example, Superior Street, or Peach Alley, in U.S. Census, *Fourteenth Census of the United States: 1920, Manuscript Schedules,* vol. 10, Pennsylvania, Allegheny County, National Archives microfilm reel 1511; Frank Takach, interview by Jim Barrett, 28 May 1976, transcript, p. 1, HAOHP.

53. Tankosich interview, p. 9; Takach interview, pp. 1–2; Yuhos interview, p. 5; Kerekac interview.

54. Anonymous black man (interview #2-2), interview by Peter Gottlieb, 16 Dec. 1974, transcript, p. 10, POHP. See also Willie C. Norman, interview by Jon Eric Johnson, 9 April 1976, transcript, p. 9, EFOOHP.

55. Kerekac interview; John Smitko, interview by Carl Romanek, 24 June 1974, POHP; Tankosich interview, p. 9; Barbara Perkovic, interview by Kate McEvoy, 16 Sept. 1975, transcript, p. 10, EFOOHP.

56. U.S. Census, *Fourteenth Census of the United States: 1920, Manuscript Schedules; Duquesne Times,* 23 Jan. 1958; Duquesne Works payroll ledger, Oct. 1933, USSC; records of the War Department, Office of the Provost Marshall General, Selective Service System, World War I Draft Registration Cards, State of Pennsylvania, County of Allegheny, Local Board #8, microfilm copy, reel 14, Hillman Library; O'Connor, *Steel-Dictator,* 3; Ruttenberg, "Steel Labor," pp. 4–6.

57. Biographical information about Amalgamated leaders is derived from U.S. Census, *Fourteenth Census of the United States: 1920, Manuscript Schedules;* World War I Draft Registration Cards, Local Board #8; inactive voter registration cards, Allegheny County, Pa., Voter Registration Records; *Duquesne Times,* 24 May 1934, 7 June 1934, and 13 March 1936.

58. Wilson, "Occupational Status," p. 52; Cayton and Mitchell, *Black Workers and the New Unions,* 159–62, 167–68; Dennis C. Dickerson, *Out of the Crucible: Black Steelworkers in Western Pennsylvania, 1875–1980* (Albany: State University of New York Press, 1986), 10–17, 85–92.

59. Cayton and Mitchell, *Black Workers and the New Unions,* 163.

60. Ibid., 166; *Amalgamated Journal,* 18 and 25 Jan., 2, 15 and 22 Feb., and 16 Aug. 1934.

61. Cayton and Mitchell, *Black Workers and the New Unions,* 187–88; *Amalgamated Journal,* 22 March 1934. The quotation is from *Amalgamated Journal,* 1 March 1934.

62. *Amalgamated Journal,* 12 July 1934, 13 Sept. 1934, and 3 Jan. 1935; U.S. Steel, Bureau of Safety, Sanitation and Welfare, *Bulletin* (Dec. 1920): 63; Phillip Bonosky, "Pittsburgh Experiment," *Masses and Mainstream* 3 (Aug. 1950): 30.

63. *Amalgamated Journal,* 12 April 1934.

64. *Amalgamated Journal,* 12 and 19 April, 28 June, 19 July, 9 and 16 Aug. 1934; AAISTW Tri-Boro Lodge #186 (Braddock, Pa.) minutes of meeting, 24 Nov. 1934, Tri-Boro Lodge 186 (Braddock) Papers (T-BL), HCLA; Cayton and Mitchell, *Black Workers and the New Unions,* 188.

65. *Amalgamated Journal,* 11 Jan. 1934, 22 Feb. 1934, 8 March 1934, 7 June 1934, 26 July 1934, 27 Sept. 1934, and 17 Jan. 1935; Tri-Boro Lodge #186, minutes of meetings, 22 and 24 May 1934, 22 Sept. 1934, 27 Oct. 1934, 24 Nov. 1934, and 12 Jan. 1935, T-BL.

66. *Amalgamated Journal,* 1 and 22 March 1934.

67. Wieck, "Steel Workers Under the NRA," p. 57; Daugherty, de Chazeau, and Stratton, *Economics of the Iron and Steel Industry,* vol. 2: 969–70.

68. David Brody, "Section 8(a)(2) and the Origins of the Wagner Act," in *Restoring the Promise of American Labor Law,* ed. Sheldon Friedman, Richard W. Hurd, Rudolph A. Oswald, and Ronald L. Seeber (Ithaca, N.Y.: ILR Press, 1994), 29–44; Raymond L. Hogler, "Worker Participation, Employer Anti-Unionism, and Labor Law: The Case of the Steel Industry, 1918–1937," *Hofstra Labor Law Journal* 7 (fall 1989): 1–69.

69. David Harvey Kelly, "Labor Relations in the Steel Industry: Management's Ideas, Proposals, and Programs, 1920 to 1950" (Ph.D. diss., Indiana University, 1976), 105–6; Stuart D. Brandes, *American Welfare Capitalism, 1880–1940* (Chicago: University of Chicago Press, 1976), 123–27; Ernest Richmond Burton, *Employee Representation* (Baltimore: Williams

and Wilkens, 1926), 29–30; National Industrial Conference Board, *The Growth of Works Councils in the United States: A Statistical Summary* (New York: NICB, 1925), 8; Daugherty, de Chazeau, and Stratton, *Economics of the Iron and Steel Industry,* vol. 2: 1005; Hogler, "Worker Participation," 5–22.

70. Sanford Jacoby, *Employing Bureaucracy: Managers, Unions, and the Transformation of Work in American Industry, 1900–1945* (New York: Columbia University Press, 1985), 180–82. The progress of the Bethlehem plan can be traced in the company's bulletin, *Bethlehem Review,* esp. 22 April 1925 and 25 Sept. 1933. The Special Conference Committee's support for employee representation can be traced in its annual reports, found in Box 1, File 9, Box 6, File 9, Box 12, File 25, and Box 17, File 7, all in Willis F. Harrington Papers, Hagley Museum and Library, Wilmington, Delaware. I wish to thank David Brody for sharing the SCC materials with me.

71. Daniel Nelson, "The Company Union Movement, 1900–1937: A Reexamination," *Business History Review* 56 (autumn 1982): 344; W. B. Dickson to Arthur H. Young, 24 Feb. 1934, Box 4, File 16, William B. Dickson Papers, HCLA.

72. National Industrial Conference Board, *Individual and Collective Bargaining Under the N.I.R.A.: A Statistical Study of Present Practice, November 1933* (New York: NICB, 1933), 23–24; *Steel,* 12 June 1933, p. 11; Daugherty, de Chazeau, and Stratton, *Economics of the Iron and Steel Industry,* vol. 2: 1005; Wieck, "Steel Workers Under the NRA," p. 83. A copy of the generic U.S. Steel ERP is found in *Steel,* 19 June 1933, p. 13.

73. *Steel* is quoted in O'Connor, *Steel-Dictator,* 137.

74. *Steel,* 19 June 1933, p. 13.

75. Lewis L. Lorwin and Arthur Wubnig, *Labor Relations Boards: The Regulation of Collective Bargaining Under the National Industrial Recovery Act* (Washington, D.C.: Brookings Institution, 1935), 87–109, 149–51; James A. Gross, *The Making of the National Labor Relations Board: A Study in Economics, Politics, and the Law, 1933–1937* (Albany: State University of New York Press, 1974), vol. 1: 7–56; *NRA Reporter* 2 (15 Feb. 1934): 61–62.

76. Lorwin and Wubnig, *Labor Relations Boards,* 142–56; *Iron Age,* 15 March 1934, p. 43H; *Post-Gazette,* 26 Feb. 1934; Federated Press, "U.S. Steel's Company Union Bluff Called; It Wilts," 3 Oct. 1934, Box 23, File DW-CSC, HOC; "Plan of Employee Representation, Carnegie Steel Co.," no date, Box 116, Exhibit 105, NLRB-Exhibits.

77. NRA, National Labor Board (NLB) press release no. 3452, 23 Feb. 1934, Box 23, File DW-CSC, HOC.

78. Robert R. R. Brooks, *As Steel Goes, . . . Unionism in a Basic Industry* (New Haven: Yale University Press, 1940), 67; Dominic DelTurco, interviewer unknown, 14 Sept. 1978, transcript, p. 5, Box 81, File 8, Beaver Valley Labor History Records, UE/L.

79. I explore the Duquesne Works ERP in chap. 4.

80. Fitch, "A Man Can Talk in Homestead," 75; Daugherty, de Chazeau, and Stratton, *Economics of the Iron and Steel Industry,* vol. 2: 995. For the treatment of Amalgamated workers at Duquesne, see O'Connor, *Steel-Dictator,* 264–65; O'Connor, "Second Battle of Duquesne," 14; Joseph T. Inglefield to Hugh S. Johnson [May 1934], Box 5, File: Carnegie Steel, McDonald and Duquesne (CSMD), NSLRB. Blacks' experiences are recounted in Cayton and Mitchell, *Black Workers and the New Unions,* 134. There would be only a few claims that workers were fired either for affiliation with the Amalgamated or, in one case, for refusal to vote in an ERP election. Not all claims proved valid. See *Daily Worker,* 26

June 1935; minutes of grievance meeting, 20 April 1937, p. 1, and 4 May 1937, p. 1, Third Step Minutes Notebook, Box 27, USSC.

81. "Telephone Conversation Between Mr. Handler and Mr. Neff at Duquesne, February 23, 1934," Box 5, Folder: CSMD, NSLRB. See numerous notarized affidavits, including those of Bodnar and Tkach, from Duquesne workers concerning intimidation during the election in Box 5, File CSMD, NSLRB.

82. "Detailed Result of Election on Revised Employee Representation Plan—February 23, 1934," Box 5, File CSMD, NSLRB; *Iron Age,* 15 March 1934, p. 43.

83. NRA, NLB press release no. 3944, 20 March 1934, Box 5, File CSMD, NSLRB; Fort Duquesne Lodge No. 187 petition, March 1934; *Pittsburgh Press,* 22 March 1934.

84. Lorwin and Wubnig, *Labor Relations Boards,* 109–13; Gross, *Making of the National Labor Relations Board,* 59–64; *NRA Reporter,* 54–56.

85. Lorwin and Wubnig, *Labor Relations Boards,* 113.

86. Wieck, "Steel Workers Under the NRA," p. 58; William Spang to Robert F. Wagner, 2 April 1934, Box 5, File CSMD, NSLRB.

87. Spang to Franklin Roosevelt, 11 April 1934, Box 5, File CSMD, NSLRB.

88. Federated Press, 18 April 1934, Box 23, File DW-CSC, HOC.

89. "Telephone Conversation Between Mr. Handler and Mr. Desverine, March 27, 1934," Box 5, File CSMD, NSLRB; NLB executive session minutes, 29 March, 10 and 26 April, 3 May 1934, Box 1, File: Minutes, Records of the National Labor Relations Board (RG 25), Pre–Wagner Act Records, National Labor Board: Records of the Executive Director, Jesse I. Miller (NLRB-Miller), NA; Daugherty, de Chazeau, and Stratton, *Economics of the Iron and Steel Industry,* vol. 2: 1053–54.

90. *Steel,* 4 June 1934, p. 10.

91. [Harold Ruttenberg] to Steve [Raushenbush], 2 April 1934, Box 6, File 7, Harold J. Ruttenberg Papers (HJR), HCLA.

92. *Amalgamated Journal,* 24 May 1934; NLB executive session minutes, 3 May 1934, Box 1, File: Minutes, NLRB-Miller; *Pittsburgh Press,* 5 May 1934; Federated Press, 3 May 1934, Box 23, File DW-CSC, HOC; Spang and Raymond Ruhe to NLB, 2 May 1934, Box 5, File CSMD, NSLRB.

93. *Amalgamated Journal,* 24 May 1934.

94. NLB executive session agenda and minutes, 16 May 1934, Box 1, File: Minutes, NLRB-Miller.

95. NLB executive session minutes, 16, 22, 29, and 31 May 1934; NLB executive session agenda, 22 May 1934, all in Box 1, File: Minutes, NLRB-Miller.

96. M. F. Tighe, report of delinquent lodges, undated, *American Federation of Labor Records, pt. 2, President's Office Files, Series A, William Green Papers,* 1934–52 (Frederick, Md.: University Publications of America, 1985), microfilm reel 28, frame 00041; Daugherty, de Chazeau, and Stratton, *Economics of the Iron and Steel Industry,* vol. 2: 953.

97. Daugherty, de Chazeau, and Stratton, *Economics of the Iron and Steel Industry,* vol. 2: 959–60; Brooks, *As Steel Goes,* 49–51; exchange of letters between Earl Forbeck, president of Amalgamated Pioneer Lodge No. 158 (McKeesport Tin Plate Co.), William Green, and Michael Tighe in Dec. 1933 and Jan. 1934, *American Federation of Labor Records, Green Papers,* microfilm reel 28, frames 00002–00009.

98. Brooks, *As Steel Goes,* 51; Ruttenberg, "Steel Labor," p. 3.

99. Brooks, *As Steel Goes,* 52–54; Ruttenberg, "Steel Labor," pp. 7–11, exhibit 6; Heber Blankenhorn, unpublished manuscript, chap. 12, "The Steelworkers Invade Washington," 6, Box 8, File 3, HEB.

100. Harvey O'Connor to Staughton Lynd, 29 Oct. 1972, Box 15, File 57, pt. 2, HOC; [Mr. Dewey], Memorandum, 1 June 1934, Box 41, File: Steel Strikes, Department of Labor Records (RG 174), Office of the Secretary, General Subject Files, 1933–41, NA; Cayton and Mitchell, *Black Workers and the New Unions,* 128; *Amalgamated Journal,* 12 April 1934; Federated Press, 19 April 1934, Box 23, File DW-CSC, HOC; [Ruttenberg] to [Raushenbush], 2 April 1934; Tri-Boro Lodge ledger book for 1934–35, T-BL; Chorry interview, p. 7; DiCola interview, 29.

101. Ruttenberg, "Steel Labor," pp. 14–17; O'Connor, *Steel-Dictator,* 200.

102. Brooks, *As Steel Goes,* 59.

103. Ruttenberg, "Steel Labor," pp. 17–31.

104. Harold Ruttenberg, "Finale [*sic*] Day of the Convention: May 1st, 1934," Box 17, File 95, HOC: Pt. II; O'Connor, *Steel-Dictator,* 198. For Duquesne Works preparations see Duquesne Works payroll ledger, June 1934, USSC; U.S. Congress, *Violations of Free Speech and Rights of Labor,* 208.

105. *Duquesne Times,* 8 June 1934; *Steel,* 28 May 1934, p. 13; Henry Budahazi to Wagner, 9 June 1934, Box 5, File CSMD, NSLRB; Duquesne City Council minutes, 18 June 1934, microfilm copy of Duquesne borough and city council minutes, reel 5075, Hillman Library.

106. Two slightly different versions of the leaflet appear in the *Amalgamated Journal,* 1 and 7 June 1934.

107. *Duquesne Times,* 8 and 15 June 1934; *Daily News,* 11 June 1934.

108. Ruttenberg, "Steel Labor," pp. 34–35, Brooks, *As Steel Goes,* 66–67. For the origins of the steel strike settlement, see Moody, "Steel Industry and the National Recovery Administration," 251–54; L. E. Block, E. C. Grace, and W. A. Irwin to Hugh S. Johnson, 8 June 1934, Box 45, File: Memo, etc., June–Sept. 1934, Donald Richberg Papers, LOC; Boris Shishkin, "Memorandum," 12 June 1934, Box 41, File: Steel Strikes, Department of Labor Records.

109. [Harold Ruttenberg], "The Special Convention of the AA's 59th: June 14, 15 . . . ," Box 22, File: AA June Convention, HOC; Adamic, "Steel Strike Collapses," 11–12; Daugherty, de Chazeau, and Stratton, *Economics of the Iron and Steel Industry,* vol. 2: 963.

110. Lynd, "Possibility of Radicalism in the Early 1930s," 43–51. Ruttenberg's reminiscences are found in Harold Ruttenberg, interview by Don Kennedy, 24 April 1968, transcript, pp. 4–5, USAOHP; Harold Ruttenberg, interview by Arthur S. Weinberg, 12 May 1968, transcript, p. 2, USAOHP; Harold Ruttenberg, interview by Rhea Lehman and Florence Joseph, 24 Feb. 1986, National Council of Jewish Women Oral History Project, AIS. For contemporary and oral history sources that emphasize the weakness of the rank-and-file movement and that discount the claim that the intellectuals attempted to steer the movement away from a strike, see O'Connor, *Steel-Dictator,* 198–200; Jessie Lloyd O'Connor, Harvey O'Connor, and Susan M. Bowler, *Harvey and Jessie: A Couple of Radicals* (Philadelphia: Temple University Press, 1988), 160; Harvey O'Connor, interview by Don Kennedy, March 1976, transcript, pp. 17–19, 22, USAOHP; Clarence Irwin, "A Leader Speaks for the Rank and File," in Brooks, *As Steel Goes,* 49–67; Ruttenberg, "Steel Labor," pp. 3–

35, and attached typewritten copies of letters from Ruttenberg and O'Connor, listed as exhibits 7, 8, 9, and 20.

111. O'Connor to Lynd, 29 Oct. 1972.

112. Lorwin and Wubnig, *Labor Relations Boards*, 115, 335–36.

113. Thomas Bell, *Out of This Furnace* (Pittsburgh: University of Pittsburgh Press, 1976), 323–24.

114. Brooks, *As Steel Goes*, 61.

115. Ruttenberg to George Soule, 6 July 1934, Box 4, File 4, HJR; Ruttenberg, "Steel Labor," p. 17; *Steel and Metal Worker,* July 1934.

116. *Post-Gazette,* 27 Oct. 1934.

117. AAISTW, "To the Officers and Members of Subordinate Lodges," 5 July 1934, Box 1, File: AAISTW, NSLRB; *Pittsburgh Press,* 17 July 1934; Charlton Ogburn to Spang, 13 Sept. 1934, Box 4, File: Carnegie Steel Co., Duquesne Plant (CSCDP), NSLRB.

118. *Steel,* 6 Aug. 1934, 22.

119. *Amalgamated Journal,* 2 Aug. 1934.

120. Ogburn to Spang, 13 Sept. 1934; DWERP, minutes of meeting, 27 Aug. 1934, Box 4, NSLRB.

121. Spang to Roosevelt, 27 Aug. 1934, Box 4, File: CSCDP, NSLRB; Ogburn to Spang, 13 Sept. 1934.

122. MAE, "Memorandum," 21 Aug. 1934, Box 1, File AAISTW, NSLRB; Ruttenberg, "Steel Labor," pp. 31, 36; Lorwin and Wubnig, *Labor Relations Boards,* 340.

123. Ogburn to Spang, 17 Aug. 1934, Box 4, File: CSCDP, NSLRB; Ruttenberg to O'Connor, 4 July 1934, Box 22, File: Amalgamated Assoc. June Convention, HJR; [Harold Ruttenberg] "Joint-District Meeting of December 30th, 1934," Box 4, File 4, HJR.

124. Ogburn to Spang, 17 Aug. 1934.

125. See Spang to Roosevelt, 27 Aug.1934.

126. Lorwin and Wubnig, *Labor Relations Boards,* 338–39; "Labor Notes: The President and Steel," *Nation,* 23 Jan. 1935, p. 107.

127. Daugherty, de Chazeau, and Stratton, *Economics of the Iron and Steel Industry,* vol. 2: 1041. Harvey O'Connor's notes from the two-day hearing are found in Box 22, File DW-CSC, HOC.

128. Ogburn, "To the National Steel Labor Relations Board," undated, Box 4, File: CSCDP, NSLRB.

129. *New York Times,* 3 Oct. 1934.

130. Statement by I. Lamont Hughes before the NSLRB, Box 23, File DW-CSC, HOC; *New York Times,* 3 Oct. 1934; *Post-Gazette,* 3 Oct. 1934.

131. *New York Times,* 3 Oct. 1934.

132. Federated Press, 3 Oct. 1934.

133. *New York Times,* 3 Oct. 1934.

134. *New York Times,* 1 Nov. 1934.

135. Daugherty, de Chazeau, and Stratton, *Economics of the Iron and Steel Industry,* vol. 2: 1041–45.

136. Ogburn to Walter P. Stacey, 24 and 26 Oct., 8 Nov. 1934; Chairman [Walter Stacey] to Ogburn, 3 Nov. 1934, all in Box 4, File: CSCDP, NSLRB; Lorwin and Wubnig, *Labor Relations Boards,* 341; *Iron Age,* 29 Nov. 1934, pp. 43, 45.

137. Ogburn to Stacey, 12 Nov. 1934, Box 4, File: CSCDP, NSLRB; Ruttenberg, "Joint-District Meeting of December 30th, 1934"; *Amalgamated Journal,* 25 Oct., 9 Nov. 1934.

138. Daugherty, de Chazeau, and Stratton, *Economics of the Iron and Steel Industry,* vol. 2: 1045–46, 1054; *New York Times,* 19 Dec. 1934; Green to Stacey, 4 Jan. 1935, Box 4, File: CSCDP, NSLRB; Blankenhorn to O'Connor, 30 July 1935, Box 11, File 64, HOC: Pt. II.

139. *Employee Representatives, General Body Committee vs. National Steel Labor Relations Board,* U.S. Circuit Court of Appeals (3d Cir.), "Petition for Review of Findings of Fact," and general docket entries, Records of the U.S. Courts of Appeals (RG 276), NA–Mid-Atlantic Region, Philadelphia; *Iron Age,* 10 Jan. 1935, p. 51, and 21 Feb. 1935, p. 53-A.

140. *Daily Worker,* 2 March 1935.

141. *Amalgamated Journal,* 12 April 1934.

142. *Amalgamated Journal,* 18 Jan. 1934. Also see issues of 23 Nov. 1933, 7 and 21 Dec. 1933, and 11 and 25 Jan. 1934.

143. *Steel and Metal Worker,* Feb. and March–April 1934; *Daily Worker,* 14 Dec. 1933.

144. Brooks, *As Steel Goes,* 54–55; Lynd, "Possibility of Radicalism in the Early 1930s," 47–48; Ruttenberg, "Steel Labor," pp. 12–14, and exhibit 10.

145. *Steel and Metal Worker,* July 1934; *Daily Worker,* 9 June 1934; "Unify the Forces of All Steel Workers for Aggressive Unionism," *Communist* 13 (July 1934): 655–63; *Amalgamated Journal,* 16 Aug. 1934.

146. John Steuben, "Recent Developments in the Steel Industry and Our Tasks," *Communist* 13 (Dec. 1934): 1234–40; "Lessons of Economic Struggles, Tasks of the Communists in the Trade Unions," *Communist* 13 (May 1934): 467; Brooks, *As Steel Goes,* 69; *Steel and Metal Worker,* Jan. 1935; Edward A. Wieck, "Report on SMWIU Convention," 5 Aug. 1934, Box 26, File 31, Wieck Collection; Bert Cochran, *Labor and Communism: The Conflict That Shaped American Unions* (Princeton: Princeton University Press, 1977), 71–77.

147. Brooks, *As Steel Goes,* 69; Lynd, "Possibility of Radicalism in the Early 1930s," 52; Ruttenberg interview by Kennedy, p. 3; Clarence Irwin to Ruttenberg, 23 Jan. 1935, Box 4, File 4, HJR.

148. Tri-Boro Lodge #186, minutes of meeting, 24 Nov. 1934, T-BL; *Amalgamated Journal,* 17 Jan. 1935.

149. Steuben, "Recent Developments in the Steel Industry," 1236.

150. *Amalgamated Journal,* 17 Jan. 1935; Ruttenberg, "Joint-District Meeting of December 30th, 1934."

151. *Amalgamated Journal,* 17 Jan. 1935; *Daily Worker,* 2 Jan. 1935.

152. Brooks, *As Steel Goes,* 69; *Amalgamated Journal,* 17, 24, and 31 Jan., 14 and 21 Feb., 17 March 1935.

153. William Spang press release, 26 Jan. 1935, Box 22, File: Amalgamated Assoc. Rank and File Jan.–Feb. 1935, HOC.

154. *Amalgamated Journal,* 14 Feb. 1935; AAISTW, *Journal of Convention Proceedings,* 1935, Pittsburgh, p. 2616; *Steel and Metal Notes,* May 1935, p. 5; Wieck, "Steel Workers Under the NRA," p. 84.

155. Tighe to Stacey, 9 and 31 Jan. 1935, Box 1, File AAISTW, NSLRB.

156. Charlton Ogburn, amended petition to the NSLRB, 14 Feb. 1935, Box 5, File CSMD, NSLRB; *Post-Gazette,* 5 and 8 March 1935; *Iron Age,* 14 March 1935, p. 46; *ERP vs. NSLRB,* general docket entries.

157. Wieck, "Steel Workers Under the NRA," pp. 128–32; Lynd, "Possibility of Radicalism in the Early 1930s," 54; Clarence Irwin and L. A. Morris to Green, 8 June 1935, *AFL Record*—*Green Papers*, microfilm reel 28, frame 00064; and AAISTW, minutes of the executive board, 22 April and July–Sept. 1935, Louis Leonard Papers, Box 10, File 6, HCLA.

158. *Daily Worker*, 2 March 1935; *Post-Gazette*, 6 May 1935; *Progressive Steel Worker*, March and May 1935, Mary Van Kleeck Collection, Box 26, File 44, ALUA; Wieck, "Steel Workers Under the NRA," p. 124; Phillip Bonosky to author, 23 Feb. 1995.

159. *Amalgamated Journal*, 18 April 1935.

160. *Post-Gazette*, 1, 6, 8, and 10 May 1935; *Daily Worker*, 10 and 24 May 1935; *Amalgamated Journal*, 9 May 1935.

161. *Daily Worker*, 6 and 19 Feb. and 3 June 1935.

162. *Federated Press Eastern Weekly Letter*, 28 March 1935, Box 24, File: Rank and File, March 1935, HOC.

163. *Daily Worker*, 18 May 1935.

164. Wieck, "Steel Workers Under the NRA," pp. 132–34; Harold J. Ruttenberg, "A Rank and File Strike," unpublished manuscript, 3 June 1935, Box 4, File 4, HJR; *Steel and Metal Notes*, June 1935, p. 5.

165. *Daily Worker*, 27 May 1935; *Post-Gazette*, 31 May 1935; *Daily News*, 31 May 1931.

166. Duquesne Works payroll records, June 1935, USSC; Duquesne City Council minutes, 3 June 1935; *Daily News*, 31 May and 1 and 3 June 1935; *Post-Gazette*, 31 May and 1 June 1935; *Duquesne Times*, 7 June 1935; Federated Press, 3 June 1935, Box 23, File DW-CSC, HOC.

167. *(Homestead) Daily Messenger*, 1 June 1935; *Daily Worker*, 3 and 13 June 1935; Federated Press, 3 June 1935; [Harold Ruttenberg] to Clinton Golden, 16 July 1935, Box 4, File 4, HJR.

168. *Duquesne Times*, 11 Nov. 1932, 9 Sept. and 10 Nov. 1933, 11 May and 9 Nov. 1934; *Daily News*, 13 Sept. 1933.

169. *Duquesne Times*, 16 Aug., 6 and 20 Sept., 18 Oct., and 1 and 8 November 1935; *Post-Gazette*, 7 Nov. 1935; Draham, "Unlikely Allies Fight for Unionization," 65–71.

Chapter 4: The Employee Representation Plan, 1933–36

1. Duquesne Works payroll ledgers, 1934–35, U.S. Steel Corp. (Duquesne Works) Payroll Ledgers and Records of the Personnel Division (USSC), 1904–80, UE/Labor Archives, Archives of Industrial Society, Hillman Library, University of Pittsburgh, Pittsburgh; Elmer Maloy testimony, NLRB Case C-142, 11 Jan. 1937, pp. 578–83, *U.S. Steel Corp. and Carnegie-Illinois Steel Corp. vs. Steel Workers Organizing Committee and Amalgamated Ass'n of Iron, Steel and Tin Workers*, Box 115, National Labor Relations Board Records (RG 25), Administrative Division, Files and Dockets Section, Transcripts and Exhibits (NLRB-Exhibits), Washington National Records Center, Suitland, Md.

2. Duquesne Works Employee Representation Plan (DWERP) requests 42 and 69, Box 4, Records of the National Recovery Administration (RG 9), Records of the National Steel Labor Relations Board (NSLRB), National Archives, Washington, D.C.; Duquesne Works Wage Committee to A. C. Cummins, 1 Oct. 1934, Box 26, File: ERP Blooming Mill, 1934–37, USSC.

3. DWERP request 217-51, Box 26, File: ERP Blooming, USSC.

4. Ibid.; R. F. Sanner to Maloy and Zuzo, 10 March 1937, Box 26, File: ERP Blooming, USSC.

5. A copy of the generic U.S. Steel ERP is found in *Steel,* 19 June 1933, p. 13.

6. I. Lamont Hughes to Employees of Carnegie Steel Co., 7 June 1933, Box 4, File: Carnegie-Duquesne, NSLRB; Maloy testimony, NLRB Case, 17 Dec. 1936, pp. 68–70; John J. Kane testimony, NLRB Case, 18 Dec. 1936, pp. 323–26; DWERP, minutes of meeting, 16 June 1933, Box 4, NSLRB.

7. DWERP, minutes of meeting, 16 June 1933; Duquesne Works payroll ledgers, 1933–35.

8. DWERP, minutes of meetings, 27 and 30 June 1933, Box 4, NSLRB.

9. Duquesne Works, "Report of Positions Excluded from Representation by the Union Under the Terms of the September 1, 1942 Agreement," 7 Oct. 1942, Box 30, File: Positions Excluded from Union Membership, USSC; Carroll R. Daugherty, Melvin G. de Chazeau, and Samuel S. Stratton, *The Economics of the Iron and Steel Industry* (New York: McGraw-Hill, 1937), vol. 2: 1021; Frank Miller Keck, Jr., "The Development of Labor Representation at the Homestead Steel Works" (master's thesis, University of Pittsburgh, 1950), 38.

10. Charles Erickson testimony in U.S. Congress, Senate, Committee on Education and Labor, *To Create a National Labor Board,* 73d Cong., 2d sess., 1934, pt. 3: 876–79; U.S. Census, *Fourteenth Census of the United States: 1920, Manuscript Schedules,* vol. 10, Pennsylvania, Allegheny County, National Archives microfilm reel 1511; Duquesne Works payroll ledgers, 1934–35; *Duquesne Times,* 11 May 1934 and 4 Oct. 1940; DWERP request 66, Box 26, USSC.

11. For a partial sample of requests centering on working conditions and athletics, see DWERP requests 16, 20, 22, 23, 26, 30, 38, 48, and 51-53; and for chipper requests see DWERP requests 1, 6, 9, 10, 21, 65, 73, 75, 82, 95-4, 108-17, and 119-28, all in Box 4, NSLRB.

12. DWERP requests 58, 90, 110-19, and 105-14, Box 4, NSLRB.

13. DWERP request 18; DWERP, minutes of meetings, 19 Sept. 1933, 5 and 26 March 1934, 17 April 1934, 22 May 1934, and 9 July 1934, all in Box 4, NSLRB.

14. DWERP requests 66, 67, 69, 96-5, 98-7, and and 102-11, Box 26, USSC.

15. DWERP request 19, Box 4, NSLRB.

16. "Minimum Hourly and Tonnage Earnings No. 2 Open Hearth Cranemen," 18 July 1934, Box 26, File: ERP, Maintenance, 1934, USSC.

17. DWERP requests 17, 42-44, 61, and 91, Box 4, NSLRB; DWERP request 63, Box 26, USSC.

18. For early wage requests among small groups of tonnage men, see DWERP requests 61, 69, and 70, Box 4, NSLRB; and DWERP requests 66, 67, and 98-7, Box 26, USSC. The superintendent is quoted in J. T. MacLeod to A. C. Cummins, 16 April 1935, Box 26, File: ERP, Open Hearth 1935–37, USSC.

19. DWERP requests 99-8 and 102-11, Box 26, USSC; DWERP request 46, Box 4, NSLRB.

20. Ibid.

21. DWERP request 93-2, Box 26, USSC.

22. Kane testimony, NLRB Case, 18 Dec. 1936, pp. 330–34; DWERP, minutes of meetings, 4 and 16 Aug. 1933, 29 Sept. 1933, and 25 June 1934, Box 4, NSLRB; I. Lamont Hughes to Cummins, 11 Aug. 1933, Box 110, Exhibit 90, NLRB-Exhibits.

23. DWERP, minutes of meeting, 28 May 1934; and DWERP request 86, both in Box 4, NSLRB.

24. DWERP, minutes of meeting, 5 Oct. 1933; Duquesne Works payroll ledger, June 1934; Kane testimony, NLRB Case, 19 Dec. 1936, pp. 359–70.

25. Erickson testimony in U.S. Senate, *To Create a National Labor Board,* 876–79; American Iron and Steel Institute (AISI), *Employee Representation in the Iron and Steel Industry* (New York: AISI, 1934), 84–86.

26. Maloy testimony, NLRB Case, 18 Dec. 1936, pp. 293–94, and 15 Jan. 1937, p. 1025; Kane testimony, NLRB Case, 19 Dec. 1936, p. 397.

27. Kane testimony, NLRB Case, 18 Dec. 1936, pp. 327, 349–57; Charles Erickson et. al., "Notice," Box 7, File W-1(a), USSC; Duquesne Works payroll ledger, 1934; DWERP representatives, "To the Employees of the Duquesne Works—Carnegie Steel Co." [Feb. 1934]; and A. C. Cummins, "To the Employees of the Duquesne Works," 17 Feb. 1934, both in Box 23, File: Duquesne Works, Carnegie Steel Co., Harvey O'Connor Collection, Archives of Labor and Urban Affairs, Wayne State University, Detroit.

28. Harvey O'Connor, *Steel-Dictator* (New York: John Day, 1935), 261–64.

29. Kane's biographical information is found in U.S. Census, *Fourteenth Census of the United States: 1920, Manuscript Schedules;* Records of the War Department, World War I Draft Registration Cards; *U.S. Steel News,* April 1957; Kane testimony, NLRB Case, 19 Dec. 1936, p. 321, and 27 Jan. 1937, p. 1387.

30. Kane testimony, NLRB Case, 19 Dec. 1936, p. 323.

31. Ibid., 327, 349.

32. Ibid., 373–79; DWERP, minutes of meeting, 23 April 1934, Box 4, NSLRB.

33. Kane testimony, NLRB Case, 19 Dec. 1936, pp. 359–70.

34. Maloy testimony, NLRB Case, 17 Dec. 1936, pp. 75–78, and 13 Jan. 1937, p. 854; Kane testimony, NLRB Case, 19 Dec. 1936, pp. 383–87.

35. Elmer Maloy, interview by Don Kennedy, 7 Nov. 1967, transcript, pp. 10–11, 26, United Steelworkers of America Oral History Project (USAOHP), Historical Collections and Labor Archives (HCLA), The Pennsylvania State University, State College; *Who's Who in Labor* (New York: Dryden Press, 1946); Maloy testimony, NLRB Case, 17 Dec. 1936, p. 75. The Maloy quotes appear in the interview by Kennedy.

36. *Duquesne Times,* 14 and 21 June 1935; Maloy interview, pp. 10–11; Maloy testimony, NLRB Case, 18 Dec. 1936, p. 318, and 13 Jan. 1937, pp. 884–85; *Iron Age,* 27 June 1935, p. 34.

37. Maloy testimony, NLRB Case, 18 Dec. 1936, pp. 298–99; DWERP, Sixth Joint Conference, 2 June 1936, pp. 5–6, Box 26, USSC; Maloy interview, p. 18.

38. Maloy testimony, NLRB Case, 18 Dec. 1936, pp. 298–306, and 13 Jan. 1937, pp. 841–51; Maloy interview, p. 18.

39. DWERP, minutes of Fifth Joint Conference, 11 Feb. 1936, pp. 3, 5–6, 12–13, Box 26, USSC; Maloy testimony, NLRB Case, 14 Jan. 1937, pp. 938, 940–43; DWERP request 135-44, in DWERP, minutes of meeting, 27 April 1936, Box 116, Exhibit 31, NLRB-Exhibits.

40. DWERP, Fifth Joint Conference, p. 20.

41. Ford, Davis, and Bacon, "Digest of Ford, Bacon, and Davis Report No. 37 . . . ," 17 Nov. 1936, p. 11, Box 45, File: Ford, Bacon, and Davis, Survey Digests of Reports, Edward R. Stettinius, Jr., Papers (STET), Manuscript Division, Special Collections, University of Virginia Library, Charlottesville.

42. AISI, *Collective Bargaining in the Steel Industry* (New York: AISI, June 1934), 11.

43. Erickson is quoted in AISI, *Employee Representation in the Iron and Steel Industry,* 85.

44. Maloy testimony, NLRB Case, 13 Jan. 1937, pp. 871–73; DWERP, minutes of meeting, 27 April 1936, Box 116, Exhibit 31, NLRB-Exhibits; DWERP, Fifth Joint Conference, p. 22.

45. DWERP request 102-11, Box 26, USSC; DWERP, Fifth Joint Conference, pp. 22, 25–26.

46. Maloy testimony, NLRB Case, 15 Jan. 1937, pp. 1074, 1081–82, and 1120; Maloy interview, pp. 18–19.

47. DWERP request 195-29 and related documents in Box 26, File: ERP Open Hearth, 1935–37, USSC.

48. Maloy interview, 19; DWERP, Fifth Joint Conference, pp. 7, 17; DWERP, Sixth Joint Conference, pp. 3, 12; Maloy testimony, NLRB Case, 17 Dec. 1936, p. 107, and 18 Dec. 1936, p. 311.

49. Maloy testimony, NLRB Case, 14 Jan. 1937, pp. 927–32, and 15 Jan. 1937, pp. 1132–34.

50. Maloy interview, 19.

51. DWERP, Fifth Joint Conference, p. 19.

52. Maloy testimony, NLRB Case, 17 Dec. 1936, pp. 88–89, and 12 Jan. 1937, p. 667; DWERP, Fifth Joint Conference, p. 17.

53. Maloy testimony, NLRB Case, 12 Jan. 1937, pp. 653–55, 664–68. See also "Meeting of Employee Representatives in Personnel Office, November 18, 1935," Box 19, File D-1(m-1), USSC.

54. Kane testimony, NLRB Case, 27 Jan. 1937, pp. 1436–38; DWERP, Sixth Joint Conference, p. 3.

55. DWERP requests 179-13, 191-25, 193-27, 213-47, 214-48, and 217-51, all in Box 26, USSC.

56. See materials related to DWERP request 184-18, especially, Carnegie Illinois Industrial Engineering Department Survey, 2 March 1936, all in Box 26, File: ERP Open Hearth 1935–37, USSC.

57. DWERP, Fifth Joint Conference, pp. 16–17, and 25.

58. DWERP, Sixth Joint Conference, p. 13.

59. For critiques of U.S. Steel's policies and corporate structure, see Thomas K. McCraw and Forest Reinhardt, "Losing to Win: U.S. Steel's Pricing, Investment Decisions, and Market Share, 1901–1938," *Journal of Economic History* 49 (Sept. 1989): 593–619; Alfred D. Chandler, *Scale and Scope: The Dynamics of Industrial Capitalism* (Cambridge, Mass.: Belknap, 1990), 131–40; "The Corporation," *Fortune* 13 (March 1936): 59–66, 152 ff.; Gertrude G. Schroeder, *The Growth of Major Steel Companies, 1900–1950* (Baltimore: Johns Hopkins Press, 1953), 112–13.

60. Robert M. Collins, "Positive Business Responses to the New Deal: The Roots of the Committee for Economic Development, 1932–1942," *Business History Review* 52 (autumn 1978): 369–91; Kim McQuaid, "Corporate Liberalism in the American Business Community," *Business History Review* 52 (autumn 1978): 342–68.

61. Myron Taylor, *Ten Years of Steel* (New York: U.S. Steel, 1938), 9–15; *Steel,* 22 Feb. 1932, p. 13; Ford, Davis, and Bacon, "Report #100," 26 April 1938, pp. 81–82, 111, Box 65, STET.

62. Ford, Davis, and Bacon, "Report #100," pp. 77–82; Taylor, *Ten Years of Steel,* 19; "Managers," *Fortune* 21 (March 1940): 64; W. J. Filbert to Stettinius, 26 Feb. 1934, Box 67, File: U.S. Steel Reorganization, Data—Filbert, STET; "The Corporation," 169 ff.

63. Taylor, *Ten Years of Steel,* 16; *Steel,* 2 Sept. 1935, p. 22; "The Corporation," 169.

64. "The Corporation," 188; McQuaid, "Corporate Liberalism," 356; *New York Times,* 2 Feb. 1934.

65. Arthur H. Young testimony in U.S. Senate, *To Create a National Labor Board,* pt. 3:

719; *Steel,* 2 April 1934, p. 19; *Iron Age,* 8 Feb. 1934, p. 41-L; Arthur H. Young, "Safety at the Quarter Century Mark," unpublished speech, no date, Arthur H. Young Papers, Management Library, Industrial Relations Center, California Institute of Technology, Pasadena; Toni Gilpin, "New Feet Under the Table: International Harvester's Industrial Council Plan," *Labor's Heritage* 4 (spring 1992): 8–18; "Minutes of the Special Conference Committee Meeting, New York, Oct. 31–Nov. 1, 1923," Box 71, File: Service Report, DuPont Administrative Files, Hagley Museum and Library, Wilmington, Delaware.

66. Young testimony in U.S. Senate, *To Create a National Labor Board,* pt. 3: 719–20; *Steel,* 2 April 1934, p. 19. The work of the IRC is traced in Raymond B. Fosdick to John D. Rockefeller, Jr., 7 May 1926; and Young to Fosdick, 5 May 1933, both in Box 16, File 127, Record Group 2, Series Economic Interests, Rockefeller Family Archives; Young to Fosdick, 24 Nov. 1933; and "Industrial Relations Counselors, Inc.," 4 Oct. 1934, both in Box 348, File 4143, Record Group 1.1, Series 200S, The Rockefeller Foundation Archives, all in Rockefeller Archive Center, North Tarrytown, N.Y.

67. Daugherty, de Chazeau, and Samuel S. Stratton, *Economics of the Iron and Steel Industry,* vol. 2: 1025.

68. Young testimony in U.S. Senate, *To Create a National Labor Board,* pt. 3: 719–29; Arthur H. Young, "Industrial Relations," paper presented at Association of Iron and Steel Electrical Engineers Convention, 24 Sept. 1935, Box 116, Exhibit 121, NLRB-Exhibits.

69. *Steel,* 30 July 1934, p. 13; Ford, Bacon, and Davis, "Digest of Ford, Bacon, and Davis Report No. 37." For Duquesne see *Duquesne Times,* 2 August and 13 Dec. 1935; Duquesne Works payroll ledger, Aug. and Nov. 1936.

70. Ford, Bacon, and Davis, "Digest of Ford, Bacon, and Davis Report No. 37," p. 7 and passim; "Minutes of Special Meeting [U.S. Steel and Ford, Davis, and Bacon executives]," 8 Sept. 1937, pp. 17–18, Box 46, STET; Carnegie-Illinois Steel Corp., "Instruction to Supervisory Forces Governing Employee Relations," 1 Sept. 1936, Box 28, File S-6(a), USSC; "Minutes of the First Joint General Conference of Employee and Management Representatives Carnegie-Illinois Steel Corporation Pittsburgh District," 12 Aug. 1936, 27, Box 116, Exhibit 37, NLRB-Exhibits.

71. Arthur H. Young, *Relations of the Supervisor to His Men* (New York: American Management Association, 1926); Sanford Jacoby, *Employing Bureaucracy: Managers, Unions, and the Transformation of Work in American Industry, 1900–1945* (New York: Columbia University Press, 1985), 185–87; Ford, Bacon, and Davis, "Digest of Ford, Bacon, and Davis Report No. 37," p. 17; Carnegie-Illinois Steel, "Instruction to Supervisory Forces Governing Employee Relationships." For Duquesne see minutes of grievance meeting, 4 May 1937, 3, Box 27, USSC; "Foreman's Club Formed at Duquesne Steel Works" [April 1935], Box 29, File C-2(a), USSC.

72. Draft of Annual Report of Special Conference Committee for 1934, Box 36, File: John D. East, STET.

73. David Brody, "Section 8(a)(2) and the Origins of the Wagner Act," in *Restoring the Promise of American Labor Law,* ed. Sheldon Friedman, Richard W. Hurd, Rudolph A. Oswald, and Ronald L. Seeber (Ithaca, N.Y.: ILR Press, 1994), 29–44.

74. *Iron Age,* 30 May 1935, p. 59-D.

75. John A. Fitch, "A Man Can Talk in Homestead," *Survey Graphic* 25 (Feb. 1936): 75; H[eber] B[lankenhorn], memo on suggested immediate investigation, no date, Box 2, File

14, Heber Blankenhorn Collection (HEB), ALUA; David J. Saposs, "Organizational and Procedural Changes in Employee Representation Plans," *Journal of Political Economy* 44 (Dec. 1936): 803–11.

76. Maloy testimony, NLRB Case, 17 Dec. 1936, pp. 78–91, and 13 Jan. 1937, pp. 855–78.

77. Ibid., 83–5, 90.

78. DWERP, minutes of meetings, 11 Sept. and 5 Oct. 1933, Box 4, NSLRB; Kane testimony, NLRB Case, 19 Dec. 1936, pp. 400–1, and 26 Jan. 1937, pp. 1327–28. For evidence that the Duquesne Works was economically viable and not considered for closure, see *Duquesne Times,* 8 May 1936; minutes of special meeting between U.S. Steel executives and Ford, Bacon, and Davis personnel, 14 Dec. 1936, Box 44, File: W. C. Bird, Jan.–March, STET.

79. Maloy testimony, NLRB Case, 17 Dec. 1936, pp. 83, 90–92, and 13 Jan. 1937, pp. 877–78; *Steel and Metal Notes* 4 (Dec. 1935): 1; Carnegie-Illinois ERP General Joint Conference, minutes of meeting, 12 Aug. 1936, pp. 12–13, Box 4, File 6, Harold J. Ruttenberg Papers, HCLA.

80. *New York Times,* 27 Oct. 1935; Daugherty, de Chazeau, and Stratton, *Economics of the Iron and Steel Industry,* vol. 2: 1029–32; Irving Bernstein, *Turbulent Years: A History of the American Worker, 1933–1941* (Boston: Houghton Mifflin, 1970), 456–57; Wieck, "The Steelworkers Under the NRA," pp. ix–x; Rose Stein, "Steel Robots That Came Alive," *Nation,* 5 Jan. 1936, pp. 160–61; *Steel and Metal Notes* 4 (Nov. 1935): 1; *Steel and Metal Notes* 4 (Dec. 1935): 1; *Steel and Metal Notes* 5 (Feb. 1936): 3; *Pittsburgh Press,* 7 Aug. 1935.

81. Maloy testimony, NLRB Case, 17 Dec. 1936, pp. 91–94; and 13 Jan. 1937, pp. 878–86; Robert R. R. Brooks, *As Steel Goes, . . . Unionism in a Basic Industry* (New Haven: Yale University Press, 1940), 13; John J. Mullen, interview by Alice Hoffman, Feb. 1966, transcript, 7, USAOHP.

82. DWERP, Fifth Joint Conference, pp. 9, 27–28.

83. Ibid., 8.

84. Ibid., 10.

85. Maloy testimony, NLRB Case, 18 Dec. 1936, p. 189.

86. Ibid., 17 Dec. 1936, p. 107.

87. Ibid., 15 Jan. 1937, pp. 97–98.

88. Clinton S. Golden to Heber Blankenhorn, 27 March 1936, Box 1, File 13, Clinton S. Golden Papers (CSG), HCLA.

89. DWERP, minutes of meeting, 27 April 1936.

90. For the relationship of the CIO with steelworkers before the formation of SWOC, see Walter Galenson, *The CIO Challenge to the AFL: A History of the American Labor Movement, 1935–1941* (Cambridge: Harvard University Press, 1960), 75–83; Golden to Blankenhorn, 21 May 1936, Box 3, File 2, CSG; [Clinton Golden], "The Steel Situation," 25 May 1936, Box 1, File 33, HEB.

91. R. Brooks, *As Steel Goes,* 87–88; Golden to Blankenhorn, Box 1, File 13, CSG; Maloy interview, 20; Kane testimony, NLRB Case, 27 Jan. 1937, pp. 1446–54.

92. Fitch, "A Man Can Talk in Homestead," 75.

93. Ford, Bacon, and Davis, "Digest of Ford, Bacon, and Davis Report No. 37."

94. Correspondence between Blankenhorn and Golden, Jan.–April 1936, in Box 1, File 13, CSG; Thomas R. Brooks, *Clint: A Biography of a Labor Intellectual, Clinton S. Golden* (New York: Atheneum, 1978), 150–53; R. Brooks, *As Steel Goes,* 9–12; Mullen interview, pp. 8–10; U.S. Senate, Subcommittee of the Committee on Education and Labor, *Violations*

of Free Speech and Assembly and Interference with Rights of Labor, 74th Cong., 2d sess., 1936, 9–26; Maloy testimony, NLRB Case, 26 Jan. 1937, pp. 1293–1304.

95. R. Brooks, *As Steel Goes,* 9–12; Mullen interview, pp. 8–10; Senate, *Violations of Free Speech and Assembly,* 9–26.

96. Maloy testimony, NLRB Case, 13 Jan. 1937, pp. 888–89; Kane testimony, NLRB Case, 19 Dec. 1936, pp. 390–92; minutes of meeting between Benjamin Fairless and ERP representatives, 13 April 1936, Box 116, Exhibit 30, NLRB-Exhibits.

97. Carnegie-Illinois ERP Central Committee, minutes of meetings, 2 and 16 May 1936, Box 116, Exhibits 32, 33, NLRB-Exhibits; Golden to Blankenhorn, 21 May 1936; Maloy testimony, NLRB Case, 17 Dec. 1936, pp. 98–102; Kane testimony, NLRB Case, 27 Jan. 1937, pp. 1455–56, 1503–4.

Chapter 5: SWOC and the Rise of Steel Unionism, 1936–37

1. Elmer Maloy testimony, 14 Jan. 1937, p. 960, NLRB Case C-142, *U.S. Steel Corp.n and Carnegie-Illinois Steel Corp. vs. Steel Workers Organizing Committee and Amalgamated Ass'n of Iron, Steel and Tin Workers,* Box 115, National Labor Relations Board Records (RG 25), Administrative Division, Files and Dockets Section, Transcripts and Exhibits (NLRB-Exhibits), Washington National Records Center, Suitland, Md. Maloy testified on December 17 and 19, 1936, and January 11 to 15, 17 to 18, and 26, 1937.

2. Ibid., 960–74; John J. Kane testimony, NLRB Case, 27 Jan. 1937, p. 1394.

3. Maloy testimony, NLRB Case, 14 Jan. 1937, p. 961.

4. Ross Leffler to all general superintendents, 25 July 1936, U.S. Steel Corp. (Duquesne Works) Payroll Ledgers and Records of the Personnel Division (USSC), 1904–80, Box 30, File #1256: Maintenance of Membership and Check Off, 1936–49, UE/Labor Archives (UE/L), Archives of Industrial Society (AIS), Hillman Library, University of Pittsburgh.

5. Melvyn Dubofsky and Warren Van Tine, *John L. Lewis: A Biography* (Urbana: University of Illinois Press, 1986), 140–43, 148–61; Walter Galenson, *The CIO Challenge to the AFL: A History of the American Labor Movement, 1935–1941* (Cambridge: Harvard University Press, 1960), 75–78.

6. CIO, minutes of meeting, 9 Dec. 1935, Box 14, File 4, Katherine Pollack Ellickson Collection (KPE), pt. 1, Archives of Labor and Urban Affairs (ALUA), Wayne State University, Detroit; David Brody, "The Origins of Modern Steel Unionism: the SWOC Era," in *Forging a Union of Steel: Philip Murray, SWOC, and the United Steelworkers,* ed. Paul F. Clark, Peter Gottlieb, and Donald Kennedy (Ithaca, N.Y.: ILR Press, 1987), 19–20; Irving Bernstein, *Turbulent Years: A History of the American Worker, 1933–1941* (Boston: Houghton Mifflin, 1970), 440–41. Although the Steel Workers Organizing Committee (SWOC) used the Amalgamated's name in its organizing work, *Amalgamated* as used in this chapter refers to the pre-SWOC union.

7. Bernstein, *Turbulent Years,* 451–53; Ronald W. Schatz, "Philip Murray and the Subordination of the Industrial Unions to the United States Government," in *Labor Leaders in America,* ed. Melvyn Dubofsky and Warren Van Tine (Urbana: University of Illinois Press, 1987), 234–57.

8. SWOC, minutes of organizational meeting, 17 June 1936, pp. 2–4, CIO National and International Unions, United Steel Workers of America Records (CIO-USWA), Department of Archives and Manuscripts, The Catholic University of America, Washington, D.C.

9. Lloyd Ulman, *The Government of the Steel Workers' Union* (New York: Wiley, 1962), 3–92.

10. Philip Murray, "The Problem Before SWOC on June 17, 1936," 8 Nov. 1936, CIO-USWA; Bernstein, *Turbulent Years*, 452.

11. Bernstein, *Turbulent Years*, 454–55; Murray, "The Problem Before SWOC."

12. *Duquesne Times*, 14 Aug. 1936 and 19 March 1937; Pennsylvania, Department of Internal Affairs, *Report on Productive Industries, 1935* (Harrisburg: Commonwealth of Pennsylvania, 1937), 103; Pennsylvania, Department of Internal Affairs, *Report on Productive Industries, 1936–1938* (Harrisburg: Commonwealth of Pennsylvania, 1940), 149.

13. *(Pittsburgh) Bulletin Index*, 27 Aug. 1936, p. 6, and 11 Feb. 1937, p. 18; Douglas Fisher, *Steel Serves the Nation, 1901–1951: The Fifty Year Story of United States Steel* (New York: U.S. Steel, 1951), 224; *Iron Age*, 18 Feb. 1937, p. 76.

14. Richard C. Keller, *Pennsylvania's Little New Deal* (New York: Garland, 1982), 121–243.

15. *(Pittsburgh) Post-Gazette*, 6 July 1936; *Steel Labor*, 1 Aug. and 5 Sept. 1936; *Amalgamated Journal*, 17 Dec. 1936.

16. Jerold S. Auerbach, *Labor and Liberty: The La Follette Committee and the New Deal* (Indianapolis: Bobbs-Merrill, 1966), 72–73, 88–90; U.S. Congress, Senate, Committee on Education and Labor, *Violations of Free Speech and Rights of Labor*, 77th Cong., 1st sess., S. Rept. 6, 1939, pt. 3: 208.

17. James A. Gross, *The Making of the National Labor Relations Board: A Study in Economics, Politics, and the Law, 1933–37* (Albany: State University of New York Press, 1974), vol. 1: 149, 170–73, 195–98, 211–12; Bernstein, *Turbulent Years*, 450–51; Murray, "The Problem Before SWOC." Early SWOC materials, including its newspaper, *Steel Labor*, carry little mention of the Wagner Act.

18. Galenson, *CIO Challenge to the AFL*, 89; Bernstein, *Turbulent Years*, 457; *Amalgamated Journal*, 25 June 1936.

19. *Iron Age* 23 July 1936, p. 72; *Steel*, 27 July 1936, p. 14; *Post-Gazette*, 6 and 20 July 1936; Pat Fagen, interview by Alice M. Hoffman, 1 Oct. 1968, transcript, p. 20, United Steelworkers of America Oral History Project (USAOHP), Historical Collections and Labor Archives (HCLA), The Pennsylvania State University, State College; Vincent D. Sweeney, *The United Steelworkers of America: Twenty Years Later, 1936–1956* (Pittsburgh: USWA, 1956), 14; Max Gordon, "The Communists and the Drive to Organize Steel, 1936," *Labor History* 23 (spring 1982): 262; Edward Stettinius, Jr., to Myron Taylor, 11 Aug. 1936, Box 63, File: Taylor Correspondence, Edward R. Stettinius, Jr., Papers (STET), Manuscript Division, Special Collections, University of Virginia Library, Charlottesville.

20. *Amalgamated Journal*, 2 July 1936.

21. Powers, *Cradle of Steel Unionism: Monongahela Valley, PA* (East Chicago, Ind.: Figueroa, 1972), 85–86, 97; Clinton S. Golden to David J. McDonald, 19 Feb. 1937, Box 59, File 15, David J. McDonald Papers (MCD), HCLA; Harvey Klehr, *The Heyday of American Communism: The Depression Decade* (New York: Basic, 1984), 229–30; *Steel Labor*, 1 and 20 Aug. 1936; Gordon, "Communists and the Drive to Organize Steel, 1936," 254–65; Bert Cochran, *Labor and Communism: The Conflict That Shaped American Unions* (Princeton: Princeton University Press, 1977), 96–97; Herb Kaye, "Communists and Steelworkers—A Look at History," *Political Affairs* 63 (Oct. 1984): 14–17.

22. Amalgamated, executive board minutes, July–Sept. 1935, and 22 April 1936, Box 10,

Files 1 and 6, Louis Leonard Papers, HCLA; Harold Ruttenberg, "Extent of Unionization," Sept. 1935, Box 6, File 33, Harvey O'Connor Collection (HOC), pt. 2, ALUA; Committee for Industrial Organization (CIO), "Summary of Situation in Steel," 13 Jan. 1936, Box 16, File 11, KPE; Robert R. R. Brooks, *As Steel Goes, . . . Unionism in a Basic Industry* (New Haven: Yale University Press, 1940), 70; [Harold Ruttenberg] to Golden, 16 July 1935, Box 4, File 4, Harold J. Ruttenberg Papers (HJR), HCLA.

23. *Duquesne Times,* 13 March 1936.

24. CIO, "Supplementary Report on Steel Situation," 13 April 1936, Box 14, File 14; CIO, "Report of Director," 18 April 1936, Box 14, File 13, both in KPE; Brooks, *As Steel Goes,* 70–72; Powers, *Cradle of Steel Unionism,* 63–65.

25. *Amalgamated Journal,* 10 Dec. 1936; *Duquesne Times,* 13 March 1936 and 3 Dec. 1959; inactive voter registration cards, Allegheny County, Pa., Voter Registration Records, AIS; Golden to Lou Davis, 29 June 1936, File 92, Beaver Valley Labor History Society Records (BVLH), UE/L.

26. "Italian-American Labor Day Celebration," 13 Sept. 1936, Box 26, File 8, Mary Van Kleek Collection, ALUA; *(McKeesport) Daily News,* 14 Jan. 1937.

27. Staughton Lynd, ed., "Personal Histories of the Early CIO," *Radical America* 5 (May–June 1971): 54–55; Roger Keeran, "The International Workers' Order and the Origins of the CIO," *Labor History* 30 (summer 1989): 385–400; Thomas J. E. Walker, *Pluralistic Fraternity: The History of the International Workers' Order* (New York: Garland, 1991), 45–50. For a breakdown of national and ethnic organizations in Duquesne, see American Service Institute, "Index of Nationality Organizations, Allegheny County, 1945," June 1945, Cabinet I, Drawer 3, File A-4; and American Service Institute, "Nationality Leaders in Duquesne," no date, Cabinet I, Drawer 4, File B-19, both in American Service Institute Records, AIS.

28. Duquesne City Council Minutes, 21 Oct. 1935, microfilm copy of Duquesne Borough and City Council Minutes, reel 5075, Hillman Library, University of Pittsburgh; *Daily News* 16 Nov. 1935; *Duquesne Times,* 12 June 1931 and 2 Jan. 1942.

29. For Salopek's ethnic, work, and residence background, see Thomas E. Hughes to R. F. Sanner, 29 June 1940, Box 26, USSC, Grievance File A-47-40; *Duquesne Times,* 4 Nov. 1938; *Daily News,* 29 Oct. 1968. Salopek's Communist Party membership is found in testimony of John Frey, U.S. Congress, House, Special Committee on Un-American Activities, *Investigation of Un-American Propaganda Activities in the United States,* 75th Cong., 3d sess., 1938, p. 238; U.S. Congress, House, Committee on Un-American Activities, *Expose of the Communist Party of Western Pennsylvania: Based upon Testimony of Mathew Cvetic (Undercover Agent),* 81st Cong., 2d sess., 1950, pp. 1245, 1328; Herb Kaye, "Communists and Steelworkers," 15; Lou Bortz, interview by author (telephone), 10 May 1993; Phillip Bonosky to author, 23 Feb. 1995. Information about Salopek's arrest and political campaign are found in *Duquesne Times,* 7 June, 16 Aug., and 20 Sept. 1935; *Daily News,* 18 Sept. 1935.

30. Powers, *Cradle of Steel Unionism,* 60, 98.

31. Dennis C. Dickerson, *Out of the Crucible: Black Steelworkers in Western Pennsylvania, 1875–1980* (Albany: State University of New York Press, 1986), 142, 144; Bonosky to author, 23 Feb. and 26 Aug. 1995; Powers, *Cradle of Steel Unionism,* 64–65.

32. Fraternal Orders Committee, *Fraternal Orders Speak for the Unionization of the Steel*

Industry: Proceedings of the Fraternal Orders Conference, October 25, 1936, Pittsburgh, Pennsylvania (Pittsburgh: Fraternal Orders Committee, 1936).

33. *Daily Worker,* 11 Jan. 1937; Dickerson, *Out of the Crucible,* 135–39; Horace R. Cayton and George C. Mitchell, *Black Workers and the Unions* (Chapel Hill: University of North Carolina Press, 1939), 198–202.

34. Galenson, *CIO Challenge to the AFL,* 86; *Amalgamated Journal,* 17 Dec. 1936; "The Great Labor Upheaval," *Fortune* 14 (Oct. 1936): 150.

35. Philip Murray, "Report to the Steel Workers Organizing Committee," 29 Sept. 1936, pp. 2–4, CIO-USWA; [Edward A. Wieck], "Summary of Observations . . . ," p. 5, Sept. 1936, Box 10, File: SWOC 1935–42, Edward A. Wieck Collection, ALUA.

36. Wieck, "Summary of Observations," p. 2.

37. David McDonald, *Union Man: The Life of a Labor Statesman* (New York: Dutton, 1969), 94.

38. SWOC, minutes of meeting, 29 Sept. 1936, CIO-USWA.

39. Wieck, "Summary of Observations," pp. 2–3; John Fitch, "A Man Can Talk in Homestead," *Survey Graphic* 25 (Feb. 1936): 71–72.

40. Brody, "Origins of Modern Steel Unionism," 20–21; McDonald, *Union Man,* 95; James Green, "Steel Workers Organize in Aliquippa, Pennsylvania, 1933–1937," *Labor's Heritage* 5 (summer 1993): 7, 18. The pages of *Steel Labor* especially emphasized collective bargaining and wage issues.

41. SWOC, minutes of organizational meeting, 17 June 1936, p. 3; Murray, "Report to the Steel Workers Organizing Committee," p. 1; Bernstein, *Turbulent Years,* 453.

42. *Amalgamated Journal,* 12 Nov. 1936.

43. Brooks, *As Steel Goes,* 119.

44. *Duquesne Times,* 16 Oct. 1936; Pennsylvania, *Pennsylvania Manual* (Harrisburg: Commonwealth of Pennsylvania, 1933), 439–40; *Pennsylvania Manual* (Harrisburg: Commonwealth of Pennsylvania, 1937), 212.

45. SWOC leaflet, Box 144, File 2, MCD; Brooks, *As Steel Goes,* 119.

46. *Amalgamated Journal,* 12 Nov. and 24 Dec. 1936; John T. Flynn, "Other People's Money," *New Republic,* 30 Dec. 1936, p. 273; *Pittsburgh Press,* 11 Dec. 1936; *Post-Gazette,* 30 Nov. 1936.

47. McDonald, *Union Man,* 94–95.

48. Membership figures for the McKeesport District of Carnegie-Illinois and U.S. Steel are found in various SWOC membership reports in Box 156, Files 2 and 3, MCD, and various SWOC organizing reports, in Organizing Reports, Local Union Section (microfilm), Roll LA 1989, HCLA. See also *Steel Labor,* 23 Jan. 1937; McDonald, *Union Man,* 102.

49. Milan Tankosich, interview by Peter Gottlieb, 16 Aug. 1974, transcript, p. 11, Pittsburgh Oral History Project (POHP), Pennsylvania Historical and Museum Commission, Pennsylvania State Archives, Harrisburg.

50. Brody, "Origins of Modern Steel Unionism," 17.

51. Golden to Heber Blankenhorn, 25 May 1936, Box 1, File 33, Heber Blankenhorn Collection (HEB), ALUA.

52. [Clinton Golden], "The Steel Situation," 25 May 1936, Box 1, File 33, HEB; Golden to Blankenhorn, 21 May 1936, Box 3, File 2, Clinton S. Golden Papers (CSG), HCLA.

53. Golden, "The Steel Situation"; [Harold Ruttenberg?], "May 30th [1936] Confab of Steel Workers," no date, Box 6, File 33, HOC; Lewis sticker, Box 10, File 17, CSG; John Chorry, interview by Alice Hoffman, Oct. 1966, transcript, p. 8, USAOHP; *Daily Worker,* 5, 15, and 18 June 1936; Dominec Del Turco, interviewer unknown, 14 Sept. 1978, transcript, p. 10, Box 81, File 8, BVLH; CIO, "Supplementary Report on Steel Situation."

54. For early SWOC criticism of the ERPs, see, for instance, "Employe Representative Believes Scheme 'Farce,'" in *Amalgamated Journal,* 25 June 1936.

55. SWOC, "Report of Officers to the Wage and Policy Convention," *Proceedings of the First Wage and Policy Convention* (Pittsburgh: Steel Workers Organizing Committee, 1937), 9.

56. Murray, "Report to the Steel Workers Organizing Committee," p. 6.

57. Murray, "The Problem Before SWOC," 2–3.

58. John J. Mullen, interview by Alice Hoffman, Feb. 1966, transcript, pp. 5, 7–10, USAOHP; George Patterson, interview by Alice Hoffman, 2 Feb. 1969, transcript, pp. 10–11, USAOHP; Elmer Maloy, interview by Don Kennedy, 7 Nov. 1967, transcript, p. 20, USAOHP; Powers, *Cradle of Steel Unionism,* 58.

59. *Amalgamated Journal,* 30 Nov. 1933 and 20 Dec. 1934; *Daily News,* 2 Nov. 1935; SWOC grievance A-78-41, Box 26, USSC; U.S. Census, *Fourteenth Census of the United States: 1920, Manuscript Schedules,* vol. 10, Pennsylvania, Allegheny County, National Archives microfilm reel 1511.

60. For Maloy's campaign card, see Box 115, Exhibit D, NLRB-Exhibits; Maloy interview, p. 16. For Kane see Kane testimony, NLRB Case, 18 Dec. 1936, p. 322. Election results are found in *Duquesne Times,* 12 and 19 June 1936.

61. Powers, *Cradle of Steel Unionism,* 58, 60; Maloy testimony, NLRB Case, 26 Jan. 1937, p. 1303.

62. Maloy testimony, NLRB Case, 17 Dec. 1936, pp. 108–18; minutes of the First Joint General Conference Employee and Management Representatives Carnegie-Illinois Steel Corp. Pittsburgh District, 12 Aug. 1936, passim, Box 116, Exhibit 37, NLRB-Exhibits. Although Kane did not serve on the Duquesne Works ERP after June 1936, the other representatives still viewed him as their representative in the central committee efforts.

63. Minutes of First Joint General Conference, 12 Aug. 1936, pp. 17, 20–27. For criticism of the overtime policy at Duquesne and other mills, see Duquesne Works Employee Representation Plan (DWERP), "Questions regarding plan for payment of overtime plan as discussed at Employee Representatives meeting July 23rd, 1936," Box 11, File W-1(h), USSC; *Amalgamated Journal,* 30 July 1936; *Iron Age,* 6 Aug. 1936, p. 62; minutes of First Joint General Conference, 12 Aug. 1936, passim.

64. Minutes of First Joint General Conference, 12 Aug. 1936, pp. 28–30.

65. Kane testimony, NLRB Case, 27 Jan. 1937, pp. 1394–97; Brooks, *As Steel Goes,* 92; *Post-Gazette,* 21 Dec. 1936; Kane to Benjamin Fairless, 9 Sept. 1936, Box 26, File 14, United Steelworkers of America, Research Department Records, HCLA; Pittsburgh District Central Committee, minutes of meeting, 25 Aug. 1936, Box 116, Exhibit 41, NLRB-Exhibits; "The Line-up of the Central Committee of the Employee Representatives of Carnegie-Illinois Steel," 24 Aug. 1936, Box 4, File 6, HJR; *Steel Labor,* 5 Sept. 1936.

66. Brooks, *As Steel Goes,* 92; Maloy testimony, NLRB Case, 14 Jan. 1936, pp. 960–74. Maloy spoke of Philip Murray to Kennedy, pp. 21–22.

67. William Theis, interview by Robert Schutte and Alice Hoffman, 8 May 1968, transcript, p. 21, USAOHP.

68. Brooks, *As Steel Goes,* 92.

69. Harold J. Ruttenberg, interview by Arthur S. Weinberg, 12 May 1968, transcript, p. 10, USAOHP. Anthony Mackey echoed Ruttenberg's assertion during an interview by Carl Romanek, 16 Oct. 1974, POHP.

70. Phillip Bonosky, typewritten "semi-autobiography," pp. 106–7, partial copy in author's possession; Bonosky to author, 23 Feb. 1995.

71. Elmer Cope to Ruttenberg, 20 Oct. 1936, Box 3, File 19, HJR.

72. Youngstown ERP, minutes of meeting, 28 Sept. 1936, Box 109, Exhibit 271, NLRB-Exhibits; Youngstown ERP, minutes of meeting, 5 Oct. 1936, Box 110, Exhibit 51, NLRB-Exhibits; Maloy testimony, NLRB Case, 17 Dec. 1936, pp. 143–59, 18 Dec. 1936, pp. 163–87; Brooks, *As Steel Goes,* 98.

73. Maloy testimony, NLRB Case, 17 Dec. 1936, pp. 144–49.

74. DWERP, "To the Employee Representatives," 1 Oct. 1936, Box 110, Exhibit 50, NLRB-Exhibits; "Meeting of Employee Representatives of Pittsburgh District Plants," minutes, 18 Oct. 1936, Box 4, File 6, HJR; Maloy testimony, NLRB Case, 17 Dec. 1936, p. 137; Brooks, *As Steel Goes,* 106; "Order of Business (Confidential)," no date, Box 4, File 6, HJR; and Ruttenberg to Joseph Timko et al., 3 Oct. 1936, Box 3, File 19, HJR.

75. Youngstown ERP, minutes of meetings, 28 Sept. and 5 Oct. 1936; Maloy testimony, NLRB Case, 17 Dec. 1936, pp. 143–59, 18 Dec. 1936, pp. 163–87, and 15 Jan. 1937, pp. 1130–31; Brooks, *As Steel Goes,* 98–99; *Steel Labor,* 20 Oct. 1936; copy of the employees' proposal that management rejected, Box 116, Exhibit 29, NLRB-Exhibits.

76. Maloy testimony, NLRB Case, 15 Jan. 1937, pp. 1130–31.

77. Pittsburgh District General Council (PDGC), employee delegates, minutes of meeting, 9 Nov. 1936, pp. 2–5, 9, Box 110, Exhibit 60, NLRB-Exhibits; Maloy interview, pp. 22–23; *Daily Worker,* 3 Nov. 1936; Brooks, *As Steel Goes,* 101–2.

78. PDGC, employee delegates, minutes of meeting, 30 Nov. 1936, pp. 10–16, Box 117, Exhibit 152, NLRB-Exhibits; PDGC, minutes of meeting, 1 Dec. 1936, pp. 17–18, Box 117, Exhibit 154, NLRB-Exhibits; Maloy testimony, NLRB Case, 18 Dec. 1936, pp. 275–78; 11 Jan. 1937, pp. 525–44; Youngstown ERP, minutes of meeting, 27 Nov. 1936, pp. 7–8, Box 110, Exhibit 68, NLRB-Exhibits; *Post-Gazette,* 2 Dec. 1936; Maloy interview, pp. 23–24; Brooks, *As Steel Goes,* 103–6.

79. PDGC (Employee Delegates), minutes of meeting, 2 Dec. 1936, Box 117, Exhibit 155, NLRB-Exhibits; Maloy testimony, NLRB Case, 11 Jan. 1937, pp. 535, 553. Maloy is quoted in *Post-Gazette,* 8 Jan. 1937.

80. *Daily Worker,* 3 June 1936; *Steel,* 8 June 1936, 14–15; minutes of First Joint General Conference, 12 Aug. 1936, p. 14.

81. Stettinius to Taylor, 26 July 1936, Box 63, File: Taylor Correspondence, STET.

82. Myron C. Taylor, *Ten Years of Steel* (New York: U.S. Steel, 1938), 38–39; Bernstein, *Turbulent Years,* 462–63.

83. Maloy testimony, NLRB Case, 18 Dec. 1936, pp. 207–9. For a copy of the agreement see Box 7, File W-1(a), USSC. For an analysis of the agreement by SWOC, see "Critical Analysis of Steel Wage Adjustment," no date, Box 4 File 6, HJR.

84. DWERP, minutes of meeting, 7 Nov. 1936, Box 110, Exhibit 55, NLRB-Exhibits.

85. Ibid.

86. Ibid., 14 Nov. 1936, pp. 5–6, Box 110, Exhibit 63, NLRB-Exhibits.

87. *Post-Gazette,* 11 Nov. 1936.

88. DWERP, minutes of meetings, 13, 14, and 16 Nov. 1936, Box 110, Exhibits 62, 63, and 65, NLRB-Exhibits; Maloy testimony, NLRB Case, 18 Dec. 1936, pp. 252–56. Petitions are found in Box 7, File W-1(a), USSC.

89. DWERP, minutes of meeting, 16 Nov. 1936, pp. 1–2; Brooks, *As Steel Goes,* 103. Copies of Department of Labor analyses of the wage agreement are found in Box 36, File: Conciliation Steel, Department of Labor Records (RG 174), Office of the Secretary, General Subject File, 1933–41, National Archives (NA).

90. DWERP, minutes of meeting, 7 Nov. 1936, p. 3.

91. Maloy testimony, NLRB Case, 18 Dec. 1936, p. 270.

92. DWERP, minutes of meeting, 16 Nov. 1936, p. 3.

93. Ibid., p. 2.

94. Raymond Hogler, "Worker Participation, Employer Anti-Unionism, and Labor Law: The Case of the Steel Industry, 1918–1937," *Hofstra Labor Law Journal* 7 (fall 1989): 1–69.

95. A copy of the unfair labor charges filed by SWOC before the NLRB's sixth region is found in Box 328, Records of the National Labor Board (RG 25), Unfair Labor Practices and Representation Case Files, NA. For Carnegie-Illinois' response, see Carnegie-Illinois press release, 16 Dec. 1936, Box 566, File: Eugene Grace, STET.

96. Maloy's and Kane's testimony, running well over a thousand transcribed pages, is found in NLRB-Exhibits. Their testimony also can be found in reports in the *Post-Gazette, Pittsburgh Press, (Pittsburgh) Sun-Times,* and *Daily News* in December 1936 and January 1937.

97. Kane testimony, NLRB Case, 27 Jan. 1937, pp. 1394–97; *Post-Gazette,* 21 Dec. 1936; Maloy testimony, NLRB Case, 17 Jan. 1937, pp. 979–87; "Maloy Unmasked," no date, Box 4, File 6, HJR.

98. *Post-Gazette,* 7 and 8 Jan. 1937; Maloy interview, pp. 23–24; *Steel,* 30 Nov. 1936, p. 16. The resolution recalling Maloy appears in Box 117, Exhibit 159, NLRB-Exhibits.

99. *Post-Gazette,* 31 Dec. 1936 and 5 Jan. 1937; *Iron Age,* 7 Jan. 1937, p. 192, and 21 Jan. 1937, p. 94; Youngstown ERP, minutes of meeting, 4 Jan. 1937, Box 109, Exhibit 281, NLRB-Exhibits. Many of the defense committee's press releases appear in Box 4, File 6, HJR.

100. *Iron Age,* 25 Feb. 1937, p. 39; *Duquesne Times,* 15 and 22 Jan. 1937 and 26 Feb. 1937; *Post-Gazette,* 10 and 24 Feb. 1937; *Pittsburgh Press,* 9 Jan. 1937. Fairless is quoted in Fairless to Owen Jones et al., 9 Jan. 1937, Box 4, File 6, HJR.

101. *Duquesne Times,* 22 Jan. 1937; defense committee leaflet, "To Our Fellow Employees of the Carnegie-Illinois Steel Corp.," no date, Box 4, File 6, HJR; *Post-Gazette,* 2 and 7 Jan. 1937; defense committee, minutes of meeting, 18 Jan. 1937, 1, Box 4, File 6, HJR.

102. Ford, Bacon, and Davis, "Digest of Ford, Bacon, and Davis Report No. 37 . . . ," 17 Nov. 1936, pp. 13–14, Box 45, File: Ford, Bacon, and Davis, Survey Digests of Reports, STET; "Minutes of Special Meeting [U.S. Steel and Ford, Davis, and Bacon executives]," 8 Sept. 1937, pp. 12–16, Box 46, STET; "It Happened in Steel," *Fortune* 15 (May 1937): 179.

103. Stettinius to Taylor, 26 July 1936.

104. DWERP requests 217-15, 143-52, and "Informal wage request—repairmen, automatic telephones, and linemen, telephones," Box 26, USSC.

105. DWERP request 4-36, Box 26, USSC.

106. See DWERP requests 228-62, 4-37, 4-38, 4-44, 4-51, 4-60, and 4-92, Box 26, USSC.

107. R. F. Sanner to K. H. McLaurin, 4 Dec. 1936; McLaurin to W. C. Oberg, 9 Dec. 1936; and A. C. Cummins to McLaurin, handwritten note regarding McLaurin to Cummins, 8 Feb. 1937, all in DWERP request 4-50 materials, Box 26, USSC.

108. For example, DWERP request 23 materials, Box 26, USSC.

109. Maloy testimony, NLRB Case, 11 Jan. 1937, pp. 545–52, and 14 Jan. 1937, pp. 946–58; Ford, Davis, and Bacon, "Digest of Ford, Bacon, and Davis Report No. 37," pp. 13–14.

110. Maloy testimony, NLRB Case, 11 Jan. 1937, pp. 545–52, and 14 Jan. 1937, pp. 946–54.

111. Ibid., pp. 548–49. In his 1968 oral history Maloy took more credit for the results of the study. See Maloy interview, p. 19.

112. DWERP requests 183-17, 191-25, 193-27, 213-47, and 214-48, Box 26, USSC.

113. Maloy interview, p. 19; Maloy testimony, NLRB Case, 11 Jan. 1937, pp. 551–52; DWERP requests 213-47 and 214-48, Box 26, USSC.

114. See material related to DWERP request 4-68 [partially mislabeled as 4-66], Box 26, USSC.

115. Maloy testimony, NLRB Case, 14 Jan. 1937, pp. 956–57; DWERP requests 4-03, 4-07, 4-15, 4-19, 4-23, Box 26, USSC.

116. DWERP requests 4-17 and 4-23, Box 26, USSC.

117. Galenson, *CIO Challenge to the AFL,* p. 656, n41. See also Wieck, "Summary of Observations," p. 8. "After all," wrote Wieck in September 1936, "if they get the representatives they do not have the mass of workers."

118. For attempts by *Steel Labor* to address skilled workers, though generally only in the context of all workers, see issues for 20 Aug. 1936 and 5 and 25 Sept. 1936.

119. See, for example, Clinton Golden, "Re: Company Unions," 13 July 1936, Box 3, File 18, HJR; Murray, "The Problem Before SWOC"; Murray, "Report to the Steel Workers Organizing Committee"; SWOC, minutes of meeting, 29 Sept. 1936.

120. Ruttenberg to John Brophy, 13 July 1936, Box 16, File 17, KPE. For a similar Communist critique see Horace B. Davis, *Labor and Steel* (New York: International Publishers, 1933), 85.

121. Ruttenberg to all staff representatives, 19 Nov. 1936, Box 9, File 21, Emil J. Lever Papers, HCLA.

122. Wieck, "Summary of Observations," p. 1; Maloy testimony, NLRB Case, 18 Dec. 1936, p. 289, and 11 Jan. 1937, pp. 556–66; *Steel Labor,* 23 Jan. 1937. After the signing of the collective bargaining agreement between Carnegie-Illinois and SWOC, Duquesne unionists would raise only five cases alleging that management had fired workers because of their union activities. All five cases dated to the pre-SWOC period, and it is unclear whether any of these workers actually were fired for union activity. See minutes of SWOC local 1256 grievance meeting, 20 April and 4 May 1937, Third Step Minutes Notebook, Box 27, USSC.

123. Organizing report for Local 1256, SWOC Organizing Reports, Local Union Section (microfilm), Roll LA 1989, HCLA; Powers, *Cradle of Steel Unionism,* 96, 98.

124. SWOC used the term *lodge* and not *local* during this early period, but *local* soon became the common usage. For the sake of clarity, I use the term *local* in all references to SWOC.

125. Organizing report for local 1256, SWOC Organizing Reports, HCLA; Dickerson,

Out of the Crucible, 144–47; Cayton and Mitchell, *Black Workers and the Unions,* 202, 207; Maloy interview, p. 35; Michael Kerekac, interview by Linda Nyden, 9 July 1974, POHP.

126. Kerekac interview; Albert Carter, interview by Major Mason, 22 July 1974, POHP; Frank Takach, interview by Jim Barrett, 28 May 1976, transcript, p. 6, Homestead Album Oral History Project, AIS; Wilbur Collins, interview by Gordon Mason, Aug. 1974, transcript, p. 3, POHP; Homer Brown, interview by Laval Murphy, 21 Aug. 1974, POHP.

127. *Post-Gazette,* 1 Feb. 1937; *Amalgamated Journal,* 4 Feb. 1937; John Bodnar, *Workers' World: Kinship, Community, and Protest in an Industrial Society, 1900–1940* (Baltimore: Johns Hopkins University Press, 1982), 150–52; Charles Bollinger, interview by Alice M. Hoffman, July 1966, transcript, p. 9, USAOHP; Powers, *Cradle of Steel Unionism,* 99–101. Organizing reports for Edgar Thomson, Homestead, and Clairton appear in SWOC Organizing Reports, Local Union Section (microfilm), Roll LA 1989, HCLA.

128. Lee Pressman is quoted in Galenson, *CIO Challenge to the AFL,* 94.

129. McDonald, *Union Man,* 102.

130. For a chronology of events see Taylor, *Ten Years of Steel,* 40–44; "It Happened in Steel," pp. 93–94, 176, 179–80; Bernstein, *Turbulent Years,* 469–73; Galenson, *CIO Challenge to the AFL,* 91–93; Dubofsky and Van Tine, *John L. Lewis,* 273–75.

131. "It Happened in Steel," 93.

132. Dubofsky and Van Tine, *John L. Lewis,* 272–77.

133. See Taylor, *Ten Years of Steel,* 40–44; John A. Fitch, "Steel and the C.I.O.," *Survey Graphic* 26 (April 1937): 188–90; "It Happened in Steel," 179; *Iron Age,* 11 March 1937, p. 88; Frederick Harbison, "Steel," in *How Collective Bargaining Works: A Survey of Experiences in Leading American Industries,* ed. Harry A. Millis (New York: Twentieth Century Fund, 1942), 523–24; Brooks, *As Steel Goes,* 107–8; Bernstein, *Turbulent Years,* 467–70; Galenson, *CIO Challenge to the AFL,* 93–96; Dubofsky and Van Tine, *John L. Lewis,* 274–77; Richard A. Lauderbaugh, *American Steel Makers and the Coming of the Second World War* (Ann Arbor, Mich.: UMI Research, 1980), 143–69.

134. Frederick Harbison, "Labor Relations in the Iron and Steel Industry, 1936–1939" (Ph.D. diss., Princeton University, 1940), 48.

135. Brooks, *As Steel Goes,* 107.

136. *Post-Gazette,* 19 March 1937.

137. Bernstein, *Turbulent Years,* 467–68; Frederick Harbison, *Collective Bargaining in the Steel Industry: 1937* (Princeton: Princeton University, 1938), 5–6.

138. Ford, Bacon, and Davis, "Digest of Ford, Bacon, and Davis Report No. 37," pp. 2–3, 8–11.

139. Remarks of Nathan Miller, 37th annual dinner of the U.S. Steel Corp., 11 Jan. 1938, Box 36, STET.

140. Fairless, Notice "To All Employees," 3 March 1937, Box 4, File 6, HJR.

141. Taylor, *Ten Years of Steel,* 41.

Chapter 6: Consolidating the Union, 1937–41

1. *(McKeesport) Daily News,* 5 March 1937; *Steel Labor,* 20 March 1937; Local 1256, minutes of meeting, 7 March 1937, United Steelworkers of America, Local 1256 Records (L-1256), Historical Collections and Labor Archives (HCLA), The Pennsylvania State University, State College. All Local 1256 minutes are found in Local 1256 Records.

2. Steel Workers Organizing Committee (SWOC), "Pittsburgh Office Reports," Box 156, File 3, David J. McDonald Papers (MCD), HCLA; Frederick Harbison, "Steel," in *How Collective Bargaining Works: A Survey of Experiences in Leading American Industries,* ed. Harry A. Millis (New York: Twentieth Century Fund, 1942), 524.

3. Harbison, "Steel," 524.

4. See Walter Galenson, *The CIO Challenge to the AFL: A History of the American Labor Movement, 1935–1941* (Cambridge: Harvard University Press, 1960); Irving Bernstein, *The Turbulent Years: A History of the American Worker, 1933–1941* (Boston: Houghton Mifflin, 1970). For a contemporary analysis that emphasized the union's weakness at U.S. Steel, see Frederick Harbison, "Labor Relations in the Iron and Steel Industry, 1936–1939" (Ph.D. diss., Princeton, 1940), 57–61.

5. B. F. Fairless, "To All Employees," 3 March 1937, Box 4, File 6, Harold J. Ruttenberg Papers (HJR), HCLA.

6. *(Pittsburgh) Post-Gazette,* 3 March 1937.

7. Carnegie-Illinois Steel Corp., "Procedure for the Handling of Present Labor Policy and Employee Requests," 12 April 1937, Box 30, File: Grievance Procedure and Correspondence, U.S. Steel Corp. (Duquesne Works) Payroll Ledgers and Records of the Personnel Division (USSC), 1904–80, UE/Labor Archives (UE/L), Archives of Industrial Society (AIS), Hillman Library, University of Pittsburgh, Pittsburgh; minutes of Local 1256 grievance meeting with management (hereafter, Local 1256 grievance meeting), 6 April 1937, Third Step Minutes Notebook, Box 27, USSC (unless otherwise noted, all grievance meeting minutes are in this box).

8. *Iron Age,* 11 March 1937, 107; *Pittsburgh Press,* 4, 7, and 8 March 1937; *Post-Gazette,* 8 March 1937.

9. *Daily News,* 5 March 1937; *Pittsburgh Press,* 5, 8, 9, 10, and 28 March 1937; *Post-Gazette,* 6 March 1937; *Iron Age,* 1 April 1937; Frederick Harbison, *Collective Bargaining in the Steel Industry: 1937* (Princeton: Princeton University, 1938), 33–34.

10. Duquesne Works Employee Representation Plan (DWERP) requests 4-88 through 4-90, 4-92 through 4-103, and 4-105, Box 26, USSC.

11. *Daily News,* 19 March 1937; *Post-Gazette,* 19 March 1937.

12. DWERP requests 4-88, 4-92, 4-96, and 4-103, Box 26, USSC.

13. *Daily News,* 19 March 1937; *Post-Gazette,* 19 March 1937; *Pittsburgh Press,* 28 March 1937.

14. *Pittsburgh Press,* 26 April 1937; *Iron Age,* 29 April 1937, p. 93; B. F. Fairless to the Employees of Carnegie-Illinois Steel Corp., 26 April 1937, Box 30, File #1256: Maintenance of Membership and Check Off, 1936–49, USSC; Order Dismissing Complaint as to Carnegie-Illinois Steel Corp., 4 June 1937, Box 328, File: Unfair Labor Practices and Representation Case Files, National Labor Relations Board Records (RG 25), National Archives, Washington, D.C.; Harbison, *Collective Bargaining in the Steel Industry,* 33–36.

15. "Procedure for the Handling of Present Labor Policy"; "Procedure for Handling Employee Request Forms," 13 May 1940; E. E. Moore to J. E. Lose, 19 May 1942, all in Box 30, File: Grievance Procedures and Correspondence, USSC. Independent grievances, interspersed at times with union grievances, are found in Box 26, USSC.

16. Elmer Maloy, interview by Don Kennedy, 7 Nov. 1967, transcript, pp. 33–34, United Steelworkers of America Oral History Project (USAOHP), HCLA; SWOC, Lodge Collec-

tions of Carnegie-Illinois as of Sept. 29, 1937, Box 156, File 2, MCD; Local 1256 Treasurer's Cash Book, L-1256; Pennsylvania, Department of Internal Affairs, *Report on Productive Industries, 1936–1938* (Harrisburg: Commonwealth of Pennsylvania, 1940), 149. For Pittsburgh district capacity levels, see various issues of *Iron Age,* March–Aug. 1937.

17. SWOC, "Steel Workers Organizing Committee Versus United States Steel (An Analytical Comparison of Employees, Membership and Collections from April 1, 1937 to September 30, 1937)"; and J. R. Jahn to Philip Murray, 18 Aug. [1937], both in Box 156, File 2, MCD.

18. Galenson, *CIO Challenge to the AFL,* 96–109.

19. E. C. B., "The Situation," *Daily Metal Trade Review,* 10 July 1937.

20. K. H. McLaurin to R. L. Leffler, 6 May 1937, Box 10, File P-4(a), USSC.

21. *Post-Gazette,* 4 March 1937; *Daily News,* 5 and 8 March 1937; Maloy interview, p. 35; Local 1256, minutes of meetings, 7 March and 7 July 1937.

22. Harbison, "Labor Relations in the Iron and Steel Industry," 37; William T. Hogan, *Economic History of the Iron and Steel Industry in the United States* (Lexington, Massachusetts: Lexington Books, 1971), vol. 3: 1142; *Iron Age,* Aug. 1937–Oct. 1939; Douglas A. Fisher, *Steel Serves the Nation, 1901–1951: The Fifty Year Story of United States Steel* (New York: U.S. Steel, 1951), 225.

23. *Duquesne Times,* 18 Feb. 1938, 3 June 1938, 4 Nov. 1938, 24 Feb. 1939, 21 July 1939, 1, 8, 15, and 22 Sept. 1939, 6 Oct. 1939; Phillip Bonosky, typewritten "semi-autobiography," pp. 108–9, partial copy in author's possession.

24. U.S. Census, *Census of Partial Employment, Unemployment and Occupations: 1937* (Washington, D.C.: U.S. Government Printing Office, 1938), vol. 3: 266; time worked by John Schorr, grievance 35-39-U materials, Box 26, USSC; R. F. Sanner to McLaurin, 14 April 1939, Box 3, File S-3(f), USSC.

25. Local 1256 Treasurer's Cash Book, L-1256; Local 1256, "Monthly Report of Membership and Fees," 1939–43, L-1256; Local 1256, minutes of meeting, 29 June 1938.

26. SWOC, "Unemployment Survey," 1 Dec. 1937, Box 3, File 11, HJR; John Grajciar, interview by Jack Severson, 21 March 1969, transcript, pp. 3, 6, USAOHP; (Homestead) Local 1397, minutes of meetings, 27 Nov. and 17 Dec. 1937, John McManigal Collection (MCM), UE/L; Frank Miller Keck, Jr., "The Development of Labor Representation at the Homestead Steel Works" (master's thesis, University of Pittsburgh, 1950), 49; Curtis Miner, *Homestead: The Story of a Steel Town* (Pittsburgh: Historical Society of Western Pennsylvania, 1989), 57; Harbison, "Labor Relations in the Iron and Steel Industry," 58, 61.

27. Dean Clowes, interview by Don Kennedy, 17 Jan. 1975, transcript, p. 24, USAOHP; Harbison, *Collective Bargaining in the Steel Industry,* 21; *Iron Age,* 5 Nov. 1936, pp. 84, 86–87; Pittsburgh District General Council (Employee Delegates), minutes of meeting, 2 Dec. 1936, Box 117, National Labor Relations Board Records (RG 25), Administrative Division, Files and Dockets Section, Transcripts and Exhibits, Washington National Records Center, Suitland, Md.; Carnegie-Illinois Steel Corp., "Instruction to Supervisory Forces Governing Employee Relationships," 1 Sept. 1936, Box 28, File S-6(a), USSC.

28. Harbison, "Labor Relations in the Iron and Steel Industry," 198.

29. Maloy interview, p. 39; P. Murray, "Instructions to Local Lodge Officers . . . ," n.d. [1937], Box 3, File 11, HJR; William Theis, interview by Robert Schutte and Alice Hoffman, 8 May 1968, transcript, p. 28, USAOHP.

30. *Steel,* 26 April 1937, p. 24; miscellaneous letters, 1937–41, in Box 30, File: Officers, Committeemen (data sheets, elections, appointments), USSC; Local 1256, miscellaneous minutes of meetings, 1937–41. For other mills see Annemarie Draham, "Unlikely Allies Fight for Unionization: Homestead, Pa., 1933–1946" (master's thesis, Indiana University of Pennsylvania, 1984), 33; Keck, "Development of Labor Representation," 38; Charles Bollinger, interview by Alice Hoffman, July 1966, transcript, p. 9, USAOHP; Charles R. Walker, *Steeltown: An Industrial Case History of the Conflict Between Progress and Security* (New York: Harper, 1950), 21.

31. Local 1256 grievance meeting, 6 April 1937.

32. For 1937–41 grievances, see Boxes 12 and 26, USSC. For grievance meetings see Local 1256 grievance meetings, 1938. For Homestead see Local 1397 shop stewards, minutes of meeting, 17 Dec. 1937, MCM.

33. Harbison, "Labor Relations in the Iron and Steel Industry," 61.

34. Duquesne Works, "History of the Bar Mill Wage Scale Changes," no date, in Box 26, grievance 26-39-U file, USSC; Ford, Bacon, and Davis, "Digest of Ford, Bacon, and Davis Report No. 37 . . . ," 17 Nov. 1936, Box 45, File: Ford, Bacon, and Davis, Survey Digests of Reports, Edward R. Stettinius, Jr. Papers (STET), Manuscript Division, Special Collections, University of Virginia Library, Charlottesville; General Superintendent to Ernest Fries, 12 Oct. 1939, in grievance 26-39-U file.

35. "History of the Bar Mill Wage Scale Changes"; Memorandum, 25 Oct. 1939; Memorandum, 12 Dec. 1939, both in grievance 26-39-U file; *Steel Labor,* 24 Nov. 1939; Local 1256, minutes of meetings, 12 and 19 Oct., 27 Nov. 1939.

36. Memorandum, 2 Oct. 1939, in grievance 26-39-U file; Memorandum, 12 Dec. 1939; handwritten note by management on back of grievance 26-29-U. Workers who earned more under the new plan, but who did not sign the union grievance, were not required to pay back wages to the company.

37. See materials related to independent grievance #19, Box 26, USSC.

38. Grievances A-51-40, A-52-40, A-53-40, A-82-41, A-102-41, all in Boxes 12 and 26, USSC.

39. Memorandum of meeting, 3 Feb. 1941, in A-52-40 grievance file, Box 12, USSC.

40. Harbison, "Labor Relations in the Iron and Steel Industry," 148; Clinton Golden and Harold J. Ruttenberg, *The Dynamics of Industrial Democracy* (New York: Harper, 1942), 174; U.S. Steel Advisory Committee, minutes of meeting, 7 May 1939, Box 42, File 2, Howard R. Hague Collection, HCLA.

41. McLaurin to W. C. Oberg, 20 Feb. 1941, Box 7, File W-1(a), USSC.

42. Memorandum of meeting between management and 40–inch blooming mill employees, 24 Oct. 1941, in Box 26, A-87-41 grievance file, USSC.

43. All the supporting documentation for the first and second bar mill cases is found in Box 26, grievance files 34-39-U and 40-40-U, USSC; *Steel Labor,* 31 Jan. 1941.

44. Memorandum of meeting between management and Fries and Leo Foremsky, 24 Oct. 1941; memorandum of meeting between management and 40–inch blooming mill employees, 24 Oct. 1941, both in Box 26, A-87-41 grievance file, USSC.

45. Grievances A-50-40, A-51-40, A-65-41, A-68-41, A-70-41, A-74-41, A-79-41, A-84-41, A-87-41, A-90-41, and A-109-41, all in Boxes 12 and 26, USSC.

46. Memorandum, 38–40-inch Mill Proposal, 1 March 1942, in Box 26, A-87-41 grievance file.

47. Ibid.; "Proposed Basis for Final Settlement of 38–inch and 40–inch Mill Wage Incentive Plans," 3 July 1942, in Box 26, A-87-41 grievance file, USSC.

48. Edward R. Stettinius to Myron Taylor, 22 June 1938; Ford, Bacon, and Davis, "Memorandum Showing the Estimated Effect . . . ," 24 June 1938; Ford, Bacon, Davis to Stettinius, 24 June 1938, all in Box 65, File F, STET.

49. Harbison, "Labor Relations in the Iron and Steel Industry," 60–61.

50. Ibid.; E. Robert Livernash, *Collective Bargaining in the Basic Steel Industry: A Study of the Public Interest and the Role of Government* (Washington, D.C.: U.S. Department of Labor, 1961), 237–38; Kim McQuaid, *Big Business and Presidential Power, From FDR to Reagan* (New York: Morrow, 1982), 11–15; P. Murray to all SWOC lodges, 14 Feb. 1938, Box 145, File 8, MCD; P.Murray to all SWOC members and lodges, 10 Nov. 1938, Box 3, File 11, HJR.

51. Local 1256 grievance meetings, 21 Sept. 1937, 20 Dec. 1938, 21 and 29 March 1939, 19 March and 18 June 1940, and 21 Oct. 1941, Box 12, USSC; grievances 21-39-U, A-49-40, A-56-40, A-57-40, A-70-41, A-71-41, A-103-41, A-110-41, and A-113-41, Boxes 12 and 26, USSC; Strike reports 2 and 3, Box 28, File S-5(b)-1, USSC.

52. Grievances 18-38-U, 22-39-U, 23-39-U, 31-39-U, 38-40-U, all in Box 26, USSC; Local 1256, minutes of meetings, 21 Dec. 1938, 22 Feb. 1939, 22 March 1939, and 10 May 1939; Local 1256 grievance meeting, 18 Jan. 1938, 15 Nov. 1938, 20 Dec. 1938; 24 Jan. 1939, 21 Feb. 1939, 31 March 1939.

53. Local 1256, minutes of meetings, 12 Jan., 23 Feb., 2 and 30 March, 18 May, and 1 June 1938; John J. Kane to McLaurin, 19 May 1938; and [McLaurin] to Kane, 20 May 1938, both in Box 5, File S-2(a), USSC; Local 1256 grievance meetings, 18 Jan. 1938; 20 June 1939; grievance 24-39-U, Box 26, USSC.

54. Local 1256 grievance meetings, 3 Feb. and 19 March 1940; Sanner to C. F. Brown, Feb. 1940; and McLaurin to Oberg, 8 Feb. 1940, both in Box 28, File T-1(d), USSC.

55. For Carnegie-Illinois' attempt to establish a plan of procedure for layoffs and comments from plant-level officials, see Leffler to all general superintendents, 13 Nov. 1937; and Leffler to all general superintendents, 23 Dec. 1937, both in Box 3, File S-3(f), USSC.

56. Livernash, *Collective Bargaining,* 98; Harbison, "Labor Relations in the Iron and Steel Industry," 161. For grievances filed alleging seniority violations in layoffs and recall at Duquesne, see 5-37-U, 11-37-U, 13-37-U, and 20-39-U, Box 26, USSC.

57. Local 1256 grievance meeting, 19 Oct. 1937.

58. For examples of low-skilled workers' using the grievance procedure for seniority cases, see 32-39-U, 35-39-U, Box 26, USSC. Tonnage promotions turned on different issues. For these jobs, training determined promotions at first. Whoever had the most turns at training on a higher job got the job when an opening occurred. When management abuses of this system from the pre-SWOC period came to light, union and management agreed to use job seniority for promotion. Thus the most senior employee on the job ladder below the opening got the job. Occasionally, however, management did invoke its ability clause. See grievances 27-39-U, A-68-41, A-78-41, A-107-41, Boxes 12 and 26; "Memorandum," 18 June 1941, in grievance 27-39-U materials, all in USSC.

59. See Robert J. Norrell, "Caste in Steel: Jim Crow Careers in Birmingham, Alabama," *Journal of American History* 73 (Dec. 1983): 675–79; Bruce Nelson, "'CIO Meant One Thing for the Whites and Another Thing for Us': Steelworkers and Civil Rights, 1936–1974," in

Southern Labor in Transition, 1940–1955, ed. Robert H. Zieger (Knoxville: University of Tennessee Press, 1997), 113–45.

60. For a similar analysis see Judith Stein, "Birmingham Steelworkers, 1936–1951," in *Organized Labor in the Twentieth Century,* ed. Robert H. Zieger (Knoxville: University of Tennessee Press, 1991), 196–97.

61. Dennis C. Dickerson, *Out of the Crucible: Black Steelworkers in Western Pennsylvania, 1875–1980* (Albany: State University of New York Press, 1986), 146; Sylvester Grinage, interview by Gordon Mason, 21 Aug.1974, Pittsburgh Oral History Project (POHP), Pennsylvania Historical and Museum Commission, Pennsylvania State Archives, Harrisburg.

62. Michael Kerekac, interview by Linda Nyden, 9 July 1974, POHP; Albert Carter, interview by Major Mason, 22 July 1974, POHP; Nate Jones, interview by Jack Bergstresser, 16 July 1991, Steel Industry Heritage Corp., Homestead, Pa.; Dickerson, *Out of the Crucible,* 149.

63. Grievance report, 2 Jan. 1943, and supporting documentation, Box 37, File: U.S.W. Local 1256 General Correspondence, 1937–66, USSC.

64. Miscellaneous letters, Box 30, File: Officers, Committeemen (data sheets, elections, appointments), USSC.

65. Industrial Relations Department, "Memorandum on Placing Colored Employees on Bricklayer Apprenticeships," Box 37, File T-2(a), USSC.

66. Maloy interview, pp. 33–34.

67. Bonosky, "semi-autobiography," 106–7; Bonosky to author, 23 Feb. 1995; John J. Mullen, interview by Alice Hoffman, Feb. 1966, transcript, pp. 14–15, USAOHP. See also, Robert R. R. Brooks, *As Steel Goes, . . : Unionism in a Basic Industry* (New Haven: Yale University Press, 1940), 251.

68. Local 1256, minutes of meetings, 28 July and 4 Aug. 1937. Fries is quoted in Local 1256, minutes of meeting, 11 Aug. 1937.

69. Local 1256, minutes of meetings, 15 Sept. 1937, 6, 20, and 27 Oct. 1937, and 3 Nov. 1937.

70. Gene and Frank DiCola, interview by Alice Hoffman, Aug. 1968, p. 14, USAOHP; William Theis, interview by Robert Schutte and Alice Hoffman, 8 May 1968, transcript, p. 28, USAOHP.

71. *Daily News,* 1 Nov. 1937; Maloy inactive voter registration card, Allegheny County, Pa., Voter Registration Records, AIS.

72. *Duquesne Times,* 9 and 30 July, 27 Aug., 3 Sept. 1937; *Daily News,* 25 and 26 Aug., 1 and 13 Sept. 1937; Duquesne City Council minutes, 6 Jan. 1935, microfilm copy of Duquesne Borough and City Council Minutes, reel 5075, Hillman Library, University of Pittsburgh; Maloy interview, p. 35.

73. *Duquesne Times,* 17 and 24 Sept., 1 and 29 Oct. 1937; *Daily News,* 11 Sept., 30 Oct., and 1 Nov. 1937; *Friday,* 27 Dec. 1940, p. 6.

74. *Daily News,* 31 Aug. and 1 Nov. 1937.

75. *Steel Labor,* 30 Sept. and 29 Oct. 1937; "Election Returns of Candidates Endorsed or Nominated by Labor's Non-Partisan League," 2 Nov. 1937, Box 1, File: 1937 Election, Pennsylvania Federation of Labor, Labor's Non-Partisan League Papers, HCLA; Tom Murray, interview by Alice Hoffman, 23 May 1966, transcript, p. 17, USAOHP.

76. Local 1256, minutes of meetings, 6 Oct. and 3 Nov. 1937; George Powers, *Cradle of*

Steel Unionism: Monongahela Valley, PA (East Chicago, Ind.: Figueroa 1972), 133; *Daily News,* 11 Sept. 1937; Bonosky, "semi-autobiography," 107; summaries of Pittsburgh Communist Party meetings, entitled "Communist," 17 and 29 July 1937, Box 5, File 75, John P. Frey Papers, Library of Congress, Washington, D.C.

77. Maloy interview, p. 35.

78. *Daily News,* 11 Sept., 22–26 Oct., and 1 Nov. 1937; *Duquesne Times,* 29 Oct. 1937; Maloy interview, pp. 33–35; *Friday,* 27 Dec. 1940, p. 6; campaign handouts and unidentified press clippings in the personal papers of Maloy, in the possession of Joan Striegle.

79. *Duquesne Times,* 5 Nov. 1937.

80. *Daily News,* 3 Nov. 1937.

81. *Duquesne Times,* 5 Nov. 1937; Duquesne Municipal Election Books, Allegheny County Voting Records, AIS; Maloy interview, p. 35.

82. *Duquesne Times,* 5 Nov. 1937.

83. *(Pittsburgh) Bulletin Index,* 11 Nov. 1937; "Election Returns of Candidates Endorsed"; *Steel Labor,* 29 Oct. 1937; *Daily Worker,* 5 Nov. 1937.

84. *Duquesne Times,* 7 Jan. 1938.

85. Local 1256, minutes of meeting, 3 Aug. 1938; *Friday,* 27 Dec. 1940, p. 6; Duquesne City Council minutes, 3 and 21 Jan. 1938; *Duquesne Times,* 7 Jan. 1938; *Post-Gazette,* 4 Jan. 1938.

86. Duquesne City Council minutes, 7 and 11 Jan. 1938, 21 March 1938, 7, 14, and 21 Jan. 1938, 4 Feb. 1938, 8 April 1938; Maloy interview, p. 37; Local 1256, minutes of meeting, 5 Sept. 1938.

87. *Friday,* 27 Dec. 1940, p. 6; Local 1256, minutes of meeting, 1 Dec. 1937; Duquesne City Council minutes, 3 and 8 July 1936, 4 Jan. 1937, and 23 Dec. 1937; *Duquesne Times,* 21 and 28 Jan. 1938.

88. *Duquesne Times,* 21 Jan. 1938.

89. Duquesne City Council minutes, 11 Jan. 1938, 2 May 1938, 29 June 1938, and 13 June 1939; *Duquesne Times,* 14 and 21 Jan. 1938, 11 Feb. 1938, 16 Sept. 1938, 16 Feb. 1940, and 12 April 1940; *Golden Shadows* (Duquesne, Pa.: n.p., 1941), n.p.; *Friday,* 27 Dec. 1940, p. 6.

90. P. Murray to "All SWOC Sub-Regional and District Directors and Staff Members," no date, Box 145, File 8, MCD; David J. McDonald to all SWOC lodges, 29 Dec. 1937, Box 145, File 7, MCD; Harbison, "Labor Relations in the Iron and Steel Industry," 58.

91. Local 1256, minutes of meetings, 1 and 22 Dec. 1937, 5 and 26 Jan. 1938, 26 and 29 Feb. 1938, 31 Aug. 1938; *Duquesne Times,* 11 Feb. and 9 Dec. 1938; McLaurin to D. A. Barrett, 6 April 1939, Box 11, File W-2(a), USSC; Hogan, *Economic History of the Iron and Steel Industry,* vol. 3: 1180.

92. *Duquesne Times,* 18 March 1938; Local 1256, minutes of meeting, 27 April 1938.

93. Harvey Klehr, *The Heyday of American Communism: The Depression Decade* (New York: Basic, 1984), 294–302; Local 1256, minutes of meetings, 15 Dec. 1937, 2 Feb. 1938, 31 Jan. 1940; 29 Feb. 1938, and 23 March 1938; *Duquesne Times,* 2 Sept. and 9 Dec. 1938 and 2 Feb. 1940; McLaurin to Barrett, 6 April 1939; Duquesne City Council minutes, 5 Dec. 1938.

94. Local 1256, minutes of meetings, 6 and 9 March 1938.

95. Eric Leif Davin, "The Littlest New Deal: SWOC Takes Power in Steeltown, A Possibility of Radicalism in the Late 1930s," unpublished paper, no date, copy in author's possession; Eric Leif Davin and Staughton Lynd, "Picket Line and Ballot Box: The Forgotten

Legacy of the Local Labor Party Movement, 1932–1936," *Radical History Review* 22 (winter 1979–80): 43–63; Staughton, "Introduction"; and Eric Leif Davin, "The Last Hurrah? The Defeat of the Labor Party Idea, 1934–1936," in *"We Are All Leaders": The Alternative Unionism of the Early 1930s,* ed. Staughton Lynd (Urbana: University of Illinois Press, 1996), 14–15, 117–71.

96. *Duquesne Times,* 25 Feb., 1938, 9 Dec. 1938, 10 Nov. 1939, 6 Jan. 1939, 5 Jan. 1940, and 4 Oct. 1940.

97. *Duquesne Times,* 22 Sept. 1939, 10 Nov. 1939, 15 Dec. 1939, and 7 June 1940.

98. *Duquesne Times,* 1, 8, and 15 April 1938, 10 June 1938, 16 Sept. 1938, 28 July 1939, 10 March 1940, and 25 April 1940; *Daily News,* 27 June 1940; Local 1256, minutes of meeting, 18 May 1938.

99. *Duquesne Times,* 30 Dec. 1938, 9 June 1939, 28 July 1939, 1 Sept. 1939, 24 Nov. 1939, 5 Jan. 1940, 22 March 1940, 17 Jan. 1941, 30 May 1941, 15 Aug. 1941, 31 Oct. 1941; Duquesne City Council minutes, 14, 21, and 28 Dec. 1938.

100. *Duquesne Times,* 7 Nov. 1941.

101. See inactive voter registration cards, Allegheny County, Pa., for George Garland, Joseph Budday, Francis Barber, Andy Olah, and John Seman, Voter Registration Records.

102. Maurice Isserman, *Which Side Were You on? The American Communist Party During the Second World War* (Middletown, Conn.: Wesleyan University Press, 1982), 32–50.

103. Ibid., 67.

104. Richard M. Fried, *Nightmare in Red: The McCarthy Era in Perspective* (New York: Oxford University Press, 1990), 52.

105. Isserman, *Which Side Were You on?* 69; *Post-Gazette,* 27 March 1940; *Pittsburgh Press,* 26 March 1940; U.S. Congress, House, *Proceeding against George Powers for Contempt,* 76th Cong., 3d sess., 1940, H. Rept. 1904, 1–4.

106. Isserman, *Which Side Were You on?* 60–62, 67; Committee for Defense of Civil Rights of Communists, *The Conspiracy against Free Elections* (Pittsburgh, Pa. [1941]), 7–11, Box 3, File: Jewish People's Committees, Community Relations Council Records, AIS. I wish to thank David Rosenberg for directing me to this document and for sharing with me his knowledge of communism and anticommunism in the Pittsburgh area.

107. Isserman, *Which Side Were You on?* 70–71.

108. *Pittsburgh Press,* 10–15 and 27 June 1940; Committee for Defense of Civil Rights, *Conspiracy against Free Elections,* 11.

109. *Daily Worker,* 5 and 24 June and 5 July 1940; *Post-Gazette,* 4 July 1940; *Daily News,* 27 May 1940; Isserman, *Which Side Were You on?* 70.

110. *Post-Gazette,* 6 June and 4 and 6 July 1940; *Pittsburgh Press,* 5 July 1940; *Daily News,* 24 July 1940.

111. *Duquesne Times,* 21 and 28 June and 3 July 1940; *Daily News,* 25, 26, and 27 June and 24 July 1940; *Pittsburgh Press,* 15 and 27 June and 1 July 1940.

112. *Duquesne Times,* 3 July 1940.

113. *Duquesne Times,* 27 Sept. and 4 Oct. 1940; *Daily News,* 13 May 1942.

114. Harvey Levenstein, *Communism, Anti-Communism, and the CIO* (Westport, Conn.: Greenwood, 1981), 51; *Steel Labor,* 24 Feb. 1939 and 28 June 1940.

115. Harbison, "Steel," 536; Feeney Busarello, interview by Alice Hoffman, 7 April 1975, transcript, p. 55, USAOHP.

116. *Post-Gazette,* 22 and 26 June 1940; *Steel Labor,* 28 June 1940.

117. Local 1256, minutes of meetings, 10 Nov. 1937, 5 and 26 Jan. 1938, 2, 9, and 16 Feb. 1938, 6, 16, 23, and 30 March 1938, 6 April 1938, and 22 June 1938.

118. *Pittsburgh Press,* 15 June 1940; Local 1256, minutes of meetings, 10 Jan. and 19 June 1940; Bonosky to author, 15 Feb. 1995; McLaurin to Oberg, 4 Aug. 1942, Box 30, File #1256: . . . Correspondence, USSC; copy of union ticket sample ballot for 1942, Local 1256 election, in author's possession. I wish to thank Phillip Bonosky for providing me with this document.

119. *Duquesne Times,* 3 July 1940. See also *Daily News,* 29 June 1940.

120. *Duquesne Times,* 12 July 1940.

121. Local 1256, minutes of meeting, 10 July 1940; *Daily Worker,* 12 July 1940.

122. *Daily Worker* 16 July 1940.

123. Local 1256, minutes of meeting, 10 July 1940; *Duquesne Times,* 19 July 1940.

124. Grievance A-47-40, Box 26, USSC; Local 1256, minutes of meeting, 21 July 1940.

125. Committee for Defense for Civil Rights, *Conspiracy against Free Elections,* passim.

126. *Daily Worker,* 4 and 5 June 1941; *Post-Gazette* 4 June 1941.

127. Local 1256, minutes of meeting, 2 July 1941.

128. *Duquesne Times,* 10 Oct. 1941.

129. Bonosky to author, 15 Feb. 1995; McLaurin to Oberg, 4 Aug. 1942; copy of union ticket sample ballot for 1942, Local 1256 election; Local 1256, minutes of meeting, 29 April 1942.

130. Local 1256, minutes of meetings, 2 and 30 April 1941, 28 May 1941, and 27 May 1942; grievances A-59-40 and A-60-40, both in Box 26, USSC.

131. Local 1256, minutes of meetings, 14 May and 26 Nov. 1941.

132. Local 1256, minutes of meetings, 4 and 18 Sept. 1940. Homestead unionists also followed this tactic. See Local 1397, minutes of meeting, 26 Aug. 1937, and Local 1397 shop stewards, minutes of meeting, 16 April 1940, both in MCM.

133. A sizable number of individuals continued to file independent grievances during 1941. See independent grievances file and individual independent grievances interspersed in SWOC grievances in Boxes 12 and 26, USSC.

134. John A. Stephens to Barrett et al., 25 Oct. 1939; William Beye to G. C. Kimball, 9 July 1937; and Moore to general superintendents, 11 Feb. 1941, all in Box 30, File #1256: Officers . . . General Correspondence, USSC; Leffler to all general superintendents, 19 March 1937, Box 10, File P-3(e-1), USSC; Brooks, *As Steel Goes,* 209.

135. Local 1256, minutes of meeting, 6 April 1937.

136. Local 1256, minutes of meetings, 30 March, 6 April, 4 and 25 May, 8 Sept., 6 Oct., 1 Dec. 1937.

137. U.S. Steel Advisory Committee, minutes of meeting, 5 March 1939, Box 42, File 2, Hague Collection; David McDonald, *Union Man: The Life of a Labor Statesman* (New York: Dutton, 1969), 122–23; Brooks, *As Steel Goes,* 165–66.

138. Local 1397, minutes of executive committee meeting, 13 July 1938, MCM; McDonald to all SWOC lodges, district and subregional directors, 4 Feb. 1939; McDonald to SWOC directors supervising U. S. Steel lodges, 4 Aug. 1939; P. Murray and McDonald to SWOC directors, 4 Aug. 1939, all in Box 144, File 4, MCD.

139. At the local level committeemen were still frequently referred to as stewards. See

Local 1256, minutes of shop stewards' meetings, 31 Dec. 1939, 28 Jan. 1940, 25 Feb. 1940, 30 March 1940, and 26 May 1940, L-1256.

140. Harbison, "Labor Relations in the Iron and Steel Industry," 137–38. Unionists who wore shop steward buttons were asked by management to remove them, because "they impl[ied], or infer[red], a condition which, in fact, does not exist." See Stephens to Barrett et al., 25 Oct. 1939.

141. John Bodnar, *Workers' World: Kinship, Community, and Protest in an Industrial Society, 1900–1940* (Baltimore: Johns Hopkins University Press, 1982), 142–43.

142. Harbison, "Labor Relations in the Iron and Steel Industry," 137–38; McDonald, *Union Man,* 124–25; P. Murray and McDonald to SWOC directors, 4 Aug. 1939; Local 1397, minutes of meeting, 8 Aug. 1939, MCM; Local 1256, minutes of meeting, 27 Sept. 1939.

143. McDonald, *Union Man,* 123; Bodnar, *Workers' World,* 143.

144. Duquesne Works, "Report on Dues Picketing, Wednesday, Nov. 15, 1939," 16 Nov. 1939; "Report of S.W.O.C. Dues Inspection [17 Jan. 1940]," no date, Box 30, File #1256: Maintenance of Membership and Check Off, 1936–49, USSC; "Report of Dues Picketing—Duquesne Works—October 14, 1940," no date, Box 28, File S-5(a), USSC; Local 1256 Treasurer's Cash Book, L-1256; Local 1256, "Monthly Report of Membership and Fees," 1939–40, L-1256; Local 1256, minutes of meetings, 25 Jan., 9 Aug., 27 Sept., 4, 11, 18, and 25 Oct., and 1 and 8 Nov. 1939.

145. Duquesne Works, "Report of Dues Picketing—Duquesne Works—October 14, 1940," no date, Box 28, File S-5(a), USSC; Edward Wadeck, interview by Carl Romanek, 10 July 1974, POHP; *Daily News,* 15 Oct. 1940; *Pittsburgh Press,* 15 Oct. 1940; Duquesne City Council minutes, 22 Oct. 1940; *Duquesne Times,* 25 Oct. 1940.

146. Local 1256, minutes of meeting, 24 Sept. 1941.

Conclusion

1. Lloyd Ulman, *The Government of the Steel Workers' Union* (New York: Wiley, 1962), 10; E. Robert Livernash, *Collective Bargaining in the Basic Steel Industry: A Study of the Public Interest and the Role of Government* (Washington, D.C.: U.S. Department of Labor, 1961), 238–43; miscellaneous Steel Workers Organizing Committee election posters and circulars, all in Box 22, U.S. Steel Corp. (Duquesne Works) Payroll Ledgers and Records of the Personnel Division (USSC), 1904–80, UE/Labor Archives (UE/L), Archives of Industrial Society, Hillman Library, University of Pittsburgh.

2. Philip Murray to Dear Brother, 8 June 1942, Box 22, USSC.

3. Local 1256, minutes of meetings, 4 March, 1 and 8 April, and 13 and 27 May 1942, United Steelworkers of America, Local 1256 Records (L-1256), Historical Collections and Labor Archives (HCLA), The Pennsylvania State University, State College; National Labor Relations Board (NLRB), "Certification of Counting and Tabulating of Ballots," no date, Box 22, USSC; David J. McDonald to all USA [United Steelworkers of America] directors, 12 June 1942, Box 25, File 4, David J. McDonald Papers, HCLA.

4. NLRB, "Certification of Counting and Tabulating of Ballots"; Local 1256, minutes of meeting, 24 Sept. 1941, L-1256; Local 1256, "Monthly Report of Membership and Fees," 1941–42, L-1256; United Steel Workers of America (USWA), "District Sheets on Checkoff," 30 April 1942, Microfilm reel 1553, USWA, Office of the Secretary-Treasurer, Records of Clinton Golden, HCLA.

5. Livernash, *Collective Bargaining,* 106, 240–43; National War Labor Board, Carnegie-Illinois Steel Corp. et al. and the United Steelworkers of America, CIO, Case No. 364, *Opinion,* 26 Aug. 1942, Box 102, File 8, MCD.

6. Nelson Lichtenstein, *Labor's War at Home: The CIO in World War II* (Cambridge: Cambridge University Press, 1982), 6, passim.

7. Jim Rose, "'The Problem Every Supervisor Dreads': Women Workers at the U.S. Steel Duquesne Works During World War II," *Labor History* 36 (winter 1995): 24–51.

8. John Hinshaw, "Dialectic of Division: Race and Power Among Western Pennsylvania Steelworkers, 1937–1975" (Ph.D. diss., Carnegie Mellon University, 1995); A. L. Norman to G. J. Connors, 22 June 1950, Box 30, File: #1256 Officers and Grievancemen (General Correspondence), USSC.

9. Jim Rose, "Anti-Communism and the Steelworkers," paper presented at conference, "United States History in the Era of the Cold War," Center for Comparative Research, University of California at Davis, May 1993.

10. Shop-floor issues at U.S. Steel in the postwar period are explored in James D. Rose, "The Struggle over Management Rights at U.S. Steel, 1946–1960: A Reassessment of Section 2-B of the Collective Bargaining Contract," *Business History Review* 72 (autumn 1998): 446–77; Victor J. Forberger, "'My Mind Is Made Up—Don't Confuse Me with the Facts': Labor Relations in U.S. Steel, The Duquesne Works from 1955 to 1965" (senior honors thesis, Carnegie Mellon University, 9 May 1988); Victor J. Forberger, "Craftsmen and Contractual Relations at the Duquesne Steel Works, 1950s and 1960s," unpublished manuscript, 30 Nov. 1992, copy in author's possession.

Index

Adamic, Louis, 67

AFL. *See* American Federation of Labor

African Americans, 74; and the Amalgamated, 5, 64; and the depression, 60; employment levels of, 16, 46; and ERPs, 106, 162; and Fort Dukane, 72–73, 75–76, 139, 142, 143–44; and Franklin Roosevelt, 94; management discrimination against, 46–49, 64, 217–19; and the mayoral election of 1937, 197–98; and the 1919 strike, 31, 75; and seniority, 48, 192–94; and SWOC, 143–44, 147, 166–67, 169, 174, 181, 191–94, 212, 218; and turnover, 46; and welfare capitalism, 26, 47; work and working conditions of, 18, 42, 46–48, 64, 162, 191–94, 217–19; and World War I, 15–16, 26, 47, 217; and World War II, 219

Aliquippa, Pa., 145, 165, 198

Allegheny Bessemer Co., 11–12, 19, 27

Aluminum Workers of America, 96, 97

Amalgamated. *See* Amalgamated Association of Iron, Steel, and Tin Workers

Amalgamated Association of Iron, Steel, and Tin Workers: and the "Big Four," 85–86, 88–89, 90, 95; and the CIO, 132, 138; and the Communist Party, 94–96; district organization of, 76–78, 85, 89, 95–96; and ERPs, 81, 103, 111, 112, 129, 135, 148; ethnic and racial composition of, 5, 64–65, 72–73, 87; first Duquesne lodge of, 11; and the Homestead strike of 1882, 11; leadership of, 67, 75, 85–86, 90, 92, 96, 138; membership figures of, 1, 67; national conventions of, 85–86, 88; and the 1901 strike, 19–20, 31; and the 1919 strike, 30, 35; and the NSLRB, 89–97, 171; and the organizing drive in 1934, 6, 64, 67–71, 84–89; racial policies of, 75; rank-and-file movement within, 1–2, 5–6, 78, 84–89, 95–99, 142; skill composition of, 5, 64–65, 72–73, 74, 87, 101–2, 113, 135; and SWOC, 137–39; and the threatened strike of 1934, 1–2, 84–89, 109, 134, 217–18. *See also* Fort Dukane Lodge

Amalgamated Journal, 84, 146

Ambridge, Pa., 69, 198

American Civil Liberties Union, 35

American Federation of Labor (AFL): and the Amalgamated, 71, 86, 88; and the CIO, 2, 137–38; and ERPs, 177; and organizing steelworkers, 30, 132, 147; and SWOC, 175, 179; and the Trades Council of McKeesport, Pa., 77, 97

American Iron and Steel Institute, 93, 110, 116

American League for Peace and Democracy, 206

American Sheet and Tin Plate Co., 123, 129, 133

American Steel and Wire Co., 141

American Union of Steel Workers, 178

American Youth Congress, 98

Armenians, 15, 31

Arnold, Pa., 198

JAMES D. ROSE earned a Ph.D. degree in history from the University of California at Davis in 1997 and has taught at the University of San Francisco, the University of California at Davis, California State University at Sacramento, and Texas A&M University. His articles have appeared in *Labor History* and *Business History Review*.

The Working Class in American History